God's Word the Final Word on Worship and Music

A Biblical Study

Dr. Dean Kurtz

Copyright © 2008 by Dr. Dean Kurtz

God's Word the Final Word on Worship and Music
A Biblical Study
by Dr. Dean Kurtz

Printed in the United States of America

ISBN 978-1-60647-323-8

All rights reserved solely by the author. The author guarantees all contents are original and do not infringe upon the legal rights of any other person or work. No part of this book may be reproduced in any form without the permission of the author. The views expressed in this book are not necessarily those of the publisher.

Unless otherwise indicated, Bible quotations are taken from the King James Version of the Bible.

www.xulonpress.com

Table of Contents

Acknowledgments iii

1   Why Study the Word on Worship and Music 1
2   Creation to the Flood 15
3   Patriarchs 37
4   Mosaic Worship 51
5   Joshua and Judges 78
6   United Kingdom 95
7   Psalms 127
8   Job, Ruth, Esther, Eccl., Song of Solomon, Proverbs 151
9   Divided Kingdom and the Disintegration of Worship 164
10   Exile and Restoration 194
11   Christ on Worship 210
12   Worship in the Early Church 234
13   Pauline Epistles 248
14   Hebrews, James, 1, 2, Peter, 1, 2, 3 John and Jude 292
15   Revelation 308
16   Conclusions 331

Endnotes 337

Acknowledgements

I am eternally grateful for three Calvarys in my life. It was on the hill of Calvary that my dear Savior redeemed me for His own glory. Nothing in my life would make any sense without that blood stained place.

The second Calvary I am thankful for is Calvary Baptist Church in Lansdale, Pennsylvania. There God taught me so much about Himself, and it was there that I was privileged to minister with many choice servants for twenty-five years. I owe much of my theological and practical ministry development to my brothers and sisters there. It was there that I met my dear friend Warren Vanhetloo who throughout the writing of this book has been a constant sharpening influence. Sitting in Dr. Van's seminary classes and watching his gentle, faithful service opened my eyes to many great truths. His dignity and respect for God's majesty helped maintain a humility about theological studies. His oft quoted verse, "The secret things belong unto the Lord our God" (Deut 29:29) was a constant reminder that God is God, and we are not.

It was at Calvary Baptist Church in Watertown, Wisconsin, my third Calvary, that God made a place for me to pull away from ministry for a brief time to finish this book. Here my friend and pastor, Bob Loggans, has supported, encouraged and challenged me to keep writing when the temptation to do otherwise was almost overwhelming. Here too I met Dr. Dave White and Angela Morris who have painstakingly edited my work. I could not have done it without them. Countless other people, in particular my friend, Mark Ring, encouraged me to write, prayed for me faithfully, sharpened me and sometimes gave me the gentle push I needed to keep this project moving forward.

Through it all, Brenda, my dear wife of nearly thirty years and my two wonderful daughters, Sarah and Colette, have hung in there with me through the thousands of hours that this project has taken. I love my three ladies with all my heart.

Most importantly I want to thank my dear Redeemer. It is God that makes unworthy sinners co-laborers with Christ.

Lord, you alone are worthy of praise.

This book is Yours; do with it whatever You want.

The errors I know are mine.

The good words, those that build up and challenge,

You alone deserve the glory. You alone are the Truth.

Thank You for letting me be a part of Your work;

thanks for the chance.

In the precious name of Jesus,

Amen.

Dean Kurtz, 2008

Chapter One
Why Study the Word on Worship and Music?

My Personal Journey

I came to personal faith in Christ as a teenager. Our choir sang the night I realized that if this life of faith was for real, it needed to be real for me. That night I bowed and prayed that God would save me from the penalty of my sin. I turned from mere religion, confessed my need of God and His forgiveness, and He saved me, not only from the penalty of my sin, but in the fullest sense, He secured my total redemption. A part of that redemption was His promise that He would "conform [me] to the image of His Son" (Rom 8:29). And a part of my redemption included the privilege of someday worshiping Him around His throne without encumbrance.

From that first night, my worship relationship began. Since then, God has mercifully given me some wonderful worship and music leadership positions. Church youth groups, school choirs, marching bands, concert bands, and other musical groups all began molding convictions in my heart. God began specifically directing me into music ministry.

Alongside of these opportunities, God began growing in me a thirst for His Word. More and more it became clear to me that denominational allegiances and Christian traditions must take second place behind the Bible. More and more I realized that the Bible alone must be my source for faith and practice. Many around me cheered me on in this growing conviction. Still, when it came to discussions about worship or music for worship, discussions were often clouded by personal opinions, or history, or denominational preferences. Many of those early discussions were built on foundational ideas that "just seemed obvious" and ended with conclusions that were diametrically opposed to each other. Surely there must be a better foundation.

I headed off to a fundamentalist Baptist Bible college. Believers around me told me that this would be the place where the Word would reign supreme. I fully expected that since I was both a music education major and a Bible major my head and heart would be directed to a thorough study of the Word as it relates to worship and music. In my naiveté, I was sure that since my passions were the Bible and music, a systematic study of what the Bible said about music would soon be forthcoming. I completed two bachelor's degrees (one in music education and the other in Bible), a master's degree in sacred music, and a doctor of ministry degree. Somehow in all that training a systematic overview of music and worship in the Word was noticeably absent.

Don't get me wrong. I was challenged with many great ideas by wonderful, godly, and passionate professors. Most importantly my thirst for the Word was continually fanned. I am eternally grateful, that during my second year of Bible College my dear friend, Dr. Frank Garlock, came to the college to speak for several chapels. I will never forget his energy and fire. When he challenged the music majors to make the study of music in the Bible a lifelong passion, I was hooked. I was looking the other day at the Bible I had in those early days filled with treble clefs in the margins and beautifully stained with blue highlighter, the color that still marks music verses in my Bibles. Still, I missed a comprehensive study of worship and music in the Bible because, to my knowledge, one didn't exist. I am sure now that it was not for lack of desire, but a more systemic problem. My music professors had little training in theology and my Bible professors had little training or concern to deal with things musical. After all, they had no formal music training. In spite of the fact that I felt a bit cheated in this foundational study, I found myself in a leadership position in my church. But, I had to ask myself, if with all my training *I* hadn't had the opportunity for such an overview of worship and music in the Word, who had?

It also became obvious to me that while many in my church had strong feelings about worship and church music, few could explain the origin, purposes, or development of worship or music in the Bible; few could offer a concise, working definition of worship using biblical principles or examples. It is this lack that has lit a fire in me. I have a passion to see God's people exposed to the biblical teaching on worship and music. Now, I readily admit that I don't have the last word on worship and music; that is found only in God's Word. For this reason I have formatted this book to help give you a tool to wrestle through these biblical topics yourself. I will explain how the book is set up a little later.

I also need you to hear that I humbly admit that neither I nor my church has a *perfect* music philosophy. We all need the continual washing of the Word to challenge us to godly change. I remember a pastor challenging me, "Dean," he said, "let's go to the Word and let it take us wherever we need to go." My heart responded, yes! But, if you and I would call ourselves "people of the Book" then we need to *continually* recommit to that search. Doing what "works," or what keeps us comfortable will not do.

When faced with contemporary questions we must look into the Scriptures for our answers. Being a Biblicist, however, demands that we work out from Scripture, to principle, and then to application. I remember sitting in a room with several pastors who all passionately wanted better worship. But where will we go for the model? The 1980's? The 50's? The "good ole days?" Public consensus? None of these are enough. How will we measure a "successful" worship program or service? We must start with the Word and then go to application, not the other way around.

Take a look at worship in the world around us. Every week millions of people go to a place of worship during the worship hour. After a call to worship, some worship songs and other worship activities, worshipers go home and critique the worship to which they have just been exposed. Yet, the ability to biblically define worship escapes them. Worship has been and will be the practice of all created sentient beings (moral beings who have the capacity to choose: men and angels). Today, worship and church music are topics of many books and much discussion. Believers all over the world are talking and writing about worship. Many believe that their worship is God-honoring, and can marshal theological ideas or even a few Bible verses in defense of their worship style or practices. But the overarching "big ideas" about worship are largely unknown to them. When pressed for answers, worshipers and those who lead them often resort to trite or incomplete definitions for worship or offer criteria for success that have little to do with the Scriptures. It is precisely this lack of knowledge and biblical training about worship that have led to many of the "worship wars" being fought today. I agree with the truism "we become what we worship." Because of this it matters profoundly who, in reality, church attendees are worshiping. Believers are becoming more and more like their *real* object of worship. Much is at stake.

Many of those involved in the ministry of music and worship in the local church have had little or no formal training in worship and church music issues. This problem, as I reflected on my own journey earlier, is systemic. Musicians and preachers alike often have little or no formal Bible training in worship or music. People for the most part have difficulty even defining worship and often do not know what the practice of worship has been through biblical history. In other words, those involved in worship as participants and their leaders have never been exposed to the meta-narrative of worship. I believe it is critical for leaders to explore worship principles and practices in the totality of the Word.

God says He is a jealous God, that we must worship Him and Him alone. "For thou shalt worship no other god: for the LORD, whose name is Jealous is a jealous God" (Ex 34:14). Worship should matter to us because it profoundly matters to God. The *way* people worship also profoundly matters to God. How much you as a worshiper know about worship in the Word should certainly affect how you approach God.

Worship is universal. In every time and in every culture man worships someone or something. When Jesus confronted the woman at the well about her relationship to God, He did not ask, "Do you worship?" or "How do you worship?" Instead, He stated a truism, "Ye worship..." (John 4:22). Jesus knew that this woman, like all of us was a practicing worshiper. The issue Jesus raised with her is the problem we are addressing in this book. Jesus said, "Ye worship ye know not what." The question is "What (or whom), exactly, are we worshiping when we gather each week for a worship service?" "What (or whom), exactly, are we worshiping when we make worship music choices for ourselves or our families throughout the week?" Every believer is called to worship the God of the Word. Further, those worshipers who find themselves in leadership positions have an even more critical need to grow in their knowledge and appreciation of worship and the music used in worship. As worshipers and ones who model/lead worship in the public service, we desperately need to know God's mind on the subject as revealed in His Word.

Similarly, Paul observed that the unregenerate "worshiped and served the creature more than the Creator" (Rom 1:25). Paul built upon this predisposition when addressing the unbelievers in Athens at Mars Hill (Acts 17:22-25). He began his sermon with a statement of the problem: "Ye ignorantly worship" (Acts 17:23). His hearers' problem is the same problem facing us today; many worship God ignorantly. I would suggest that believers as well as unbelievers can fall prey to ignorant worship practices. The pages of Scripture are filled with them.

Increasing our knowledge of and appreciation for biblical worship and music is admittedly a journey. No person will ever worship with complete knowledge in this lifetime. It is possible, however, to understand through precept and example *more* about the kind of worship God desires.

Throughout this book I will write about worship *and* music. Please understand that worship and music are *not* interchangeable terms. Worship can and should happen without music. Music, as will be discussed later, is not always a part of a worship *act* (though all music should be "to the glory of God," 1 Cor 10:31). It is impossible, however, to have worship in the fullest sense without music eventually playing a role. For this reason music selected for worship must be even more carefully examined. Further, I would suggest that discussions about church music best happen within the context of worship overall.

Music has always been and continues to be, a powerful force in the life of the church. Throughout the church age, music has played an important role in teaching and reinforcing doctrine. As the centuries have marched on, worship and the music used in worship continue to be the topics of discussion by the world's greatest theologians. I don't think there has ever been a time in history, however, when music has played a *greater* role in influencing human beliefs and behavior than today. Technology has made music almost omnipresent. The church is inundated with sacred music choices. Church members can purchase or download "Christian" music in every conceivable musical genre. Having made a musical choice, these musicians become their teachers and intimate counselors (Col 3:16). We listen until we have completely memorized the songs and have allowed them to "indoctrinate" us with their teaching. Society's attitudes about music also affect how believers view worship music. For example, online search engines put music under entertainment alongside TV, movies, horoscopes, games, and other nonsense. Believers are often unaware that the Bible paints a radically different picture about the purpose and place of music.

Thankfully, we are not without guidance. From Genesis to Revelation, the Bible is replete with examples and principles governing worship and music. These general principles about worship and music and the many specific examples inform every believer if we will only listen. Those of us who believe that the Bible alone should formulate our beliefs and practices should thirst to know how the Scriptures define worship and how principles and practices we observe in its pages can help us bring the kind of worship God is eager to receive. Those who are a part of the worship and/or music leadership of the church should be particularly concerned about knowing and living these principles. Indeed, all believers should be able to articulate a biblical definition of worship and list principles that can guide their own practice. Every believer should have enough biblical knowledge to discern whether his participation reflects a biblical model for worship. Without this knowledge laymen and vocational ministers alike will draw conclusions about worship that are simplistic or even heretical. While every believer should know what the Bible says about worship and music, those in leadership in the church have an even more critical need to know and obey the truth.

I am aware that a biblical model for worship has been the subject of discussion by many pastors and theologians. I would never pretend to be the final word on worship or music myself. God's Word is the final authority on worship and music. What I can do is offer you a tool for your own study. Worship leaders (by this I mean all those who stand before God's people and with their words or songs direct our thoughts toward God) are limited in their ability to effectively minister to the Lord and others if they lack a basic understanding of Biblical principles governing worship and church music.

Ministry to the Lord? Yes, Acts 13:2 is one of many places that illustrates this ministry to the Lord. In fact, the ESV (*English Standard Version*) translates it "worshiping to the Lord." Strong's offers this definition of the word found in this passage.

> 3008 λειτουργέω [*leitourgeo*] v. From 3011; TDNT 4:215; TDNTA 526; GK 3310); Three occurrences; AV translates as 'minister' three times. **1** to serve the state at one's own cost. 1A to assume an office which must be administered at one's own expense. 1B to discharge a public office at one's own cost. 1C to render public service to the state. **2** to do a service, perform a work. 2A of priests and Levites who were busied with the sacred rites in the tabernacle or the temple. 2B of Christians serving Christ, whether by prayer, or by instructing others concerning the way of salvation, or in some other way. 2C of those who aid others with their resources, and relieve their poverty.[1]

This is also the sense in which the word λειτουργεῖν (*leitourgein*) is used in Hebrews 10:11 "Every priest standeth daily... ministering." Just as mortals can "bless the Lord" (Ps 103:1) they can also minister, not only *for*, but *to* the Lord. One way we do this is to, "with one mind and one mouth glorify God, even the Father of our Lord Jesus Christ" (Rom 15:6). Church music has often been thought of as primarily a ministry to other people, a ministry that God in some way is glad (or grieved) to see. Regrettably, music and worship choices are often made by first considering the desires of the unsaved and unchurched or secondarily by listening to the desires of church members. But ministering first and foremost to the Lord in our worship is a shift in focus that will have profound implications.

My passion is to help you identify and then teach principles that are set forth by example and precept in both Testaments. These governing principles are <u>transdispensational</u> (seen universally in all of God's dealings with men as recorded in the pages of Scripture) and transcultural (transcending cultural boundaries).

Where I am Coming From

I accept that the canonical Scriptures are the verbally and plenarily inspired Word of God and inerrant in the original writings. The sixty-six books of the Old and New Testaments are the complete and divine written Revelation of God to man. For this reason I believe the Bible should guide all matters of belief and practice. I am passionate to communicate the Bible's story about worship and music, particularly as it applies to the church today. This also differentiates me from those who are Process (God is becoming)[2] in their view of God or worship practices. I view the biblical teachings about worship and music as superior to the traditions or practices of historic or contemporary churchmen as helpful as they may be in their own right.

Second, I believe in a dispensational (various stewardships of revelation) hermeneutic (the way in which the Bible is interpreted). I embrace the need to see God's revelation as an unfolding revelation. Therefore the specific *practices* of worship may very well look different in various dispensations, but the governing *principles* behind these practices are transdispensational. This position contrasts to a process theologian's view of the developing changes of worship through the ages. I believe we see in the Scriptures an unfolding and further clarification of universal worship concepts. Distinction in the worship *practices* of previous dispensations must be considered while still identifying *concepts and principles* that are evident on this side of Calvary. For this reason an examination of the worship principles in all of God's dealings, past and future, are instructive for believers today. God has never changed and will never change or "become" as process theologians imagine. Worship principles *can* be identified and practical application *can* be made in church music on the basis of transdispensational principles.

I have come to embrace the need for an exegetical, theological, and finally practical approach to studying the Scriptures. Biblical principles about worship and music must be identified through careful exegesis, concepts or principles stated carefully, and then applied with cultural sensitivity and personal integrity. Certainly, conclusions and applications will vary somewhat, but just as certainly universal principles will also be apparent. Contextualization, making practical applications in specific cultural contexts, cannot be ignored; neither can "relevance" become an excuse for blending essentially pagan worship practices and philosophies (syncretism) into our worship of the Lord. Our world has largely bought into the lie that there are no absolutes (existentialism), that there is no truth or beauty. Making practical, culturally sensitive applications should not keep us from being truth-bound.

Since we will be looking at several narratives, I think it is important to understand that some very interesting things have been said over the years about worship using narratives as the basis for such assertions. You should further understand that extracting doctrine from narratives, especially Old Testament narratives is challenging. The question to keep in mind when looking to a narrative is, "Is the action in this narrative descriptive or prescriptive?" In other words, just because Moses or David did or said something does not mean God approved or is calling us to do the same today. If God didn't give His express approval, perhaps neither should we. Always look for the direct response of God not just the next action listed. Further, even if God clearly approves or disapproves in the narrative, other New Testament texts must be considered before conclusions can be made, and applications suggested.

I will at times refer to an "abstraction ladder," a term that is increasingly popular not only in theological circles but also among linguists. I believe that when a direct command is made that is applicable to our present dispensation of revelation, it should be obeyed without question. These are mandates. I also believe there are times when legitimate application can only be made as we "travel up the abstraction ladder" and discern the principle or concept behind the event or command. For example, although we are no longer obligated to offer up the first born lamb without blemish, we might travel up the abstraction ladder and state the more general principle that our offering of self should be acceptable to God. This is what Paul does when he uses OT cultus (worship practices)[3] language in Romans 12:1-2. He makes the abstraction that believers should offer themselves to God. As a general rule we should take all NT commands as directly applicable. All trips up the abstraction ladder should be as short as humanly possible.

Third, it is a blessing to know that God can indeed be pleased as believers worship Him in spirit and in truth. Furthermore, God is actively seeking worshipers, not just worship. The church corporately and believers individually are invited to worship. What God commands, He guides and empowers believers to accomplish. Believers *can* learn to worship in spirit and truth, and our loving God invites us to such a relationship.

Fourth, I am convinced that there *is* truth, and that truth exists outside of man's appreciation for or acknowledgement of it. By extension, I also believe that there is beauty that exists outside of man's appreciation for or acknowledgment of it. Since there is truth, there is beauty. I am not saying that mortal man can *fully* know all that is true any more than he can *fully* know all that is beautiful. I simply mean that there *is* a standard that exists in the mind of God beyond the limitations of human intellect or appreciation. Some truth and beauty are readily apparent. Some definitions for truth and beauty have been given to us in the Bible, God's Special Revelation. I believe the very fact that there *is* truth and beauty outside of man is in itself a refining concept.

So what about quotes from historic or contemporary thinkers? What about secular studies? I use them on a very limited basis because I believe our warfare is spiritual and that the Holy Spirit using the Word has the only power for deep and permanent change. There *are* times when believers are called upon to exercise wisdom in making an intelligent "best guess" determination about truth or beauty based on broad principles and observation. It is here where God's general revelation can be helpful. Even then we must have a certain desperate dependence on the Lord as we make these wisdom choices.

Fifth, I embrace the truth that worship affects all parties involved. From God, as primary recipient, to the worshiper himself, and even to the unbelieving observer of worship, the Bible clearly states that all parties are impacted. This is not to say, however, that worship is *primarily* for people, believers or unbelievers. Worship should be supremely about the pleasure of God. It is this hierarchy of priority in worship that is rightfully in the public discussion. Worship has both horizontal as well as vertical implications.

Sixth, although music is primarily considered a form of entertainment in our day, the ancients saw music more broadly for what it is: a powerful form of communication. Music, specifically singing, is an extension of speech and thus a form of communication not just a form of entertainment. Singing and speech became separate, discernable forms later in human history. I agree with William Wickes and others when they assert that "From time immemorial the reading of the sacred books in the synagogue has been a kind of cantillation, or musical declamation."[4] Even before the practices of the synagogue, music was intended to be used in teaching and recalling God's great acts (Ex 15:1-19; Deut 31:19-32:43). For this reason and others I believe these poetic sections were at least, "singable." I will at times deal with these sections in this broader sense.[5] For example, when God chose to make His legal covenant with Israel (Deut 31-32), He commanded it be rehearsed and remembered in song.[6] The semantic (specific meanings of words) overlap of singing and speaking will be discussed later but I mention it here because present prejudice puts such a wide chasm between speech and music that some seem to want to deny the obvious; both speaking and singing "teach and admonish" (Col 1:28 cf 3:16).

Seventh, I view God's relationship to all creation and specifically to man as doxological in nature. In other words, God created all things, including man, for His glory. God ultimately provided for man's redemption so that man might fulfill the higher purpose of bringing glory to Him in worship. God wants men to worship Him so He provides a means of forgiveness, enabling man to offer to Him the worship He deserves and desires. Redemption allows mankind to have a relationship of fellowship with God, a fellowship characterized by worship. This "fellowship of worship," is the aim of God's soteriological activities (related to salvation). It is not enough to center our lives around the gospel our center should be the greater glory of God. John Piper said succinctly, "Missions exists because worship doesn't."[7]

I will be using the word R(r)evelation in at least four ways. First, at times I refer to the single canonical book of Revelation. I will always capitalize it. Second, there will be times I will use the word to refer to the sixty-six canonical books for the Old and New Testaments, God's special written Revelation. I will also capitalize the word when I use it in this sense. Third, I may also use the term to refer to general or natural revelation (Ps 19:1; Rom 1:20). Fourth, I may also use the term in a *very* broad sense. As we communicate about God in words and actions we are in a sense, revealing God to others. Many contemporary writers have been using this term in their worship studies. Matt Redman (and others) uses the term this way in his chapter "Revelation and Response."[8] In this last sense I am using the term very loosely to refer to times when we are "revealing" God to others. Paul and Peter both talk about revealing or "showing forth" God as believers walk and talk (2 Cor 4:7; 1 Pet 2:9). In each case I will try to make the sense clear.

Book Format

You may wonder why I don't come right out and give you a formal definition of worship, or walk you through all the definitions of words used in the biblical languages. What I want is for the Word to wash over you progressively. My prayer is that you will begin to discover, as I did, elements of worship and perspectives about worship as you slowly immerse yourself in the Word. I will share with you some more formal definitions later but you will benefit most from letting the Scriptures speak. Understanding how to worship in spirit and in truth is a journey of discovery, one that will not end for me until I stand in God's heavenly throne room. One that I hope for you will be stimulated by this book.

I have chosen to set up most chapters in four sections. First, I am going to list for you what I have come to believe are significant passages regarding worship or music. I may have missed or excluded some verses you believe ought to be there or I may include some verses you think are a stretch, but my best efforts are presented for your perusal. For me, this is the most important part of each chapter. If you simply discard the rest of the book and study through the passages listed, I believe God will do a work in your life for which I would be eternally grateful to have been a part.

After the listing of passages, I am going to identify a few passages that I consider to be representative or significant for a more in-depth exegetical treatment. Each passage will then be split up into three sections. The first will come under the title **Exegetical Considerations.** I want to admit here that I rely heavily on the work of others in this section. I am especially thankful for Logos Bible Software and the help it has been to me personally. This section is not meant to be a complete treatment of the entire passage. I only highlight some points I consider to be important to our study. I realize that the selection or treatment of these passages may cause some to take exception, but I offer them with sincerity and hope that this will stimulate thought and discussion. It is easier to critique than invent and easier to refine than produce. I invite you to stand on my shoulders, do better, and see higher. *(Please don't kick me in the nose while you are up there!)*

The next section for each passage is a recap of the exegetical material into what I consider transdispensational, transcultural principles. These **Principles to Apply** are intended to succinctly and logically make connections between the text, which is time bound, and our own time. I trust they will serve as a bridge between the exegetical considerations and the applications and musings I offer next.

Last, I make an attempt to draw **Applications** out of the Scriptures. Some of my thoughts will relate directly to the passage and be the primary application of the passage. Other ideas are personal thoughts on the general principles I see. Our job is not complete until we endeavor to live out the Scriptures in practical ways. We are not done until our knowing becomes doing. Here I expect there to be the greatest divergence of thought. This is why I have organized the material as I have. We can disagree over application. We may have some latitude when it comes to discerning and stating the principles to apply. There may even be some divergence of thought in the business of exegesis but we must not close our eyes to the Word. What breaks my heart are those who seem uninterested in digging deep into the Word before making applications.

If we and the people we minister with are going to know how to minister to the Lord and others we need to have His Word on the matter. I am encouraged by an ever-increasing desire in the church for Word-based ministry that is not driven by tradition alone. Let us commit to looking to the Word and letting our applications grow out of the Scriptures.

With some exceptions I examine the Biblical material in canonical order. I deviate from this when it makes sense to address it in a more or less dispensational or historical order. For example, not all the material about music and worship in creation is available in Genesis, so in chapter one I bring some other passages dealing with pre-creation and creation into the discussion. We will examine material in Psalms as a whole and not in each Psalm's historic context.

I desire nothing more than that you would dig into the Scriptures yourself and then "get real" about how we ought to live the Word we say we believe. You might think about buying a notebook and journaling as you work through this material. If you have the Spirit in you and the Word before you, you have all you need for life and godliness. Now to the study.

Chapter Two
Creation to the Flood

I would strongly urge you to read chapter one if you have jumped to this chapter for reasons of your own. This whole presentation will make much more sense if you know how I plan to proceed with this wonderful and challenging study. Remember, I am convinced that the application questions about music should be asked within the greater context of worship.

Deciding what passages to include in this chapter was challenging. Subsequent chapters you will find to be more canonical/historical. I myself am much more comfortable with the other chapters because they lend themselves better to the exegetical, theological, practical format I explained in chapter one. Having said that, let's begin.

A. In the beginning...
   1. Gen 1:1 The preexistence of God, worship in the Trinity
   2. Zeph 3:17 God as singer
   3. Rom 1:20-21 Creation as the starting point in worship
   4. Ps 19:1 Reason for creation; the doxological end of all things

B. Creation of "the other" sentient (moral) beings
   1. Job 38:6-7 Creation and music
   2. Isa 14:11-15 Cosmic conflict over the object of worship
   3. Eze 28:13 Angelic beings generally and Lucifer specifically

C. Creation of Man
   1. Gen 1:26-27 Image of God in man
   2. Gen 2:23 First poem/song recorded
   3. Gen 3:8 Life in "the cool of the day"
   4. Gen 3:21 The "clothing" of Adam and Eve by God

D. Early Worship or Music Events
   1. Gen 4:3-9 First recorded worship cultus[1] (liturgy or worship practice) of Cain and Abel
   2. Gen 4:21 Origin of instrumental music
   3. Gen 4:23-24 Lamech's song
   4. Gen 8: 20-21 Noah's worship
   5. Gen 11:4 Was the tower of Babel a ziggurat center for worship?

From this section I have chosen to consider passages around three areas: First, the musical nature of God (Gen 1:1; Zeph 3:17) and by extension the musical nature of all sentient being created in His image; second, the worship of Cain and Abel; and third, the worship of Noah.

Our Musical World

Gen 1:1; Zeph 3:17; Rom 1:20-21; Ps 19:1
Exegetical Considerations

Genesis 1:1 does not go about to prove the existence of God but assumes God the Trinity is the uncaused cause of all things. The text does nothing less than emphatically declare that God is the cause of all we know, see, or hear. All good and perfect gifts come from our great Creator Father (James 1:17). At the end of creation God Himself gives His commentary; everything was "very good" (Gen 1:31). Man, of course has twisted some of the good things God has created and manipulated them in ways that reflect rebellion, but they were in their original state completely consistent with God's declaration; God's creation was a fitting reflection of His beauty and glorious nature.

One might ask why God would create this vast universe. The answer can be seen in at least two passages. Psalm 19:1 says that the celestial bodies universally declare the glory of God and show His handiwork. The Psalm goes on to say that paradoxically this "language" transcends words or speech and is universal (Ps 19:3). Creation itself calls for men to give God glory. Paul expands on this in Romans 1:20. Creation universally glorifies God by

Creation to the Flood

showing His eternal power (ἀίδιος δύναμις, *aidios dunamis*) and Lordship or divine nature (θειότης, *theiotes*). God shows Himself by His created acts. In response, all creation, and specifically all created sentient beings, are intended to respond in worship.

Most are aware of the tragic disobedience of the first couple; they broke that worship relationship with God. It was no surprise to God that man was hiding in shame and terror. God knew what man had done, now the "fellowship of worship," once the daily activity of mankind (happening in the cool or literally the "breeze" of the day),[2] needed to be restored. God revealed Himself to man and confronted him about his sin. This self-disclosing, divine initiative by God (it was God who came) showed His desire for a worship relationship with mankind (a relationship characterized by worship).

[margin note: a little odd]

At some early point, even before the creation of man, God created all angelic beings. They were able to celebrate God's great acts and did so with singing. Job mentions in his poetic song that as God was forming the world, music celebrated the event. TWOT (Theological Wordbook of the Old Testament) mentions that in the "poetic song of praise in Job 38:7 ... [that] the 'sons of God'"[3] sang and shouted for joy (רוע). Walvoord and Zuck also mention the place of praise using music when God made His new creation:

> Job was absent when **the morning stars** (possibly Venus and Mercury; "morning stars" were mentioned by Job in 3:9) **sang** and **the angels** (lit., "the sons of God"; cf.1:6; 2:1) **shouted** with **joy** over God's Creation of the earth. The stars' singing is a poetic personification, not a reference to the noise made by stars as detected by radio astronomy. In Psalm 148:2-3 angels and stars are together commanded to praise the Lord.[4]

Or as John E. Hartley says, "On the occasion of laying the earth's cornerstone, the morning stars were assembled as an angelic chorus to sing praises to God for the glory of his world. At the moment the stone was set in place the sons of God i.e., the angels broke out in joyous singing, praising God, the Creator."[5]

Creation to the Flood

Angelic beings have demonstrated throughout time their ability to express themselves using the powerful communication tools of speech and music (Rev 4:8-9; 5:9, 12; 14:2-3).[6] Fallen angels, most notably Lucifer, retained their communicative abilities after they fell. Paul warned Timothy, "Now the Spirit speaketh expressly, that in the latter times some shall depart from the faith, giving heed to seducing spirits, and doctrines of devils" (1 Tim 4:1). There is no reason textually or logically to exclude music from the list of ways angels, elect or fallen, communicate. Two specific passages of scripture describe Lucifer, his fall, and his character. In both cases music is referred to specifically or by inference in the greater context.

In Ezekiel 28:2-19, the prophet chides the King of Tyre. In describing the King, Ezekiel compares him to Lucifer himself. In this description Satan (made clear by vs. 13 "Thou wast in Eden") is described in terms of his beauty.[7] Verse 13 lists a number of precious stones that make up his "covering." Then the passage states that Lucifer was created with "tabrets and pipes." The question among Bible translators is should תֹּף (*top*) and נֶקֶב (*neqeb*) be translated "settings and socket" (NASB and others); or should they be translated "tabrets (timbrels or tambourines) and pipes" (KJV and others)? Much of the discussion comes down to a question of whether the context insists that *top* be translated something other than "tabrets," which is the preferred translation in the 17 other times תֹּף (*top*) is used, or must it be understood as "beat" as one might beat gold to make a setting. I believe the word selection "setting" is exceedingly unlikely. The context does not *demand* this word at all, it only reflects the prejudice of some who believe "beats" presents an "easier reading." Just as Ezekiel is using physical jewels to describe Lucifer's beauty, he is using musical instruments to illustrate the truth that Lucifer is musical. The use of the instruments as a way of describing Lucifer's beauty is not difficult to understand.

BDB (*The Enhanced Brown-Driver-Briggs Hebrew and English Lexicon*), a respected lexicon among theologians, lists Ezekiel 28:13 as one of the places *top* should be translated timbrel or tambourine. Later, I have quoted for you their decision to opt for a jeweler's term for the second more obscure *neqeb* term.

תֹף timbrel, tambourine; abs. ת׳ Gn 31:27 pl. תֻפִּים Ju 8|11:34 +; תֻפֶּ֫יךָ Ez 28:13, תֻפַּ֫יִךְ Je 31:4;—*timbrel*, held and struck with hand, especially by dancing women, often with other musical instr.:—sign of merriment, gladness Gn 31:27 (E) Jb 21:12, revelry Is 5:12; מְשׂוֹשׂ ת׳ 24:8 cf. Je 31:4 Ez 28:13 (CO *setting*) triumph Ex 15:20 (E) Ju 11:34 1 S 18:6 Is 30:32; used by prophets in ecstasy 1 S 10:5; in praise of 2 S 6:5, 1 Ch 13:8, 81:3; 149:3; 150:4. – Vid. Prince[8]

נֶקֶב... term. techn. of jeweller's work, prob. some hole or cavity (Hi. Sim. Co. Berthol; ToyHpt leaves untransl.),—only pl si. תֻפֶּ֫יךָ וּנְקָבֶ֫יךָ Ez 28:13 thy sockets and thy grooves (Da), or thy settings and thy sockets.[9]

The second word in question, נֶקֶב (*neqeb*), is used in this form only here. The etymologically close verb form, נָקַב (*naqab*) gives the idea of boring holes, mining, or piercing.[10]

Although unanimity on the translation of musical instruments for the two words in this passage does not exist, there is no clear reason to depart from the more normal understanding of the word by the original Jewish audience. תֹף (*top*) is translated "timbrel or tambourine," a musical instrument, in all other usages. I see no convincing reason to translate it otherwise. If it is an instrument, as I believe it assuredly is, then the immediate context of נֶקֶב (*neqeb*) would argue for a translation of a musical instrument with bored holes like a pipe or flute. Rabbi Mosha Eisemann offers this translation, "Your [Lucifer's] skill in making instruments, or your musical ability, was bred into you at the moment of your birth."[11] I believe these two words should be understood as musical instruments that, although not literally on Lucifer's body, are used to illustrate the beauty of Lucifer's musical nature just as the jewels illustrate his visual beauty.

In a similar passage, the prophet Isaiah compares the King of Babylon to Lucifer in Isaiah 14:4-23. I also take the position on this passage that it has a dual meaning. Isaiah is essentially calling the King of Babylon the Devil. Satan's heart of rebellion and pride are described. In Isaiah 14:11 the prophet declares that the "music" (NASB) הֶמְיָה (*hemya*) or "noise" (KJV) of the "viols" (KJV) or better "harps" (NASB and others) נֶבֶל (*nebel*) of the rebellious will be judged. Lucifer is a communicative being, as are all angels. There is every reason to presume that this innate ability to communicate includes their ability to communicate musically.

Man was also created a communicative being and that included his ability to communicate with music. After God created man, He immediately began to communicate with him. First, God blessed בָּרַךְ (*barak*)[12] him; thus initiating a relationship with him (Gen 1:28a). Then God launched into a description of mankind's service for Him (Gen 1:28b-30). All of this occurred in one day (Gen 1:31). The conservative Bible interpreter is left with no other conclusion than that man's ability to communicate was innate. A reading of Genesis 1-3 shows an immediate interchange between God and Himself (Gen 1:26), God and mankind (Gen 1:28; 2:23), woman (*mankind*) and Lucifer (Gen 3:1-3), God and Lucifer (Gen 3:14), and man and woman (assumed in Gen 3:6). In other words, there was free and immediate communication between all three sentient beings. Communication was given by God to sentient beings primarily to facilitate their relationship to Him and secondarily with each other. This relationship initiated by God was to be characterized by creatures giving glory to their Creator God.

Genesis demonstrates that God created men with the capacity and propensity to worship (see also Rom 1:20-23). The structure of Genesis 3:8 indicates a habitual, calm, and common approach by God as He came to fellowship with man.[13] "And they heard the voice of the Lord God walking in the garden in the cool of the day: and Adam and his wife hid themselves from the presence of the Lord" (Gen 3:8a). TWOT states "'לִפְנֵי (*lipne*) 'in the presence of, before'" is the most frequent usage of *pene* (plural construct) with a prefixed preposition. Literally, the phrase means 'at/to the face of.'"[14]

This "face to face" relationship included mankind's innate ability to communicate to God in speech or music. The Hebrew uses both prose and the poetic form in this section (Gen 1:27; 2:23). Adam's first recorded words are set in poetic form (Gen 2:23), a form that could be sung. Those who assume that God or Adam were unable to sing as well as speak read back into the passage a predisposition that is not supported by Hebrew word usage or other narrative texts that would soon follow. We are created in the image of a musical God (Gen 1:26; cf. Zeph 3:17). This musical nature is universal among men and angels. This is supported theologically, logically, and anthropologically. Wherever man is found, some form of music exists.

[Margin notes: "very weak." and "How is the musicality of angels supported anthropologically?"]

Principles to Apply

- God is eternal and self-sufficient needing nothing, including worshipers, to be complete.
- God is a musical God. He communicates musically.
- When God chose to create the universe, He did so to display His own worth. His glory, eternal power, and Godhead or divine nature, are universally communicated to mankind.
- God both initiates a relationship with mankind by virtue of his creation and facilitates that relationship by giving sentient beings the gift of communication in speech and music. This relationship is one that is to be characterized by worship.
- Angelic beings, both fallen and elect, possess the ability to communicate through the powerful tool of music.
- Satan is a musical being and actively seeks to deceive, influence, and destroy men (1 Pet 5:8).
- God and mankind could have "face-to-face" fellowship. Man's sin marked the end of that open relationship. Man can no longer come "face to face" with God without divinely approved mediation and an appointed mediator.
- Man must come to God on God's terms and receive the needed forgiveness for the fellowship of worship to be restored.
- The powerful and unique gift of music gives all sentient beings (men and angels) the ability to express emotional sentiments of "heart, soul, mind and strength." God masterfully and wisely created man in His own image, an image that includes the

ability to commune and communicate on a deep intellectual and emotional level using the tool of music.

Applications

Throughout the Word, the very act of creation is given as a reason to worship. This is repeated throughout the Psalms and is appealed to again in the eternal state (Rev 4, 5).

Music is a uniquely fitted, God-given gift that men and angels should use in responding to God's call to worship. Yet, when we open an internet search engine or look at a newspaper for information about music, that information appears in the entertainment section giving us a narrower understanding of music's purposes. Most people today view music as primarily a form of entertainment; early man saw music more broadly as a form of communication.

The origin of music is inextricably tied to the origin of language. In a leading scholarly secular work, *The Origins of Music*, the writer states that "in fact the distinction between speaking and singing is best thought of as a difference in degree rather than a difference in kind."[15] Egon Wellesz, another respected secular writer, conjectures that "although we must reject the hypothesis that speech is protomorphic music, it is still possible to speculate whether the very ancient 'sound language' may not represent the common source of both speech and music."[16]

Historically, the most commonly held position among those who do not believe in a divine origin is that music evolved from speech patterns.[17] Though among evolutionist there is no clear consensus on which appeared first, speech or music, there is agreement that they came from the same source. In light of the biblical testimony (Adam's first recorded words were written in poetic form), I conjecture that Adamic communication may have made little or no distinction between music and speech. Even today many of the oriental languages, those linguists consider the oldest, are pitch sensitive. I realize this is based on anthropology and logic and not specific exegesis so feel free to temper this argument. I make the point because in my mind we make too sharp a distinction between speaking and singing, minimizing the influence of music on our belief systems and behavior.

Although most music scholars look upon all religious theories of the origin of music with some disdain, there are several striking similarities between other religious accounts and the biblical data. Many religious systems offer myths about the origin of music. Wellesz says,

> A close connection between gods and music in Mesopotamia is significant. One of the most ancient gods, Ea, the ruler of the deep, had his name written with a sign which stood for drum. Ramman was conceived as the 'spirit of sonorous voice.' One of the names of the goddess Ishtar, the virgin mother, was 'the soft reed pipe'.[18]

However erroneous the details in these non-biblical accounts, the parallels between them give testimony to a divine origin of music, just as various flood accounts in ANE (Ancient Near Eastern) religions give testimony to a world-wide flood.

Music was not created or invented by man. Music was given to all sentient beings in the original creation by God, who Himself actively communicates through music. Secular evolutionary musicologists also attest to the truth that music is interestingly universal.[19]

I must wonder how this gift from God, The Supreme Moral Agent, given to moral angels and moral men, who communicate moral messages, can possibly avoid taking on moral attributes. Stay with me on this, I'm asking you to think it through. I can't deal with this completely but in light of music's beginning, let me summarize several factors that argue for the moral nature of music: the Divine origin of music, the universality of music in human culture, the uniqueness of music among sentient beings as opposed to other created beings, the physics of universal tonal and rhythmic constants within cultural diversity, and the observable power of music to transcend mere facts.[20]

Writers like David Nelson who oppose the moral character of music miss the point entirely. He says "... I do not believe that music itself has the capacity to be immoral. I have yet to encounter an argument, ancient or modern, that adequately demonstrates how musical notes, rhythms, timbres, and such are immoral or evil."[21] Although the elements of music (notes and rhythms, timbre and volume, or in the case of visual art: lines, curves and colors) may be thought of as morally neutral, when a moral being combines these elements into an understandable whole, the music reflects the musician and his intentions. I readily admit that communication in the arts involves many elements, including the social conditioning of the receptor and the cultural referents of the time and society.[22] Interestingly, Nelson states on the next page that in his estimation, "we should admit that some music is simply bad and thereby not suitable for worship."[23] *"bad" does not equal "immoral."*

Arguing for music's moral character is not to say that culture does not play a role. Consider the human conscience; it reflects both the image of God in man on one hand and the results of the conditioning of culture on the other hand. Because every man has a conscience given to him by God (Rom 1:19), his moral choices reflect some universal as well as some cultural elements. Further, even immoral people can communicate in objectively moral ways. You see, even though the things wicked men do are of no eternal value ("even the plowing of wicked is sin" Prov 21:4) people are not always, in every way as bad as they can be. For this reason, no cultural aberrations erase the truth that conscience is universal. Similarly, music is universally present among humans and communicates more universally than any other medium. It is an innate part of God, men, and angels, and music is afforded eternal tenure; it will forever adorn the throne room of God (Rev 15:3-4).

Kurt Woetzel in his unpublished notes for the National Leadership Conference, February 23, 2006, introduced an interesting idea. He proposed that every man has a "musical conscience." When considering the question of universals in music perhaps this is a better concept than using the word "morality" when discussing this topic. Mankind is "hard wired" with certain musical sensibilities. *Wow. really?*

When thinking about music's moral nature, I think it is also important to remember that music, unlike inanimate objects such as a gun or a bottle of alcohol, does not exist except as a form of communication between moral agents. Really, music has no direct parallel. The closest comparison would be other forms of

Creation to the Flood

communication like speaking or perhaps visual communication. Music is only produced by moral agents who intend for their music to be perceived by other moral agents.

[margin: um, wrong. we can sing entirely for ourselves.]

Music is certainly universal as a communication tool in the world. For this reason music is not so much an element of worship as it is a vehicle for the elements of worship. I agree with others who have said that singing is really no more an element of worship than speaking, yet somehow it often appears in lists of worship elements.[24] Let me explain. Prayer is an element of worship which can be facilitated through singing. Yet believers are often surprised by the idea that when they sing a song *to* God it is by every definition, a prayer. Testifying to others of God's great acts is an activity that is clearly commanded in both Testaments (Ps 51:15; 1 Pet 2:9). Music is a singularly powerful, effective, and divinely decreed means of testifying of God's great acts. When believers sing, they are testifying. Music is more memorable and potentially more influential than teaching using the spoken word. When "reading" the Scripture or "preaching/teaching" God's Word, singing and speaking can happen interchangeably. John Frame, a theologian with whom I respectfully disagree in some areas, offers some helpful historic insights on this point. He states:

[margin: So is language, but that doesn't mean everyone understands each other.]

[margin: really a shallow understanding of the function of music.]

> In our time, we tend to see music mainly as entertainment, or perhaps as "art for art's sake". Matters of historical importance, however, like congressional bills and international treaties, are always written in prose. To put them into poetry or music would seem to trivialize them.... But the use of song for this purpose would not have seemed odd in the ancient world. The most important things were commonly expressed in poetry and music. So we see that God's Word is typically poetic when something of great, lasting importance is taking place.... Part of the reason for this is that in ancient Near Eastern societies, there was less literacy and less distribution of written texts than we have today. In such a society, most people's access to important documents was through the memory. And, as we have seen, poetry and music aid the memory by presenting words vividly and in easily remembered form.[25]

It has been my experience that singing is often presented as a noble activity, but one which is certainly less important than speaking. Let me challenge your thinking on this point. Though I take exception to the man-centeredness of much of what is defined as emergent worship, writers in this movement are also addressing this dichotomy. Sally Morganthaler, author of *Worship Evangelism, Inviting Unbelievers into the Presence of God*, wrote a forward in *Emerging Worship* in which she states that she wants to "move preaching from the centerpiece to one among many pieces."²⁶ The emergent worship movement is largely a reaction away from what Morganthaler calls "predictable and monotone nonspecificity via hundreds of subcultural praise choruses." [Sic]²⁷

Please don't misunderstand, I am not suggesting that speaking, especially preaching, should not be central in the propositional delivery of truth but rather that what is needed is a more concerted effort to infuse what we say *and* sing with the truth of the Word. We must all embrace the reality of the power of music to permanently and powerfully affect every area of our lives. Anyone who finds himself in a leadership role in worship generally or music specifically, especially the pastor as primary worship leader, must select music that is rich in the Word and carefully consider the influence of musical teachers on the flock of God (2 Pet 2). Let's be honest, what we sing or listen to dozens of times will have a greater impact on our belief system than a spoken message we hear once. God has given mankind a powerful tool for good or evil; music must be used thoughtfully and judiciously.

Musicians and theologians, to the detriment of both, have often talked and thought in separate, unrelated worlds. The interrelationship between the origins of language and music is a case in point. Music anthropologists, ethnomusicologists, and evolutionary musicologists inextricably link the origins of music and speech. My research into the theories of the origin of ancient music has caused me to even more strongly believe that Adam sang as freely as he spoke.²⁸ The archeological and linguistic evidence suggests that poets and prophets had a harp in their hand and not a scroll. To the ancients, the thought that poetry would be read and not intoned would have been ridiculous. I realize that biblical genre issues have only recently become matters of concern for scholars, but I believe we need to appreciate the fact that the majority of the Bible is in the poetic genre and much of that was likely sung. This may be a revelation to traditionalists, but I am confident that your research into the way ancient poetry and prophecy were delivered will bring you to the same conclusions. This is one of the reasons the music choices we make are of utmost importance. As Ulrich Leupold asserts, "poetry recited was unknown in antiquity."[29]

Let me summarize. A look at creation passages makes several powerful points:

- God initiates true worship. God needs nothing, but created this universe, including men and angels, to show His own glory; a resplendent glory that should cause us to give Him the worship that He alone is worthy of.
- God facilitates a worship relationship by giving His created beings the communicative gifts of speech and music.
- Although speech and music elements are a part of the created order they have been put in the hands of men and angelic beings who can choose to glorify God with those gifts or not.
- Since all angelic beings are musical by nature we would be wise to discern what Lucifer is up to in the musical world in which we live.
- In modern times we separate music and speech and often see music as simply a form of entertainment. Our culture stands out of sync with the biblical evidence.
- Believers are commanded in both Testaments to actively use this powerful form of communication.
- The Bible makes no clear distinction in purpose or end result between what is spoken and what is sung.

How might these creation concepts affect our life and ministry? Principally, God does not need our worship, yet He still chooses to invite mankind to have a worship relationship with Him. He seeks to have this worship relationship with us and facilitated that worship by making us after His image: an image empowered to communicate both in speech and singing. Fulfill your purpose!

For those who lead in worship, it is of fundamental importance that you embrace the fact that it is God that initiates worship.

Reveal God; He will call, and if people choose to come, worship will follow. Cajole, trick, stimulate, or manipulate, through music or whatever, and you will have the kind of worship pagans have been practicing in false worship all these many millennia: trying to win the attention or favor of their god. <u>Start planning public worship, or for that matter private worship, by showing God for who He really is. Our highest goal in leading worship is to say "Here is God!"</u>

Both the speaking *and* singing parts of the service are critically important. This is heightened by the fact that technology has made music almost omnipresent. The music we sing together and the music people listen to outside the services has an incredible effect on Christianity today. Our musical choices influence how we perceive our walk with the Lord should be fleshed out. It is often in our songs that we begin to form in our minds the identity of the Trinity, the personhood of God. Choose wisely.

While you are mulling over the implications for the above paragraph combine it with the truth that Satan and his angelic hordes are also musical. Dr. Warren Vanhetloo made the following summary comments in his email "Cogitations" number 432, February 14, 2007:

> Don't underestimate the presence and power of Satan and demons. Lucifer was an anointed cherub of God (Ezek. 28:14), is beautiful and musical (Ezek. 28:12-13), is proud (Ezek. 28:17; 1 Tim. 3:6), wants to be like God and steal His throne (Isa. 14:13-14), is intelligent (2 Cor. 2:11; 11:3), possesses memory (Matt. 4:6), will (2 Tim. 2:26), and desire (Luke 22:31), is full of wrath (Rev. 12:12), and has great organizational ability (1 Tim 4:1; Rev. 2:9, 24). God exhorts us to be cautious of spirits (1 John 4:1) lest we be taken in by the wiles of such a clever enemy.

For this reason let me implore you to be discerning and exercise great caution when it comes to the musical teachers you are using or promoting. This spiritual battle is not easy and there will certainly be differences between sincere believers but it is a battle worth fighting.

Genesis 4:3-8 Worship of Cain and Abel
Exegetical Considerations

This account is the first recorded public worship act. The opening phrase in the AV "And in the process of time," indicates that this offering was a part of the normal course of events in man's short history. The Hebrew term מִנְחָה (*minchah*) is the most general word for tribute, gift, or offering in Biblical Hebrew.[30] The grammar indicates that both Cain and Abel were in the habitual practice of bringing their offering to the Lord.

As the text continues, Abel's offering is contrasted with Cain's offering. Cain showed no particular effort in bringing his worship offering. By contrast, the Hebrew use of the disjunctive clause "But Abel brought, also he..." indicates a contrasting carefulness about Abel's offering.[31] BDB also suggests that the construction is "pointing back to the subj. and contrasting it with something else: Gn 4:4 הבל גם־הוא Abel, *he also*..."[32]

The passage points out that Abel's offering was "of the firstling" and included "the fat thereof" (Gen 4:4). Both statements show that Abel's offering was different in essence. NT references to this worship event give us insight into Abel's heart. His heart was "righteous" and his offering was "more excellent" (Heb 11:4). It is also possible that Abel's offering showed the means by which mankind may approach God in worship: the blood of a substitute. Though non-bloody sacrifices were given to God, they did not stand alone. The bloody sacrifice demonstrated the price that had to be paid so that the worshiper could stand before a holy God.

Cain, by contrast, was "corrupt" (Jude 11) and "wicked" (1 John 3:12) in his heart, and his offering reflected it. God accepted Abel's offering and did not accept Cain's. Again, Hebrews comments on this event, indicating both the heart *and* actual offering.

> "By faith Abel offered unto God a more excellent **sacrifice** than Cain, by which he obtained witness that he was righteous, God testifying of his **gifts**: and by it he being dead yet speaketh," (**emphasis** mine). Heb 11:4

How, exactly, God showed His approval in Genesis is unclear. Perhaps God caused Abel's offering to be consumed as He did in later biblical accounts.

It is also unclear from Genesis how men were to know what was an acceptable sacrifice. The instruction could have come from God directly, from Adam and Eve, or from Abel (Luke calls Abel "the first prophet" in Luke 11:50-51). However the instruction came, God made it clear to Cain that if he had done "well" (Gen 4:5) God would have accepted his offering just as readily as He accepted Abel's.

The question is sometimes asked, "Was it indeed the content of the offering or was it not simply the wickedness of Cain's heart which caused God's rejection?" It seems clear from the passage above that the *essence* of the offering was indeed in view. However, I would suggest that it is a moot point. Cain's heart gave rise to the decision to disregard whatever worship instructions God said he should have understood. The essence of Cain's offering was simply a reflection of Cain's heart.

The first recorded public offering in worship ended tragically from a human point of view. Cain's worship was rejected by God. Cain's ability to fellowship with God was evidently and dramatically broken. Cain vented his displeasure upon his brother by killing him. Abel became the first martyr (Luke 11:51). If Abel himself was the "mouthpiece" of God, and it was he who had communicated the truth(s) about worship that Cain rejected, this may have been the motive for Cain's actions. Cain may have "vented" his anger on the messenger. Cain for his part was unrepentant, subsequently punished by God, and fathered a race of men characterized by rejecting God.

By contrast, God took pleasure in Abel's offering and clearly expressed His approval (Gen 4:4). Some may not characterize it as a "successful" worship service because it did not result in Abel's (the worshiper's) prosperity and happiness. But God was obeyed and Abel is eternally exonerated in the Scriptures.

Genesis is the book of beginnings and origins. Many of the worship concepts discussed throughout this book are seminally contained in Genesis. This is certainly true when it lays the foundational concepts in this worship "event."[33]

Principles to Apply

- God is very pleased to accept some people's worship but will not at all accept other people's worship. We must worship on God's terms. *good*
- The consequences and effect of worship are very significant. Worship matters. How man worships matters morally and eternally, personally and corporately.
- Both the heart of the worshiper and the essence of his offering have importance. God deserves worship on His terms and one of those terms is the offering of a careful and costly offering.
- From the giving of the law to the teachings of Christ to the golden crowns offered up before the throne, the concept of the acceptable offering endures. God is pleased to accept costly, bloody sacrifices as worshipers approach Him on His terms.

[Margin note: I think the modern equivalent of the "different essences" is "Christ" or "Not Christ".]

Applications

The existential philosophy that permeates the landscape of our post-modern day gives rise to the idea that any worship done in Christ's name is acceptable to God. As we will see later, Christ Himself rebuked this idea. From the very beginning of recorded public worship God made it clear that *how* we worship matters to God. One of the reasons confusion exists today is because leaders have neither adequately understood nor effectively communicated the concept of the stewardship of revelation we see demonstrated in this passage. Let me explain.

The Bible teaches that every person is accountable to respond in obedience to the revelation God has given. It is only the rebellious who think they can approach God on their own terms. Now, balance that truth with the fact that God works in our lives incrementally. And, praise God, He always works with manifold mercy and grace. In the walk of the believer we call this patient working of God sanctification. God patiently reveals Himself as believers grow in their understanding of His holy Word.

So, does God accept the worship of an immature believer? Yes, to the degree that the believer is being obedient to the sanctifying work of the Holy Spirit. As God convicts, He works in us and grows us. Each believer is then a steward of a greater and greater amount of revelation. Believers have the Bible and the Holy Spirit. As time goes on all believers should grow in their knowledge of their Bridegroom, Jesus Christ and how to worship Him. Paul and the writer of Hebrews challenged their readers to grow up in their knowledge of Him (1 Cor 3:1-3; Heb 5:11-14). Your worship should change as you understand more about our Lord and the kinds of worship gifts that bring Him pleasure. Hmm.

On the matter of audience, I believe it is important to center our minds on the concept of priority in worship. Much more will be said later in the Word about this but even here in Genesis 4 the priority of God in worship is evident. These two brothers were bringing an offering *to God*. When we read the narrative today we may need to remind ourselves that there were no congregations or "seekers" to consider. Don't get me wrong; I am not saying there are not applications to be made when considering people in or around worship today. There certainly are. I am reminding you that from Genesis on, worship reflects a hierarchy of priority with Jehovah God at the top. If worship is not first and foremost about approaching God on His terms for His pleasure, then it is very easy to picture another god and promote another gospel.

For those who function in a leadership role when public worship choices are being made, let me encourage you to do a couple of practical things. As you are faced with the weekly task of organizing and working with people you love, don't forget to start your planning with a practical prayer, "God, first of all, what do *You* want to hear in this worship service?" It seems like this prayer reminder should go without saying, but the truth is, the pressures of ministry can shove the preeminence of God in worship right out the window. Let me suggest that you examine your next "worship event" in terms of what you are bringing to God. hmm.

Another idea that could revolutionize your public worship is to begin keeping a journal of the concepts and principles that characterize God-approved worship. My deepest prayer is that this book will stimulate a growing awareness and desire for the kind of worship the Lord desires. Your personal study and a commitment to knowing and following the characteristics of God-honoring worship will bring about lasting change.

All of us who are involved in worshiping the Lord publicly and privately need to wrestle with what represents costly sacrifice. Those who are more gifted must fight the temptation to throw out an old favorite and rely on raw talent instead of conscientiously preparing a sacrifice with the level of care that is worthy His name. Certainly our Creator God, who has now become our redeeming Savior, is worthy of a life lived wholly for His glory. Raise the bar! With the time and talents you have, make a commitment this week to ask God to receive as a gift of your love for Him your "sacrifice of praise." Be a person of great faith and commit to offering a more excellent sacrifice, a sacrifice like Abel's.

Genesis 8:20-21 Noah's Worship
Exegetical Considerations

In response to the unbridled sin of mankind, God moved to curse the earth with a flood (Gen 6:5-7). Noah was unique from the world around him, so He and his family were the special recipients of God's grace and were saved from the flood (Gen 6:8). After the flood waters receded, Noah and his family came out of the ark to replenish the earth and begin their new life with another service of worship.

Some call Noah "the second head of the human race."[34] Still others have called him the first of the patriarchs.[35] Others call him a kind of "second Adam."[36] He certainly worshiped in a pivotal time in human history. The worship act we have recorded in Genesis 8:20-22 must be seen in the context of Noah's entire lifetime. It was this life of faith that is described as righteous (צַדִּיק s*adiq*) and blameless (תָּמִים *tamim*) (Gen 6:9). Noah's godly life of faith did not escape God's notice (Gen 6:8 cf. Heb 11:7). It was this life of faith that caused him to walk with God and why God disclosed His purposes to him. Having experienced God's self-disclosure, Noah was motivated to consistently serve and obey God for over twelve decades.

Noah stood with the entire living human race before a world that had been washed clean by the miraculous hand of God. As earth's only family left the ark, Noah was led to offer a total burnt offering.[37] The first structure Noah built after the flood was not a house or a barn, but rather an altar (מִזְבֵּחַ *mizbeah*). Since the time of Cain and Abel, men knew to build sacred places, altars, for the express purpose of meeting with God and bringing Him sacrifices. On that altar Noah offered up one of every clean animal that God had commanded him to take on the ark (Gen 8:20). The value of this sacrifice should not be underestimated. Not only were these animals one-seventh of his entire domesticated flock, but they were also his, indeed his whole family's "breeding stock." "Wild" resources would have been unavailable. This offering was incredibly costly.

Noah had seen God reveal Himself in powerful ways. First, God revealed His plan to destroy the world and gave Noah specific instructions to escape the coming judgment. Noah responded in fear (Heb 11:7), and this fear motivated him for 120 years of obedient service as he and his family worked to complete the ark and prepare for God's judgment. Second, God destroyed the world before Noah's eyes, further revealing His eternal power and godhead. As Noah acknowledged God's mercy to his family, he offered a sacrifice that was appropriate. God revealed Himself to Noah and he responded by offering up costly worship.

After the offering of worship the Lord "reacted" by dramatically showing His approval. The desire of any true worshiper is that his offering be a "sweet aroma" to God. Certainly, God knew what He was going to do after the flood, and there is no indication that God "changed His mind" at the offering of Noah, but God acknowledged that the offering pleased Him and in that context further commissioned and blessed Noah as he and his family looked ahead to the future (Gen 8:21-9:17). The Noahic covenant was given in the context of Noah's costly worship.

Noah's whole life was in a sense a spiritual worship. Worship can be defined as both a single act and life in its totality. Which was the greater sacrifice, Noah's 120-year leap of faith in building this oddity called an ark, or his "foolish waste" of one-seventh of his and his family's domesticated animals? Some of the current furor over worship is due to the confusion over acts of worship and a life of worship. Acts of worship must grow out of a context of a life of worship. What is so clearly taught in the NT is beautifully demonstrated in this early passage.

A worship spiral is demonstrated in this passage. Noah was both responding to God and revealing God to those who saw his worship act. Each time God reveals Himself, men have the opportunity to respond to that revelation and offer back to Him acts and life choices that reflect their adoration. With each successive response by the worshiper, God is further revealed, offering yet another opportunity to respond.

Principles to Apply

- God is pleased to accept costly worship, for it is an appropriate response to God's self-revelation. In this narrative and in subsequent dispensations the bloody sacrifice is evident.
- Over and over again God demonstrates His blessing and plan for mankind in the context of worship.
- God-honoring worship acts happen in the context of a life of obedience.
- Worship is both a response to God and a revelation of Him to a watching world.

Applications

Noah's sacrifice was a profoundly costly act of worship. It was tied to the perceived worth of God. I say perceived because God is supremely worthy of costly worship whether men perceive it or not. We may stand to lose a lot in our sacrificial worship, but any price pales in comparison to God's worthiness. Readers of the NT are certainly familiar with the worship language used to describe Christ's sacrifice on the cross and the believer's sacrifice of himself. Let this truth wash over you. The things Christ may be asking you, your family, or your church to do right now may seem too costly or too risky. As you continue to study worship in the Word, you will be reminded again and again that He is worthy of your costliest sacrifice.

The interrelationship between worship and revelation is not always clear. As God reveals Himself we need to "react" to that revelation both with acts of worship and with life choices of obedience. Both acts of worship and life choices reveal to others around us what our God is like. Which is the cart and which is the horse? I am not sure it really matters. To offer acts of worship without a life of obedience is odious. But to throw ourselves at service without heartfelt words and acts of worship is equally unthinkable. Both should abound. Preacher, endeavor to teach your flock the balance between acts and lifestyle and to live that balance yourself. To neglect either is a mistake.

Chapter Three
The Patriarchs

In this chapter we will again look at some foundational considerations that will resurface many times in our study. I made the decision to launch into an abbreviated discussion of culture in this chapter. The whole subject of culture is a book in itself but please consider some initial thoughts in this historic context. Before we jump into this time period, let me encourage you recommit yourself to allowing God's Word to wash over you and to challenge your traditions and prejudices about worship.

1. Gen 12:7; 13:4,18 Abraham built altars to the Lord
2. Gen 14:18-20 Abraham's tithe to Melchizedek
3. Gen 17:3,17; 18:2 Abraham bowed before God
4. Gen 19:1 Lot bowed himself before the angels
5. Gen. 22:1-19 The worship of Abraham and Isaac
6. Gen 24:26,48,52 Abraham's servant bowed in worship
7. Gen 26:24-25 Isaac's altar and acts of worship
8. Gen 28:13-22 Jacob saw the Lord and worshipped
9. Gen 31:19,30,32,34 Rachel stole her father's idols
10. Gen 31:54 Jacob offered sacrifices and established a treaty with his father-in-law
11. Gen 33:20 Jacob's altar "El-elohe-Israel"
12. Gen 35:1-3,7,14 God spoke to Jacob, Jacob built "El-bethel"
13. Gen 46:11 Israel's altar at Beer-sheba
14. Gen 48:12 Joseph bowed himself before Israel

Gen 12:7; 13:4, 18; 14:18-20 Abrahamic Worship
Exegetical Considerations

Several concepts are worth noting about Abraham's worship. Abraham continued the tradition evident since man's earliest worship: building altars for sacrifice to the Lord (Gen 12:7-8; 13:4, 18). Giving costly, bloody sacrifices (Gen 14:20) can be traced back as far as recorded history. Tremper Longman suggests the concept of an altar *assumes* a bloody sacrifice for "sin had to be accounted for before a person entered the holy place."[1] Further, the verbal root for "altar" (זָבַח *zabah*) literally means sacrifice. I am not convinced that in every subsequent reference a sacrifice *must* be in view, but the connection is worth consideration.

This passage is the first time the Scriptures use the word "tithe" (מַעֲשֵׂר *maaser*). It occurs in the context of God defeating Abraham's enemies and rescuing Lot. There is much we don't know about the event's principal character, Melchizedek. What we do know is that Melchizedek "blessed the most high God" (Gen 14:20) and was the recipient of Abraham's costly offering of the tithe. This tithe offering was given to the King/Priest Melchizedek before any such giving was codified in the Mosaic Law. Why or how Abraham knew to give the tithe or acknowledge Melchizedek's superior position remains a mystery.

The phrase "bless the Lord," first used in Genesis 14:20 also holds a great deal of mystery. The basic understanding of the word (בָּרַךְ *barak*) is a superior conferring or wishing special favor upon another. Fathers blessed their children, kings blessed their people or were a blessing to their people, and certainly God is the only and ultimate source of all blessings to mankind. It was natural that Melchizedek (a superior in some perceivable sense) would bless Abraham. However, it is a mystery how any human being could "bless the Lord" though the phrase is mentioned over 50 times in the Scriptures. God is over all things and needs nothing that a mortal could "confer" or "wish" upon Him. Yet, Melchizedek "blessed the Lord," as we are commanded to bless the Lord even now.

It is also during the life of Abraham that the first occurrences of bowing (שָׁחָה *shachah*) are used in Genesis.[2] This term is translated both "bow" and "worship" by any number of Bible translations. David Peterson offers this summary:

> Part of the ritual of worship came to stand for the whole, so that bending over to the Lord came to represent devotion and submission to him as a pattern of life. Particularly by means of sacrifice and praise in the temple cult at Jerusalem. God's dominion over the whole creation, his gracious rule over his

chosen people, and his kingly presence in their midst was acknowledged....The reference is either to spontaneous acts of adoration or to the expression of homage in obedience to his commands.[3]

It is also important at this early stage to underline the fundamental difference between pagan worship and the true worship we are seeing in the Word. In all worship, true and false, a similar makeup of ingredients occurs. All worship involves deity, worshiper, sacrifice, revelation (by some definition), and response. It is the order of worship that differs. Pagan worship works something like this:

1. The worshiper wants or needs something from the deity. He desires to build some kind of "credit" or favor with his god.
2. The worshiper initiates some activity to manipulate the god into doing what the worshiper wants. The activity usually involves some sort of sacrifice.
3. The worshiper believes the deity "responds" in some way by revealing himself/herself.

The worship we see exampled in these and other passages looks much different.

1. It is God who reveals Himself to the worshiper. He is the "Initiator."
2. The worshiper responds in humility to the revelation with a spontaneous or purposeful sacrificial offering.
3. The worshiper sees God reveal Himself further, often as God addresses the needs of the worshiper.

Some fundamental differences between pagan worship and Jehovah worship are evident. Noel Due in his very helpful book describes it well stating:

The principle of 'Cainite worship' (to coin a phrase) is one of self-justification. For those who worship according to the line of Cain, worship is about a means to an end – the end being one's own blessing, the means being on one's own terms.[4]

At its core, pagan worship is an attempt to grab hold of a god and manipulate him or her into doing something or giving something to the worshiper. True worship is a whole hearted, obedient response to the self-disclosure of God. Abraham's altar building and the sacrifices surrounding them occurred in response to God's self-disclosure. God spoke or acted and the worshiper in gratitude or awe offered up his worship.

I believe it is important to point out that cultural dynamics begin to evidence themselves even more clearly during this time period and certainly in various elements of the Mosaic period to follow. We know little of the cultural environment Abraham was called out of in Ur. Nor do we know what specific elements of the culture Abraham felt free to embrace or reject. What we do know is that whether the culture approved or not, some elements of the culture Abraham was to reject. For example, fathering children by a handmaid was common cultural practice. Abraham would have done well to avoid it. This culturally accepted practice contradicts the model family we read about in Genesis. "Therefore shall a man leave his father and mother, and shall cleave unto his wife: and they shall be one flesh" (Gen 2:24). Polygamy may have been "allowed" in the culture but it did not reflect a biblical model.

It may have also been common for the Pharaoh to want Sarai for his harem or for Abraham to tell the half-truth that she was his sister but these cultural practices were to be rejected. "Culture" can be defined as the belief system and practices that govern a people group. The culture surrounding Abraham was something with which he should have interacted with greater caution.

Among other ANE religions, elements appear somewhat similar to Abraham's worship. This is only natural. The common root of historic truth since the flood is revealed. Everyone who stepped out of the ark knew the same truth. The fact that some choose to twist common truth slightly, or to pervert it altogether, explains both the similarities and differences in the cultural

The Patriarchs

landscape. It has been popular in some worship discussions to espouse the idea that because there were similarities or because some similar ANE practices predate Abraham, God simply adapted to the culture. Similarities, however, point to a common fountainhead of historic reality not to God adapting to the cultural practices of men. Commonality could also point to Lucifer's skill as a counterfeiter. The Bible texts, by contrast, picture God as initiator not imitator. For example, though circumcision was practiced by other groups to some extent, consider these two commentary entries regarding the practice.

> Elsewhere Scripture refers to circumcision as a symbol of separation, purity, and loyalty to the covenant. Moses said that God would circumcise the hearts of His people so that they might be devoted to Him (Deut. 30:6). And Paul wrote that "circumcision of the heart" (i.e., being inwardly set apart "by the Spirit") evidences salvation and fellowship with God (Rom. 2:28-29; cf. Rom. 4:11).[5]

> In the OT a spiritual idea is attached to circumcision. It was the symbol of purity (Isaiah 52:1). We read of uncircumcised lips (Exodus 6:12, 30), ears (Jeremiah 6:10), hearts (Leviticus 26:41). The fruit of a tree that is unclean is spoken of as uncircumcised (Leviticus 19:23).[6]

> God initiated circumcision with Abraham as a sign of the unique "culture" that was to accompany the believers of his time. God did not look around to see if pagans were practicing circumcision and then institute it for His people. He commanded the practice for His own purposes irrespective of its practice in the greater culture. The extent to which circumcision may have been practiced by some cultures did not dissuade God from regulating this part of the culture of His chosen people. Read further on this in the application section.

41

Principles to Apply

- From man's earliest time he knew or was told that memorials were important. The form of memorials has changed but the need for them has not and will not change.
- Costly, bloody sacrifices (or as Paul builds on in Romans 12:1-2, life giving sacrifices) are an appropriate response to the revelation of God.
- Humble, submissive posture (bowing) is the natural response of obedient worshipers.
- "Culture" is the byproduct of the belief system of a people group. This begins to be more clearly seen and regulated as time goes on and revelation expands.

Applications

It would be easy to think memorials were just something for the Old Covenant, but the need for memorials is seen in every dispensation. The Lord commands believers today to observe two ordinances: baptism and communion. In both cases these present day memorials picture the costly, bloody sacrifice of the Lord Jesus. We will forego a more complete discussion of these ordinances until they are more naturally dealt within the NT context. Let me say here that when the Lord's Supper *is* observed, we need to make every effort to make the form an accurate reflection of the reality. Some have suggested that "full worship" cannot occur if communion is not observed *each* service.[7] Although I am not ready to make that leap in application, I am very much in favor of reminding each worshiper of the supremacy of the bloody event of Christ's death on the cross at every event we call worship, private or corporate. Even in the eternal state memorial images and meals are present (vial offerings Rev 5:8; marriage supper Rev 19:9).

However mysterious it may be, the Bible reveals that men *can* bring gifts that God is happy to receive; and in giving them, we bless God and become one of God's "well-wishers." Abraham was so overwhelmed by what God had done for him in defeating his enemies that he "blessed the Lord" by offering up his praise to God and by giving his monetary offering. Getting this into the heads and hearts of people is, admittedly, a work that only God the Spirit can accomplish in His children. If you embrace this yourself and live with the conviction that you too can bless the Lord it will certainly result in teaching and activities that are sensitive reflections of that heart. If you understand, for example, that your tithe, and above that, your offering is a response to God's goodness and a concrete way in which you can bless the Lord, you will find ways to teach and example this for your people. The offering time in each service is a great place to creatively teach this concept of selfless gift giving to God.

I also want to remind you that the idea of tithing or giving monetarily is not simply a leftover from the Law. Giving precious gifts to the Lord is seen literally from Genesis to Revelation. Although there are many abuses of it in our day, giving needs to be seen as an act of worship and not as a way to collect funds for the church budget. Like all forms of worship it is both revelatory (it shows a watching world how highly we value our God) and a response to the wonderful provision of God. In Abraham's case it was a victory in battle and an enormous store of material wealth. For the Macedonians it was a realization that God had given them slightly more financially than another believer who needed it; they "first gave their own selves" which effectively "prov[ed] the sincerity of [their] love" (2 Cor 8:1-8). Because material offerings are a reaction, it may be helpful to schedule the offering after some kind of reminder of the goodness of God - *as if we needed one* – or at the end of the service.

Outward acts such as bowing and sacrifice should mirror inward attitudes of humility, submission, and adoration. Discussions over form and heart often attempt to divorce the connection between the outward and the inward. Abraham bowing before the Lord was an outward act that clearly reflected a heart of submission. God is the supreme King, so the outward act of bowing is both natural and appropriate. This is what NT writers build upon later. Outward acts of worship (form) are the natural outworking of inner spirit worship (heart).

We see the posture of bowing in worship from Genesis to Revelation. Though evangelicals at times seem to have an aversion for anything that non-evangelicals may do, bowing is clearly a transdispensational practice. Although it is true that one can "stand up on the inside" while bowing on the outside that is hardly a reason to abandon something practiced in every dispensation. I would suggest that you look for opportunities to invite those who are physically able to bow with you in worship. Though most church architecture makes public bowing a challenge, assuming the posture of worship on an occasional basis is worth the effort. I believe it communicates much. Bowing is both revelatory, as a witness, and a fitting response. Surely nothing is preventing you from incorporating bowing into your private and family worship.

As to God's relationship with culture I am convinced that God exists above or, perhaps better, independent of human cultures. In other words, elements in every culture are sub-ideal when compared to a biblical norm or what might be called a "kingdom culture"—how life will be when Christ reigns as King. When it comes to worship and music issues, a study of heavenly worship and music (Isa 6; Zeph 3:17; Luke 15:7 and especially the book of Revelation) are helpful in seeing the worship ideals of God. Worship in the heavenly kingdom can provide supra-cultural principles. This will be discussed in more detail in chapter 13 as we examine the question of meat offered to idols in 1 Corinthians 8 and 10. Let me say in summary that I must disagree with those who say culture, as it is defined by anthropologists, is morally neutral. Culture is the outworking of a people group's belief system—by definition, their morality.

I believe there is something refining in understanding that the standard for culture exists outside of man. I would go further and suggest that these "supra-cultural" ideas are precisely what Christ had in mind when He taught us the beatitudes. We long for all cultures to be submitted to King Jesus when He will rule supreme. In the meantime let's commit to seeking to know what elements of the cultures around us *best* reflect Christ's wishes and live redemptively with those that do not.

On a related matter, I want to mention here for your consideration the differences between pop culture and folk culture. Resisting the temptation to launch into a discussion that would turn into a book in itself, I will encourage you to do some thinking on your own about this idea. Calvin Johansson was the first one who introduced me to the concept that the part of culture that is commonly shared between people (folk culture) is different than "pop" culture. In his very helpful chapter, "The Gospel and Contemporary Culture" he differentiates pop culture and its music, from folk culture which exists within mass culture (global in its scope) and the music reflected in it. He suggests:

> The word popular needs to be defined. It is a neutral term which simply means 'something that is in demand.' However, in order to understand what we mean by the word pop, the word popular will be used as a technical term, indicating that which is distinctly manufactured for widespread acceptance. It is intended to mean that which is created to be popular rather than that which incidentally has become popular.[8]

Folk music in the strictest sense is musical styling which is participatory in nature, arising without known composers, and for this reason has wide acceptance. It communicates broadly held feelings and beliefs about basic living. It is most distinguished from pop music because commercialism is absent.[9] Not always easily distinguished from pop music, folk music's simplicity and accessibility to people means it *can* be an appropriate vehicle for communicating the immanence or "accessibility" of God's person. It is less helpful as a vehicle to show the transcendent side of God. It is no surprise then that over the past century it has been the evangelist who has emphasized folk elements in their ministries. The gospel song, with its simple chord structure, easily singable melodies, and simple texts was written in what must be defined as a folk music styling. Churchmen and local church musicians, when they are allowed, have shown a greater tendency to use musical forms that are more transcendent in character, more "high church."

For what it is worth, it is my opinion, that although folk music is immediately accessible, by the fifth or sixth selection it begins to show its lack of depth. This is not a criticism. Folk music has done what it does best: emphasize that God is a God who is immediately accessible, which of course is a very good thing! Music and texts which are more complex and transcendent (but still understandable) may take some time to become "ours" but have the benefit of greater staying power [?Untrue]. Both the "musical vocabulary" of common folks and more complex musical stylings, combined with simple spiritual truths and the deeper ideas of the mature should be included in the music of worship. Both are essential in accurately picturing the many sides of God.

I ask you to consider this matter of communicating God's person within different cultural contexts. I would not say that music is *completely* universal in *all* its meanings. I would say that even though we aren't given special revelation at this time to quantify beauty, we *are* given hints into God's definition of beauty as we observe His creation. It is the existence of such an objective standard of beauty outside of mankind that is refining and disciplining: refining, because it calls people to a process; disciplining, because it makes God the "bench mark" of beauty and not man himself. We should desire to grow in our ability to reflect God's beauty in our music.

Let me continue. Musical symbols go through subtle changes as people are exposed to them. Music is sometimes perceived differently by different people because of the change in "baggage" that accompanies the referent (the idea that the symbol, sound or word denotes). Music is really only performed once. Every subsequent time and place music is performed it goes through subtle changes in meaning because of associations nuanced by the previous listening. We must also be aware of the desensitization that results from man's depravity and his constant exposure to sinful practices. As I mentioned in chapter one, the conscience is universally present and evidences many universal elements. Society and our personal experiences can, however, affect conscience; though just as certainly there are universals. Similarly, society and our personal experiences can also affect our perception of musical genres, though just as certainly there are universals. Technology and globalism have increased not decreased the probability of universals in musical communication.

When interacting with other cultures I have found it helpful to focus on the biblical texts, move to general principles and then insist that the "insider" of the culture make the specific applications under the control of the Spirit. Exporting Americanisms will not do.

Both language and music evidence universals. The very fact that one can define and translate from one language to another is testimony of universals in language.[10] This is apparent in music as well when physical motions and emotion (dancing, marching, crying, laughing, etc.) are observed. Age and location have little or no effect on how a person responds to rock music for instance. John Makujina applies this to rock music when he says:

> Whereas one may argue that a certain combination of musical elements can take on various meanings (and I think these meanings are far more restricted than most), it is rather difficult to find a non-sexual or otherwise wholesome connotation for the flexions of rock-related aphrodisiac dancing and stage acrobatics.[11]

Emotions are understood and expressed quite uniformly between cultures and the music that reflects these emotions is usually correspondingly understood. This is even further reinforced in light of the world-wide influence of Hollywood. The sound tracks of movies do not change between continents. If anything, the emotions expressed in music are becoming more, not less universal in our ever shrinking world. Let me leave this volatile and challenging discussion with a call to moderation and further thought. There are two ditches. One is to imagine that contemporary culture in all its elements must necessarily be evil. The other is to accept the post-modern existentialism that insists all questions of culture, including worship or music choices, are simply matters to be determined by the "group;" what the postmodernists call the group's metanarrative (overarching story). This ditch is populated by people who imagine that "music is purely cultural." Music is not purely cultural. Satan is the prince of the power of the air in our world and has twisted culture along with its musical and emotional expressions. Believers are called to be discerning and exercise wisdom as they relate to the culture around them. "And be not conformed to this world, but be ye transformed by the renewing of your mind" (Rom 12:2).

Genesis 22:1-19 Abraham's Supreme Worship Test
Exegetical Considerations

Without a doubt God's call for Abraham to offer his son as a burnt offering in an act of worship (Gen 22) was the most dramatic test of Abraham's life. Anyone familiar with the whole of Abraham's story understands that he did not obey perfectly in every test, and when he didn't he was rebuked. It is equally clear that this sacrifice of Isaac was not an isolated act. Abraham's life gave testimony to his desire to live for God.

Consider again the order of this historic worship event. It was God who revealed Himself to Abraham and commanded him to give his beloved son as a sacrifice: "offer thy son, thy only son Isaac, whom thou lovest" (Gen 22:2). Abraham's worship was in response to God's self-revelation. Abraham's subsequent obedience to God in this narrative dramatically illustrates his understanding that his offerings must be given obediently. Abraham was willing to offer exactly what God instructed him to offer. He was committed to worshiping God on God's terms.

We see in Genesis 22:5 that Abraham was acting in faith (Heb 11:17-19). He told the men: "I and the lad will go yonder and worship, and come again to you." Abraham expected to return from the mountain with Isaac and demonstrated that he understood that worship was about giving his all. Abraham's "present" and "future" were wrapped up in the person of his son Isaac and he was willing to trust God to fulfill His promises and to meet his needs. He did not focus on how he might personally benefit from his worship.

Principles to Apply

- Offerings of worship must be given in the context of obedience. Any single worship act of obedient, costly sacrifice must occur within the context of a life of obedience.
- The sacrifice in worship of all a person is or will be is both profoundly sobering and at the same time unquestionably "reasonable."

- Ultimately, even if only in heaven, God does bless the obedient worshiper, often giving them additional revelation or a specific charge to service.

Applications

Early in my music ministry, I was challenged to see myself as not simply a "music man" but as a leader in the greater arena of our people's worship. I was cut to the heart. Although I had attended institutions that believed the Bible should be the basis on which faith and practice were built, I knew virtually nothing about worship. I empathize with Robert Webber when he shared this testimony:

> I graduated from three theological seminaries without taking a course in worship. Even though I was planning to become a minister, no one ever sat down and said, 'Look, worship is one of the most central aspects of your further ministry. Now is the time not only to learn all you can about the subject, but also to become a worshiping person so you can offer mature leadership to your congregation.[12]

Faced with this same challenge I walked down to the seminary library. But before I pulled down one of the many books about worship on the shelves, I was moved to pull down a *Strong's Concordance*. I flipped open the page where the word "worship" was found, made a copy of the page, put it in my Bible, and left for home. The next day I opened up my Bible to start my journey of the study of worship. The fact that Genesis 22:5 is the first time the English word is used dramatically illustrated to me the fundamental concept that worship is a recognition of God's supremacy and is demonstrated by laying my most precious gifts on the altar of sacrifice. I remember as if it were yesterday the realization that what I might "get out" of worship was a distant second, if it should even have a place at all. Worship is about abandoning my pursuits in order to pursue pleasing God supremely. I cannot think of a more practical, profound application to make when considering this narrative. It is something that should change your worship and become a fundamental concept that you share with your people. We live in such a consumer driven age, and that fact has colored our approach to worship generally, and service preparation specifically. Do yourself and your congregation a favor; dethrone the consumer!

The next statement might sound like double talk but the fact is that God *did* bless Abraham, and He still blesses those who worship Him today. Much like loving your wife selflessly brings certain selfish gains. "He that loveth his wife loveth himself" (Eph 5:28). What could be better than two people trying to out-give each other in a marriage relationship! In the biblical model, acts of worship, just like acts of marital intimacy, are to be other-oriented. This doesn't mean that one should ignore the pleasure of such intimacy, just that the pleasure of the other is to take priority in our motives and actions. When worshipers come to God on His terms and for His pleasure, certainly worshipers experience many wonderful benefits. We must remain vigilant that these wonderful blessings don't turn us into the selfish bride of our wonderful Bridegroom.

As the worship metanarrative continues, succeeding patriarchs follow Abraham's example and continue building altars, bowing before the Lord, and offering costly sacrifices (Gen 26:24-25; 28:13-22; 33:20; 35:1-14; 46:11; 48:12). The nation of Israel grew and eventually found itself in captivity in Egypt. God heard the cry of the nation and sent a deliverer, Moses.

Chapter Four
Mosaic Worship

This chapter has its own set of challenges. It is difficult to decide which verses one might include in the concordance section because of the sheer volume of material. It is also difficult to decide which passages to highlight for more in-depth exegesis. For this reason I am going to make some general observations about Mosaic worship and the sacrificial system and then deal with some specific narratives concerning Moses. I hope this will serve to summarize and limit this chapter.

You may be tempted to skip ahead to some of the NT passages we will deal with later, but in order to understand Paul's writings about NT worship one must have some understanding of this time period. Paul, the apostle to the Gentiles, used Mosaic worship language quite frequently. Reading Hebrews or Revelation without a good grasp of Mosaic worship is virtually impossible.

A. Exodus Event

1. Ex 3:2,4-6,10,12 Moses' commissioning worship service
2. Ex 3:18; 4:22-23,31 and 5:3,8,17;7:16;8:1,8,20,25,26-27,29; 9:1,13;10:37,8,11,24-26 4:23,31; 5:1,3,8,17; 7:16; 8:1,8,20,25,26-29; 9:1,13; 10:3,7-11,24-26;12:31 Israel's release from bondage and the purpose of the exodus
3. Ex 12:5,25-27 Institution of the Passover
4. Ex 13:15 Sacrifice of the first-born
5. Ex 14:31-15:21 A song of deliverance, full involvement
6. Ex 16:10 Glory of the Lord appearing in the cloud
7. Ex 16:22-23 Breaking of the Sabbath
8. Ex 17:15 Moses built an altar, Jehovah Nissi
9. Ex 18:12 Moses and Jethro worship
10. Ex 19: 10-11,14,16 Moses worshiped God in the mount
11. Ex 20:3-5, 7-8,20,23-26 Giving of the 10 commandments

B. Giving of the Law

1. Ex 22:20 Judgment for false worship
2. Ex 23:13, 18-19, 24-25, 32-33 Regulations about false worship
3. Ex 24:1-11 God's call to worship
4. Ex 25:2-3, 8, 22 Willing offering; Immanuel's tabernacle
5. Ex 26 Building of the Tabernacle
6. Ex 27 The altar and court
7. Ex 28 Dedication of the priests
8. Ex 29:42-46 The special meeting place
9. Ex 30:9, 10 Command against "strange fire"
10. Ex 32 The false worship of Israel
11. Ex 33:9-10 Moses and the Tabernacle
12. Ex 34 Second giving of the tablets; judgment for false worship (13-17)
13. Ex 35:5, 24, 29; 36:3 Willing offering
14. Ex 37-39 Tabernacle materials
15. Ex 40:27-35 Dedication of the tabernacle; the special worship place; "I will meet you there"
16. Lev 1:2, 3, 8-10, 13-17 Worship requirements "Holiness to the Lord"
17. Lev 2 Meat offering
18. Lev 3 Peace offering
19. Lev 4-6 Sin offering
20. Lev 7:12-27 Thank offering
21. Lev 8:27ff Wave offering
22. Lev 9:22-10:3, 9-13, 19 True worship of Moses and Aaron; false worship of Nadab and Abihu
23. Lev 17:7; 18:21;19:4-5; 20:2-3, 7 Worshiping like the heathen forbidden
24. Lev 19:4-8, 12 Motivation of the fear of the Lord
25. Lev 20:2-6, 23 Condemnation of false worship
26. Lev 21-22 Requirements of the priests
27. Lev 22:24, 29, 32-33 Sacrifice that is fitting before the Lord
28. Lev 23:8, 12-15, 18-20 Various offerings
29. Lev 24:16 Death of the blasphemer
30. Lev 26:1-2, 30-31 False worship condemned
31. Lev 27:9, 11, 26, 30 Things devoted to the Lord

32. Num 3:4-8 Nadab and Abihu commentary
33. Num 4:4, 24, 27, 28, 35, 39 Service of the Kohathites
34. Num 5:15ff Jealousy offering
35. Num 6 Nazarite
36. Num 6:23-27 Blessing in the poetic form
37. Num 7 Offering of the princes
38. Num 8:11, 13, 15, 21, 24 Priests' offering
39. Num 10:10 Peace offering
40. Num 11:25-29 Possibly unison prophecy sung
41. Num 15 Heave offering
42. Num 16:9-10, 15, 22, 35, 38-40, 46 Judgment of Korah
43. Num 18 Charge to the priests and Levites
44. Num 21:17 Song of the wells
45. Num 22:31, 41; 23:1-6, 14-17, 29-30 Balaam falls down before the angel of the Lord; Balaam's three sacrifices
46. Num 25 Israel bowed down before the pagan gods (Baal-peor), God judged
47. Num 28-29 Observation of various offerings
48. Num 31:16, 17, 29-30, 41, 52 Israel's false worship; Balaam slain by Eleazar
49. Num 33:52 Israel to destroy all images that remind them of false worship
50. Deut 4:16-28 Warnings about the temptations of false worship
51. Deut 5:7-12 Restating of 10 commandments
52. Deut 6:2, 5, 13-16 Fear and love the Lord
53. Deut 6:13 Compare with Matt 4:9-10
54. Deut 7:4-6, 16, 25-26 True worship must be separated from pagan worship
55. Deut 8:6, 10, 19, 20 People blessed the Lord; God promises judgment on false worship
56. Deut 9:10-12, 16, 18, 21, 25 Moses recounted the golden calf episode
57. Deut 10:8, 12, 20-21 Levites' job is to walk in God's way, love and serve Him
58. Deut 11:1, 13, 16-17, 22, 27-28 The greatest command in the OT, to worship the Lord
59. Deut 12: 2-8, 11-14, 17-18, 26-27 Special place of sacrifice; 30-31 (also 18:9-12,20 and 20:18) Israel is to destroy all

images that remind them of false worship, commanded not to ask the question "how did these nations serve their gods?"
60. Deut 13:2, 4, 6-11, 13, 17 Warnings about the temptations of false worship; judgment pronounced on false worshipers
61. Deut 14:21 Call to holiness; don't seethe the kid in its mother's milk
62. Deut 15:21 Sacrifice without blemish
63. Deut 16 Passover worship; 21-22 God hates false worship
64. Deut 17:1-5 Judgment pronounced on false worshipers
65. Deut 18 Levitical offerings
66. Deut 23:3 Amorites and Moabites restricted from worship
67. Deut 26:10-13 Command to worship with the first fruits
68. Deut 27:5-7, 15 Uniqueness of Jehovah worship; curse pronounced on those who craft a graven image
69. Deut 28:14, 36-37, 47-48, 58, 64; 29:16-21, 25-27 Warnings about the temptations of false worship; judgment pronounced on false worshipers
70. Deut 29:16-21; 25-27 Condemnation of false worship
71. Deut 30:6 Love and worship from the heart
72. Deut 30:16-20 Life and death – true worship and false worship
73. Deut 31-32 The teaching power of music

General Considerations Regarding Mosaic Worship

Separate from False Worship

The Mosaic Law is replete with regulations about approaching God. This is nothing new as we have already seen. From the giving of the Decalogue (Ex 20:1-11, 20, 23, 26), which commits the first four commandments to worship regulations directly, to the particular regulations of the rest of the Law, God commanded His people to approach Him on His terms (Ex 22:20; 23:18,24-25).

Among the commands regarding worship are the repeated and clear commands for Israel to completely disassociate the worship of Jehovah from the worship of the pagans they displaced. The second giving of the Law outlines the posture of separation that Israel was to maintain. Israel was to "utterly destroy…overthrow…burn…hew down…and destroy the names of them (gods) out of that place"

(Deuteronomy 12:2-4, 8, 11-14, 17-18, 26-27). The passage states further:

> When the Lord thy God shall cut off the nations from before thee, whither thou goest to possess them, and thou succeedest them, and dwellest in their land; Take heed to thyself that thou be not snared by following them, after that they be destroyed from before thee; and that thou enquire not after their gods, saying, How did these nations serve their gods? Even so will I do likewise. Thou shalt not do so unto the Lord Thy God: for every abomination to the Lord, which he hateth, have they done unto their gods; for even their sons and their daughters they have burnt in the fire to their gods. What thing soever I command you, observe to do it: thou shalt not add thereto, nor diminish from it (Deut 12:29-32; see also Deut 13:2, 4, 6; 17:1-4; Lev 17:7; 18:21; 19:4; 20:2-6; 26:1-2).

God did not want the worship of Israel to be patterned after the worship of the surrounding pagan nations (see further Leviticus 17:7; 18:21; 19:4-5; 20:2-3,7). They were not to be "creative" in their worship of Jehovah if such "creativity" compromised the essential integrity of worship. I am not saying that Israel was not to be concerned with "reaching" the cultures around them. God intended for the nation of Israel to act as mediator to the rest of the world as a "kingdom of priests" (Ex 19:6). Israel's testimony to the world was achieved only within the context of God-centered and God-regulated worship. Consider D. A. Carson's synopsis.

> The first 'religious' command here (16:21–22) repeats Deuteronomy's strong opposition to the symbols of Canaanite worship (cf. 7:5); only the God of Israel is to be worshipped. The second (17:1) contains another basic principle of true worship, namely that only undamaged animals should be sacrificed to God (*cf.* 15:21). To *sacrifice* an imperfect animal was no sacrifice at all, because it was of little value to the worshiper. True worship implies real self-sacrifice (see Mal. 1:6–8). Thirdly (2–7), the need to root out any who would lead astray to false religion is repeated. This law is in substance like that of ch. 13, but here the judicial means of proceeding is stressed (5–

7). The *gate* (5) was where the judges sat. The punishment is so severe because the crime is a breach of the first commandment, and would destroy the covenantal relationship of the whole people with God.[1]

A fundamental difference exists between the worship of Jehovah and all other pagan worship. The religions of the world attempt to manipulate their god to do something for the benefit of the worshiper. True worship is a response to what God has already done. It is not about earning favor but responding to the unearned grace of the Giver of all things. The law at times may read like God is telling the Israelites that if they want Him to do things for them, they need to offer the correct incantations. This could not be further from the truth. Israel was the unique recipient of the favor and deliverance of God. He acted first; they did not get His attention by their worship. After God acted, they were "inclined" to worship. In fact, for worship to please God at all it had to come first from a willing heart. The rubrics of the law were simply God's gracious insights into the kind of worship that pleases Him; worship an Israelite must be willing to bring "of his own volition" (Lev 1:3).

I have been struck recently with the fact that conflicts over worship sometimes come when people are wrestling with a counterpoint; worship should be both a wholehearted *response* to God and a *revelation* of God. Our responses *reveal* God to a watching world and remind us of His person. The OT saint was called to worship wholeheartedly, but God also made it clear that when he worshiped, his worship was a "reflection," if you please, of the Person of God. God wants it all: wholehearted purity. As politically incorrect as it may be, Mosaic Law illustrates that purity in worship "trumps" participation because worship forms reveal God's character to mankind, a character God is unwilling to have tarnished. Over and over again the motivation for a specific regulation is given to the worshiper; "I am the Lord" (Lev 11:44-45; 18:4-6, 21, 30 and 15 times in Lev 19 alone!).

The new nation lived within the rubric of offerings, sacrifices, and feasts as they sojourned in the wilderness and as they began to possess the new land. The ever present temptation toward syncretism in worship, which God had so clearly warned against, required constant vigilance.

Mediated by the Priests

Although the nation acted as mediator to the world, God also instituted a relationship of mediation within the nation itself. Priests mediated and instructed individuals about God and how they were to come before Him. The priest's role in the nation can be seen in the list of passages above (read especially Leviticus 21-22). The priests' dress, manners, lifestyle, and even diet, functioned as illustrations of the nature, character, and desires of God. The priests both aided the worshiper in presenting his gifts to God and became a visible "revealer" of God to the nation.

The priest's position is noteworthy in four ways. First he occupied his office by virtue of his birth; he did not choose to be a mediator. Second, because of his birth, he was uniquely God's. Third, because he was uniquely God's, he was to be holy, or sanctified for the Lord's purposes. Last, his position and holiness allowed him a unique relationship with God; he was able to draw closer to Jehovah than others in the nation (Num 16:5).[2] NT writers draw on these concepts for believers today. We will discuss them further in this study, especially as we consider Hebrews in chapter 14.

The Sacrifices Themselves

Since the contrasting offerings of Cain and Abel in Genesis 4, both the heart and the actual offering have been significant. Leviticus opens up with a simple summary phrase: "If any man of you bring an offering unto the LORD, ye shall bring your offering...." (Lev 1:2). Chapter after chapter includes various regulations that were to be followed with exacting detail. Offerings were to be made by willing participants (Lev 1:3; 19:5), but the sacrifices themselves were also be costly, offerings without blemish (Lev 3:1, 6; 4:3), and of the first born (Num 3:13). The offering itself was to reveal the heart of the worshiper and the character of the Object of worship, God. Walvoord and Zuck state:

To take a defective **sacrifice to the LORD** (Deut. 17:1; cf. 15:21) was to bring something into the sanctuary that was foreign to the worship of **God,** just as Asherah poles and sacred stones were foreign to genuine worship. Such a sacrifice was **detestable to** the Lord. To offer less than the best to God was to "despise" His name (Mal. 1:6-8). Offering a less-than-perfect sacrifice was, in effect, failing to acknowledge Him as the ultimate Provider of all that is best in life. Also it was a failure to acknowledge the vast gulf that exists between the perfectly holy God and sinful people.

The priests were normally responsible to maintain pure worship at the sanctuary (i.e., no fertility symbols or defective sacrifices), but the ultimate responsibility rested with the judges. If the priests failed, it was necessary for the judges to intervene.[3]

Within the Context of Relational Integrity

I am struck with the fact that much of the worship language and specific worship acts are interspersed with very practical, even at times homey, regulations in the law. Leviticus 19 for example starts with a stern warning to "be holy," then moves to the command that Israelites honor their parents, then their need to turn from false idol worship, then to regulations about proper peace offerings, then to leaving the corners of the fields for the poor, etc., etc. Worship is both an act and a lifestyle. Or better, acts of worship must be done within the context of an obedient life marked by relational integrity. To the Israelite, worship was not just something they *did;* it was a part of the very fabric of their lives—of who they were. They brought their sacrifice, left some grain in the field for the poor, paid their tithe, dealt ethically with their neighbor, sang their songs of remembrance, sowed their unmixed seed according to the law, "went to Temple on the Sabbath," were careful when butchering, and on and on it goes. Worship was not the musical part of the service one hour a week. Acts of worship were a part of a whole life of worship;

This leads naturally to another observation. God's commands are simply a reflection of His own holy nature. God does not arbitrarily call some activities sin. He knows that certain activities or attitudes are destructive by their very nature. God is not being prudish or overly restrictive in these Mosaic worship practices; He is guarding the integrity of the message that various worship activities would reveal about Him. Worship is based on who God is as a person not on what wonderful blessings a believer might receive. Even the song of testimony we will see in Exodus 15 is centered on the clear teaching of who God is.

I also want to mention here something about the seemingly strange restrictions of God in light of this last paragraph. Why couldn't the Israelites yoke together an ox and a donkey for plowing, or weave together wool and linen? Although we cannot be entirely certain, some have suggested that "they may have had a symbolic function in teaching the Israelites something about the created order. Or the mixtures mentioned in these verses may reflect certain pagan cultic practices."[4] Still others state more emphatically that "the essence of the crime (Zeph 1:8) consisted, not in wearing a woollen [sic] and a linen robe, but in the two stuffs being woven together, according to a favorite superstition of ancient idolaters (see on Lev 19:19)."[5] Whether created order, or more likely, associations with pagan worship these prohibitions made it clear that all of life was to be lived on purpose.

Last, let me mention again the importance of the rite of circumcision. The rite of circumcision was positively tied to the self-identity of God's chosen people. Israel was unique, and not *just* unique, uniquely God's. In light of the many phallic symbols that were ever present among the false religions around them, I wonder if circumcision might not have also been a private reminder of what they were *not*; they were not like the false worshipers that lived around them.

Mosaic Narratives

Moses was a prophet, patriarch, political leader, intercessor, and law communicator. I will remind you that doing theology while examining narratives can be difficult. When God speaks or acts directly, we can more clearly see a normative principle that can be applied. What we cannot do is assume that just because Moses (arguably one of the godliest men to walk the earth) did something it automatically means we should do it as well. So with this caution in mind let's examine our first passages.

Ex 3:18; 4:22-23,31 and 5:3,8,17;7:16;8:1,8,20,25,26-27,29; 9:1,13;10:37,8,11,24-26 4:23,31; 5:1,3,8,17; 7:16; 8:1,8,20,25,26-29; 9:1,13; 10:3,7-11,24-26;12:31; 12:5,25-27 Israel's Release from Bondage and the Institution of the Passover

Exegetical Considerations

When God revealed Himself to Moses, calling him to the great task of delivering His people, Moses responded in fear, humility, and obedience (Ex 3:2-6, 4:20). In the context of Moses' worship, God commissioned him to deliver His people from bondage and lead them in worship on the mountain of His calling (Ex 3:2-4,10,12).

From the very birth of the nation, it was obvious that God had more in mind than simply its collective redemption. God wanted a worship relationship with the new nation. The exodus was not an end in itself. Over and over again in Moses' (and Aaron's) pleas for deliverance before Pharaoh, God reminded the people that they were being redeemed so that they could "serve," (עָבַד) Ex 4:23; 8:8,20; 9:1,13; 10:3,7,8,11,24; 12:31 (*the latter [12:31] is translated "worship" in ESV and NASB*). They were being called to a worship "feast" (וְיָחֹגּוּ) (Ex 5:1; 10:9). They were redeemed to "sacrifice" (וְזִבְחָה) (Ex 3:18; 5:3,8,17; 7:16; 8:1,25-29; 10:25-26).

The Hebrew term (עָבַד *abad*) is often used to refer to men serving men; but here, later in the Decalogue, and still later referring to Levitical temple worship, "serve" is used synonymously with worship. God did not just save Israel to deliver them from the slavery of Egypt, but for the greater purpose of showing His glory to the world and allowing people the opportunity to enjoy a relationship of worship with Him. God was doxological (bringing glory to Himself) in His soteriology (redemptive acts).

In the context of God's deliverance of His people, He instituted the bloody, family-centered memorial worship service of the Passover (Ex 12:27, 31). This special worship event was to mark the beginning of months for Israel (Ex 12:2). The Passover introduced the giving of Mosaic worship practices.

Principles to Apply

- Redemption is not an end in itself. Believers in every age are redeemed from sin to a life of worship.
- The interchangeable use of the terms "feast," "sacrifice," and "serve" show the many sides of the complex term "worship." Worship is our whole life, as well as a specific act or activity. An act of worship is to be a representation of the whole of worship.
- Memorial meals and specific activities are not strictly New Testament phenomena. Multi-sensory activities have always been a part of worship acts.

Applications

The whole purpose of God granting man redemption is to manifest His own glory and allow people the opportunity to worship Him and even *further* manifest His glory. God is not simply a fire escape! Our people need to hear again and again that they are not the center of the universe and God has a greater plan for them now that He has redeemed them. Be counter-cultural; live to worship, worship to bring pleasure to God! The multiplicity of words used to describe this historic event, ("serve," "worship," "feast," and "sacrifice") are all terms with which grace-age livers are familiar. These are things we are called to as well. Because worship is the reason God has redeemed us, worship needs to be a part of every believer's beginning discipleship. Let's admit it, worship is a very confusing term today. Determine to teach your people, especially young believers, what the Bible says about worship. My prayer is that this book will stimulate your thinking as a church leader, but I also know that this book is probably not for the average person in the pew. There are probably better materials for helping the average layman than this more in depth book. You might want to consider some materials I have developed, or better yet, write your own from your own study. By all means help your people see that they were redeemed to worship now and for eternity.

For reasons that I do not fully understand, the word "serve" as we use it today has become divorced from the idea of worship. I have heard some say "we gather to worship" on Sunday mornings and then scatter to "serve the Lord." On the other hand some think worship *acts* are of no consequence; that we should busy ourselves with activities of "service," and not "waste time" adoring our Savior. When NT writers used the word "service" their original audience understood it meant both lifestyle and specific acts of adoration and intimacy. The Greek term is often used to explain the worship activities of the temple (Luke 2:37; Acts 7:42; Heb 10:2). The LXX (the Septuagint is the Greek translation of the OT) uses the term "serve" (λειτουργεῖν) when the tabernacle and temple worship activities of the priests are described (Num 18:6-7). Worship is a heart attitude and an act of devotion, a life lived serving God.

I often think of the Indian parable of the blind men and the elephant. As each blind man reached out to ascertain and define what this elephant was, they all accurately described a part of the whole. None were technically wrong in their description, but all failed to see how the whole fit together. Make sure that your definition of worship and the expectations you have about worship take into account the whole picture. I trust that by this point in the book you are formulating a working definition of worship. I will give you mine later.

The redemptive act of the exodus was the most commonly cited event of the nation as it began its conquest of the Promised Land. Perhaps even more significantly, Passover was the highest holy day of Israel's year which Christ used to illustrate His own death for another nation, a nation of "kings and priests" that would be His own church (Matt 26;17-29; Rev 1:6). Worship acts and ongoing worship relationships were preceded by bloody sacrifices. Even in heaven we will be constantly reminded that it was the Lamb that was slain for us. Your church's focus should continually be brought back to the

Lamb of God, our Sacrifice, and the price that was paid for this relationship we now enjoy.

Ex 14:31-15:21 Israel's Song of Victory
Exegetical Considerations

When Israel was finally redeemed out of Egypt, Moses wrote a song of celebration (Ex 15:1-21). Several foundational concepts can be seen in this first recorded song of public worship in the new nation. First, it was sung by the whole congregation with their enthusiastic participation. God dramatically revealed Himself as He defeated Israel's enemy. The nation responded to His revelation by offering up this song of praise:

> And Israel saw that great work which the Lord did upon the Egyptians: and the people feared the Lord, and believed the Lord, and his servant Moses. Then sang Moses and the children of Israel this song unto the Lord and spake, saying... (Ex 14:31-15:1).

The second significance is that the song was directed to the Lord. This may seem like a minor point, but if you put yourself in the story, you understand the drama of singing before the blazing manifestation of the great Redeemer God; the Shekinah glory. Though the song itself uses both first person and third person terminology, God was seen as the primary audience.

Notice third the interchangeable use of the verbs "sang" (יָשִׁיר *sir*) and "spake" (וַיֹּאמְרוּ *amar*) (Ex 15:1). Although we often think of singing and speaking as something significantly different, the Hebrew makes no such distinction. What they sang to the Lord, they spoke to the Lord; they "sang, saying."

Fourth, the content of the song was a poignant reminder of God's dramatic deliverance. Music, by God's design, was the emotionally empowered vehicle for the Israelites to remember God's character and His mighty acts. Moses' song was a full and accurate description of the actions of God in Israel's deliverance, showing both God's power ("The Lord is strength" Ex 15:2) and personal intimate care

("He is become my salvation" Ex 15:2). God is pictured both as transcendent and tender. This song pictures God fully.

Last, Miriam brings up two interesting topics. First, she acted as a "prophetess" or "mouthpiece" (נְבִיאָה *nebiha*) for God as she led the women in enthusiastic worship through music (Ex 15:20-21). This is the first in a number of occasions when the root word *nabi* (literally, mouthpiece) or its derivatives are used to refer to people who act as a mouthpiece by using music as their means of communication. Moderns tend to think of music in terms of its entertainment value and not primarily as a means of communication generally, nor as a fitting vehicle for Divine revelation. We will not fully investigate the relationship of music and the prophetic office but the Bible considers music as well as speech a valid means of communication while acting in the prophetic office.

This is also the first time the English word "dance" is used in the AV. Again, dance could be the subject of a book by itself. I will resist dealing with it in a full sense until the various passages present themselves in context. Several words are translated dance with several shades of meaning. Here, (מְחֹלָה *meholah*) is used. Allow me to make some general comments about dance at this time.

- The dances we read about in the Bible seem to be spontaneous. The group of Hebrew words can also be translated to writhe, skip, or leap.
- There is every indication in this passage and others to follow that such dancing was segregated by sex. When it was not, it was often bad news (see Ex 32).
- Spontaneous physical movements when music is present among same gender participants had no sexual implications, even as these activities among Jews today do not.
- Dance was probably accompanied by rhythm instruments and/or other musical instruments, with the associative meaning of being so joyful that one is "beside themselves." It can also be the spontaneous physical reaction that accompanies immorality (Ex 32:19; Jdg 11:34; 21:21; 1Sam 18:6; 21:12; 29:5; SS 7:1).

- Whatever might have been done, dance was not done in the context of public worship in either Testament.

Principles to Apply

- Content-rich songs showing both God's transcendence and closeness should be a part of the believer's joyful reaction to God's great acts.
- Although the primary audience of worship is God Himself, music undoubtedly and purposely affects, even physically, all those who sing or hear it.
- Those who sing God's praises are acting as mouthpieces of God just like those who speak God's praise.
- Participation in worship is to be wholehearted and universal among believers.

Applications

More than once I have been involved in a conversation when someone begins to share his ideas about what was right or wrong with a particular song or song service. In my mind I often ask the question "What is it exactly that you liked or objected to, and what Bible passages do you look to for your model?" There is no better model for congregational music than the model of the Word. I am not saying that we should be singing only the Scriptures, although this is woefully lacking. What I am saying is that just like a look at the prayers of the Bible can inform our prayer life, the songs of the Bible, like the song in Exodus 15, should inform our "song life." Our music should show the immensity and immanence (nearness) of God. As a practical matter, take a month's worth of services in your church and honestly ask yourself how balanced it is both textually and musically. Now be brave and do the same for your family and your own personal listening. Are you getting a biblically accurate view of God based on the music you are listening to?

We are going to deal often with the matter of audience. This song was directed to the Lord but it was also intended to be instructive. Sometimes this issue is a matter of degrees. Private singing is almost exclusively for the Lord's ears: a song He is too often deprived of.

Congregational singing, even when it is a first-person prayer has very strong horizontal implications. And, of course, every song, even those we might by definition call "secular," should be sung with God's "scruples" in mind and always for His glory (1 Cor 10:31). Some songs are primarily between people with our Heavenly Father listening in, giving His approval, or not. Other songs should be sung with a desire to be intentionally focused on God alone.

On the matter of Miriam's dance, I think it is wisest, based on the whole of revelation, to abstract Miriam's dance and make the application that our praise should be a wholehearted response to God's great acts. This is a narrative and making direct application to sacred dance today is ill-advised for several reasons. We will deal with dance again when examining David's dance.

Positively, I can say that heart, soul, mind, and strength should all to be involved in expressing our love to God. Let me remind you of several greater principles delineated later in the Word that should shed light on Miriam's dance. Whatever spontaneous physical responses may be present in our worship, they can never be sexual. Miriam may have moved her hands and feet while leading this huge crowd of ladies, but to suggest that the sexually intimate parts of her body were involved would be out of character with the passage and the whole of Scripture. Paul reminds Christians that we are the Lord's and sexual impurity must always be excluded (1 Cor 6:18-20).

To whatever degree wholehearted worship may be reflected in the spontaneous physical responses of the believer outside the formal public gathering we know that all public worship in the NT must be done to edify (1 Cor 14). When thinking about a more direct parallel for our time, the closest contemporary activity I can conceive is what spontaneously happens after the basketball team wins the league championship. This is a far cry from the choreographed liturgical dance of our day or the lustful mixed gender gyrations in some church quarters. Let me lovingly remind you of our task; understand the Scriptures for what they say, get to the principle, and then wrestle with how to apply it today.

Exodus 24:1-11 The Worship of the New Nation

Exegetical Considerations

The Sinai event (Ex 19:1-40:38) constitutes a shift from clan based worship led by the patriarchs to new worship practices as a nation. God showed the world His desire to dwell among a people with whom He would have a unique worship relationship. As God's representative "Moses went up unto God, and the LORD called unto him out of the mountain" before the new nation (Ex 19:3-8). Exodus 24 inaugurated this profoundly new relationship. In this worship event, God invited the whole nation into a covenantal relationship of worship with Him. Then, uniquely, God invited certain particular mediators to a special relationship with Him. They included Moses, Aaron, Nadab, and Abihu (the priests), and the elders (Ex 24:1). As representatives of the nation as a whole, God revealed Himself and called His people to fellowship with Him on His terms. Moses, as the singularly intimate mouthpiece of God, acted as the prophet to declare God's words to the people (Ex 24:2-3). The people's response was clear; "All the people answered with one voice, and said, 'All the words which the Lord hath said will we do'" (Ex 24:3). This declaration clearly underscored their commitment to worship in the context of complete, personal obedience. By the way, it is possible, I believe even likely, that this declaration was sung. Music naturally serves the purpose of unison proclamation. The Hebrew construction, קוֹל אֶחָד, translated "lifted up their voice" appears one other time in 2 Chronicles 5:13 at the dedication of the temple.

"It came even to pass, as the trumpeters and singers *were* as one, to make one sound to be heard in praising and thanking the LORD; and when they **lifted up their voice** (קוֹל אֶחָד) with the trumpets and cymbals and instruments of musick, and praised the LORD, *saying*, For he is good; for his mercy endureth for ever: that then the house was filled with a cloud, even the house of the LORD" (**emphasis** mine).

I believe it is likely that the Israelites accomplished the feat of unison affirmation by using a musical phrase. The passage also allows for coordinated unison speech, though it is hard to conceive how this might have been accomplished.

Other worship elements were also present. An altar was built (Ex 24:4), animals were sacrificed (Ex 24:5), the book of the covenant was read (Ex 24:7), people wholeheartedly responded in affirmation (Ex 24:7), Moses sprinkled the people with the blood of the sacrifice (Ex 24:8) and the leaders experienced a unique display of God's glory (Ex 24:9-11,15-18). This event represented a sort of "ratification" of the treaty between God and the nation Israel.

Principles to Apply

- God intends all believers to be active participants in worship. Throughout time, even as God provides a mediator, He invites all of His creation to come to Him.
- A commitment to purity and obedience to the revealed Word of God has always been the prerequisite of true worship.
- Over and over again the bloody sacrifice was in view when true worship was to begin.
- Worship involves man's response to God and in man's response God is further "revealed" or made known.

Applications

The whole of the Law was really an invitation; God inviting His people to come to Him. They could come and enjoy a special relationship as they came on God's terms. Though God was omnipresent, He ordained a unique place for His glory to be shown and His people to enjoy His presence.

> This shall be a continual burnt offering throughout your generations at the door of the tabernacle of the congregation before the LORD: where I will meet you, to speak there unto thee. And there I will meet with the children of Israel, and the tabernacle shall be sanctified by my glory. (Ex 29:42-43)

Though the Israelites needed the mediation of the priests, they were all invited to worship. I have made it abundantly clear that I believe we have humanized God far too often in our worship, but let me say with equal clarity that if we do not make worship and music choices that clearly communicate God's desire to meet with "whosoever" we have failed just as miserably. God calls us to worship on His terms and for His pleasure, but He *does* call us and as our loving Bridegroom He tells to "enter into the joy of your Lord." As ambassadors we need to show God for the holy God He is and at the same time make worship choices that communicate in meaningful ways that He *can* be known.

OT worshipers were constantly reminded with the sights, sounds, and smells of the sacrifice, that substitutionary death was a necessary part of worship. Consider the bloody Passover event specifically. NT believers as well should always remember that although we now come boldly to our Father's throne, it is only because of the bloody sacrifice of our Savior. We, however, live in a time and place when death is quite sanitized. We are removed from my parents' world when having meat meant you were personally involved in ending the life of an animal. In my parents' generation, it was not uncommon for the family to care for the body of a deceased loved one as many do in other countries even today. Moderns rarely see death that up close and personal. Think again on the death of Christ. His death is the only way our worship is made possible. Let me challenge you to imagine the very unsanitized death of a perfect Jesus who died so that we might have the privilege of a worship relationship with the God of the universe. While you're at it, help the people you lead in worship imagine it as well.

Exodus 32 False Worship Revealed
Exegetical Considerations

Within days after the giving of the law, Israel turned to false worship (Ex 32:1-28). Several things can be observed about this false worship. First, false worship grew out of the faithless heart of the people who demanded that their spiritual leader give them what they wanted (Ex 32:1). Aaron's "heedership" empowered the people to forsake the Lord (Ex 32:2-4). Second, while Aaron was enabling the people to worship falsely, he was still contending that this false worship would be "a feast to the Lord" (Ex 32:5). In fact, the actual activities of the false worship appeared very much like the worship we just examined. There were burnt offerings and peace offerings (Ex 32:6 cf. Ex 24:5), the people brought material offerings (Ex 32:2-3 cf. Ex 25:2-3), and, certainly, the people responded "wholeheartedly" (Ex 32:6, 19, 25 cf. Ex 24:3, 7; 25:2). But, noticeably absent from this false worship was the clear presentation of the Word and a commitment to wholehearted obedience to the entire law we saw in Exodus 24. Also clearly evident in Exodus 32 was the unabashed desire to have their lustful desires fulfilled. The people's false worship provoked God to express His displeasure clearly and dramatically (Ex 32:9-11).

Consider the characteristics of the music that accompanied this worship. Joshua, still on the periphery of the camp, observed that the music of this false worship was like shouting and warfare (Ex 32:17-18). In fact, it was not clearly identifiable as music until Moses and Joshua moved closer to the people. The false worship was further characterized by a lack of restraint (Ex 32:25). BDB defines פָּרַע as to "*let go, let loose*, people, i.e. remove restraint from them."[6] Some translators believe that the people were ". . . literally naked, as the Egyptians performed some of their rites in that indecent manner."[7] The Expositor's Bible Commentary adds, "It would appear that there was a type of religious prostitution connected with the people's worship of the golden calf."[8] Keil and Delitzsch believe they worshiped "in the same manner in which the Egyptians celebrated their feast of Apis (*Herod* 2, 60, and 3, 27)."[9] God called the false worshipers completely "corrupted" (Ex 32:7). The unbelieving peoples around the Israelites participated in these aberrations of true worship which the Israelites had chosen to imitate. It is universally accepted among anthropologists that music was very much a part of Egyptian worship and that of all the religions of the Ancient Near East.

To gain the most from this passage you need to put yourself in the story. Moses and Joshua were coming down the mountain from a fresh experience in God's presence. God shattered this intimate time with the bad news that the nation was involved in idolatry (Ex 32:7-10). During their relatively short absence the people had already forsaken God and began worshiping falsely (Ex 32:8). To Joshua the worship music was not "just exciting" but violent; it sounded like the noise of war. Those elements in the music that predominated were shouts of distress not joyous examples of exuberant true worship. Keil and Delitzsch offer the following entry:

> When Moses departed from God with the two tables of the law in his hand (see at Ex. 31:18), and came to Joshua on the mountain (see at Ex. 24:13), the latter heard the shouting of the people (lit., the voice of the people in its noise, רֵעֹה for רֵעוֹ, from רֵעַ noise, tumult), and took it to be the noise of war; but Moses said (v. 18), *"It is not the sound of the answering of power, nor the sound of the answering of weakness,"* i.e., they are not such sounds as you hear in the heat of battle from the strong (the conquerors) and the weak (the conquered); *"the sound of antiphonal songs I hear."* (עַנּוֹת is to be understood, both here and in Ps. 88:1, in the same sense as in Ex. 15:21.)[10]

Although we do not know many things about the musical characteristics of this false worship, those things we do see in the "halo data" (observable data surrounding the activity) of the event are at the very least, worth examining. I reserve my applications of this event for the section below.

Those who had not corrupted themselves were commanded to destroy all those who were involved in false worship (Exodus 32:27-28). This command specifically mentions slaying "every man his brother, and every man his companion, and every man his neighbor" (Ex 32:27).

For the sake of time I will not deal with Leviticus 9:22-10:19 but God's equally stern judgment on Nadad and Abihu for their "strange fire" further underscores God's intolerance of anyone who would not wholly glorify and sanctify Him before His people (Lev 10:3).

Principles to Apply

- No matter how effective the teacher or how dramatic and pure previous public worship may have been, some people will choose to fall into false worship.
- False worship may in many ways mimic true worship. Worship leaders may be involved in elements of false worship even while calling it an activity "for the Lord."
- Music surrounding false worship may reinforce or even stimulate the immorality associated with it.
- For the sake of His own integrity, God judges false worship.

Applications

God has used a couple of circumstances in my life to remind me that as much as a leader may desire to demonstrate pure worship before his people, they still have choices to make. God-centered worship in the past holds no guarantee for the future. The sights and sounds of the Sinai event were every worship leader's dream. Surely this obviously successful worship service would so impress the people of God that settling for lesser false worship would hold no appeal. But the desire to imitate the way they always did it in Egypt, the allurements of the sensual, the impatience or boredom of the doubters, the whispering of the Evil one, the weakness of Aaron's leadership all conspired to make this seem like the right thing to do. Leaders, *every* service is worthy of our conscientious, spiritual preparation. But, no matter the conscientious preparation, every person in the congregation must make a choice to follow the Lord. As Pastor E. Robert Jordan once told me "Dean, people choose to worship or not; you can't make them."

Yet, worship choices must be made. When Israel chose to worship God with purity, they enjoyed the blessings of relationship. Leviticus 26:3-13 says: "And I will set my tabernacle among you: and my soul shall not abhor you. And I will walk among you, and will be your God, and ye shall be my people." If they chose to worship themselves and would not draw near to God, God would destroy them and their false worship. Later, in Leviticus 26:30-31 we read: "I will destroy your high places, and cut down your images, and cast your carcasses upon the carcasses of your idols. And my soul shall abhor you...and I will not smell the savour of your sweet odors."

Satan is the master deceiver. Although I have seen dramatic demonstrations of the reality of Satanic forces in our world, I believe he is most commonly very subtle. False worship may look very much like true worship. If we are to avoid it, I believe we need to look for a commitment to the centrality of the Word, and second a commitment to God-centered, not people-driven decision making in worship and music issues. I understand, and have clearly said that the human side of the equation is important, but only secondarily so. Don't fall for Satan's repeated lie that it's "the people" that make me violate purity in my worship. That was Aaron's lame excuse (Ex 32:22-24). Why God allowed Aaron to continue in a place of leadership is a mystery of the grace of God. Let us not be of his number in these important issues.

I want to address the issue of music in this passage with great caution. On one hand I am disappointed that most of the writers I have read on this passage fail to mention music at all. On the other hand, since we are dealing with a narrative, I am reluctant to make too much of the insights Moses and Joshua make to the music involved in this worship. The Bible gives us no sound, no recordings of how worship music did, should, or should not sound. Of course, God in His providence *could* have revealed this to us, but He did not. His divine intention is to leave this for us to discern. It becomes a test, a test of our love and commitment to seek God's pleasure, a test of how well our knowledge of Him and His creation grows, and a test of whether we will let our knowledge of the Lord inform and shape our decisions. As I mentioned above we are sometimes left to consider the "halo data" surrounding an event.

Although it would be simpler to jettison this whole idea of "halo data" or association all together, we will see again in the NT that we do not have that option. I am sorry, life might seem easier if we could ignore the fruits connected to teachers if we were not called to examine motives and lifestyles, but as we will see, these commands remain as challenging imperatives. So, I challenge you, consider what the "halo data" of this passage can tell us about the nature of the music of false worship. Examine the fruit and consider the accompanying activities and attitudes of these false worshipers. Joshua thought it sounded like shouts of war: neither victorious nor desperate, just violent and orgiastic. As they came upon the reality, Joshua's impressions were all too accurate. Can initial impressions be wrong and apparent associations misleading? Yes, but wisdom living would call us to great caution when the obvious and overt in music literally screams out to us of violence and all around those sounds are signs of idolatry and out of control behavior. Thoughtfully consider these ideas as you look at trends and movements today.

Allow me to stretch you a bit further. The music accompanying this false worship stimulated, caused, or was at least associated with the violence and aural disarray that would have more logically been present in an ancient battle scene. This was certainly not the beauty of ordered music more fitting godly worship. It has been interesting to me over the years to think on the question, "Do you suppose the music is the horse pulling the cart or the cart being pulled by the horse?" As I look over the whole of the Bible on this interrelationship between worship and music, I personally lean toward music's causative role. Whatever your opinion, it seems that sensual, pleasure-driven, even violent music is very often the bedfellow of false worship. Avoiding music that accompanies such movements, even if some leaders claim it is "a feast to the Lord," is just the wise thing to do.

Deuteronomy 31-32 The Power of Music
Exegetical Considerations

God's last command to Moses regarding his public ministry was to put the covenant treaty between God and the Israel in the form of a song and teach it to the children of Israel so that as they were drawn away in false worship. This music would serve to testify against generations of Israelites and remind them of God's character and actions (Deut 31:12-13, 18-32:47). It may seem unusual that a song was a part of God's plan to ensure the fidelity of Israel's worship (Deut 31:19, 21) but you will see several powerful truths regarding music in this narrative.

Notice that God chose music as the tool to remind His people about Himself. This song was to be taught to and sung by every one of the children of Israel (Deut 31:19, 22, 30). It was not to be just tacitly heard. The purpose of the song was to teach and to "testify as a witness" as they sang to themselves and to those who heard them. The phrase "put it in their mouths, that this song..." (Deut 31:19) leaves no doubt that music is to be actively sung, not just listened to.

Merrill says "the song itself was a reiteration of the essence of the covenant history and text, a statement of faith they affirmed and to which they recommitted themselves every time they sang it."[11] The song was strong in content, speaking of the nature and acts of God (Deut 32:3-43). Joshua was also involved in instructing the people regarding this song along with Moses (Deuteronomy 32:44).

I think it is also important to notice the interchangeable use of the verb (דָּבָר *dabar*) word, speaking, speech and the noun (שִׁירָה, *sira*) song. What they sang to God they said to God. It was no less the clear teaching of the Word when they sang. This is yet another powerful reminder that the "teaching" of the Word of God does not begin after the singing ends.

Principles to Apply

- Music is designed by God to be a powerful ally in combating false worship and retaining the truths of God.
- The songs of God's people should be accurate portrayals of the acts and attributes of God.
- God's people are to actively sing to the Lord so that the truths of the songs may witness and give counsel to them.
- God commands music to be used as an unforgettable reminder of the acts of God. This song is not to be listened to, but actively sung by the people of God.

Applications

Someone asked me one day, "In your opinion, what is the thing we just 'don't get' in our church?" Excusing the colloquial grammar, without hesitation I said, "The thing we don't get is that music is a powerful teaching tool and that the musicians our people listen to are having a greater impact on the lives of our people than anything else we do." That may seem too strong to you. But think about it. When we endear our people, especially our young people, to a musical teacher, they buy the CD or go online, download the music, and listen to it a few dozen times until it is completely memorized. Now, these ideas are permanently imprinted on their minds. What a powerful tool for good! What a powerful tool for evil! As many of you know from personal experience, the music you listened to forty or more years ago is no less in your mind. I believe we just "don't get this" in Christianity today. God help us to actively and conscientiously use the powerful tool of music in our lives and ministries.

Satan is no doubt fully using the power of music to permanently impact the belief systems of unsuspecting believers and unbelievers alike. As we consider his agenda we understand that he can be either blatant or subtle in his attacks. Not only does music have the power to keep us from false worship by reminding us of the truths of God, it also has the power to attract us to false worship. This truth about music is a double-edged sword. The world knows this truth as well. Music attaches information quickly, permanently, emotionally, and can bypass the cognitive, going right for the volition of the listener. Filmmakers and advertisers make full use of music's power all the time.

Let me add finally that once again the content of the song in this passage ought to act as a template for music writers today. Let's look to build music programs whose goal is the full and accurate disclosure of the acts and attributes of God sung in ways our people, all our people can sing together.

As we leave this time period, I hope your definition of worship and your understanding of music is beginning to crystallize. I trust you are beginning to discern a few more of the biblical principles of both worship and music choices. We are all accountable to know God's Word on these issues and make choices that reflect our love for Him. I remind you of our process. The exegetical considerations you must wrestle with. The Bible says what it says; we need to grow in our understanding of the texts with which we must wrestle. Next, it is not enough to leave the passages in the world of the original audience; we must attempt to discern principles to live by. Last, we must come up with ways to be "doers of the Word and not hearers only" (James 1:22). Our job is not done until we make our best attempt to live out the truth. God bless us all in our journey toward "the Way, the Truth, and the Life." We all have another step to take.

Chapter Five
Joshua and Judges

The passages I have chosen from this time period may challenge some fundamental ideas you have about music as a form of communication. What you will do with some of the ideas presented may cause you to do some "outside the box" thinking. Be wise, but let your mind be sharpened by the way things were when these passages were written.

In this chapter, you will also come face to face with whether this matter of worship is worth quarreling over in the first place. Remember that the Canaanites were being displaced because they were false worshipers. The Israelites were sternly warned to avoid their new neighbors' sins at all costs. Oh, that we would maintain that same zeal.

1. Deut 32:44 Joshua accompanied Moses in singing the covenant treaty
2. Josh 5:13-15 Joshua worships Captain of Host
3. Josh 7:6 Joshua bowed before Ark of the Covenant
4. Josh 8:30-35 Joshua lead worship after Ai
5. Josh 10:13 First reference to the book of Jasher, a series of songs chronicling military victories
6. Josh 22:5, 10-34 Misunderstanding and cautions regarding the "altar" by Jordan
7. Josh 23:7-8, 16 Warnings about the temptations of false worship judgment pronounced on false worshipers
8. Josh 24:14-24 Call to pure, sincere worship
9. Jud 2:2, 5, 11-14, 17, 19; 3:6-10 Warnings against false worship and the subsequent worship of Baalim by the Israelites
10. Jud 5 Debra sang a song as "prophetess"
11. Jud 6:10,21,24-26,28,30-32 Gideon called to fearlessly destroy false worship
12. Jud 7:15 Gideon worshiped after the dream

13. Jud 8:27, 33 Gideon made an ephod which is worshiped, leaving a legacy of idolatry
14. Jud 9:4, 27, 46 False worship of Baal-berith by Gaal
15. Jud 10: 6,7,10, 13, 14, 16 Judgment for false worship
16. Jud 11:24, 31, 34 Jephthah's vow
17. Jud 13:16, 19-23 Manoah's vision and worship
18. Jud 15:16-17 Song of Samson
19. Jud 16:23, 24 Worship of Dagon
20. Jud 17:3-5, 10, 12-13; 18:14, 17-20, 24, 30-31 Micah's false worship with the hireling levitical priest who later served the tribe of Dan
21. Jud 20:18, 26, 27 Israel sought God in worship
22. Jud 21:4 Israel's worship
23. I Sam 1:3-4, 19, 21, 25, 28 Elkanah's worship
24. I Sam 2:1-10 Hannah's song
25. I Sam 2:11-19, 22-33 Samuel's worship contrasted with the worship of Eli's sons
26. I Sam 3:1, 13, 14 Eli's judgment
27. I Sam 5:2-5 The Ark of the Covenant and the temple of Dagon
28. I Sam 6:4-5, 8, 13-15 Ark returned to Jerusalem
29. I Sam 7:3-4, 9-10, 17; 8:8 Samuel spoke judgment and exampled proper worship, Samuel called Israel to forsake baalim and ashtaroth
30. I Sam 9:12-14, 19, 25 Breaking down the high places
31. I Sam 10:5-6, 8, 10-13 The school of the prophets and music
32. I Sam 11:7, 15 Worship at the anointing of Saul
33. I Sam 12:10, 14, 18, 20, 24 Samuel called Israel to forsake false worship and seek the Lord

Subsequent passages dealing with Samuel's relationship to Saul as King will be examined under chapter 6, United Kingdom.

I have chosen three passages in the life of Joshua to highlight in this chapter. They are Joshua's call, the brief mention of the book of Jabesh, and the conflict over the erection of the memorial pillar at the end of the major conquests. Other significant passages you might consider studying on your own are the elements included in Joshua's worship in Joshua 8:30-35 and his final challenges in Joshua 23-24.

Judges illustrates the conflict over the object of worship and the dramatic judgment of God when false worship occurs. In this section I have chosen to only highlight the song of Deborah in Judges 5. It would also be worth your time to study Gideon's stand against false worship (Judg 6), his positive example (Judg 7), and his poor worship choice in making the ephod (Judg 8). The hireling Levite in Judges 17-18 is also an interesting case study. I will deal with the demise of the Ark of the Covenant and its return when we consider King David in the next chapter.

Joshua 5:14-16 Joshua's Worship
Exegetical Considerations

God instructed Joshua to prepare the people to worship by circumcising the men and celebrating their redemption from Egypt by observing the Passover. Remember the significances of this event we discussed in the last chapter. As we have seen before and will see again, God used the context of worship to further reveal His will. Once again the cyclical pattern of revelation, response in worship, further revelation, and further response in worship is seen. In this narrative, God revealed His commands (Josh 5:2); worshipers responded in obedience (Josh 5:3-5), God was further revealed through the observation of the Passover (Josh 5:10-12); God in that context miraculously revealed Himself as the "Captain for the Host" (Josh 5:14); Joshua fell before Him in worship (Josh 5:14), and God further revealed His Lordship (Josh 5:15).

Joshua would have seen this response in worship before. Falling on one's face is a natural response to power and lordship. Taking off one's shoes, on the other hand may seem unusual. Keil and Delitzsch give the following insights into the practice.

> The command of God to Moses to put off his shoes, may be accounted for from the custom in the East of wearing shoes or sandals merely as a protection from dirt. No Brahmin enters a pagoda, no Moslem a mosque, without first taking off at least his overshoes (*Rosenm.* Morgenl. i. 261; *Robinson,* Pal. ii. p. 373); and even in the Grecian temples the priests and

priestesses performed the service barefooted (*Justin,* Apol. i. c. 62; *Bähr,* Symbol. ii. 96). When entering other holy places also, the Arabs and Samaritans, and even the Yezidis of Mesopotamia, take off their shoes, that the places may not be defiled by the dirt or dust upon them (vid., *Robinson,* Pal. iii. 100, and *Layard's* Nineveh and its Remains). The place of the burning bush was holy because of the presence of the holy God, and putting off the shoes was intended to express not merely respect for the place itself, but that reverence which the inward man (Eph. 3:16) owes to the holy God.[1]

Freeman and Chadwick suggest that it may have had an even deeper significance in light of the location of this experience.

> When God descended on Mount Sinai, the mountain itself became so holy because of his presence that He told Moses: "Put limits around the mountain and set it apart as holy," and tell the people: "Be careful that you do not go up the mountain or touch the foot of it. Whoever touches the mountain shall surely be put to death" (Exodus 19:23, 12). At the bush, God told Moses to take off his sandals because: "where you are standing is holy ground." The commander (captain, KJV) of the Lord's army told Joshua: "Take off your sandals, for the place where you are standing is holy." Same reason as with Moses: the place or ground where they were standing was holy—made holy by the presence of God. So it is probable that being told to take off their sandals was not because of demanded respect, and certainly not worship on their part because they had been told to do it, but because nothing man-made—and therefore unclean—was to be between the feet of God's creature and the holiness that God's presence made the ground.[2]

It is quite likely that the parallels between Joshua's experience and the commissioning of Moses were significant not for Joshua alone but also for the people. The Israelites would now know that Joshua, like Moses (also an octogenarian at the beginning of his leadership tenure), had the unique blessing of a face-to-face visible encounter with a manifestation of God (Ex 3:1-6). This event must have been a significant memory for both Joshua and the people.

This worship event served as a poignant reminder that although Joshua was to serve as the human leader of Israel's military forces, the "commander of the host" (whether the host referring to an angelic host or the nation itself) was someone Joshua needed to bow before. Not only was God's holiness manifested but also His lordship and sovereignty. This would be tested when Joshua is given the unorthodox commands for military victory against Jericho in the near future.

Principles to Apply

- Obedience to God's commands and the observation of worship activities like the Passover both reveal the character of God and act as an appropriate response to Him. Both revelation and response are integral parts of worship.
- Outward acts like bowing, memorial observations, and submissive service provide visible manifestations of a heartfelt understanding of God's attributes; in this case God's holiness, lordship, and power.

Applications

Warren Weirsbe makes some interesting parallels to Paul in Ephesians and this narrative. Although clearly an application and not the main point of the passage, I believe Weirsbe illustrates some transdispensational concepts when he states:

> The sequence here is significant: first *humble worship*, then *holy walk*, then *heavenly warfare*. This parallels the "spiritual postures" found in the Epistle to the Ephesians. Joshua first bowed the knee (Eph. 3:14); then he submitted to a holy walk (4:1, 17; 5:2, 8, 15); and then he went out to battle the enemy in the power of the Lord (6:10ff). Like Joshua, we have already been given our inheritance (described in Eph. 1–2) and we must overcome the enemy in order to claim it for ourselves and enjoy it.[3]

One of my seminary professors used to say "read until you start hearing the echoes." Hear the echo that worship is about responding to God and accurately revealing Him. That is why I believe our worship choices matter so much. God wants us to respond to Him, and God needs to be revealed, portrayed, and displayed before a watching world accurately and completely. This means that on both sides of this worship equation we must do everything within our power to worship in ways that reflect an understanding and respect for God supremely, coupled with an understanding and respect for the people God has called us to lead: a daunting task worthy of our passionate prayer and careful consideration.

Take this time as well to ask the Lord for a fresh look at your need to not just hear about God in some sterile, academic way, but also to personally live in light of who He is. For those of us on this side of the cross, this is something we can experience every time we enter into His presence as blood-bought, adopted children. Go there often; see Him clearly.

Joshua 10:13 The Book of Jasher
Exegetical Considerations

I want to take this opportunity to mention briefly the Book of Jasher cited first in this passage, again in 2 Samuel 1:18, and, as is generally agreed, again in Numbers 21:14 called the "book of the wars of the Lord." The practice of singing a ballad recounting victory in battle was a common practice in antiquity as we have seen already in Exodus 15. In *The Biblical Knowledge Commentary* this entry summarizes the consensus among scholars: "In Josh 10:13 (**The Book of Jashar** [sic] is a Heb. literary collection of songs written in poetic style to honor the accomplishments of Israel's leaders; [cf. David's "lament of the bow" in 2 Sam. 1:17-27].)"[4] *Harpers Bible Handbook* offers the possibility that in addition to these citations there may be another, stating:

> ...1 Kings 8:12-13, where the Septuagint (LXX) adds, 'is it not written in the book of songs,' a reading that is perhaps due to a simple transposition of two Hebrew consonants. The

nature of the 'book' has been a matter of discussion from pre-Christian times. It was apparently a collection of archaic poetry which, though well known in ancient Israel, has not survived, perhaps because it was transmitted primarily in oral form by professional singers.[5]

Last I would draw your attention to this entry in the *Easton's Bible Dictionary*, which says:

> **JASHER** — upright. "The Book of Jasher," rendered in the LXX. "the Book of the Upright One," by the Vulgate "the Book of Just Ones," was probably a kind of national sacred song-book, a collection of songs in praise of the heroes of Israel, a "book of golden deeds," a national anthology. We have only two specimens from the book, (1) the words of Joshua which he spake to the Lord at the crisis of the battle of Beth-horon (Josh. 10:12, 13); and (2) "the Song of the Bow," that beautiful and touching mournful elegy which David composed on the occasion of the death of Saul and Jonathan (2 Sam. 1:18–27).[6]

Principle to Apply

- The use of music to communicate in emotional and memorable ways has precedents both historically and biblically.

Applications

I am taking time to mention this passage to once again reinforce the point that storytelling through music was an important part of retaining truth in the ancient world. The book of Jasher was an important part of how military victories were announced, celebrated, and remembered. The singing of epics and other important truths is something we have lost in our culture today, though perhaps some cantatas or oratorios may come close. If you would like to see this change it will mean thinking outside the box of our present world. How this is actually fleshed out will be new territory. It will very likely mean that your paradigm for thinking about the role of music in your personal life and your church will undergo some change. Music in our day is rarely a story of historic significance or theological substance. Good testimonies, wonderful simple sentiments, yes, but rarely is our music, "secular" or "sacred" (however those terms are defined), complex in storyline or content. Yet, those things that we have sung to us, and certainly those things we sing are more memorable than what we read, what we see, or what we have spoken to us. In relation to the totality of human history, only recently have songs relating significant data been neglected.

The days of nine stanza hymns like "O God Our Help in Ages Past" dealing with doctrine or sacred history in substantive ways are gone. People seem stretched when called upon to sing all three stanzas of most of our current hymns. Don't misquote me, I am not saying that songs with simple sentiment or colloquial, indigenous testimony songs are bad. They are very right! Only that the potential of music to deliver truth is largely under-used in our present environment. Let me also add that even if we embrace a model of music that strives to be more substantive in text, we must still live in the world in which we find ourselves. Let's commit to looking for growth in the substance of our music and let's do it in such a way that we do not lose our people or ignore the wonderful simple music that should certainly be a part of what we sing.

Joshua 22 Opposing False Worship at Any Cost
Exegetical Considerations

With the major military campaigns ended, the Eastern Tribes (Reuben, Gad, and the half tribe of Manasseh) were excused to return to their families on the eastern side of Jordan. Joshua called the tribes to fidelity in worship with this challenge in Joshua 22:5:

> But take diligent heed to do the commandments and the law, which Moses the servant of the Lord charged you, to love the Lord your God, and to walk in all His ways, and to keep His commandments, and to cleave unto Him, and to serve Him with all your heart and with all your soul.

Obedience to the law, love for the Lord, obedience to all the commandments of the Lord, a desire to draw close to the Lord, and full-hearted service give a convincing and succinct reiteration of many of the worship concepts we have already discussed. Joshua 22 records one of the high points of Israel's history. Joshua commends the tribes' service (Josh 22:1-4) and blesses them (Josh 22:5-9). As the Eastern Tribes left their brothers to return to their families on the east side of Jordan, they built an altar (Josh 22:10). Other patriarchs had done the same and although sacrifices were only now to be done at the central altar in the tabernacle (Deut 12:4-14; Lev 17:8-9) building an altar was not strictly condemned.

Israel responded to this altar building swiftly, for they thought the Eastern Tribes had built a false altar to the Lord (Josh 22:10, 19-24, 29). They responded by gathering an army to kill their comrades if they were found to be false worshipers (Josh 22:12-14). Before the war began, a delegation was sent. Among them was a prince from each Tribe, and the priest Phinehas. It was Phinehas who dramatically judged the false worship and fornication of Baal-Peor, recorded in Numbers 25. The false worship of Baal-Peor resulted in the death of 24,000 people.

The sequence of events of the trial looked something like this: The accusations were made by the prosecution. The episode at Baal-Peor was specifically mentioned (Josh 22:15ff). The Western delegation offered to make provision for them on the west side of Jordan (Josh 22:19). They reminded them that the whole nation was judged in the matter of Achan (Josh 22:20); reinforcing the truth that the nation's corporate guilt was not something inconsequential.

The defense of the Eastern Tribes was to call on "El, Elohim, Jehovah" (אֵל אֱלֹהִים יְהוָה) Himself to judge (Josh 22:22a). They agreed that capital punishment would be justified for such a heinous crime (Josh 22:22b-23). The truth was, however, that the Eastern Tribes had built a memorial for the very purpose of preserving true worship among those who lived to the east of Jordan (Josh 22:24, 28-29). Their concern was that subsequent generations would refuse to allow the Eastern Tribes to participate in the pure worship of Jerusalem. Preserving the true worship of Jehovah was their stated purpose. They decided to build this altar as an additional safeguard since they were already required to return to the tabernacle three times a year for sacrifices and feasts (Ex 23:17). The Western delegation responded by accepting their explanation (Josh 22:30-32) and giving a favorable report to the Western Tribes (Josh 22:32-34).

Whether they should have built this altar in the first place is a matter of disagreement among Bible scholars. We see nowhere in the passage that building this altar was a response to God's command to them. History proved that the Easterners were among the first to forsake the Lord (1 Chron 5:25-26). Admittedly, the Westerners fared only slightly better. For both parties involved, this worship matter of building a memorial altar was viewed as a life and death situation. Preserving pure worship was the stated goal of both groups.

Principles to Apply

- Avoid false worship at all cost, in your own life and in the lives of others around you.
- What is really at stake in worship and worship music choices is nothing less than how people understand the nature, attributes, attitudes and actions of God Himself.
- In matters of worship practices, a zeal for purity in worship should be combined with open and forthright communication, and followed by unity whenever possible. Discerning the true motives and actual practices of others is essential in making proper biblical judgments.

Applications

Some people wonder, why all the concern over worship? I hope you come away from this narrative with a greater understanding of why worship is such a big deal. More than one person has wondered out loud why I would pull out of active ministry and spend a year trying to put these materials in print form. If there were another way I certainly would have chosen it. It's a compulsion really, a fire in me. I trust it is a compulsion that is Spirit led and Spirit controlled, but a compulsion nonetheless. I invite you to enter into the journey for truth in these matters as well. It will be a bumpy journey and some, perhaps many, will misunderstand your intentions or ideas. I am prepared for that inevitability. Are you?

I am reminded of another story we dealt with in the last chapter. Let me quote again what Aaron proclaimed in Exodus 32:5-6: "Tomorrow is a feast to the Lord, and they rose up early on the morrow, and offered burnt offerings, and brought peace offerings..." Yet, later in Exodus 32:26-28 the narrative says Moses...

> ...stood in the gate of the camp, and said, who is on the Lord's side? Let him come unto me. And all the sons of Levi gathered themselves together unto him. And he said unto them, Thus saith the Lord God of Israel, put every man his sword by his side, and go in and out from gate to gate throughout the camp, and slay every man his brother, and every man his companion, and every man his neighbor. And the children of Levi did according to the word of Moses; and there fell of the people that day about three thousand men.

In Joshua 22 and in Exodus 32, the matter of pure worship was so important that battle lines were drawn or blood was shed. Friendship, camaraderie, even family relationships took second place to the matter of proper worship.

One might suggest several central propositions from this narrative. *Aggressively go after false worshipers. Don't jump to conclusions. Send delegations before making war. Get the facts.* I would suggest that the big idea of the narrative is that worship matters; it is worth shedding blood over or taking the time to build memorials to safeguard pure worship for future generations. Throughout Israel's history God jealously guarded worship. Remember, God consumed Nadab and Abihu (Lev 10:1). Remember one of the most impassioned moments of Christ's ministry when He threw over the tables of the temple and declared, "This is my Father's house" (John 2:16). Remember that Paul said some are weak and some sleep because they worshiped unworthily (1 Cor 11:30). And be reminded that finally, John in Revelation writes of a time when the only Worthy One will finally break the seals on the book and send His angelic servants to hunt down false seals on the book and send His angelic servants to hunt down false worshipers once for all, forcing every knee to bow before Him who alone is worthy of worship (Rev 9:14-21).

During the time of the Judges, false worship is what brought God's judgment (Jud 2:2, 11-12-17, 19; 3:10; 10:6, 13, 16). Only when false worship was eradicated and true worship restored was God willing to rescue His people and send deliverance. The immoral activities of the time of the Judges were the result of false worship.

Judges 5 Song of Deborah
Exegetical Considerations

The *New American Commentary* offers an excellent entry on this passage that I believe lays some important groundwork in this matter of the similarities and differences between prose and poetry.[7]

I draw your attention first to the entry where Block says:

> most (scholars) agree that - along with the Blessing of Jacob (Genesis 49), the Song of the Sea (Exodus 15), the oracles of Balaam (Numbers 23–24), and the Blessing of Moses (Deuteronomy 33) - Judges 5 ranks among the oldest monuments of Hebrew literature.[8]

Next, see this helpful comparison of prose and poetry:

> Judges 4–5 offers a rare presentation of a single event in two versions, one prose (chap. 4), the other poetic (chap. 5). Indeed these chapters offer students of OT literature an invaluable resource for examining the differences between ancient Hebrew poetry and prose. Although the distinctions are not absolute, the typical features of the two major categories of Hebrew literature may be summarized as follows:

Feature	Prose	Poetry
Diction	Common diction, employing words and spellings used in everyday speech and commerce	Elevated literary diction, archaic expressions, and rare words
Grammar	Common grammar and syntax, with distinctive prosaic elements	Creative grammatical and syntactical forms, often lacking the prosaic elements.
Style	Logical and chronological description, heavily dependent upon coordinating and subordinating clauses, dialogue, plot development, etc.	Impressionistic and often abstract description, heavily dependent upon the heightened use of parallelism
Tone	Controlled and relatively realistic, though deliberately and artistically composed	Emotionally charged, with heavy reliance on hyperbole and other figures of speech
Aim	To inform, educate, entertain, indoctrinate	To celebrate, commemorate, inspire

The only parallel to this juxtapositioning of prose and poetic accounts of the same event in the entire OT is found in Exodus 14–15, which recounts and celebrates the Israelite crossing of the Reed [sic] Sea.[9]

Judges 4 and 5 illustrate the repeating cycle of false worship, God's judgment of false worship, repentance, deliverance and again more false worship. In this particular narrative God was allowing dominance by Jabin king of Canaan. I would like to focus on the musical aspects of this narrative.

This is interesting because the oldest texts were set in the poetic form, which in antiquity was consistently intoned. These passages use the term אָמַר, *amar* (say) to refer to saying something through singing. Walvoord also refers to this ancient practice.

> This ancient poem (Jud 5), which may have been initially preserved in a collection such as "the Book of the Wars of the LORD" (Num. 21:14) or "the Book of Jashar" (Josh. 10:13), is literally a victory hymn (well known in examples from the 15th to 12th centuries B.C. in Egypt and Assyria).[10]

Deborah's song has been recognized as one of the most powerful poems of antiquity even by secular scholars.[11] Carson even suggests it may have been one of the songs included in the Book of Jasher discussed above.[12] As both prophet and judge (אִשָּׁה נְבִיאָה) Deborah is much like Miriam in Exodus 15:20. Her role as a prophetess may have similarly been connected to her proclamation as a singer. Block concludes his introductory material regarding this passage with an interesting observation.

> Two introductory questions of intention remain: (1) Why was this song composed in the first place? (2) Why did the author of the Book of Judges insert it here? The answer to the first depends upon the generic classification ascribed to the poem: as history it informs; as a ballad it entertains; as a heroic ode it inspires; as a hymn it calls for celebration. As a poetic recital of historical events, this ode offers the reader/hearer a glimpse into the early history of Israel.[13]

Principles to Apply

- Music can be used to communicate historic and/or theologically important concepts in an emotional and memorable way.
- The role of prophet includes the proclamation of truth using both prose and music.
- Women can be used to proclaim the truths of God through testimony and praise.

Applications

I have once again highlighted the place of music in this narrative, realizing that many may still wonder if we should take music seriously enough to include it in the proclamation of significant truth. Remember that in Deuteronomy 31-32 the Israelites were directly commanded to remember God's works through singing; here in Judges 5 we see another example of using music to record a significant historic event.

I am going to take this opportunity to further develop the contrasts between prose and poetry (that which the ancients sang or intoned). I have spent a great deal of time and energy in this book trying to make the case for substance in our music and to reinforce the point that what we sing we are also saying. The contrast between prose and poetry outlined above in the *New American Commentary* clearly demonstrates some differences between prose and poetry. They both have their own strengths and weaknesses. Genre studies like this have recently made some leaps forward. Evangelicals have begun to explore the idea that genre should make a difference in how we understand a passage and should also inform us as to how we might best proclaim it. I am attempting to bring forward this idea to the genre of music in the Word.

Understand that early in man's history, perhaps in the garden, the difference between singing and speaking may have been indiscernible. The semantic overlap may have been more complete; a "sound/language." Today the semantic overlap between singing and speaking is more distinct, though among the more ancient oriental languages, distinctions are still strongly tonal. Still, even today some mediums do overlap in English.

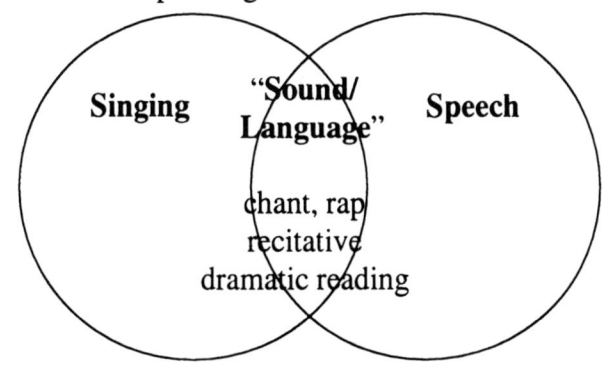

Singing | "Sound/Language" | Speech

chant, rap
recitative
dramatic reading

As to purpose and effect the Bible pictures a larger overlap. This concept can also be seen when we examine Paul's use of prose vs. poetry in the epistles that we will explore more fully later. Below, I offer a chart illustrating some of the ways in which I believe speech and singing are similar to and unique from each other. You will find that it is similar to the observations made by Block above.

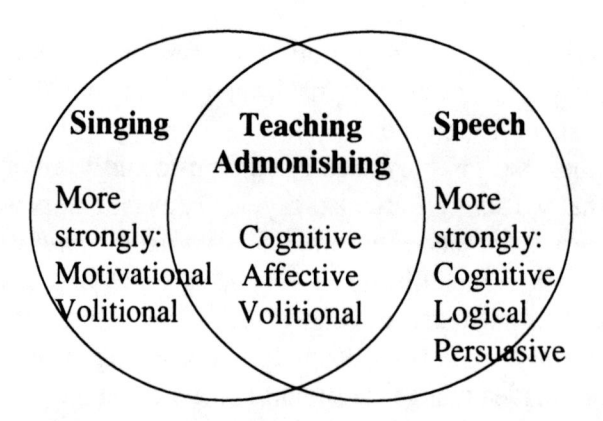

```
   Singing        Teaching         Speech
                 Admonishing
   More                            More
   strongly:     Cognitive         strongly:
   Motivational  Affective         Cognitive
   Volitional    Volitional        Logical
                                   Persuasive
```

Singing, it seems to me, is more suited to the function of prophet and speech to the function of the teaching priest, though both used the tools of music and speech.

Speech seems best suited to a more propositional presentation of truth or a presentation where an authority exercises his role and in essence is saying, "I am your spiritual leader, you need to do this for these reasons."

Singing is best suited to a motivational reminder of God's truth. Music goes right for a volitional response in the listener. At times, as in the case of instrumental music, bypassing the cognitive altogether and going right for the will. Music lends itself to expressions that are filled with emotion, even passion. Music in the Bible is predominantly prayer, testimony or creed (celebration of a truth). Prose is predominantly linear; a logical delineation of truth or persuasive logic.

The role of the musical prophet in Greek culture is even better documented. Consider the following quote in TDNT (*Theological Dictionary of the New Testament*).

Belief in a link between the divine Muse and the human poet is found in the earliest Gk. poetry, where it is obviously traditional and finds its simplest expression in the appeal to the Muse, Hom. Il.,1, 1, esp. 2, 484–492 etc. The Homeric poet-singer feels that in his work he is dependent on the divine (θεὸς ... δῶκεν ἀοιδήν, Od. 8, 44); by contact therewith he is a θεῖος ἀοιδός, Od., 1, 336; 8, 43 etc. The gift sought from the Muse is not only song (τέρπειν Od., 8, 45) but also the content of the past which is to be depicted. The Muses have seen and know all things (ἴστε πάντα Il., 2, 485) and they remind the singer (μνήσασθαι, 492), who is first the hearer and then the poet and speaker in the endowed power of presentation. Continuing this view, but breaking free from the epic of chivalry, Hes. with a new claim to truth (ἀληθέα γηρύσασθαι, Theog., 28) finds the relation of the poet to the Muse in his personal experience of calling by the Muses, who breathe into him the divine voice, 22–34 → 350, 4 ff.[14]

Understand that each time we sing, we act as a "mouthpiece" for God. For this reason we must take the musical life of our congregation seriously. Remember too that when you promote a singer by whatever means, you may be endearing your people to that powerful teacher. Do so with the greatest caution. Positively, we should give our people musical tools to help them remember God's great acts on our behalf. I am certainly not advocating a denigration of speaking in ministry but an elevation of singing and its role in the believer's life.

Before we leave this chapter, remember that Samuel, the last of the judges, called Israel to leave false worship (1 Samuel 7:3-4). As a part of Samuel's mission he started a "school of the prophets" (1 Sam 10:5, 10-11). These men can be seen prophesying "with a psaltery, and a tabret, and a pipe, and a harp." As "mouthpieces" of God, they too used music as one of their tools in teaching Israel (1 Sam 10:5).[15] It is in this context that the transition to the United Kingdom (and our next chapter) is introduced.

Chapter Six
United Kingdom

With the rocky start of Saul and the disappointing ending of Solomon notwithstanding, this time period represents the zenith of formal worship for the nation. Many lessons await you in this chapter. Although I have chosen to deal with Psalms separately, many of them were written during this historic time period. You will learn much as you look past the actual practices of the period and seek to gain insights into the principles behind them.

1. 1 Sam 13:9, 12-13 Saul intruded into Samuel's office and offered sacrifices. Saul's lineage will not continue to rule
2. 1 Sam 14:35 Saul built an altar but may not have sacrificed on it, he was not censured
3. 1 Sam 15:15, 21-25, 30-31 Saul seeks to worship after his disobedience
4. 1 Sam 16:2-5 David is anointed in the context of Samuel's worship
5. 1 Sam 16:16-23 Music of David comforted Saul
6. 1 Sam 18:6,7; 21:11; 29:5 Song of the women regarding military victory
7. 1 Sam 18:10-11; 19:9 David continues to play for Saul in spite of Saul's violence
8. 1 Sam 19:20-24 Saul again "prophecies," very likely singing (cf. 1 Sam 10)
9. 1 Sam 26:19 David defends himself to Saul and accuses Saul of driving him out, encouraging him to serve other gods
10. 1 Sam 30:16 David's enemies are eating, drinking, and dancing
11. 1 Sam 31:9-10 Saul's head and armor are paraded in Ashtaroth's (Dagon's) temple Cf. 1 Chron 10:10-11
12. 2 Sam 1:17-27 David's lament song over Saul and Jonathan
13. 2 Sam 3:33-34 David's lament song over Abner
14. 2 Sam 5:21 After a defeat in battle David and his men get rid of their idols Cf. 1 Chron 14:8-14

15. 2 Sam 6:1-23 First and second attempts to bring the ark back to Jerusalem Cf. 1 Chron 13, 15-16
16. 2 Sam 12:20 David worshiped after the death of his son
17. 2 Sam 15:8, 12 Absalom vowed to "serve the Lord" and has sacrifices offered in an attempt to steal the crown
18. 2 Sam 15:32 David's personal worship on the mount
19. 2 Sam 19:35 David lamented that in his old age he can no longer hear music
20. 2 Sam 22:1-23:7 Final songs of David
21. 2 Sam 24:18, 21-25 David's costly sacrifice and the purchase of the land where the Temple would be erected Cf. 1 Chron 21:18-30
22. 1 Kings 1:40 Music at the coronation of Solomon
23. 1 Kings 3:2-4 "Solomon loved the Lord…only he sacrificed and burnt incense in high places"
24. 1 Kings 3:15 Solomon worshiped in Jerusalem after his vision from God
25. 1 Kings 5-7 Details for the building of the temple Cf. 2 Chron 1-4
26. 1 Kings 8:1-66 Dedication of the temple and Solomon's praise, prayer, and song. Cf. 2 Chron 5-8:18
27. 1 Kings 9:6-9 God appeared to Solomon and challenged him to forsake false worship
28. 1 Kings 9:25 Solomon's thrice annual practice of worship
29. 1 Kings 10:12 Musical instruments in temple worship
30. 1 Kings 11:2-10, 33 Solomon's wives and their influence toward false worship
31. 1 Chron 5:25 The judgment for false worship upon the eastern tribes
32. 1 Chron 6:1-80 Levitical musician families and the high priestly line described Cf. 1 Chron 23-24
33. 1 Chron 9:33-34 The musician Levites description and responsibilities
34. 1 Chron 22:1-19 David challenged Solomon to build the temple and explained the purpose for the glories of the temple
35. 1 Chron 23:5-6, 13, 30-31 David established temple worship and music ministry
36. 1 Chron 25-26 Musician Levite families commissioned

37. 1 Chron 29:1, 6, 9-10, 13, 20-22 David worshiped God as he sets up Solomon as king
38. 2 Chron 1:3, 6 Solomon anointed at a "high place" and offers sacrifices
39. 2 Chron 2-4 Solomon described his plans for the Temple and furnishings
40. 2 Chron 9:11 Musical instruments and their excellence described

I Samuel 15:15, 21-25, 30-31 Saul's Intrusion into Priestly Worship
Exegetical Considerations

By way of introduction, it is important to remember that Saul had been anointed king and given the signs of the Holy Ghost's special anointing by spontaneously and uncontrollably prophesying, very probably through singing praises as were the prophets that he joined (1 Sam 10:5-13). Two incidents previous to 1 Samuel 15 show Saul intruding into the priest's office. The first was clearly a violation (1 Sam 13:9-13). The second, building an altar (1 Sam 14:34-35), was not strictly condemned but manifested Saul's cavalier attitude about worship. For his first infraction in the matter of the offering, the future succession of his kingly line was taken from him. 1 Samuel 15 represents the third similar public worship event recorded.

In this narrative Saul had clearly been commanded by the Lord through Samuel to "utterly destroy" the city of the Amalekites (1 Sam 15:2-3). 1 Samuel 15:9 reveals that Saul had other plans: "But Saul and the people spared Agag, and the best of the sheep, and of the oxen, and of the fatlings, and the lambs, and all that was good, and would not utterly destroy them: but everything that was vile, and refuse, that they destroyed utterly." There was nothing kind, or spiritual, or humanitarian about Saul's selective obedience. His stated desire, to bring a sacrifice of what should have been utterly destroyed, thinly veiled his genuine desire. His worship decisions revealed a Cainite worship philosophy: self-centered and self-directed worship. Samuel's message exposed this decision for what it was.

And Samuel said, when thou wast little in thine own sight, wast thou not made the head of the tribes of Israel, and the Lord anointed thee king over Israel? And the Lord sent thee on a journey, and said, go and utterly destroy the sinners, the Amalekites, and fight against them until they be consumed. (1 Sam 15:17-18)

First, Saul was too important in his own eyes (1 Sam 15:17). Second, the Lord anointed Saul as king, and because he was not self-made, he should not have been self-directed (1 Sam 15:17). Third, it was God that sent Saul on a specific mission; a mission he should have completely fulfilled (1 Sam 15:18). Saul's pride manifested itself in a disregard for obedience. Saul was offering worship as a means to another end, his own of self-aggrandizement and self-promotion.

Saul's disobedience, rebellion, insubordination, and rejection of the Word were manifested in Saul's attempt to worship his own way (1 Sam 15:22-23). Saul's sacrifices were not pleasing to the Lord because they were done within the context of disobedience, not obedience. To further heighten the travesty of this worship, Saul's sins of rebellion and stubbornness are compared to divination (קֶסֶם *qesem*), iniquity (אָוֶן *awen*), and idolatry (תְּרָפִים *terapim*). The first and last of these terms specifically referring to organized false worship were meant to show the connection between a disregard for God's express commands and more obvious overt false worship practices. Those who practiced divination or idolatry were to be destroyed (Deut 18:9-14). Saul's rebellion and stubbornness are essentially false worship. He was putting something or someone before Jehovah God.

Saul "confessed" his transgression but gave this excuse: "I feared the people, and obeyed their voice" (1 Sam 15:24). Notice Saul's insincere request to Samuel revealing his lack of repentance, for his true motive for worship continued to be people-centered. Saul said to Samuel: "I have sinned: yet honor me now, I pray thee, before the people and before Israel, and turn again with me, that I may worship the Lord thy God" (1 Sam 15:25, 30). It is now that Saul's judgment was sealed. Saul violated God's command and disregarded the need for absolute obedience. This violation of God's law regarding worship signaled the beginning of the end of Saul's reign (1 Sam 15:24-29).

Principles to Apply

- Worship must occur in the context of obedience.
- Although God desires sacrificial worship, attitudes of rebellion, disobedience, and stubbornness make such sacrifices as odious as overt false worship.

Applications

Isn't it enough if we have professionally performed music in beautifully appointed buildings with awe-inspiring lights and sound? Isn't God pleased when we bring the very best we can possibly muster to Him in worship? Or, how could we question the value of worship that unites people? After all, shouldn't we be trying to listen to the people and give them what will unify them around worship?

The difference between Saul's purportedly valuable sacrificial worship (he saved the best) and Noah's truly valuable sacrificial worship was obedience. That is why I am so excited that you have committed to picking up this book and growing in your understanding of how to obey the Lord and please Him in your worship. Noah moved with godly fear and carefully obeyed all that God had commanded him. Saul, on the other hand, was moved with a fear of people and disregarded God's commands in favor of what he believed would unite the people around himself.

Seeing these sentences before me on my computer screen drives me to my knees. How many times have I hungered for a perfect performance or a flawless musical sacrifice, instead of hungering and thirsting after righteousness? How many times have I sat down to prepare a worship service fearing people more than I fear God? I have wondered if my music and worship choices would satisfy the factions in my church more than whether I had fully surrendering my stubborn heart to do His will supremely, and to obey His leading in my choices, no matter the cost. I wonder too, how many times I have excused my own attitude of rebellion or stubbornness, thinking it is not as bad as God says it is, when it really is like witchcraft, and iniquity, and bowing before an idol. God, help me to value obedience to You above all. Let's commit to giving God a greater delight than sacrifices and burnt offerings–let's give Him our obedience.

1 Sam 16:16-23 David Plays before Saul
Exegetical Considerations

Because of Saul's disobedience, David had been anointed the next King. God's Spirit which had rested on Saul empowering him for his position, now rested on David (1 Sam 16:13). David Payne succinctly observed that "It is no coincidence that David's experience of receiving the Spirit of God is at once followed by Saul's loss of it."[1]

Saul's servants observed Saul's depression and recognized a universal understanding that music had the power to affect men's spirits. They suggested that Saul authorize them to bring in an appropriate individual to meet this need (1 Sam 16:16). *The New Bible Commentary* makes an interesting observation about this time period:

> This passage and ch. 17 show how two separate talents of David brought him to Saul's attention, making him a permanent member of the royal court (18:2). The first talent was his skill as a harpist, and the second was his military ability.... By itself, his ability on the battlefield might not have brought him to Saul's notice; it was his skill as a harpist which brought him to the royal court.[2]

God in His sovereign wisdom brought David into the royal court. From a human perspective, however, it was David's reputation as a musician. How or why Saul's servants knew about David's abilities as a musician is unclear. The other characteristics mentioned, especially his valor and description as a "man of war," may have reference to his exploits with the bear and lion which he mentions later (1 Sam 17:34). He was brought into the court because music's power to affect people was universally acknowledged by Saul and his servants.

Robert Bergan suggests:

David's music greatly affected Saul, who was helped on a number of occasions. The Hebrew verb forms in v. 23 suggest that Saul was attacked numerous times by the tormenting spirit; Scripture records two such additional instances (18:10; 19:9), and likely there were others.[3]

It is clear that the combination of the words harp (כִּנּוֹר *kinno*) and music (נָגַן *nagan*) (of stringed instruments) combined with the further clarifying word (יָד *yad*) (to play with the hand) indicate purely instrumental music. The effect of this music on King Saul was evident; David's playing made Saul well in every way (1 Sam 16:16-17 cf. 16:23). The Hebrew literary device of multiples in 1 Samuel 16:23, "so Saul was refreshed, and was well, and the evil spirit departed from him," reinforces the fact. Although I cannot prove from this passage what parts of the music specifically target each area, I can with certainty affirm that music affects listeners mentally, spiritually, volitionally, emotionally and physically.

Principle to Apply

- Music, including purely instrumental music, affects the whole person.

Applications

I have included this narrative to remind you of the power of music as a medium for change in others. To make that point a generation or more ago would have seemed absurd. Yet today, some have the idea that music doesn't rise above a matter of taste or perhaps cultural conditioning. As I look over at my bookcase I see scores of books, old and new, authored by saved and unsaved alike, from medical, psychological, theological, or historic perspectives almost all of which readily acknowledge for clinical or anecdotal reasons that music affects listeners. The only volumes that argue otherwise are recent copyrights that somehow believe *their* music must be the exception, simply because they wish it so. Please, I don't mean to be unkind; it is just that I have no idea what

I could possibly add to the discussion on this matter. I believe a thorough enough job has been done to prove the point that music by its very nature and purpose makes a difference in people. God, the supreme Moral Agent shared the ability to communicate with music with moral agents, men and angels. Communication must of necessity reflect the morality of the communicator. Let's not be willfully ignorant.

Since music affects those who hear it, the real question is, how? Here, since I am in the application section, I am going to offer some purely personal ideas. I would suggest that you begin by looking at some very basic components. Instead of looking for a secret code from the Scriptures or a music theory book, knowable only by the musically elite, I am convinced all believers have the tools to make wise musical choices. But we may need to be less scientific, less Baconian[4] in how we think. We are using the wrong paradigm when we think we need to prove exactly what sound always produce the exact same scientifically provable outcomes. Instead, the Bible calls us to look at fruit; the fruit of our musical teachers and their listeners. Believers in both Testaments are called on to be wise and look around at how people are being affected by the teachers (yes, even musical teachers) who surround them every day. Paul said: "For the time will come when they will not endure sound doctrine; but after their own lusts shall they heap to themselves teachers, having itching ears." (2 Tim 4:3) And earlier...

> This know also, that in the last days perilous times shall come. For men shall be lovers of their own selves, covetous, boasters, proud, blasphemers, disobedient to parents, unthankful, unholy, without natural affection, trucebreakers, false accusers, incontinent, fierce, despisers of those that are good, traitors, heady, high-minded, lovers of pleasures more than lovers of God; having a form of godliness, but denying the power thereof: from such turn away. (2 Tim 3:1-5)

Take note of the fact that most of the characteristics we are called to examine require that believers get beyond the surface facts to more subjective criteria. Music affects every person. Look for the fruit that accompanies the music. I realize this goes down sideways in many circles, but there are times when as unpopular or unscientific as it may seem, observing how people live and what influences, yes, including what musical influences, are in their lives is all the reason we need to eliminate its use. We will look at this further in the NT, so let me encourage you to reserve judgment on this issue.

On a completely different matter, I want you to consider the greater context of this section in the book of Samuel: the demise of Saul and the rise of David. As I have stated previously, in light of the musical context of 1 Samuel 10 and the use of the word prophet *(nahbi)* when referring to music participants, I believe that one of the outward evidences of the Holy Spirit is a song of praise. This is even clearer when you look at Ephesians 5:18-21. King Saul evidenced his special anointing of the Spirit by prophesying with the other prophets as they played their instruments. This is repeated in 1 Samuel 18:10 as David played. The fact that David is now evidencing the Spirit through musical praise may be another way the writer of this passage is showing the shift of spiritual leadership from Saul to David.

2 Samuel 6:1-23; 1 Chronicles 13:1-14, 15:1-16:42 Return of the Ark
Exegetical Considerations

In looking over this narrative many things can be learned. There are also some things that have been said about this narrative that I think are ill-informed. Unlike some narratives where God dramatically shows His approval, even during the second attempt, God does not give His endorsement. For students of the Word this event gives a glimpse into the contrast between the book of Samuel and the later writing of the Chronicles. The Chronicles, written at the end of the Israel's exile, gives some unique clarifications. We'll start first with setting the stage for this event.

Remember that the ark was in its present location because the Philistines had captured it in battle and returned it on an ox cart after it appeared to them to be the source of God's unique chastening power (1 Sam 5:2-12). There in Bethshemesh it was desecrated by some men who were slain (1 Sam 16:19). Some disagreement exists among translators about the number of those killed, (50,070, 1400, 70) but in any case this event further illustrates and perhaps foreshadows the need to respect God's commands regarding the ark's treatment. After that episode it was moved to Kirjathjearim and remained there 20 years (1 Sam 7:1-2).

Beginning with 1 Chronicles 13:1-4, we see several statements giving foreboding foreshadowing. First notice the absence of any prayer by David seeking God's specific direction about returning the ark and notice by contrast where he *does* seek for direction:

> And David consulted with the captains of thousands and hundreds, and with every leader. And David said unto all the congregation of Israel, If it seem good unto you, and that it be of the LORD our God, let us send abroad unto our brethren every where, that are left in all the land of Israel, and with them also to the priests and Levites which are in their cities and suburbs, that they may gather themselves unto us: And let us bring again the ark of our God to us: for we enquired not at it in the days of Saul. And all the congregation said that they would do so: for the thing was right in the eyes of all the people (1 Chron 13:1-4).

Notice also the numbers involved. David wants the whole nation to be brought together under his leadership through this event. "...that they may gather themselves unto us." David also contrasts his kingdom by debunking his predecessor. "...for we enquired not at it in the days of Saul." Next, David attempted to transport the ark on a new cart as the Philistines had transported it earlier (1 Sam 6:8), instead of having the Levites carry it as prescribed by God (Ex 25:14; Deut 12:29-32).

When a careless, though perhaps well-meaning Uzzah, reached out to steady the cart, God struck him dead (2 Sam 6:6-7). Some have suggested that Uzzah may have been one of the caretakers for the ark the many years it stayed in the house of his father Abinadad (1 Chron 13:7). Naturally, this interruption to David's plan angered him and filled him with fear and disappointment (2 Sam 6:8-9). The ark was brought to the house of Obededom, a Levite, who would properly care for the ark until it would later find a more permanent home.

Several months later David, still with a company of several thousand, retrieved the ark with the proper Levitical protocol and with animal sacrifices (1 Chron 15:12-13, 26). Again, the musicians were engaged in the processional.

David's dance has been the topic of much discussion surrounding worship. Other more in-depth studies of this topic have been done, but since it is very much a topic of current concern in worship I would offer the following perspectives. First, the specific word (כָּרַר *karar*) has only two occurrences, both in this passage. The AV translates it as "dance" both times. It has a secondary understanding of to whirl, dance, whirling, dancing. Two closely related words are used: (מְחֹלָה *machowlah*) occurring eight times, and (מָחוֹל *machowl*) which occurs an additional six times. The verb contains two basic ideas: first, whirling around in circular movements (reflected in the derivatives *mahol* and *mehola*) and second, writhing in labor pains (reflected in *hil* and *hila*). The Chronicler uses different words, here contrasted by Keil and Delitzsch. "1 Chron. 15:29–16:3. V. 29 and 1 Chron. 16:1–3 agree in substance with 2 Sam. 6:15–19a, only some few words being explained: e.g., מְרַקֵּד וּמְשַׂחֵק, v. 29, instead of מְפַזֵּז וּמְכַרְכֵּר (Sam.), and אֲרוֹן בְּרִית יהוה instead of אֲרוֹן יהוה (Sam.)"[5]

The variant word used in Chronicles, (רָקַד *raqad*), is also used in Job 21:11, "little ones like a flock, and their children dance," Psalm 29:6 "He maketh them also **to skip** like a calf," Psalm 114:4 "ye **skipped** like rams," and Ecclesiastes 3:4 "a time to mourn, and a time **to dance**," (**emphasis** mine). The use of this word by the Chronicler makes it clear that nothing of a choreographed or sensual manner was occurring and that David's dance would not have been related to dance as we commonly know it today.

Jeremy Montagu in his book *Musical Instruments of the Bible* (which includes much more than just a complete discussion of musical instruments), deals with dance quite exhaustively. He suggests that (מָחוֹל *mahol*), used in Psalm 30, 149 and 150, may actually have been a musical instrument and not dance at all.[6]

Much like the term "waltz" in modern music can refers to a musical genre rather than an actual dance; *mahol* may refer to a musical instrument originally associated with these spontaneous physical movements the AV translates as dance. In my opinion this would fit the context of these Psalms more easily. In any case, to suggest that this passage is somehow a biblical defense for the modern practice of cross-gender, choreographed, modern dance is not justifiable textually or contextually. I do have some ideas about application which I will share below.

Returning to the narrative, we read that Michal rebuked David for publicly celebrating in an "unkingly" way (2 Sam 6:20-23; 1 Chron 15:29). David's response, "It was before the Lord, which chose me before they father, and before all his house" (2 Sam 6:21), as well as the Chronicler's specific mention of Michal being the daughter of Saul (1 Chron 15:29), further illustrate the political implications of the text. Remember, part of the overall context is the demise of Saul and the rise of David. Some have conjectured that Michal's childlessness was the unique chastisement of God for her criticism of David's worship and infer that any criticism or censure of the worship of others today will be similarly chastened by God. The text reads more naturally without this contrived idea. McCarter chooses a more "normal" reading in light of the greater context (Saul's demise and David's rise) and simply says Michal was "excluded from his [David's] bed,"[7] which of course resulted in her remaining childless.

Upon entering Jerusalem, David commissioned the Levitical priestly singers and delivered a psalm of praise to Asaph to be sung as the ark returned (1 Chron 16:7-42). This psalm calls on God's people to remember God's actions and "give unto the Lord the glory due unto His name" (1 Chron 16:29). This song appears as Psalm 105 with little variation in the first sixteen verses. Several other psalms may have found their genesis in this event or these psalms may have been previously conceived and simply quoted by David here. Once again, this song praises God for His power and providence in Israel's history.

Principles to Apply

- Borrowing the religious practices of pagans and/or ignoring worship practices that are revealed by God have disastrous consequences.
- Wholehearted worship in the context of obedience can be God-honoring. We must be cautious in this narrative because God has not specifically revealed His approval of David's actions.
- Filling our songs with the acts and attributes of God should be a part of the music of every believer.

Applications

Let's begin first with the matter of the ark and the method of transportation employed. It was never the intention of God for Israel to borrow ideas for worship methodology from the pagans around them; this was strictly prohibited in the Law. Yes, there were practices common to the cultures that surrounded believers in both Testaments, things that were part of everyday life, which in no way contradicted the laws of God and were not necessarily identified with evil. But even these were to be continually and critically examined. Borrowing the idea of transporting the ark on a cart from the Philistines was...well...just plain foolish. Creativity is restricted by the Lord's commands. Today we should learn principles and practices that we see as normative in the NT and try to live them out, not follow the latest, greatest marketing survey for what will work. Was putting the ark on a cart a good idea *before* Uzzah grabbed the ark? No, even when it looks like it is "working," worship models should come from the world *above* us, not the world *around* us. Get your good ideas from the Scriptures, not by looking to modern day Philistines.

What about David's dance? God is silent in this narrative about His specific approval or disapproval. If you are looking to defend dance as a practice, go somewhere else, like Psalm 150. There, you will still have to wrestle with whether it is a musical instrument or not. If you are certain it is physical movement accompanying music, the understanding of the word in its original context will only allow you to say it was a spontaneous activity. What we see going on today does not parallel the biblical dance we see in this narrative or the rest of Scripture. This specific event *may* give us some insights into spontaneous physical reactions of joyful believers. Even then, we must remember that dance is nowhere mentioned as a part of any of the corporate worship of the temple, synagogue, or church. For this reason I would suggest we "abstract" the concept of "wholehearted" worship from this narrative instead of making a direct application (transference) of dancing for today. And for clarity, let me say again that this event is wholly distinct from the choreographed, sexually oriented, contemporary understanding of the word as moderns use it today. This event today might parallel how a same-gender athletic team might react after a victory. An observer might say a team member was "beside himself with excitement, jumping and skipping around spontaneously." David's procession was characterized by exuberant celebration as the nation rejoiced in their new found unity (1 Chron 15:27-28; 2 Sam 6:14-16).

You might wonder what "dance" could possibly have to do with "writhing." The connection is not as curious as it might seem on the surface. Both activities are a spontaneous reaction to an event. For example, when David said "Thou hast turned for me my mourning into dancing" (Ps 30:11), he may have been referring to this or another time in his life. David at times "mourned" (מִסְפֵּד) spontaneously under the judgment of God. David now "danced" (לְמָחוֹל) spontaneously under the blessing of God. The two activities, mourning and dancing, are used antithetically in both Testaments (Jer 31:13; Eccl 3:4; Lam 5:15; Mat 11:17; Luke 7:32).

This event happened in the context of a theocracy, so direct applications can be difficult. Although not everyone will agree with my assessment, in my mind this event has all the trappings of being *primarily* a political event. Thirty thousand people were called to attend, the previous administration is debunked, people exuberantly celebrated, a parade was given, and a feast was enjoyed at the end. Yes, God was exalted and it is true that sacrifices were offered by the priests, but I still think this is best understood as *primarily* a national event, for which God was rightly praised, not *primarily* a worship service.

When I think about physical response that may occur in the context of public worship I am reminded of the concepts outlined in

1 Corinthians 11-14 that we will look at later. In summary, let me say here that worship should be wholehearted, mutually edifying, and spirit-controlled, not sensual or self-focused in any way. The other ditch to fall into is to imagine that all physical responses in worship are necessarily sensual and self-focused. Again, we are to show our love for God with heart, soul, mind, and strength. We should not imagine that we are restricted from all physical involvement just because abuses are common. If you have further questions about David's actions or his relationship with Michal, I suggest two sources in the footnotes below that I have found very helpful.[8]

Before we leave this narrative I want to reinforce a recurring theme. The songs of God's people were songs full of the acts and attributes of God, many of which we will see in detail in the next chapter on Psalms. David is a tremendous example that exuberant, spirited worship happens authentically when it is based in truth. Surely Christ's words from John 4:24 are ringing in your ears, "they that worship Him must worship Him in spirit and in truth." Worship must be based in truth, but apathetic worship, uninvolved worship, unengaged worship, emotionless worship, are all oxymoronic. Do what edifies the saints and love God with heart, soul, mind, and strength! God wants it all: spirit and truth, wholehearted and edifying.

1 Chron 6:1-47; 9:33; 16:4-7, 37-42; 23:5-6, 13, 30-31; 25:1-7
Temple Worship Music
Exegetical Considerations

Under David's leadership as king, the ministry of the temple musicians was instituted. These Levitical musicians were "chief(s) of the Levites" (1 Chron 15:16) and were expected to minister in their offices with the same purity and care as any other Levitical priest. Their activity is called "prophecy" (1 Chron 25:1-3). They are considered the "mouthpieces" or "seers" of God (1 Chron 25:5; 29:30; 2 Chron 35:15). The Levites were actively "forthtelling" the truths of God. Thompson offers this further explanation about the use of the term prophesies:

> The nature of their prophesying is not spelled out. But the Levites, or at least their leaders, are referred to with prophetic

terminology such as the verb "prophesy" (vv. 1-3) and the noun "seer" (v.5). At least we are to understand that through the ministry and music of the Levites, God revealed his will to the people, and the people gave thanks and praise to him (v.3; cf. Num 11:25-30).[9]

The New Bible Commentary also refers to the prophecy and music connection stating:

> Heman is called the king's seer here (5), and Asaph and Jeduthun are similarly styled elsewhere (2 Ch. 29:30; 35:15); there is clearly a connection between prophesying and music-making, though the word *supervision*, which like 'prophesying' is mentioned three times in vs. 1–3, shows that in biblical times (cf. 1 Cor. 14:26–33) speech or song could be inspired without being ecstatic or uncontrolled.[10]

The number and selection of the musician priests is also significant. Richard Larry gives the following entry:

> The importance of music in temple worship is illustrated first by the fact that 4,000 of the 38,000 Levites of David's time were assigned to praise God as singers and musicians (cf. 23:3–4). It is also illustrated in the facts that musicians were drawn from each major levitical family, that like the priests they were organized in 24 different shifts (with plenty of time for practice and preparation!), and that the leader of each shift is identified by name.[11]

The significance of these musical Levites and the level of organization and skill are certainly exemplary. It is also significant that some of these Levites were employed in their musical activities fulltime rather than coming only by course which was the practice of most. 1 Chronicles 9:33 says: "And these are the singers, chief of the fathers of the Levites, who remaining in the chambers were free: for they were employed in that work day and night." They were involved in this ministry because of God's direct providential choosing – they were born into the position.

This is not to say that individual abilities had no bearing on specific occupation, it certainly did. Notice how some individuals were singled out for specific jobs "according to the order of the king" (1 Chron 15:2, 6). Some were given specific tasks like those who "instructed in the songs of the Lord, even all that were cunning" (1 Chron 25:7). We are even given the specific leadership duties of Chenaniah. 1 Chron 15:22 says: "And Chenaniah, chief of the Levites, was for song: he instructed about the song, because he was skilful." In this same chapter he is mentioned as "the master of the song with the singers" (1 Chron 15:27). Temple musicians functioned according to family structure but leadership and skill played a role in specific duties.

Three times a year, at the three major feasts, all the Levites would gather in Jerusalem. Other times during the year they came by courses (1 Chron 6:31-33): 24 groups reporting for 2 weeks of special ministry a year, and all of them ministering a full week during the Feast of Passover and the Feast of Booths.[12] When they were not functioning in their roles at the Temple, they were dispersed among the people in their Levitical villages.

It is worth noting that although they had a significant and honored role in the teaching of the people of God, they were partners, you might say junior partners, in the ministry with the priests. They did not specifically offer the sacrifices on the altar and were not among the high priests. Thompson offers this commentary on 1 Chronicles 23:

> The duty of the Levites was to help Aaron's descendants in the service of the temple. The Levites were assigned cultic responsibilities, particularly in the area of providing music for the services.
>
> The Levitical duties listed here were only on the periphery of the temple cult and reflect less responsibility than in 9:28–32. They appear to be subordinate to the priests, for they are to stand beside the sons of Aaron, that is, to assist them morning and evening when offerings were presented in the temple. Part of their duty was to provide thanksgiving and praise in the temple, that is, to carry out musical duties. ...The details of God's relationship with his people are significant in every age.

Organization and planning is not necessarily contrary to sincerity in worship... These chapters also remind us of the many tasks and the many people necessary for proper worship and service (cf. 1 Cor 12:14–31).[13]

Principles to Apply

- Musicians are influential spiritual leaders.
- Those who minister in music act as spokespersons for God.
- Organization and clear delineation of responsibilities are hallmarks of biblical worship ministry.

Applications

Although I do not believe that the worship of the Temple is *the* model for believers today, I believe we *can* see some instructive concepts. Let me begin by drawing upon the fact that although talent seemed to be a factor in choosing which people would function in which leadership roles, raw talent was not the sole criteria. There was no nationwide talent search for the best singers in Israel. If a great Gentile singer decided to attach himself to Israel, he was not catapulted into music ministry just because "he had an awesome voice." The tenor of these passages and even the specific words chosen by the writers in Chronicles and later by Ezra and Nehemiah, point to the importance of these musicians' roles as teachers and prophets not as entertainers. These men were Levites first and foremost, not performers to be idolized. Unfortunately, we live in a world where music is understood as primarily a form of entertainment, hence the titles "Christian Entertainers" or "Christian Artists." Today, even when the most sincere believers come to church, they are often unwittingly conditioned by our culture to critique the music for its aesthetic or entertainment value.

I must restate that music was and is for every believer. Yes, some will instruct, organize, lead, or compose, but their function should not overshadow the greater good–the edifying, teaching, and admonishing of the whole body. The end of effective worship leadership is not celebrity but ministry. A good painting draws attention to the subject, not the artist. The artist gains notoriety precisely because he transports the viewer into the world of his painting and does not draw attention to himself.

Put yourself into the world of the Levite temple musician. When he stood to minister in music, he saw before his very eyes the manifest glory of God blazing above the mercy seat. As he sang and played, he was aware of God's unique presence in the Temple. As he instructed and ministered in music, he did so with people he knew and loved. In my perfect world it is this kind of relationship, this kind of role, this kind of servant's heart that should characterize the "musical prophets" we listen to as well. The aloof "Christian Artist," whom I cannot know, who wants to sell me something, who desires to impress me with his or her persona, is not the biblical model we see in either Testament. Musicians *are* prophets, teachers, workmen, and servants (1 Chron 25:1); we must respect and/or judge them as such.

I know we live in a radically different world. No one in the biblical world had the ability to recreate music on demand, to download the latest song and listen to it, perfectly the same, dozens of times. Because listeners and "performers" looked at each other face-to-face, music was a participatory activity even as a listener. So when believers were called to look discerningly into the lives of their teachers and prophets, the task was easier. You see, the beliefs, agendas, skills, motives, and accountability structures of our teachers really *do* make a difference, or at least they should. So in our fallen world, so radically different from the world of the text, what can we do? I would suggest first of all that we abandon the idea that there is an easy answer to this. If we are really people of the Book, we need to take what the Bible says about prophets and teachers and be as discerning as possible. Find out what you can about what drives this musician. I will wait until we are in the NT to suggest a specific paradigm for our musical teachers, but let me say here that these things *do* matter and that the Bible has something to say about our musical teachers and prophets.

As far as Levitical music providing a model for organization and excellence let me quote McConville in *The Daily Study Bible Series*. I believe he makes some keen observations and natural connections between the OT and the NT when he says:

... it is instructive to observe the fastidious care with which the tasks of the Temple's service are surrounded.

(b) *Order and excellence.* Almost more important than the subject-matter of the Levites' duties is the orderliness which is here associated with them (cf. 1 Chr. 6:32). Everyone played his part, it seems, exactly as it was laid down that he should. From this it emerges that the search for "decency and order" in worship was not the invention of Paul (1 Cor. 14:40), but is something inherent in worship itself. Worship can be sublime and spiritual without becoming disorganized; and the converse is probably not true.

Associated with orderliness is the pursuit of excellence. Notice how many references there are in these chapters to skill and ability (e.g. 25:7; 26:6, 9, 30ff; 27:32). This skill is particularly associated with the musical duties of the Levites, and is therefore easy for us to identify with. ... If we would have music, let us channel all available talent into it, see that the musicians have sufficient resources for their task, and that a proper atmosphere exists for them to make their contribution.[14]

Before I leave this section let me make one final suggestion. Hopefully you are wrestling with building the best biblical model for worship and music you can for your sphere of influence whether it is church, school, or family. Let's build a great one. After all, the model for the moral life of the believer is "a perfect man, unto the measure of the stature of the fullness of Christ" (Eph 4:13). God never compromises on the model. Yet, God in His patient mercy lovingly calls us to "grow up into Him in all things" (Eph 4:15). As you look at the musicians around you, who may very well fall exceeding short of the lofty goals of the servants we see in these Temple passages, commit to showing them the next step by the way *you* live. Help them incrementally grow into the fullness of Christ.

More will be said about David in chapter 7 when we deal with the Psalms. I would invite you to investigate some of the many passages listed above that we will not be able to deal with here. As we transition to the reign of Solomon, I remind you of David's tireless effort to prepare and organize the various ministers in the

Temple and his willingness to amass materials for the building of the Temple structure. When David crowned Solomon as king he reminded him in the following passage of his responsibility to build the Temple. The NKJV translates 1 Chronicles 22:5:

> Now David said, "Solomon my son is young and inexperienced, and the house to be built for the Lord must be exceedingly magnificent, famous and glorious throughout all countries. I will now make preparation for it." So David made abundant preparations before his death.

The reasoning was clear enough; the wealth and beauty was to accurately portray the glory of the God Who had chosen to manifest His unique presence in it. Chapter after chapter describes what could arguably be the greatest gathering of wealth and artistry in history (1 Chon 22, 28, 29; 2 Chron 1-6). "And the house which I build is great: for great is our God above all gods" (2 Chron 2:5). Many have conjectured as to what the actual temple may have cost in terms of 2008 numbers but conservative estimates put the cost at between $100 and $150 billion.[15] That's right, billion! It may have been the largest concentration of wealth in one relatively small area that the world has ever seen. Estimates of the amount of gold at 2008 prices alone would tip the scales at over $60 billion. By comparison, Bill Gates, the richest man in the world in 2007, was only worth a meager $56 billion. Hiring 153,600 skilled laborers (1 Kings 7:13–17; 2 Chron 2:17–18) at 2008 prices and employing them for the seven years to complete the project could have cost over $4.5 billion. Whatever the exact cost of this magnificent building, it was certainly unrivaled in its day.

Let me make it clear that the Temple was *not* a model for church buildings today. The Temple on earth in the OT was not simply a gathering place for worshipers; it was the place God had chosen to put His name and manifest His visible presence on earth. 1 Chronicles 29:1 says: "For the palace *(Temple)* is not for man, but for the Lord God" *(italics mine)*. In Solomon's dedicatory prayer he makes two poignant statements regarding this. First, no building could contain the fullness of God. Second, since God chose to manifest His presence in this earthly Temple and in that sense "dwell" in a unique visible way in the Temple, praying toward the Temple was in reality praying to God. 2 Chronicles 6:18-20 reads:

> But will God in very deed dwell with men on the earth? Behold, heaven and the heaven of heavens cannot contain thee; how much less this house which I have built! Have respect therefore to the prayer of thy servant, and to his supplication, O LORD my God, to hearken unto the cry and the prayer which thy servant prayeth before thee: That thine eyes may be open upon this house day and night, upon the place whereof thou hast said that thou wouldest put thy name there; to hearken unto the prayer which thy servant prayeth toward this place.

Understanding the significance and value of the Temple structure has, I believe, some amazing implications for the Temple on earth today, NT believers. We will explore those later. Before we look at the Temple dedication event, let me also add that the earthly Temple structure is really an antitype of the "real" Temple which is the unique presence of God in heaven. J. A. Thompson said:

> On the one hand, no building, not even the whole earth, could contain God. He dwells in thick darkness, and indeed he fills all. On the other hand, in some special way God would be here, in this temple, more than in any other place. Perhaps this helps us understand the mystery of the incarnation of God in Christ—while God fills the whole universe, he also is specially present in the person of Christ. This is why Jesus referred to his body as a "temple" (John 2:20–21).[16]

Just as God spoke of His unique presence being in the tabernacle by saying: "the tabernacle of the congregation before the LORD: where I will meet you, to speak there unto thee" (Ex 29:42), so now, His unique presence is in every true believer. It is a true mystery of God's grace that today believers are the Temple of the Holy Spirit where His unique presence dwells. But the majesty and glory of any earthly Temple, even Solomon's Temple will fade when we stand in the eternal, heavenly Temple where God sits on His throne. Now, let's examine the dedication of the Temple.

2 Chron 5:1-7:11; 1 Kings 8:1-66 Dedication of the Temple
Exegetical Considerations

Having diligently, sacrificially, carefully, and meticulously completed this magnificent building project, Solomon was ready to assemble the nation for the dedication. The timing of the event corresponds with the Feast of Tabernacles, a weeklong feast where all the Levites would have been present (2 Chron 5:11). Obeying Mosaic Law, the priests (referred to simply as Levites in Chronicles 5) who were able to bear the ark and bring it to its permanent resting place carried out their duties. After delivering the ark, the Levitical musicians, aided by the priests surrounded the altar. The service described in 2 Chronicles 5:12-14 says:

> Also the Levites which were the singers, all of them of Asaph, of Heman, of Jeduthun, with their sons and their brethren, being arrayed in white linen, having cymbals and psalteries and harps, stood at the east end of the altar, and with them an hundred and twenty priests sounding with trumpets:) It came even to pass, as the trumpeters and singers were as one, to make one sound to be heard in praising and thanking the LORD; and when they lifted up their voice with the trumpets and cymbals and instruments of musick, and praised the LORD, saying, For he is good; for his mercy endureth for ever: that then the house was filled with a cloud, even the house of the LORD; So that the priests could not stand to minister by reason of the cloud: for the glory of the LORD had filled the house of God.

Notice the Levitical families involved since David installed them. We know that 120 priests were playing trumpets, an amazing sound to imagine, but they were also joined by the other Levites who numbered 4,000 in David's day (1 Chron 23:3-4). Whatever their exact number, the music was a fitting picture of the transcendent majesty of God. The Chronicler gives special attention to the unified singing. Keil and Delitzsch refer to this when they offer this translation: "V. 13*a* runs thus literally: "And it came to pass, as one, regarding the trumpeters and the singers, that they sang with one voice to praise and thank Jahve." The meaning is: and the trumpeters and singers, together as one man, sang with one voice to praise"[17] As the sounds of praise, "For He is good; for His mercy endureth forever" (2 Chron 6:13b) filled the air; God responded by filling the Temple with His glory. This was worship for which God dramatically, visibly, and powerfully showed His approval. In fact, the presence of His glory temporarily suspended the offering of sacrifices. Although God calls the Temple a place for sacrifice (2 Chron 7:12), it was to be primarily a place where prayers were sung and spoken. God promised to "attend unto the prayer that is made in this place." Christ in Matthew 21:13 quotes Isaiah 56:7 passionately making this point clear.

Notice as well the content of this brief song text points both to God's holiness (goodness) and mercy. Both of these truths are once again emphasized. It is precisely the interrelationship between transcendence and immanence Thompson referenced when he wrote:

> These verses raise the question of the relationship between the transcendence and immanence of God (cf. 2:45). God's transcendence is fully acknowledged, but the temple was the place of prayer where Israel could meet God. It was, in fact, both a place for the offering of sacrifices (2:5) and for the offering of prayer. The prayer asks God to hear from heaven, his dwelling place, and when he hears to forgive both his servant Solomon and his people Israel.[18]

The next event in the chronology of this event is Solomon's prayer and praise from a platform set up in the center of the outer court (2 Chron 6:13). Although Solomon was speaking, the congregation also participated. Notice, they stood with him (2 Chron 6:3), offered offerings (1 Kings 8:62), and feasted for a full 14 days in celebration (2 Chron 7:9). Later, when the people observed the descending fire of God, "they bowed themselves with their faces to the ground upon the pavement and worshiped, and praise the Lord saying, for He is good; for his mercy endureth forever" (2 Chron 7:3). There is every indication that they sang this praise together as they were taught to do by the priests and Levites. This short text may have been part of a larger one, perhaps the entire Psalm of David from 1 Chronicles 16 discussed above. This phrase also appears in Ezra 3:11, Ps 100:5; 106:1; 118:1, 29; 136:1; 145:9; and Jer 33:11. In each of these passages the entire song could be in view.

The content of Solomon's prayer and praise is divided into three sections. The first section is a testimony of praise for God's gracious hand in allowing Solomon to build the temple with the materials from his father David (2 Chron 6:1-11). Standing with hands raised to heaven, demonstrating his guiltlessness, then kneeling in humility on the platform before Israel, Solomon starts the second section which is his prayer (2 Chron 6:13-39). This prayer shows with beautiful balance both God's transcendence, "the heaven of heavens cannot contain Thee" (2 Chron 6:18), and God's immanence, "hear Thou from heaven; and when Thou hearest, forgive" (2 Chron 6:21). This section is set up like the covenant-treaty we studied together earlier (Deut 31-32).

The last section (2 Chron 6:40-42) is a fitting song Solomon sings to the Lord before the congregation (also seen in Psalm 132:1, 8-10). At the singing of this praise God responded by sending fire from heaven to consume the burnt offerings and sacrifices (2 Chron 7:1). Then, the glory of the Lord filled the temple so completely that not only were the priests prevented from sacrificing, but all the people saw it and worshiped the Lord, joining in song:

> And when all the children of Israel saw how the fire came down, and the glory of the LORD upon the house, they bowed themselves with their faces to the ground upon the pavement, and worshipped, and praised the LORD, saying, For he is good; for his mercy endureth for ever (2 Chron 7:3).

When commenting on this passage, McConville writes: "The descent of fire upon the burnt offering puts God's final seal of approval upon the newly-established arrangements for worship (as built, 1 Chr. 21:26; cf. also Lev. 9:23f.)."[19] When the cloud had diminished, the priests resumed their duties, the Levites continued in their music ministry (2 Chron 7:6) and Solomon offered a staggering number of sacrifices, "twenty and two thousand oxen, and an hundred and twenty thousand sheep" (1 Kings 8:63). These "peace offerings," would have been eaten by the people (cf. on 1 Chron 29:21), supplying the meat for fourteen days of feasting (2 Chron 7:9, 10).

Principles to Apply

- Although anything earthbound can only be a veiled reflection of God's person, God has chosen to reveal Himself in both Testaments through Temples–buildings, Christ Himself, and now believers.
- Music is used as a tool to reveal God to man and as a tool for man to respond to God.
- God is pleased when His people offer sacrifices, most notably the sacrifices of praise.
- Both the transcendence and the immanence of God need to be evident in how we reveal God, and in how we respond to Him.

Applications

Is our worship really all about making sure our worship choices reveal God accurately to a watching, listening world or do we only need to concern ourselves with making choices that help people respond wholeheartedly? While we are at it, are we revealing and responding in ways that give a balanced view of God and our relationship to Him? It makes your head spin doesn't it? Every worship choice, even our choice of voice inflection as we speak, makes a difference in our understanding of the Lord. Every choice we make either helps or hinders our ability to respond wholeheartedly. Mixed into this important discussion is the need to reveal God as both transcendent and immanent.

In the next chapter we are going to examine a template for our music: the book of Psalms which will show us again the need to preserve this dynamic balance. For now, I want to challenge you in this area of transcendence and immanence. One of the purposes of the Temple was to reveal God accurately. The awesome size and jaw-dropping beauty of the structure would have stopped you in your tracks. Beauty does that. When describing the details of the Tabernacle or Temple, the inspired writer would explain the reason for such a thing; it was simply "for beauty" (Ex 28:2, 40; 2 Chron 3:6). And why? Because beauty stops us from being caught up in the mundane things of life and prompts us to pause and praise the thing or person of beauty. Beautiful things *can* become the object of our admiration, or they can help us praise the Creator of all that is beautiful. Buildings and the "stuff" of worship have the potential of becoming idols in themselves or helping us see God. The large gathering in the ornate building with the wonderful, majestic, intricate music show us a side of God we must see. The small family gathering with simple, transparent, humble voices shows us an equally important side of God.

Leaders, our task is impossible without God's Spirit guiding our every choice. For our task is to know God in all His fullness and know the people we serve so completely that we both reveal God and empower our people to respond to Him with integrity. Please, before you give up all together in light of this lofty model, remember again that "He knoweth our frame; He remembereth that we are dust," (Ps 103:14). He came to us with a way to approach Him. He is good! And His mercy endures forever! Praise the Lord.

I am humbled and challenged by the thought that I, as a believer, and my church, as a group of believers, are called the temple of the Holy Spirit, the unique place where His manifest presence is to dwell; the touch point between God and the world. Let that truth wash over you and consider it again when we study it together in the books of Corinthians, Hebrews and Ephesians.

I only wish Solomon had made the choices necessary to see this pinnacle of worship the norm in Israel for generations. Unfortunately he let other things get in his way. Consider our last narrative in this chapter.

1 Kings 11:1-11 Solomon's End
Exegetical Considerations

For those of us who are familiar with Solomon's writings, it seems almost unfathomable that a man who had experienced two direct revelations from God, the singular blessing of a peaceful and prosperous kingdom, and so many insights into wise living could fall prey to foolishness. What a warning to us all! Chronicles, a book written later than Kings, does not mention the fall of Solomon but the Chronicler's purpose was different and his audience already had the book of the Kings which explained why they were in captivity. Chronicles served to give hope and remind the nation how things should be reorganized in the land once they had returned.

1 Kings 10 explains that Solomon had already begun his decline by multiplying riches and military might. Chapter 11 explains how he violated the law in the matter of his wives. In all three areas Solomon attempted to live above the law and violated Deuteronomy 17:16-17 where we read:

> But he shall not multiply horses to himself, nor cause the people to return to Egypt, to the end that he should multiply horses: forasmuch as the LORD hath said unto you, Ye shall henceforth return no more that way. Neither shall he multiply wives to himself, that his heart turn not away: neither shall he greatly multiply to himself silver and gold.

It is unclear what Solomon's original motivation for compromise may have been. By this time in his life he would have been scarcely 50 years old.[20] Was it the desire for the political protection that these marriages would bring? Was it the prestige that his large harem would bring? Was it the sexual pleasures of such an arrangement? Whatever his reasons it was precisely what Proverbs 5:20–23 and 6:20–24 taught against. Not only was the polygamy ill-advised, but he married the pagan women of the nations that he had conquered–Moabites, Ammonites, Edomites, Zidonians, and Hittites (1 Kings 11:1-2). It is clear that this was more than a political alliance because the text explains "Solomon held fast in love" (דָּבַק שְׁלֹמֹה לְאַהֲבָה) to these wives. The words "cleave in love" or "hold fast in love" (דָּבַק לְאַהֲבָה) appear three other times, each time calling believers to cleave in love to the Lord alone (Deut 11:22, 30:20; Josh 22:5). Solomon's affection for his wives rivaled his love for the Lord, clouded his judgment and weakened his resolve. We must be clear: God held Solomon completely responsible. He was not trapped, but rather made his own choice not only to enter into these unholy alliances, but to empower his wives to practice their false worship openly. Eventually this tolerance led to his wholesale participation in their false worship practices. So what was the cause? "...His heart was not perfect with the Lord..." (1 Kings 11:4). Weirsbe comments: "But Solomon had a divided heart—he loved the world as he tried to serve God. What a tragedy that the man who built the temple to the one true God should begin to worship at heathen altars."[21]

Who were these gods Solomon worshiped? He worshiped the fertility goddess Ashtoreth, a sex goddess. He also worshiped Molech, an astral deity with the body of a man and the head of a calf. Under Molech's arms would be built a fire, and upon his outstretched arms would be laid children to be burned to death in worship (Lev 20:2–5; 2 Kings 23:10; Lev 18:21; Jer 32:35). And there was Chemosh which, like Molech, was probably also an astral god. Besides these deities, Solomon worshiped other gods equally violent and licentious (1 Kings 11:8).[22]

Sexual perversion, violence, and infanticide have frequently accompanied the false worship we see in the Scriptures. These practices flowed out of Solomon's heart, a heart that was not fully yielded to God in true worship. Paul House gives this insightful comment in *The New American Commentary:*

> Of all the sins recorded in Scripture, God takes idolatry the most seriously, for no other sin has the capability of wrecking the entire covenant by itself. When this sin is committed, God acts swiftly, justly, and redemptively, as Israel discovers in Exodus 32–34; Numbers 20; and the entire Book of Judges. It is natural, then, to read that God "became angry with Solomon." The Lord has revealed himself to Solomon, blessed

him, and honored him. In return Solomon has turned his back on the Lord.[23]

Solomon fell progressively. He married ungodly women, he loved them, he loved them above God, he tolerated their false worship, he empowered them to worship their gods, he became accustomed to false worship, and finally he participated in false worship himself. It was not one gigantic step but a series of small ones. As he clave to his wives in love, Solomon, of necessity, had to stop cleaving to God. His moral decline was a reflection of his spiritual decline. The object of his worship had shifted. No other sin is greater than the sin of false worship. It led Solomon to all the others.

Principles to Apply

- All false worship is essentially a heart that cleaves to something other than God.
- Even the very wise can be pulled into false worship if they allow compromise.
- Moral perversions are the natural outcome of a flawed object of worship.
-

Applications

I have been cut to the heart studying this passage. I see too much of Solomon in me. I am approximately the same age as Solomon when he evidenced his destructive slide. Like him, in many ways God has allowed me to prosper materially (at least compared to the majority of the world), physically, and to some degree spiritually. And although I have never experienced Solomon's dramatic revelations, I have something Solomon did not have—I have the completed canon of Scripture. Though I can't boast Solomon's riches I feel relatively secure financially. At times I have the liberty to spend money purely for the pleasure a purchase may bring. I am tempted to look to myself for direction, for satisfaction, and to indulge my passions. I often find to my shame that my heart, like Solomon's, is not perfect toward God. I turn my gaze away from the worship of God alone and allow the lesser god of self to ascend the throne of my affections.

Many start out with a red-hot passion to worship God with heart, soul, mind, and strength. They seek the Lord wholeheartedly in worship, but as the years of sameness press on, they become disillusioned. Keeping our hearts with all diligence is not easy at any age. Have you too begun to look to human resources, to personal wealth, or to allegiances with those who are not friends of pure worship? So many believers my age have fallen to the same allures that Solomon fell to. Sadly, few believers finish strong.

Consider too how Solomon responded to the false worship around him. God called his people down through the ages to be separate from all that defile. Ephesians 5:11 implores us to "Have no fellowship with the unfruitful works of darkness but rather reprove them." Instead of separating himself from the false worship around him, Solomon thought he must get along and overlook to be successful; after all, he lived in a changing world. As the years march on there is a certain resignation that sweeps over us like a thickening cloud. If we refuse to aggressively thrust the light into our lives, especially as we grow older, darkness will undo us. It is, in reality just the fear of man that slowly replaces a godly fear of the Lord. I am also deeply convicted that, like Solomon, I can write and talk about pure worship and about using the tool of music in a biblical way in my life without really living it. It is not in talking but in running that victory is achieved. Build the biblical model for worship and music well—be radically biblical. Then, you and I must take steps to grow into that model. It is not enough to lead by preaching precept alone; we must be the "lead doers" of the Word. Others will follow where you are *going*, not where you are telling them they need to go. Paul reminded the Corinthians that although knowledge is good, it can also just puff us up (1 Cor 8:1). Sometimes in my life, knowing can masquerade for doing.

The next chapter will be a look at Psalms and then the wisdom literature. Chapter 10 will be a continuation of the history of Israel that Solomon is responsible for veering off course. Remember that the worship choices we make have a great deal to do with how the next generation worships. Choose wisely, be uncompromising, live real.

Chapter Seven
The Psalms

Selecting the passages to include in this concordance section has prompted me to remind you of my rationale for including these in the first place. God's Word is the final word on worship and music. What men may have to say is important only to the degree it helps us understand God's revelation. It is ironic that one of the most thorough treatments of the importance and supremacy of the Word, Psalm 119, is set to music, an area where opinion and personal preference, and not the Word, often rule supreme. Stay in the Word!

Before looking at the verses I have listed below I confess again my own uncertainty about what verses to include. Worship should begin with revealing God and seeing Him clearly for who He is, but in the verse list below I have not included all the verses that encourage us to "declare" or "make known" our God, to "exalt" Him. If worship involves seeing God clearly then our services should be based on and driven by the need to show Him clearly in the worship choices we make.

Based on a clear observation of who God is, we need to "react" to what we see. This reaction is really what the "fear the Lord" is all about, yet, I have not included all of those verses in the Psalms either. You will notice that I have made the decision to include them in future references. My rationale behind this is to that you, the reader, would allow this concept to grow on you a little. This realization came to me over time, so I introduce it here to you with the prayer that the timing is right for this idea in your thinking. Pray with the Psalmist, "Make me to understand the way of Thy precepts: so shall I talk of Thy wondrous works" (Ps 199:27).

You may be reading all the passages I have identified in the previous chapters, but if you haven't (which I know is highly likely), this might be a good time to dive into the texts themselves and do some study on your own. Remember, I am not the final word on worship and music, God's Word is. If you read Psalms with a heart to know God's mind and purposes for our worship and

The Psalms

music you will have a wonderful foundation for your worship and music model.

1. Ps 2:11 Serving God with both fear and joy
2. Ps 4:5 Offer the sacrifices of righteousness
3. Ps 5:7 "...in thy fear will I worship"
4. Ps 5:11 Shouting because of God's power in defeating the enemy
5. Ps 6:5 The grave cannot praise
6. Ps 7:17 Commitment to sing praise
7. Ps 9:1-2,11,14 Wholehearted worship among the people, showing God's praise
8. Ps 13:6 Reason for singing His praise
9. Ps 15:1 Those who can abide in God's tabernacle
10. Ps 16:4 The blood offering of the idolater
11. Ps 16:7 The psalmist blessed the Lord
12. Ps 18:3, 6, 49, 49 God is worthy of praise among the heathen
13. Ps 19:1 ff The heavens declare the glory of God
14. Ps 20:2-3 Psalmist called for God to remember and accept his acts of worship
15. Ps 20:5 "Sing for joy" or shout to God
16. Ps 21:13 Exalting the Lord, singing His praise
17. Ps 22:3 God inhabits praise, He is the theme
18. Ps 22:22-30 Who will praise the Lord? All creation
19. Ps 26:6, 7, 12 Bless the Lord by publishing His works around the altar with pure hands
20. Ps 27:4-6 The beauty of the Lord in His house followed by sacrifices of praise
21. Ps 28:7 Praising with song
22. Ps 29:1, 2, 9 Give to the Lord the glory that is due
23. Ps 30:1, 4, 9, 11-12 Remember and give joyful, wholehearted thanks
24. Ps 31:21 The reason to bless the Lord
25. Ps 32:7 God gives songs in the night
26. Ps 32:11 Be glad in God and show it with shouts of joy
27. Ps 33:1-3, 8 Fear the Lord and offer praise with a new song
28. Ps 34:1-3 Magnify and bless the Lord together continually
29. Ps 35:18, 27-28 Shout and speak of God's righteousness

The Psalms

30. Ps 40:3 God's new song of praise that many will see
31. Ps 40:6 God's desire for more than mere acts of worship
32. Ps 40:16 Magnifying the Lord
33. Ps 41:13 Blessing the Lord
34. Ps 42:4-5, 8, 11 The psalmist's desire to praise and his song the night
35. Ps 43:4-5 Praising God joyfully with the harp
36. Ps 44:8 Boasting of God
37. Ps 44:20-21 Calling for God's judgment upon himself if he seeks other gods
38. Ps 45:11, 17 Praising and worshiping God for His beauty
39. Ps 46:10 God's promise to exalt Himself over the whole earth
40. Ps 47:1, 5-7 Commands to praise to God for His power over Israel's enemies
41. Ps 48:1, 9-10 Praising God in His temple because of His greatness
42. Ps 49:4 Opening up dark sayings with music
43. Ps 50:5 Sacrifices given as a covenant
44. Ps 50:8-15, 23 God shows the place of sacrifices in worship under the law
45. Ps 51:14-19 Forgiveness followed by singing, praise, and sacrifices
46. Ps 52:9 Praise because of God's work
47. Ps 54:6 Freely sacrificing (acts of worship) is good in the context of obedience (lifestyle of worship)
48. Ps 56:4,10-12 Commitment to praise
49. Ps 57:7-11 Commitment to praise through music
50. Ps 59:16-17 Reasons to sing God's praise
51. Ps 61:8 Commitment to praise.
52. Ps 63:3-5 How and why the psalmist will praise and bless the Lord
53. Ps 65:1 Praise waits for God
54. Ps 65:13 Even nature "sings" in praise of the Creator
55. Ps 66:1-4, 8, 13-15 Command and commitments to praise with music
56. Ps 67:3-5 All people should praise; a call to missions
57. Ps 68:3-4, 19, 25-26, 32-34 Commands and commitments to praise with music

58. Ps 69:12, 30-34 Lament portion of the Psalm mentions the "song of the drunkard," command and commitments to praise with music contained in the ending
59. Ps 70:4 Those who are blessed should magnify God.
60. Ps 71:6-8, 14-15, 22-23 Commands and commitments to praise with music
61. Ps 72:9, 11, 15, 18-19 All should praise and bless the Lord
62. Ps 74:18, 21 Foolish blaspheme, poor and needy should praise
63. Ps 75:1,9 Command and commitments to praise with music
64. Ps 77:6 Songs in the night
65. Ps 78:4, 58-60 God establishes His testimony to be praised by every generation. His judgment upon false worship is sure
66. Ps 79:13 God's people need to show forth His praises to all generations
67. Ps 81:1-3, 9 Commitment to sing aloud and God's command for purity in worship
68. Ps 84:4 A blessing pronounced on those who dwell in God's house and praise Him
69. Ps 86:9-12 All nations will praise and glorify God as does the psalmist
70. Ps 87:7 Singers and instrumentalists
71. Ps 88:10 Shall the dead praise?
72. Ps 89:1, 5, 7, 15 Singing of God's mercy and greatness to all generations
73. Ps 92:1-3 It is proper to praise continually
74. Ps 95:1-7 Singing and worshiping
75. Ps 96:1-9 Singing and worshiping with a new song
76. Ps 97:6-7, 12 Commands and commitments to praise.
77. Ps 98:1, 4-6 Commands and commitments to praise joyfully with a new song to the Lord
78. Ps 99:1-3, 5, 9 Worshiping in fear of a holy God
79. Ps 100:1-2, 4 A joyful noise of singing and a pure heart as worshipers enter God's courts
80. Ps 101:1 Sing of mercy and judgment
81. Ps 102:15-16, 18, 21 The heathen will fear God's name and glory as He is revealed
82. Ps 103:1-2, 20-22 Bless the Lord

The Psalms

83. Ps 104:1, 31, 33, 35 Bless the Lord, Commands and commitments to praise with music
84. Ps 105:1-3, 45 Commands and commitments to praise with music
85. Ps 106:1-2, 12, 19-20, 28-31, 36-40, 47-48 Rehearsal of God's works as the reason to worship. False worship recalled.
86. Ps 107:1-2, 8, 15, 21-22, 31-32 "Oh that men would praise the Lord"
87. Ps 108:1-5 Commands and commitments to praise with music among the nations
88. Ps 109:1, 30 Active praise among the multitude
89. Ps 110:4 The priesthood of Melchizedek is mentioned
90. Ps 111:1-2, 10 Wholehearted praise
91. Ps 112:1 Command to praise
92. Ps 113:1-3, 9 The Lord's name is to be praised
93. Ps 114:7 "Tremble at the presence of the Lord"
94. Ps 115:1, 4-8, 17-18 Contrast of true and false worship
95. Ps 116:17, 19 "The sacrifice of thanksgiving"
96. Ps 117 A call to praise
97. Ps 118:1, 14, 19, 21, 24, 27-29 Commands and commitments to praise with music
98. Ps 119:7, 54, 62, 108, 164, 171, 175 Praise for and with the Word
99. Ps 122:4 Jerusalem, a place of thanksgiving to the Lord
100. Ps 126:2 Singing used as a tool for testimony
101. Ps 132:3-8, 16 David's desire to worship at God's footstool and build the temple
102. Ps 134 Blessing the Lord at night in the temple with hands lifted up in innocence
103. Ps 135:1, 3, 15-21 Commands and commitments to praise with music. False worship contrasted
104. Ps 136:1-3, 26 Call to give thanks
105. Ps 137:2-4 "The Lord's song in a strange land"
106. Ps 138:1-5 Wholehearted, unashamed worship
107. Ps 139:14 Reasons to praise
108. Ps 140:13 The righteous will give thanks
109. Ps 141:2 Lifting innocent hands at the evening sacrifice

110. Ps 142:7 Delivered for the purpose of praise
111. Ps 144:1, 9 Bless the Lord with a new song of praise
112. Ps 145:1-7, 10-12, 21 Commands and commitments to praise with music
113. Ps 146:1-2, 10 Commands and commitments to praise with music
114. Ps 147:1, 7, 12, 20 Praise and thanksgiving are appropriate
115. Ps 148 A psalm of praise for all that God is.
116. Ps 149:1-6, 9 A new song of praise by God's saints
117. Ps 150 Commands and commitments to praise with music

Because of the nature of the Psalms I am going to digress from our usual format. To begin, I am going to discuss some general observations about this beautiful songbook. Next, I will move to what we can learn from the overall content and the recurring ideas in the Psalms. Last, we will look at what the texts teach us specifically about music and worship.

General Observations

Hundreds of volumes have been committed to understanding and appreciating all that is written in this songbook. Let me begin by stating the obvious. Psalms is a collection of inspired songs. I feel compelled to start here because this fact is often lost in the present generation of Bible exegetes. We have some wonderful resources for studying the literary structure and actual content of the Psalms, yet writers, preachers, and professors sometimes minimize the obvious need to sing these wonderful texts. In our present evangelical world we rarely sing the Psalms but rely on reading the text divorced of its intended medium.

Until the 1800's, Psalm singing was an integral part of the worship of almost all Christian groups. Even as late as the Reformation the ability to sing the entire Psalter (poetic versions of the Psalms) was expected of anyone ordained to Christian ministry.[1] Roman churchmen and reformed pastors alike followed their liturgies as they sang, intoned or occasionally recited the whole Psalter weekly. Still, some in our generation believe that since Psalms is an OT book it has little application for NT believers. Even for those who embrace the richness of Psalms for believers, some ignore the fact that the Psalms were intended to be sung and not just studied for content. Don't misunderstand, I am not suggesting that focusing on the meaning of these rich texts is not necessary, but that understanding is the beginning. We should also be singing these truths to ourselves and others, not just analyzing them for their grammar and syntax. Each Psalm was birthed as a song and intended to be sung. They have been sung for millennia. Only with the advent of the gospel song was Psalm-singing eclipsed by other song types.

Allow me to include a practical application to this truth. If you agree that singing the Psalms is a part of obeying the NT (James 5:13), then we need to identify accessible Psalm settings, encourage musicians to give us more, and gradually, lovingly introduce them into our personal, family, and church repertoire. You can start by looking for Psalms in the hymnals you have. A helpful resource for some very singable Psalm settings is *Hymns of Grace and Glory*, (Ambassador Emerald International at www.emeraldhouse.com.) Even with the resources we have at our disposal, I think we need a growing repertoire in this area. At risk of stirring up a whirlwind of controversy I believe we need more understandable Psalm settings in contemporary English, set to singable tunes, tunes that non-choir members can sing by the second or third stanza—a daunting task for any gifted songwriter.

We have seen in each of the historical periods that the writing and singing of Psalms is not limited to book of Psalms. Psalms appear throughout the biblical narrative. Music in the biblical world was a part of life, a normal part of how people communicated to God and others throughout their lives. It was not just something they listened to others "perform," nor was it limited to times of formal worship. Oh, that we would return to that day, a day when the songs of God were a part of the daily ebb and flow of the life of every believer.

The content of our songs should also be informed by this wonderful book. No single book is richer in teachings about the acts and attributes of God. Luther and Watts, for example, used the Psalms as models for their hymns. Generations of believers have sung these songs to remind them of the fullness of who God is and how He acts. I repeat that it is very important to sing simple truths, but our view of God needs to be informed by the depth the book of Psalms provides. Look at your ipod or the last six weeks of your church's music and hold up those songs to the model of the Psalms.

Having said that, I feel compelled to offer two balancing truths. The Psalms were written under the superintending hand of God. The Psalmists were "borne-along" by the Holy Spirit so that what was written in the original language was exactly what God wanted written. Modern songwriters and translators cannot claim such inspiration. Second, and perhaps because of the first truth, our music, as well as our lives will never *fully* measure up to the models we construct. Can you live with that dynamic in your life? Look long at the model of the Psalms, and then commit to growth toward that model. We need to humbly admit that no person and no church has a perfect music philosophy. We all need the continual washing of the Word to challenge us to godly change. Let me challenge you as I was challenged: let's go to the Word and let it take us wherever we need to go. If you, like me, would call yourself a "Biblicist," than we need to continually recommit to that search. Doing what "works" or what will keep you comfortable will not do. Furthermore, being a Biblicist demands that we work out from the Scripture to principle, and then to application. We all want "better worship" I am sure, and that means we must start with the Word and then go to application, not the other way around.

Emotions in the Psalms

Another amazing feature of Psalms is the breadth and depth of emotion that gives a voice to every true believer. We are not just challenged to be rich in content; we are also encouraged to be "real" about our worship of the Lord, to be engaged emotionally. Emotions can be communicated through written text, to a greater extent through speech, but most powerfully through text set to music. Some of the emotions expressed in Psalms include:

- A godly fear of the Lord: "Ye that fear the LORD, praise him." (22:23a) See also Psalm 2:11; 5:7; 33:8, 18; 76:7; 85:9; 86:11; 89:7; 96:4, 9; 112:1; 114:7.
- Joy and gladness: "I will be glad and rejoice in thee." (9:2) See also Psalm 9:2; 20:5; 35:7; 47:1; 66:1-2; 70:4; 95:1-2; 100:1, 4; 104:34.
- Despair: "O my God, I cry in the daytime, but thou hearest not; and in the night season, and am not silent." (22:2) See also Psalm 13:1-2; 42:5; 69:1-3; 73:1-15.
- Gratitude or thankfulness: "O give thanks unto the LORD; for he is good: for his mercy endureth for ever." (118:29) See also Psalm 13:6; 26:7; 68:3, 19; 147:7; 149:2,5.
- Relief: "And now shall mine head be lifted up above mine enemies round about me: therefore will I offer in his tabernacle sacrifices of joy; I will sing, yea, I will sing praises unto the LORD." (27:6) See also Psalm 28:7; 32:7.
- Resoluteness: "He shall not be afraid of evil tidings: his heart is fixed, trusting in the LORD." (112:7) See also Psalm 29:2; 34:1; 35:28; 50:14; 56:10-12; 57:7; 65:1; 71:22-23; 108:1-3; 149:2,5.
- Awe: "Who can utter the mighty acts of the LORD? who can shew forth all his praise?" (106:2) See also Psalm 33:8; 66:3; 68:35; 72:18-19: 99:1-5; 148:7-13.
- Confidence: "My soul shall make her boast in the LORD: the humble shall hear thereof, and be glad." (34:2b) See also Psalm 44:8; 52:9; 59:16-17; 140:12-14.

This list is only representative. You can find virtually every human emotion expressed or confessed in this glorious book. I have broached this subject before, but be warned, you will hear about it again! Our music should not only accurately portray the Person of God, but our music should also be an accurate reflection of the Christian experience. We need to make this truth a plank in our worship and music model.

May I lovingly tell on us as Bible believers? Hanging around the next generation I hear a recurrent theme. Some of the music that has been the mainstay of evangelicals for the last generation comes across as trite (I hope I am not being unfair or that my brush is not too broad). Allow me to repeat a quote I gave in chapter one. Sally Morganthaler, author of *Worship Evangelism, Inviting Unbelievers into the Presence of God*, wrote a forward in *Emerging Worship* by Dan Kimball. In it she states that she wants to "move preaching from the centerpiece to one among many pieces."[2] The emergent worship movement is largely a reaction away from what Morganthaler calls "predictable and monotone nonspecificity via hundreds of subcultural praise choruses."[3] Although I strongly disagree with much of post-modern worship and music, I feel we must address this accusation and strive to avoid triteness in our musical choices. I think it can be seen in both text and music.

First, think text. Although there *are* times when "I am happy in service of the King, I am happy, oh so happy," this text and others like it are just not a realistic reflection of the whole of Christian service. If this text is used, it must be balanced with the reality of the *rest* of our service for the King. Paul pictured his service, though always joyous, as still very much a sacrifice. Some of our texts are just not an accurate reflection of the biblical warfare we are called to fight.

Perhaps it is a matter of the subtle changes words go through in time. Service for our King *is* joyful, but this text comes across as trite to many. Remember, language goes through changes over time. When I was a child, Fred Flintstone had "a gay old time" (and if you remember that jingle, you are old!) but today this phrase means something very different. Seriously, we must continually evaluate the contemporary meaning of our worship texts. Ask yourself, "do these texts give us an accurate and balanced view of the Christian experience?" Again, look at the bigger picture of a month's worth of music, not a single text, and strive for progress in your life and ministry.

Second, think not just about text but also about "musical vocabulary." We will discuss this in more detail when we look at 1 Corinthians 14, but understand this maxim: the music we marry to text also communicates, sometimes more powerfully than the text itself. This truth cuts many ways. First we must wisely deal with issues surrounding music's ability to communicate trans-culturally and trans-generationally as it stimulates and modifies behavior nearly universally (though the incessant conditioning of a depraved society may mitigate music's universality). Next we must also wrestle with issues of communication through association—the identification of non-musical ideas communicated through musical referent. Whether talking about innate effects or associational issues, music *is* saying something, and it needs to complement and communicate the message of the text clearly. Sometimes, in an effort to be "relevant" we become insensitive to the music's associations in the world around us or blinded to its innate properties. Sometimes the musical vocabulary we choose becomes associated with things that trivialize, even contradict the message. I see this happening when we make worship choices that reflect pop elements, which quickly become dated (is God groovy?), instead of striving for clear communication in an indigenous musical language that maintains commonality of expression. This is the truest understanding of folk music in the classic definition of the term; it is not pop music.

The Psalms on Worship and Music

Not only can we learn much by the model Psalms provide for us, but Psalms also has some profound things to say about music and worship specifically. I admit again that this list is not exhaustive, but I hope thought-provoking.

- Singing in the Psalms is often presented as first and foremost directed to the Lord. I am not saying that Psalm singing was not or should not be a public declaration. I affirm that singing has very strong horizontal implications, but singing in worship should predominantly be an intensely vertical experience. When we sing, and especially when the text is a prayer, we need to remember that God is listening to our songs. He is our primary audience. Others will hear the believers' praise and prayer and will benefit from it, but if it is not first for the ears of the Lord, we lose our worship center. One of the classic verses that shows this vertical direction in singing with its horizontal implications is Psalm 40:3. "And he hath put a new song in my mouth, even praise unto our God: many shall see it, and fear, and shall trust in the LORD." See this relationship also in 7:17; 9:1-2, 11; 18:49; 30:12 57:7-11; 68:32. Again, this relationship is repeated in Paul's admonitions to NT believers (Col 3:16 and Eph 5:19).

- First and foremost music is directed to God, but certainly it is also a tool for making God and God's ways known to others. "Therefore will I give thanks unto thee, O LORD, among the heathen, and sing praises unto thy name" (18:49). "I will declare thy name unto my brethren: in the midst of the congregation will I praise thee" (22:22). See also 9:1-2,11; 18:49; 22:22-29; 59:16; 78:4-6; 79:13; 89:1; 105:1-5; 107:22,32; 108:3; 40:3; 57:5-11; 111:1-22.

- Praise and worship are based on a cognitive realization of the specific act or attribute of God; it is based on God's worthiness. The sheer number of references to this is convincing. "I will praise the LORD according to his righteousness" (7:17). "And now shall mine head be lifted up above mine enemies round about me: therefore will I offer in his tabernacle sacrifices of joy; I will sing, yea, I will sing praises unto the LORD" (27:6). "The LORD is my strength and my shield; my heart trusted in him, and I am helped: therefore my heart greatly rejoiceth; and with my song will I praise him" (28:7) (emphasis mine). See also 13:6; 18:3; 21:13; 29:2; 30:4; 33:1; 34:1; 35:27-28; 47:5-7; 50:14; 54:6-7; 56:10-12; 59:16-17; 66:1-4; 81:1-3; 92:1-3; 98:1, 4-6; 99:1-5 101:1.

- Let's NOT "just praise the Lord" but instead praise the Lord for something specific, something we know. In our study we have seen godly people responding to God with great emotion but they did so with understanding. We should feel our worship intensely but first we must know the God we worship. Jesus addressed this with the woman at the well. "Ye worship ye know not what" (John 4:22). The songs of praise we sing need content and emotion. Or better, emotion flowing from content.

- The cry I hear from so many quarters is, "we want worship that people will 'get into.'" Ok, I think I understand, and I hope what is really being said is that worship services need to help people respond wholeheartedly. If we are concerned about the model we see in the Word, the solution must still be based on

The Psalms

substance, on showing people God and not manipulating them emotionally or musically. If we show people God, and they truly know and understand what the Word says, worship will follow.

- Singing and praising are "reactions" to God's good acts. This is very much related to the previous point. How often we see a call to praise followed by the word "for" and then an attribute and action of God. Too often contemporary songs that call us to exalt or praise the Lord leave us hanging with no specifics. Psalms shows us texts that base our praise on specific things God is, or is doing. "...Praise him; all ye the seed of Jacob, glorify him; and fear him, all ye the seed of Israel. For he hath not despised nor abhorred the affliction of the afflicted" (22:23b-24a). "Praise ye the LORD. O give thanks unto the LORD; for he is good: for his mercy endureth for ever" (106:1). The entirety of Psalm 107 is built on the repeating pattern of declaring the actions and attributes of God and then calling the worshiper to react to this truth. "Oh that men would praise the Lord for His goodness, and for His wonderful works to the children of men!" (107:8, 15, 21, 31). See also 27:6; 28:7; 32:11; 48:10; 51: 14-15; 52:9. You might read the Psalms and circle every time "for" or "because" appears in the text.

- The psalmists often committed to continual praise in their lives. "I will bless the LORD at all times: his praise shall continually be in my mouth" (34:1). "Let them shout for joy, and be glad, that favor my righteous cause: yea, let them say continually, Let the LORD be magnified, which hath pleasure in the prosperity of his servant. And my tongue shall speak of thy righteousness and of thy praise all the day long" (35:27-28). "Let all those that seek thee rejoice and be glad in thee: let such as love thy salvation say continually, The LORD be magnified" (40:16). (See also 44:8; 61:8; 71:6, 8, 14; 75:9; 77:6; 104:33-34; 145:1-2; 146:2.)

The Psalmists understood how music aided our ability to pray without ceasing, meditate on the Word, and rejoice evermore. Having a song of praise or prayer "playing" in our heads and hearts

The Psalms

as we go through our day is one of the surest ways of obeying these commands.

Music is a unique gift that has special attributes. The Psalmists, under God's divine direction understood this and made specific mention of many of the unique attributes of the power gift of music.

- Music has the ability to surround the Psalmist with songs (רׇנִּי, exuberant shouts) of deliverance. "Thou shalt compass me about with songs of deliverance" (32:7).
- Music has the power to remind the believer of God's lovingkindness in the middle of the night. "Yet the LORD will command his loving kindness in the daytime, and in the night his song shall be with me, and my prayer unto the God of my life" (42:8). "Let the saints be joyful in glory: let them sing aloud upon their beds" (149:5).
- Music has the ability to shed light, explain, or open up, truths ("dark sayings"). "I will incline mine ear to a parable: I will open my dark saying upon the harp," (49:4).
- Music is a wonderful vehicle for remembering God's Word. "Thy statutes have been my songs in the house of my pilgrimage," (119:54). As we have already seen, various commentators have stated: "in ancient times laws were put in verse, to imprint them the more on the memory of the people."[4] (See again Deut 31:19-21.) For believing "pilgrims," God's laws are to be our songs. I wonder, if we had only our songs how much of God's law we would know.
- Instruments were used to accompany worship and praise. "Praise the LORD with harp: sing unto him with the psaltery and an instrument of ten strings. Sing unto him a new song; play skillfully with a loud noise" (33:2-3). "I will also praise thee with the psaltery even thy truth, O my God: unto thee will I sing with the harp, O thou Holy One of Israel" (71:22). "Make a joyful noise unto the LORD, all the earth: make a loud noise, and rejoice, and sing praise. Sing unto the LORD with the harp; with the harp, and the voice of a psalm. With trumpets and sound of cornet make a joyful noise before the LORD, the King" (98:4-6). See also Psalm 43:4; 108:2; 144:9;

147:7149:3; 150:3-5. I believe the use of instrumental music has the unique ability to intensify emotion. As a practical matter, it is important not to lose the reason for the emotion: the greatness of God.
- I also want to take this opportunity to debunk the silly exegesis that says since there were drums in the Bible that means any style of playing those drums is biblical. Just because an instrument is listed doesn't mean it was played in the same way you heard the latest "Christian artist" play it.
- The phrase "new song" is used in Psalms 33:3, 40:3, 96:1, 98:1, 144:9 and 149:1. Although it can mean new chronologically, it is used most often to describe something that is new in kind or purpose. TWOT offers the following definition:

> חָדָשׁ (hadas). New, new thing, fresh. This adjective, usually attributive, describes, as in English, a variety of physical objects (e.g., house, wife, cords, sword, garment, cruse, meal offering, king, gate, etc.). It is also used for non-material things as name (Isa 62:2), song (Ps 149:1), covenant (Jer 31:31), God's mercies (Lam 3:23), heart and spirit (Ezk 36:26). While suffering, Job longed for the time when his glory was "fresh" in him (Job 29:20).[5]

It is no wonder the Apostle Paul gave specific instructions for the church at Ephesus and the church at Colosse to include singing, specifically singing of psalms, as a part of the teaching and admonishing ministry (Eph 5:19; Col 3:16). Nor is it a mystery why believers through the ages have encouraged churches to continue the practice of singing the songs of this inspired, balanced hymnal.

Physical Responses in Psalms

I want to take some time to deal with some specific questions that I have been asked over the years regarding physical responses in worship. "When we are worshiping, is it okay to raise our hands, clap, shout, or bow down in worship?" Let me start by pulling apart the question a little bit.

The question usually (I believe in my memory, always) comes up in the context of *public* worship. I have never had someone ask me if it was okay to respond physically in demonstrative ways in *private* worship. I see no restrictions in private worship on how you might choose to respond as long as it respects your growing knowledge, respect, and love for the person of God.

The second element of the question that I think needs our consideration is whether it is "okay." Believers are called to live above the juvenile question of "am I allowed?" or "is it okay?" We are to mature into making choices that edify, make for peace ("Let us therefore follow after the things which make for peace, and things wherewith one may edify another." Rom 14:19), contribute to our growth (2 Pet 1:5-8), and generally glorify our God (1 Cor 10:31). A much better question would be "When we are worshiping publicly, will raising our hands, clapping, shouting, or bowing down edify, make for peace, contribute to our growth, or generally glorify our God?" (A little wordy and contrived, I know.) Sometimes our questions reflect a sincere heart to know, other times, they reveal our self-centered or man-centered desires.

I remind you here that public worship choices are not *just* about our response to God, they are also about how these choices "reveal" God to me and to others. We want to respond to God in ways that He will take pleasure in and reflect well on Him, not in ways that are primarily about what *I* can take pleasure in. Beyond that fundamental desire to please God in our responses, we also need to remember that this reinforces *my* understanding of the person of God, *and* the understanding of those who may observe my worship.

I would suggest that there are basically two ways of "doing theology." We can ask a specific contemporary question and then look back at the Bible for answers. When we are building models for life and ministry, we start with the Bible looking for God-approved practices and concepts, state non-time-bound principles, and work forward to how we can best apply those principles. When some people are faced with a worship question, they are satisfied to appeal to "common sense," common practice, or historic precedence without ever reasoning from the Scriptures to the question. Even then, this bottom up theological process is easily flawed. For example, it is easy to assume that the practice of raising hands in church is the same practice we read about in the Bible. So if the contemporary issue is hand raising, we look at the Bible, see hand raising practiced, and make certain assumptions. Let's consider these response questions in the light of a top down theological process.

Lifting Holy Hands

Remember: First, exegete the Scriptures, second, get a hold of the timeless principle, third, make the application. I'll tell you right off that I believe it is important to be a Biblicist no matter what people might call you—legalist or liberal. So if the Bible teaches lifting hands, we need to do it! Several examples of it are found in Scripture (1 Kings 8:22; 2 Chron. 6:13; Ezra 9:5; Ps. 28:2; 63:4; 88:9; 134:2; 141:2; Lam. 2:19 and others). And we have this NT admonition: "I will therefore that men pray every where, lifting up holy hands, without wrath and doubting." (1 Tim 2:8). Since we have the NT command, it is applicable for the church today. We know that the practice was common in ancient times. But what was the practice?

It literally meant "open palmed," "(כף *kap*) **the palm of the hand, hand** (opened or turned upward so as to expose the hand, in contrast with *yad* "hand" in general, whether open or closed in a grasp or fist); flat of the hand."[6] Raising open palms to the Lord was done to signify "I am innocent, I have nothing to hide, I am clean" similar to what you might do spontaneously if an officer drew his weapon. Or what you might have done as a child when your Mother asked you if your hands were clean. We would spontaneously open our hands in a gesture that showed our innocence, that we have nothing to hide. The practice in prayer is explained in the rest of the verse, showing that there is no human ("without wrath") or divine (without "doubting") problem to deal with as we pray. Walwoord says:

> Moreover, these prayers were to be offered with lifted **hands.** This was a common OT practice (cf., e.g., 1 Kings 8:22; 2 Chron. 6:13; Ezra 9:5; Pss. 28:2; 141:2; Lam. 2:19). It

was also common in the pagan mystery religions of the first century and in the early church. Paintings on the walls of the catacombs in Rome portray this posture. The hands were to be **holy** (*hosious*, "devout, undefiled"), signifying an internal cleanness on the part of these spiritual leaders. Further, such leaders must be men of sound relationships, not characterized by **anger** (*orgēs*, "outbursts of temper") **or disputing** (*dialogismou*).[7]

Keener adds:

> Hands were normally lifted or outstretched for both praise and supplication in the OT, Judaism, the ancient Near East and the Greco-Roman world. Diaspora Jews usually washed their hands before prayer, so "pure [or holy] hands" became a natural image for genuine worship (cf. also Ps 24:4).[8]

So, I would suggest that what Paul is going after is the heart condition of holiness expressed in a physical posture that showed innocence. With a guiltless heart, we should pray to God. This common physical posture in prayer of holding your palms out to God and face toward heaven expresses that there is nothing between you and God.

Praying with your face toward heaven and your palms open before God was to be done "everywhere" (in every place - ἐν παντὶ τόπῳ). Always make sure in *public* worship that you are not drawing attention to yourself and that this activity is truly edifying. What others are doing when they wave their hands during worship outside of praying is something different than what the Bible (Paul) commands in this passage.

When considering OT references to hand raising (63:4; 68:31; 134:2; 141:2; as well as Lev 9:22; Isa 1:15; Lam 3:41 and others) commentators are divided on what, in addition to holy prayer, might be in view. For example the two entries below give contrasting opinions of what the Psalmist might be referring to in Psalm 63:4. In the quote below, Knight suggests that the Psalmist is lifting hands to lay them on God:

Then again, when one person *blessed* another, he used not only his lips to speak, but his hands, which he placed on the head of the other. Here then is the daring picture of a man actually laying his hands on the head of God![9]

Mathew Henry suggests:

> This we must have an eye to in our work and warfare; we must lift up our hands to our duty and against our special enemies in God's name, that is, in the strength of his Spirit and grace, Ps. 71:16; Zech 10:12.[10]

As a practical matter, when leading public worship, I have chosen to neither legislate ("let's all lift our hands now!") nor restrict ("Hey, you there, put your hands down") but to focus on the general principles behind the practice, encouraging people to approach God with purity.

In secular culture, hand-raising, which differs from the biblical posture of "open palms," is a fairly common spontaneous reaction. It is done during rock concerts, after a goal or basket at an athletic competition, or in a prideful display. What I have normally seen in Christian worship, people raising hands while singing, seems to happen regardless of whether the song is prayer or not. I rarely see people with open palms during spoken prayers. I have to wonder how many people practicing hand-raising today are doing so in an effort to obey God's Word.

Charismatics have practiced hand-raising for their own theological reasons. Many believe that God's power (kingdom authority) flows into the worshiper's hands empowering them for divine service or healing. Some people explain that raising their hands toward God is like a child raising his hands to an earthly parent in surrender or an expression of need. This seems like nice sentiment but without any scriptural basis. You might promote it for your own reasons, or you might disallow it because of pagan or religious associations and practices, but understand this is not the *biblical* meaning or practice of lifting your hands to the Lord.

Below are some interesting blog comments in defense of modern hand-raising that seem representative in contemporary

The Psalms

worship. Notice the reliance on personal opinions and feelings not on the Bible or scriptural principles when they comment:

> It just feels natural to me. It is my physical acknowledgement of his presence. I really don't care what anyone has to say, I know that most times when I have lifted my hand that my focus was always on God and his attributes of mercy, kindness, love and goodness. For me reflecting on his character and his works in my life make me worship-and that is one of the ways I worship, by lifting my hands to God!

> When I raise my hands, it is a physical signal to me to tune in.

> I have read in *Charisma* magazine that hand raising was the sign of the Pentecostal Spirit's presence, but I have also seen pagans raise their hands in the same way. I have seen cults doing the same.

> A Baptist friend says that when he attends a CCM concert, and the audience begins to raise their hands, he can sense a mighty rush of the Spirit's presence.[11]

Clapping

Clapping is also an interesting study, mainly because of the dramatic difference between current cultural practices and biblical practices. I divide current practices into two distinct categories: clapping as applause and using the hands as percussive musical instruments—a rhythmic accompaniment. The AV translates the following words as "clap."

Strong's number H4222, מָחָא *maha: clap*

> "Let the floods **clap** their hands: let the hills be joyful together" Ps 98:8
> "For ye shall go out with joy, and be led forth with peace: the mountains and the hills shall break forth before you into

The Psalms

singing, and all the trees of the field shall **clap** their hands." Isa 55:12

"For thus saith the Lord GOD; Because thou hast **clapped** thine hands, and stamped with the feet, and rejoiced in heart with all thy despite against the land of Israel" Ezek 25:6

Strong's number H5221, נָכָה *nakah: strike be struck be struck destroy destroyed be destroyed kill killed afflict be afflicted defeat vicious blow*

"And he brought forth the king's son, and put the crown upon him, and gave him the testimony; and they made him king, and anointed him; and they **clapped** their hands, and said, God save the king." 2 Kings 11:12

Strong's number H5606, סָפַק *sapaq, sapaq: clap strike punish*

"Men shall **clap** their hands at him, and shall hiss him out of his place." Job 27:23

"All that pass by **clap** their hands at thee; they hiss and wag their head at the daughter of Jerusalem, saying, Is this the city that men call The perfection of beauty, The joy of the whole earth?" Lam 2:15

Strong's number H8628, תָּקַע, תּוֹקְעִים *towqeim, taqa: handshake*

"O **clap** your hands, all ye people; shout unto God with the voice of triumph." Ps 47:1

"There is no healing of thy bruise; thy wound is grievous: all that hear the bruit of thee shall **clap** the hands over thee: for upon whom hath not thy wickedness passed continually?" Nah 3:19

Psalm 47:1 is the single place clapping is given as a command to believers. When considering this verse, take note of these points. First, clapping here is an agreed upon signal between two people. Some suggest that it is "...striking hands with someone else (serving a function similar to our handshake)."[12] A "high five," if you please, *might* be a contemporary, contextualized example. Or, it could be striking your hands together as a final confirming gesture. Second, the thing being agreed upon is that God will surely bring judgment on the heathen through the nation of Israel. The rest of the Psalm continues on with that theme and bears out this understanding. "For the LORD most high is terrible; he is a great King over all the earth. He shall subdue the people under us, and the nations under our feet," (47:2-3). This example, along with most other occurrences, demonstrates dominance and authority.

Notice that *none* of the above occurrences exactly fit our contemporary practices. We do not clap to show dominance or to strike an agreement but to affirm or say "thank you." If you decide to clap in public worship, you should know the Bible gives no such admonition. The Bible does not teach the practice of clapping as we use it in contemporary society. There are no references to it in the NT. We might better define what we do as applause. The English word "applause" literally means to give praise. The real questions are "Since applause is not practiced in the Bible, is it appropriate in Christian worship? If so, for whom, how, or when should believers applaud?"

One of the better discussions I have read on this topic appears in Paul Jones's book *Singing and Making Music*. In chapter 3, "Applause: for Whom Are You Clapping," Jones discusses current socio-cultural meanings and how or when applause might be appropriate. As a means of praise or acknowledgement of people, it might be useful. Consider Paul's admonition to give honor ($\tau\iota\mu\grave{\eta}\nu$) to whom honor is due (Rom 13:7). Interestingly, Paul does not use the word praise ($\check{\epsilon}\pi\alpha\iota\nu o\nu$) (Rom 13:3) which is "an expression of high evaluation"[13] to refer to this activity. Because of the way applause is used in todays culture (the referent meaning), I think applauding God in worship is a distraction away from the greatness of God. It is my observation that people are not so much applauding God in contemporary worship as they are applauding people. I believe it is better to respond by saying "Amen" (1 Cor 14:16) after elements of worship. Applause has the effect of pointing to people in a worship service and not to God. It is odd to take a bow after being applauded for a song in worship (a culturally acceptable response by a performer after applause) that is supposed to draw attention to the Lord.

At times during a church gathering applause could be the right thing to do. We may want to honor someone to whom honor is rightly due (Rom 13:7). But, we need to be careful that we are applauding them and not confuse applause with worship. As a minimum, let's not say that the Bible is calling us to practice it.

I would suggest that clapping, i.e. using hands as "musical" instruments is a slightly different question. I think this accompaniment to singing should be regulated by the same principles that might regulate the use of any musical instrument (an issue we will deal with again in the NT). It must be appropriate, we must discern what it communicates in our culture, and it must be edifying. I repeat again that the contemporary practice of clapping is not what the Bible teaches, so other principles must be applied.

Shouting to the Lord

Shouting to the Lord is also a response mentioned in the Psalms (41:11; 47:1; 60:8; 65:13; 66:1; 81:1; 95:1-2; 98:4, 6; 100:1; 108:9). This verb family appears 42 times in the OT. It is any loud vocal or instrumental sound, so it can have a variety of emotions attached with it. The Greek verb forms are also translated shout or cry out and cover a wide variety of emotions from Christ's agonizing cry on the cross (Mt 27:46) to the call to musical praise around the throne (Rev 5:12-14). As we respond in worship today, it is important to encourage people to express emotions that honor the Lord and are under the "governorship" of a mind fully engaged in truth. A loud, wholehearted response to God in worship can be an appropriate response just as easily as not.

Bowing

We have already discussed bowing in the context of worship and will again as it appears in many texts dealing with worship. It is the posture of humility, a posture of humble response that reveals the Lordship of God. It is the posture of worship most common when the worshiper is overwhelmed with the self-disclosure of our thrice-holy God. It is the response of the saints of the ages when they see the Worthy One on His throne (Rev 4-5). It is a posture we should be quick to assume in private worship, and unafraid to assume in public worship, more than we do. Of all the responses we have discussed, I believe this one is most called for in our culture. I know it is one I need to assume regularly. Humility and submission should be the hallmarks of our lives.

As we leave Psalms, I am humbled by the truth that although the Word is knowable it is also beyond our ability, certainly my ability, to do justice to its truths. I hope my flawed and limited treatment will serve the Lord in a way that will cause your thirst for the Bible's truths to outweigh all others. In the next chapter we will look at the other wisdom literature in an effort to discern what Solomon and others can teach us.

Chapter Eight
Job, Ruth, Esther, Ecclesiastes, Song of Solomon and Proverbs

In this chapter I call on the wisdom of others to show us insights into worship and music. This chapter will be one of the briefest, but a couple of poignant reminders in these books are apparent. I dealt in some detail with Job 38:6-7 in chapter 2 with the implications of the musical nature of moral beings so I will not repeat that treatment. What you will see is the place of music in both the religious and "secular" lives of the nations. Much thinking and open discussion must occur around this volatile subject. Commit yourself to prayerful consideration.

1. Job 1:5-6 Job offered burnt offerings
2. Job 1:20-21 In the midst of trials Job bowed and worshiped
3. Job 21: 11-12 The presence of music seems to show there is no trouble
4. Job 21:15 Serving the Almighty
5. Job 29:13 The widow who is cared for sings for joy
6. Job 30:9 Job in his misery is the song of the fool
7. Job 35:10 God is the one who gives songs in the night
8. Job 38:7 The angels sing and praise at creation
9. Job 42:8 Job offered sacrifices for his friends
10. Ruth 1:15 Ruth is invited to go back to her gods but refused
11. Prov 2:5; 19:23; 22:4 The interrelationship between worship and "the fear of the Lord," Proverbs repeatedly teaches the importance of fearing the Lord.
12. Prov 15:8 Worship from the wicked is an abomination
13. Prov 21:3 Justice and judgment must accompany worship
14. Prov 21:27 Worship from the wicked is an abomination
15. Prov 25:20 Singing songs to a heavy heart
16. Prov 29:6 The righteous are characterized by singing and rejoicing
17. Eccl 2:8 Music without the Lord is an empty idol

18. Eccl 3:4 There is a time for dancing
19. Eccl 3:14 God acts so that men would fear Him
20. Eccl 5:1 Words are referred to as a type of sacrifice
21. Eccl 7:5 Better to hear rebuke than the song of fools
22. Eccl 7:18; 8:12-13 Blessings upon those who fear God
23. Eccl 9:2 Whether one sacrifices or not their end is the same
24. Eccl 12:13 The conclusion of the book is to fear God and keep His commandments
25. S of S 1:1 King Solomon writes a song of human love. God's name is not specifically mentioned

Job 1:5-6, 20-21; 40:8 The Worship of Job
Exegetical Considerations

I have selected three passages in the book of Job that reflect his own worship practices and attitudes. The consensus among Bible scholars is that Job lived either before or during the lives of the early patriarchs. In some ways, this narrative is better understood in the context of those previous studies. Job acted as a mediator and priest for his family in the first chapter (Job 1:5-6), and later for his friends (Job 40:8). No mention of the Law or even of Abraham occurs; yet, as we have seen as early as Genesis 4, sacrifices offered in worship and intercession for others were common concepts in worship. Carson says in summary fashion: "As head of the family, Job acts as priest, offering sacrifices in case his children had accidentally said or done anything irreligious."[1]

The story of Job has been a source of comfort and challenge for all of us who have or are going through trials. One of the startling challenges is that while Job is reeling from the almost inconceivable series of blows in his life, he stops to fall to the ground before the Lord and worship. The word for worship or bow down used in this passage is וַיִּשְׁתָּחוּ. Of this word, Robert Alden in the *New American Commentary* says:

'Worship' is יִשְׁתָּחוּ, a *histaphal* (*IBHS* § 21.2.3d) that expresses repeated, reflexive, or reciprocal action, in this case repeated bowing or falling both prostrate and supine.[2]

Keil and Delitsch add:

He does not, however, act like one in despair, but, humbling himself under the mighty hand of God, falls to the ground and prostrates himself, i.e., worshiping God, so that his face touches the earth. הִשְׁתַּחֲוָה, *se prosternere*, this is the gesture of adoration, προσκήνησις.[3]

Historically, linguists have suggested that הִשְׁתַּחֲוָה is a Hithpael verb form from the root שָׁחָה. Recent scholars have suggested that based on studies in Ugaritic the root is more likely חָוָה. *A Biblical Hebrew Reference Grammar* (1999) takes the position:

> For a very long time הִשְׁתַּחֲוָה was regarded as a Hithpael form of שָׁחָה in which metathesis had occurred. However, research into Ugaritic, a Semitic language closely related to BH, has clearly indicated that it is a relic from an earlier stage of the language... The most common meaning of this verb stem חָוָה is 'to bow'.[4]

For those who might be interested, TWOT also has a very lengthy treatment of this word. In either case the lexical meaning of the two roots is the same. The words should be translated "bow down," "prostrate," or "worship": the action representing the attitude. The activity of putting one's face to the ground is an action that reflects an attitude of humble submission and honor to the one being bowed to. The common usage of our English word "worship" helps us little with what worship should mean, but the Hebrew reader would have understood a great deal about the attitude of worship by the word itself. This word is used to describe one of a series of verbs; Job got up, he tore, he shaved, he fell, he worshiped.

Perhaps the opposite of this worship was Job's wife's suggestion—"Curse God and die" (Job 2:9). Indeed, Job refers back to the declaration of truth he made earlier in Job 1:20-21 in response to this solicitation to sin. God gives and takes and He is worthy of worship in either case. Job worships not because he is happy or excited but because God's character demanded it; God is sovereign and good. Worship for Job was not...well... a great many things moderns have attached to their English word worship.

The fact that Job worshiped in the context of his tragedy is really a further extension of his life practice of worship. Job offered sacrifices, another act of worship that reflected a heart conviction about God's worthiness of costly sacrifice. His sacrifices came after his children's celebration (Job 1:5-6), and later as intercessor for his friends (Job 40:8-9).

Principles to Apply

- Outward acts such as bowing and sacrifice should reflect an inner life of true worship.
- Worship must be an acknowledgement of God's divine character and should occur even in the most desperate of circumstances. Worship cannot be primarily defined as a positive feeling on the part of the worshiper.

Applications

Let me begin by repeating that what we do in worship affects what we believe about God. And what we truly believe about God is revealed in the activity of our worship. Job saw God for who He was and feared. For this reason, he offered the sacrifices of worship and assumed the posture of worship. Knowing reflected upon Job's doing. Our worship acts also serve to reflect to others the truth about God. It is foolish to think that worship should be all about people doing whatever pleases them. Can I worship and be sad? Yes, sometimes our greatest worship happens when, with our face to the ground, we submit to God and acknowledge His sovereignty and goodness in spite of the seeming "reality" we see in our limited humanity.

This painful and humanly tragic narrative reminds us that our acts of worship *do indeed* make a difference in the lives of others. This recurring principle is seen in positive ways in Job's life. His family and friends learned about God in the worship choices Job made and so have countless generations since then. I love

Wiersbe's comment: "Anybody can say, 'The Lord gave' or 'The Lord hath taken away;' but it takes real faith to say in the midst of sorrow and suffering, 'Blessed be the name of the Lord.'"[5] When we choose to bless and worship God, our worship choices can also have a profound effect. God allows us to make many worship choices, and each choice impacts us and our sphere of influence. Stay conscious of your leadership influence. Lead by worshiping even in the midst of your own pain.

Prov 1:7; 2:5; 19:23; 22:4 The Fear of the Lord
Exegetical Considerations

As I alluded to in chapter 7, a clear interrelationship between worship and "the fear of the Lord" is in the Word. Mentioned 14 times, fearing the Lord is *the* concept on which the whole of wisdom is built. So I am going to take this opportunity to expand upon your ever increasing definition of worship. I have suggested that worship is seeing God clearly for who He is and responding with heart, soul, mind, and strength in offering up sacrifices of praise and service to Him within the context of an obedient life. If it truly starts with seeing God clearly, as we have seen in numerous passages, then what is presented in worship should stimulate a reverent awe; a fear at standing before a transcendent God. In fact, when God miraculously appeared before people throughout history, they naturally and spontaneously responded by falling on their faces in fear.

Of course there are different kinds of fear, and not all fear is godly. TWOT suggests five different categories when commenting on the Hebrew word:

> ...biblical usages of *yare* are divided into five general categories:1) the emotion of fear, 2) the intellectual anticipation of evil without emphasis upon the emotional reaction, 3) reverence or awe, 4) righteous behaviour or piety, and 5) formal religious worship. Major OT synonyms include *pahad*, *hatat*, and *harad* as well as several words referring to shaking or quaking as a result of fear.... In the Piel, *yare* means "to make to fear" (II Sam 14:15; Neh 6:9, 14, 19; II Chr 32:18). In the Niphal, the meaning is passive, "to be feared" (Ps 130:4). The Niphal

participle is frequently used to describe things as "terrible," "awesome," or "terrifying." This is a good example of the gerundive character of the Niphal participle, "to be feared" (GKC, 116e). It may describe places (Gen 28:17), God (Ex 15:11), God's name (Deut 28:58), God's deeds (Ex 34:10), people (Isa 18:2), and the Day of the Lord (Joel 2:31 [H 3:4]).[6]

God came to the Israelites with a message that should have alleviated some fears (Gen 50:19-20). It is obvious that there are generally two kinds of fear, since fear is both condemned and encouraged. Context determines whether fear is a beneficial or detrimental attitude or emotion. The problem is the inadequacy of our English word. For example, without many qualifiers we would never use the term fear to describe a positive relationship with say, one's father or someone in authority. In fact, our western minds typically view fear as always a negative emotion. I will refrain from dealing with fear in the NT until we arrive there in our study, but again we will see that fear has two distinct connotations.

Fear can be seen in several worship narratives as we have seen (Lev 9; Deut 5; as well as Isa 6 and others). The term is sometimes used as a synonym for right living. Leviticus 25:17 says, "Ye shall not therefore oppress one another; but thou shalt fear thy God." It is precisely this fear that God rewards when in Exodus 1:17 we read, "And it came to pass, because the midwives feared God, that He made them houses." In Joshua 22:25 fear is used to express the totality of the worship ritual centered in Jerusalem. The Eastern tribes worried that their children might "cease from fearing the Lord" (see the greater context). As confusing as it may appear, "fearing the Lord" became so synonymous with worship acts that at times it is used to refer to worship cultus itself (cf. Deut. 6:2; 8:6; 10:12-13; 31:12-13), even when pious living is absent. II Kings 17:33 gives us a rather startling contradiction by saying, "They feared the Lord, and served their own gods." When describing the syncretistic worship of Israel, the Northern kingdom "feared" the Lord in respect to their worship practices, while not "fearing" the Lord in respect to righteous obedience. If one doesn't appreciate this fact the text makes little sense as we read:

So they feared the LORD *(cultus)*, and made unto themselves of the lowest of them priests of the high places *(lifestyle)*, which sacrificed for them in the houses of the high places. They feared the LORD *(cultus)*, and served their own gods (lifestyle*)*, after the manner of the nations whom they carried away from thence. Unto this day they do after the former manners: they fear not the LORD *(lifestyle)*, neither do they after their statutes, or after their ordinances, or after the law and commandment which the LORD commanded the children of Jacob, whom he named Israel; With whom the LORD had made a covenant, and charged them, saying, Ye shall not fear other gods, nor bow yourselves to them, nor serve them, nor sacrifice to them *(cultus and lifestyle)* (II Kings 17:32–35). *(Italics mine)*

This usage notwithstanding, the fear of the Lord was both motivator and the result of living in light of who God was as a person. TWOT summarizes by saying: "Fear of various sorts may be caused by God's great deeds (Ex 14:31; Josh 4:23–24; I Sam 4:7–9), by judgment (Isa 59:18–19), and God's law (Deut 4:10) as well as by various human agencies (I Sam 7:7; 15:24)."[7] Acts of worship should happen in the context of this fuller understanding of a life of worship.

Solomon understood that worshiping God meant that people must first see Him in His fullness and having seen Him must respond with proper reverence, contrition, humility, obedience and service. Living in light of what we see when we look full on the person of the Godhead might be a helpful definition for the totality of worship. I agree with Aitken when he says, "Here in Proverbs, therefore, the expression "the fear of the Lord" touches the pulse of Israel's religious faith and practice in all its vitality, embracing reverence for and devotion to God, and, above all, loyalty and obedience to him."[8] In Isaiah 8:13 we read "The Lord of Hosts, Him you shall regard as holy; let Him be your fear, and let Him be your dread."

Principle to Apply

- The fear of the Lord, along with being the basis upon which all wisdom and knowledge is achieved, interacts with the greater idea of worship.

Applications

We have talked often about the need to see God both as immanent and transcendent. This is where worship must begin. I would suggest that those of us who believe we can know God personally through an intimate relationship with God have lost touch at times with the reality of our need to properly fear God. Some, I am afraid have made the mistake of thinking that our *standing* in Christ, which ought to give us great boldness, eliminates the need for us to appreciate the transcendent greatest of our heavenly Father. Some of the ministries that taught me so much about the joy we have in Jesus have at times forgotten to consistently show me a balanced Trinity. Even in my family I wonder how well I have done in communicating the fullness of the Godhead, especially in instilling a fear of the Lord. I believe my family knows God is approachable, but do they understand His transcendence? Do I?

As I look at the slice of Christianity I am most familiar with, I think we could do a better job teaching the fear for the Lord. How bold, you might say. But tell me, can you list three songs in your hymnal or even your broader Christian listening that refer to the fear of the Lord? I can't. Because we are in Jesus and are the recipients of so many wonderful privileges, it is easy for us to forget that they are indeed privileges. When we boldly enter the throne room of God, we must remember He still sits as King of kings and Lord of lords. I will save some of my "thunder" for our study of the fear of the Lord when we look at what the NT says about this important topic. Let me remind you of Solomon's conclusion in Ecclesiastes. "Let us hear the conclusion of the whole matter: Fear God and keep His commandments: for this is the whole duty of man" (Eccl 12:13).

Song of Solomon 1:1
Exegetical Considerations

I address this book with a great deal of consternation. I feel I must include a short treatment of it to stimulate some further study on the topic and, I confess, to prove to myself and you that we can talk about things we don't have all the answers for yet. It will become obvious in this section why I am so nervous. You might be driven to respond to what I write. Do so charitably and I will applaud you. There are at least three, perhaps as many as seven, ways to interpret this book. I will tell you right up front that I believe we should interpret this literally as a love song between King Solomon and his Shulammite bride. Yes, the church is the bride of Christ and human love can be a wonderful illustration of divine love, but I believe that the Song of Solomon is *primarily* a song of married love.

It never ceases to amaze me how many people are shocked to learn that Song of Solomon is, indeed, a song. This raises a number of questions, some of which I can only leave as questions for now. Was this song ever "performed" publicly? If so, wouldn't it have been "pornographic"? Was it even *intended* to be performed publicly by others or is it merely a template for couples to interact with privately? Why isn't the name of God mentioned specifically in the book? Why is it in the Bible at all? What can we learn from it today?

One question I will interact with here is why it was included in the canon of Scripture in the first place. Many have suggested that it must be interpreted allegorically because surely God would not give us such an explicit book. Sadly, we live in a world where the wonderful gift of sex has been torn from its exalted state in marriage and relegated to the cheap and ugly world of the prince of darkness. God by His inclusion of this song reminds the world that inside of the bounds of marriage sex is more than permitted, it is celebrated. God intended for it to be a glue that would bind a man and a women in an enrapturing experience that confirms the joys of commitment and the "good gift" that each partner becomes to the other in marriage (Prov 19:14; cf. Prov 31:10–31; Eccl 7:26). Willmington says, "In explicit but tasteful and beautiful imagery, Song of Songs celebrates both the emotional and physical aspects of marriage."[9]

What better genre to express this good gift than through music, the language of emotion.

Solomon composed over 1,000 songs (1 Kings 4:32). This song merits the exalted status of being the "Song of Songs:" the best song of all. Whether it is the best because of its subject matter or because of its masterful composition is up to us to contemplate. The pattern of the song has been compared with other love songs in the Ancient Near East. Duane Garrett says "Song of Songs has a number of parallels in the Egyptian love poetry of the Chester Beatty collection."[10] Later he points out:

> A neglected point in the study of Song of Songs is that it is not only the similarities but also the *differences* between the Song and ancient Egyptian, Canaanite, and Mesopotamian texts that bring out its meaning. It has already been noted that
>
> Song of Songs contains no aphrodisiac prayers for success in love. Also, contrary to the cultic and funerary interpretations, it has no allusions to love play among the gods. It never implies that the sexuality of the couple has any cultic or ritual significance or that their joining promotes the mythical powers of fertility in the renewal of nature.[11]

Herein lies the reason I believe God's name is *not* mentioned. The false worship of the ancient world tied sex to worship. Sex was thought to have brought the pleasure of the gods, bringing favor upon the worshiper. None of this is even faintly implied in this song. Garrett says again, "There the joy of love between man and woman is a wonderful but fleeting pleasure. It has no ritual powers. The effect of this is to make sexual love natural and in fact restrained because it is in its proper sphere."[12]

This does not mean that God is unconcerned with sex within the confines of marriage. On the contrary, as I have already said, God is here giving human love a place right among, though separate from, other songs in the Word. The principle purpose of wisdom literature is skillful living. In our working definition of worship then, human love would be a part of the obedience that must characterize every true worshiper. A couple's sexuality is a part of humanness; both Testaments acknowledge this. Proverbs teaches that it is the Lord who provides a wife and calls a husband to be ravished by her love and satisfied with her sexually (Prov 5:19; 18:22; 19:14). But we should not imagine that sex can have any part in the worship of Jehovah. God is to be feared and worshiped with great purity. Psalm 86:8-11 reminds us:

> Among the gods there is none like unto thee, O Lord; neither are there any works like unto thy works. All nations whom thou hast made shall come and worship before thee, O Lord; and shall glorify thy name. For thou art great, and doest wondrous things: thou art God alone. Teach me thy way, O LORD; I will walk in thy truth: unite my heart to fear thy name.

Now to the matter of the song's public performance. We have already discussed the singing of poetry in venues we moderns think unusual, such as the establishment of treaties (Deut 31-32), or a graphic war song (Jud 5), or an imprecatory song (Ps 109, 143, 69). I expect all these were sung, but they may not have all been sung *publicly*. Music as entertainment is very common today, music performed by people in their everyday lives is relatively rare, but music performed privately is uncommon indeed. Although it might seem strange for a husband and wife to sing to each other in private today (now, don't laugh) it may have been exactly what the Song of Songs is supposed to inspire wise believers to do today. It is also interesting, as Jamison points out, that the early church fathers, "Origen and Jerome tell us that the Jews forbade it to be read by any until he was thirty years old."[13]

Principles to Apply

- God has given believers an example of an intimate song of married love.
- This song of human love maintains the separation between erotic love and the worship of God.

Applications

As I have already mentioned, I believe human love is something we are "allowed" to celebrate in song. Let me regress by suggesting a couple of working definitions that might help us in our discussion. I would define sacred music as music and text that is directed to or communicates about God or the Christian experience. I believe we might define secular music as music and text that is directed to or communicates about some element of God's creation. With these definitions one could conceivably have sacred music that serves its purpose well (or not) and one could have secular music that communicates appropriately, in a god-honoring way, (or not). In other words you can have "bad" sacred music if it is addressed to or is about God but does a poor job of accurately portraying God. Just because music is about God doesn't make it "good." Man can twist and pervert the tool of music even when he is talking about God just as he can use God's name in a vain or blasphemous way. In the same way mankind can communicate in appropriate ways musically, even when the communication is not "sacred" as we have defined it. I understand those who want to reinforce the idea that God must be glorified in all our activities and argue that all of life should then be thought of as "sacred," but I still believe these definitions can help us in our discussion.

With that behind us, I believe there is a place for godly secular music. Song of Solomon is not the only example. In the Bible we see songs about wells and military victories. The questions I wrestle with is how public those songs should it be, in what context they should be sung, and what "details" should be included? I have heard some god-honoring wedding songs that expressed with dignity and modesty the joy of married love. I have also heard songs sung publicly, even in churches, in a style appropriate only for the bedroom. What a married couple does in private, the intimacies they may say or sing to each other, are their business and the Lord's. We do privately with God's blessing what would be pornographic if done publicly. We may sing privately what would be pornographic if sung publicly. Don't let Satan deceive you into thinking that singing sensually is fine as long as it's a secular theme.

Even more, don't let Satan deceive you into believing that mixing a singing or speaking style that would be appropriate in the bedroom of a married couple with sacred text is any different than the temple prostitution of false worshipers. This has been the tool of Satan in false worship since the beginning and we are willfully ignorant if we believe such practices are not a part of false worship today.

Is there a place for explicit singing in the life of the believer? Yes, it is in the bedroom, between a husband and his wife, no place else. I know this would seem strange to most of us, but as I have said regarding the Psalms—we do not often sing intense, substantive songs in private, and we are the poorer for it.

Chapter Nine
The Divided Kingdom and the Disintegration of True Worship

As you consider this slice of Israel's history I believe you will see many parallels to what we are facing in our time. You will see a time when worship was incredibly divergent; you will also see many characteristics of false worship. I believe this study is also important because Jesus Himself often referred to the prophets of this time period. We will look at them in detail later but if you are going to quote the NT about worship you need to be informed about this time period.

As you approach this time period, you will also be reminded that God has never desired outward acts of worship devoid of a life lived in holy obedience. It may surprise you what God declares about godly worship. Let God tell you what He told the nation through His prophets during this time.

1. 1 Kings 12:26-33 False worship of Jeroboam
2. 1 Kings 13:1-5, 33-34; 14:9, 15, 23 The prophet's ministry and Jeroboam's judgment for his false worship, cf. 2 Chron 11:15
3. 1 Kings 15:11-14 Asa takes a stand against idolatry, but not completely Cf. 2 Chron 14:3-5 and 2 Chron 15:8, 11-18
4. 1 Kings 16:19 Zimri judged for his idolatry
5. 1 Kings 16:26 Omri judged for his idolatry
6. 1 Kings 16:31-33 Ahab and Jezebel lead in false worship of Baal
7. 1 Kings 18:18-40 Contrast of the false worship of Baal and the true worship of Elijah.
8. 1 Kings 19:18 Elijah assured that there were many who did not bow to Baal
9. 1 Kings 22:43 Jehoshaphat followed the Lord but does not remove the high places, cf. 2 Chron 17:3, 6; 19:3 and 2 Chron 20:18-22, 28-29, 33
10. 1 Kings 22:53 Ahaziah judged for his false worship

The Divided Kingdom and the Disintegration of True Worship

11. 2 Kings 1:3, 6, 16 Ahaziah rebuked by Elijah for enquiring of Baalzebub
12. 2 Kings 3:2-3 Jehoram put away the image of Baal but did not wholly follow the Lord, cf. 2 Chron 21:11, 13
13. 2 Kings 3:15 The prophet Elijah requested a musician to minister
14. 2 Kings 3:27 The king of Moab sacrificed his son as a burnt offering
15. 2 Kings 5:17-18 Naaman's pledge to worship Jehovah, and his request for leniency regarding bowing in the house of Rimmon
16. 2 Kings 10: 18-31 Jehu destroys Baal worshipers and images but did not fully depart from the sins of Israel in worshiping at Bethel and Dan
17. 2 Kings 11:17-18: 12:3 Worship of Baal removed by Jehoiada under king Johoash, but the groves were not removed
18. 2 Kings 13:6 Jehoahaz partially followed the Lord but allowed the false worship at Bethel and the groves to remain
19. 2 Kings 14:4 Amaziah partially followed the Lord but allowed the false worship at Bethel and the groves to remain
20. 2 Kings 15:4 Azariah partially followed the Lord but allowed false worship at Bethel and the high places to remain
21. 2 Kings 15:35 Jotham partially followed the Lord but allowed false worship at Bethel and the high places to remain
22. 2 Kings 16: 3-4, 10-15 Ahaz maintained false worship and sacrificed his son
23. 2 Kings 17:7-12, 16-18, 29, 32-41 "They feared the Lord (cultic practice), and served their own gods" not fearing the Lord (in obedience)
24. 2 Kings 18:4, 22; 19:18 Hezekiah removed high places, restored true worship, and affirmed the powerlessness of the idols, cf. 2 Chron 29:4-5, 7-8, 11, 14-36; 30:8, 14-22, 27; 31:1-12; 32:12
25. 2 Kings 19:37 Sennacherib is killed while worshiping Nisroch
26. 2 Kings 21:3-7 Manasseh established false worship
27. 2 Kings 21:21 Amon maintained false worship
28. 2 Kings 22:3-6, 17; 23:4-25 Josiah, with Hilkiah, put down some idolatrous practices and partially rebuild the Temple

The Divided Kingdom and the Disintegration of True Worship

29. 2 Chron 11:15 Jeroboam threw out the Levitical priests and instituted false worship
30. 2 Chron 13:8-11 Abijah rebukes Israel's false worship and called for reunification
31. 2 Chron 14:3-5 Asa pulled down idols
32. 2 Chron 15:8, 11-18 Asa and the prophet Oded recommit to worshiping God alone
33. 2 Chron 17:3, 6, 8; 19:3 Jehoshaphat took down the groves and high places, didn't seek after Baalim, and sent a team of Levites including a singer, to teach the people
34. 2 Chron 20:14 Musicians listed among those upon whom the Spirit descended after Jehoshaphat's prayer
35. 2 Chron 20:18-22, 26, 28-29, 33 God worked a mighty victory as the Israelites sang praises under the leadership of Jehoshaphat
36. 2 Chron 21:11, 13 Jehoram encouraged false worship
37. 2 Chron 23:13, 17-18 Singing over the overthrow of wicked Athalia and Baal altars broken down as Joash with Jehoiada sought the Lord in worship
38. 2 Chron 24:7 Testimony of the treachery of Athalia in false worship
39. 2 Chron 24:14, 18 Restoration of worship under Jehoiada and the quick return to false worship after his death
40. 2 Chron 25:14-15, 20 Amaziah worshiped false gods and is judged
41. 2 Chron 26:16-21 Uzziah the king intruded into the priest's office and was judged with leprosy
42. 2 Chron 28:2-4, 23-25 Testimony of Ahaz and his idolatry
43. 2 Chron 29:4-5, 7-8, 11, 14-36; 30:8, 14-22, 27; 31:1-12; 32:12 Hezekiah restored worship and charged the priests to lead worship rightly
44. 2 Chron 33:3-7, 15-17, 19 Manasseh's false worship, repentance and true worship
45. 2 Chon 33:22 Amon's false worship
46. 2 Chron 34:3-7, 12, 25, 33; 35:1-3, 6, 8-16 Josiah's worship revival and restoration of temple worship music
47. 2 Chron 35:25 Jeremiah sang a lamentation for Josiah
48. 2 Chron 36:14 Zedekiah's leadership back into false worship

49. Isa 1:11-15; 2:8-9, 11, 17-18, 20 The false worship of Israel is condemned
50. Isa 5:1 Poetic/musical structure clearly shown here and is used several times throughout the book
51. Isa 5:12 Music is a part of the licentiousness of the people
52. Isa 6:1-8 Isaiah's vision and worship
53. Isa 8:13 Set God apart and fear Him alone
54. Isa 10:10-11 Condemnation of idol worship
55. Isa 12:1-6 A psalm of praise for the future day when God will reign
56. Isa 14:11-14 Lucifer the proud and powerful musician
57. Isa 16:10-11 A time of judgment is a time when music ceases
58. Isa 17:7-8 God will exalt Himself above the idols of Israel
59. Isa 19:1, 3,19, 21 The idols of Egypt and their judgment
60. Isa 21:9 The idols of Babylon and their judgment
61. Isa 23:15-16 "...Tyre sing(s) as a harlot"
62. Isa 24:8-9 A time of judgment is a time when music ceases
63. Isa 24:14-16 Singing will return when righteousness returns "...sing for the majesty of the Lord"
64. Isa 26:1ff A song for the restoration
65. Isa 27:2, 9, 13 A song of judgment when God will purge Israel and restore right worship
66. Isa 28:5 God will be the standard of beauty in that day
67. Isa 29:1, 13, 23 Israel drew near with their mouth only
68. Isa 30:18, 22, 29 God is to be exalted and idols torn down, then a song of joy
69. Isa 31:7, 9 God will purge Israel and restore right worship
70. Isa 35:2, 6, 10 God will restore music after judgment
71. Isa 36:7 Hezekiah's stand against false worship is derided
72. Isa 37:38 False worship of Nisroch by Sennacherib
73. Isa 38:18-20 Commitment to sing to the Lord in the song of Hezekiah
74. Isa 40:18-20, 25; 41:29 The folly of idols and their makers
75. Isa 42:8, 10-12, 17 Call for Israel to worship and sing to the Lord
76. Isa 43:7, 10-11, 21-24 God created man so that he could fellowship through worship

77. Isa 44:9-10,12-19,23 Folly of false worship and a call to true worship with singing
78. Isa 45:16, 20, 23 False worship will be judged
79. Isa 46:1-2, 5-8 The folly of the false worship of Bel and Nebo
80. Isa 47:12-13 Judgment on false worship
81. Isa 48:5, 9-11, 20 God says He will defer His anger and "will not give my glory to another" but will be declared in the earth with song
82. Isa 49:3, 7, 13 God will be worshiped in song
83. Isa 51:3, 11; 52:8-9; 54:1; 55:12 God will purge Israel and restore the song of true worship
84. Isa 56:4,6-7,11 Worship for God and not self
85. Isa 57:5-7 False worship condemned
86. Isa 58:1-14 Worship that is outward and self seeking
87. Isa 60:1, 6-7, 13-14, 18, 21 Worship that is pure and God centered
88. Isa 61:3, 8, 10-11; 62:9 Worship in the kingdom
89. Isa 63:7 Isaiah's commitment to praise
90. Isa 64:11 Lament at the destruction of the place of worship
91. Isa 65:3-5, 7, 11, 14 False worship, the reason for judgment contrasted with joyful singing
92. Isa 66:3, 17, 19-20, 23 Worship that is man centered and the promise of pure worship in the future
93. Jer 1:16 Judgment of false worship
94. Jer 2:19-20, 27-28; 3:2, 6, 9, 21 Folly of false worship
95. Jer 5:19, 22, 24 Israel worshiping and fearing other gods, not the Lord
96. Jer 6:20 God rejects the worship of Israel
97. Jer 7:1-2, 6, 9, 11, 18, 21-22, 31; 8:2, 19 False worship is condemned
98. Jer 10:14 Idols are without life
99. Jer 11:10, 12-13, 17 Judah shamefully serving other gods
100. Jer 13:10-11 As a marred girdle is good for nothing so is a nation that refuses to show forth God in worship
101. Jer 14:12 Obedience must accompany worship sacrifices
102. Jer 16:11, 13 God cast off His people because of their false worship

103. Jer 17:1-2 Intergenerational implications of false worship
104. Jer 17:14, 26 God is the praise of the righteous
105. Jer 19:4-5, 13 False worship exposed
106. Jer 20:13 Jeremiah's psalm of praise and command to sing praise to the Lord
107. Jer 22:9, 28 False worship exposed
108. Jer 25:6 False worship
109. Jer 26:2 Jeremiah commanded to prophesy to those who come to worship
110. Jer 31:4, 7, 12 God will restore singing and worship in the kingdom
111. Jer 32:29-30, 34-35, 38-40; 33:9, 11, 18 False worship the reason for judgment and the future, restoration of fear of the Lord in their hearts
112. Jer 35:15 Call to repentance from false worship
113. Jer 43:13; 44:3-5, 8, 17-19, 25 Judgment pronounced upon false worshipers
114. Jer 48:35-36 God will stop the false worship of Moab
115. Jer 50:2, 17-18; 51:52 God will judge the false worship of Babylon
116. Jer 51:17-18 Vanity of false gods
117. The entire book of Lamentations is a series of funeral dirges or songs
118. Lam 2:6-7 God violently takes away the worship center from Israel
119. Lam 3:63 Jeremiah is the theme of a song of reproach
120. Lam 5:14-15 Singing and dancing cease as judgment ensues
121. Eze 1:24-2:3; 3:12, 23-24 The worship and commissioning of Ezekiel
122. Eze 5:11 False worship is the reason for God's judgment
123. Eze 6:4-6, 9, 13; 7:20 God will judge false worship
124. Eze 8:3-6, 10, 12, 16 God showed Ezekiel false worship, God is a jealous God
125. Eze 11:13 Ezekiel fell down before God
126. Eze 14:3-7 God will judge false worship so that all will know that He alone is God

The Divided Kingdom and the Disintegration of True Worship

127. Eze 16:17, 20-21; 18:6, 11; 20:7-9, 16, 18, 21, 24, 28-29, 31-32, 39-41; 22:3-4, 8 God condemned false worship
128. Eze 21:21 King of Babylon judged for false worship
129. Eze 22:26-28 God condemned impure worship that does not make a difference between the sacred and the profane
130. Eze 23:30, 37-39, 49 God judged His people because of false worship
131. Eze 26:13 God's judgment will cause music to cease
132. Eze 28:2, 13-14, 18 Lucifer the master musician and perverter of worship
133. Eze 30:13; 33:25 God will judge false worship so that all will know "that I am the Lord"
    Eze 33:32 Ezekiel will be like a musician who is loved but who's message is unheeded
134. Eze 36:18, 25; 37:23 God judged His people because of false worship
135. Eze 40:42-44; 43:2-5, 44:4, 10, 12, 15-16, 23-24, 27; 45:4, 17; 46:2-3, 9, 12-13; 48:9-11 Music and worship in the restored millennial Temple
136. Hosea 2:8; 4:6, 13, 14, 16, 19 God judged His people because of false worship
137. Hosea 3:1, 4-5; 9:4 During God's judgment there is no worship
138. Hosea 6:6 Even in the OT God was looking for more than just outward worship
139. Hosea 8:4, 11-14; 9:1, 4; 10:1-8; 11:2; 12:11; 13:1-2, 4 God judged His people because of false worship
140. Hosea 14:2-3, 8 A call to true worship of the heart and life
141. Joel 1:13; 14:14 Mourn because the offering has ceased
142. Joel 2:26 If you have plenty, praise the Lord
143. Amos 2:8 God judged His people because of false worship
144. Amos 4:4-5 A mocking call to bring your defiled offering to God
145. Amos 5:21-26; 6:5-6 God refuses the false worship of His disobedient children
146. Amos 8:3, 10 God will turn the music of worship to bitter judgment
147. Jonah 1:16 Men feared God and offered sacrifices

148. Jonah 2:9 The psalm of Jonah and commitment to offering the "sacrifice of thanksgiving"
149. Micah 1:7 God judged His people because of false worship
150. Micah 5:13-14 God judged His people because of false worship
151. Micah 6:6-8 What God really wants in worship
152. Nahum 1:14 God judged His people because of false worship
153. Habakkuk 1:16; 2:18-19 The vanity of idol worship
154. Habakkuk 3:1, 3, 18-19 The prophet's psalm upon the Shigionoth
155. Zeph 1:5-6, 9 God judged His people because of false worship
156. Zeph 2:11; 3:4, 9 God will judge false worship and restore true worship
157. Zeph 3:17 God will sing with joy over restoration

1 Kings 12:26-33 False Worship of Jeroboam
Exegetical Considerations

When we left the discussion of the United Kingdom under Solomon, the worship landscape of Israel already showed serious signs of decay. Several reasons why Solomon's actions affected his ancestry are apparent: the splintered family structure, Solomon's unavoidable distance from his many children, the divided loyalties caused by different mothers worshiping different gods, even the emotional damage that would have occurred knowing your parents allowed one of your siblings to be sacrificed to Molech, and the list could go on. The fact that Solomon's children did not wholly follow the Lord is no surprise.

Rehoboam's foolish decision to increase an already unbearable tax burden on the nation steeled the will of Jeroboam to secede from the kingdom. Rehoboam was left with two tribes centered in Jerusalem while Jeroboam led the ten remaining tribes to the north. I will assume here that you are familiar with the basic chronology of the divided kingdom and proceed to focus on some selected narratives.

Jeroboam reasoned that he must establish a worship center outside of Jerusalem or the nation would at some point desire to reunify. 1 Kings 12:27 says, "If this people go up to do sacrifice in the house of the Lord at Jerusalem, then shall the heart of this people turn again unto their lord, even unto Rehoboam." Notice in the verse below his motivations and where he went for counsel for these worship decisions.

> Whereupon the king took counsel, and made two calves of gold, and said unto them, it is too much for you to go up to Jerusalem: behold thy gods, O Israel, which brought thee up out of the land of Egypt (1 Kings 12:28).

His next step was to reinstitute a historic Israelite practice: the worship of golden calves. The similarities to the narrative we studied together in Exodus 32 are striking. Aaron listened to the people, received their gold, and "fashioned it with a graving tool, after he had made it a molten calf: and they said, these be thy gods, O Israel, which brought thee up out of the land of Egypt" (Ex 32:4). Jeroboam may have reasoned that false worship was, after all, what the nation had wanted since its inception. Jeroboam simply gave the people what they wanted all along. Many have suggested that the calves were designed not so much as idols themselves but as places where God or gods could "ride:" a virtual seat (perhaps like the mercy seat) upon which deity would dwell.[1] Setting up syncretistic religious practices and making them sound orthodox has often been employed over time. It is easy to reinvent a past false worship practice and claim historic precedent, but more on this later.

The twin calves were set up at Dan and Bethel, both cities that had religious significance for the nation. From Jeroboam's perspective they were suitable Temple substitutes. He could have marshaled several historic and even some "spiritual" arguments for Bethel's adequacy as an alternative worship location. After all, several times Bethel *was* the location for pure worship; Jeroboam had history on his side. Dan on the other hand had pagan heritage. In fact it remained a center for Baal worship throughout Israel's history. Elwell summarizes, "The cultic worship of Baal at Dan survived even Jehu's drastic purge (2 Kgs 10:28–31)."[2] As is often the case, the nation gravitated to the lesser location. 1 Kings 12:30 says, "the people went to worship before the one even unto Dan."

Having settled on a substitute location and substitute temple furniture (i.e. the calves instead of the mercy seat), Jeroboam moved on to the personnel. 1 Kings 12:31 says Jeroboam "made priests of the lowest of the people, which were not of the sons of Levi." Notice the two-fold sin: usurping God's choice in who would serve as priests (the Levites), and among the non-Levites, choosing those who held no other significance. To complete the sacrilege, Jeroboam sets up another substitute: a user-friendly cultus, including offerings, sacrifices in multiple high places, and competing feast days (1 Kings 12:32-33).

Principles to Apply

- Making worship choices centered on the pleasure, convenience, or the political advantage of the worshipers is never right.
- False worship often imitates true worship in many of its elements.

Applications

Motives are slippery things; the text says "Jeroboam said in his heart...." His fellow Israelites of course, could not see his heart. They only knew that Jeroboam said these worship alternatives were for their own good, their collective convenience, and their political survival. He made the worship convenient and attractive. We look back and have the advantage of the Bible's perspective on the event; Jeroboam's contemporaries did not. It all sounded good to them.

Motives are slippery things; we, like the Israelites cannot see men's hearts. We are left to look on outward things. Always be guarded when a worship choice has its genesis in "well, you know people today really want..." or "don't you think we need to accommodate the way our people are?" or "this is really just what we've always done." Any number of variations on these logical "people first" themes exist around us. If we're honest, all of us can confess decisions we have made whose genesis is the same. Yes, people matter to God; but even more profoundly, God should matter to people. We are called to be God's people. Let's never enthrone "the people's god."

How can we tell? We can tell when we start like Jeroboam did: we think in our own hearts and ask for counsel, but not of the Lord. As a start, at least pray and ask God what He wants to hear as you sit down to plan your next service or make your next CD purchase. I am sure you want to grow in your worship or you would not be reading this book. The place to start is in the Word, with a sincere heart to know, and a committed will to obey what God reveals. We must slay convenience and political expediency with the sword of the Word and cast our lot with obedience and God-centered worship.

Consider well the fact that Jeroboam's worship (and Aaron's for that matter) was fashioned to look amazingly similar to obedient worship. After all, weren't calves under the laver in the Temple? What's the difference? Aren't you being a little inconsistent? A preacher once told me that if the desire for consistency *drives* your decisions you will eventually radicalize. It is a good thing to strive for consistency, but I have also seen that argument push people to such extremes that the end result is the same compromise they said they wished to avoid in the first place. Beware of "isn't this just the same as that?" Get into the Word yourself and let His Word be your model builder, it is always superior to man's best "wisdom." Counterfeits will abound; know the real thing.

1 Kings 18:18-40 Contrast of the False Worship of Baal and the True Worship of Elijah
Exegetical Considerations

This passage is an amazing example of the instructive contrasts between the worship of Jehovah and the pagan worship of Baal. Begin first by seeing the accusation Ahab makes. He claims Elijah is a trouble maker. Throughout the Word, especially as we see the ministry of the prophets, truth tellers are often pictured as stirring up division. In reality, as in this specific narrative, it is errant leadership that is to blame. Elijah said, "I have not troubled Israel:

but thou, and thy father's house in that ye have forsaken the commandments of the Lord, and thou hast followed Baalim" (1 Kings 18:18). The conflict on the mountain was ultimately not between Elijah and Ahab or Elijah and the prophets; it was between Jehovah and Baal. In the elaborate test that followed, the prophets represented characteristics of false worship that have evidenced themselves in every age.

False worshipers wanted something from their god, and the way to get it was to pray, prophecy (*naba*, likely corporate singing in this context), dance (accompanied by music), cut themselves, or do other things to convince the deity to reveal himself or herself. Pagan worship in this passage is portrayed as something man must do to get a god(s) to do great things.

By contrast, consider Elijah's worship. His actions actually seem counter-productive, working against the manipulation of God. True, the altar was built according to God's instruction and the timing of the offering was purposeful, but consider the contrasting elements of Elijah's prayer. We read in 1 Kings 18:36-37:

> And it came to pass at the time of the offering of the evening sacrifice, that Elijah the prophet came near and said, Lord God of Abraham, Isaac, and of Israel, let it be known this day that Thou art God in Israel, and that I have done all these things at Thy Word. Hear me, O Lord, hear me, that this people may know that Thou art the Lord God, and that thou hast turned their heart back again.

Elijah's desire was not the manipulation of God; Elijah simply wanted God to be revealed. Specifically, he desired to show the people God's power and that he was being obedient and speaking God's Word. Elijah wanted the people to know God and in knowing Him, respond in obedience and forsake all other gods.

Elijah was not preaching against activity or outward worship, but apathy, infidelity and a lack of commitment to God alone. When God was seen in all His glory, the people did indeed respond. First by an *act* of worship, assuming the posture of worship, humbly falling on their faces, then by an *action* of obedience to His Word in slaying all those who promoted false worship (1 Kings 18:39-40; Deut 13:1–11).

With great regularity, God took exception to anyone offering sacrifices except in

Jerusalem. It remains a mystery to me that even though this sacrifice occurred outside of the Temple, God gave His obvious approval by sending down fire. God, of course, can suspend any regulation; He is the sovereign King. Perhaps the reason is, as Carson points out:

> Circumstances here were not normal, for the very survival of Yahweh's worship in Israel, indeed the survival of Israel itself, was at stake. The issue was no longer where Yahweh might be worshipped, but whether Israel would continue to worship him at all—whether Israel would remain Israel.[3]

I wish Elijah would have left this victory encouraged in all that God could do. We know that many before Elijah and many since, experience discouragement, even depression after powerful spiritual victories.

Principle to Apply

- Obedient worship focuses on revealing God and responding to that revelation, whereas pagan worship focuses on manipulating the deity to do the bidding of the worshiper.

Applications

I don't want a single line in this section to be fueled by proud self-righteousness or in any way to be mean-spirited. I embrace the fact that I, and those I may take exception to on worship issues, are on a journey. God's Word truly is the final Word on worship and music. I do not claim to have the final word myself. When I stand before God's throne, there will, without a doubt, be things I believe that will need to be corrected. Jesus said, "I am the way, the truth, and the life" (John 14:6). All the rest of us need the light of His Word to shine into our lives.

Since the beginning there have been worship wars. They will not end until, once for all, the King of kings throws all false worshipers into the pit of His eternal judgment. I remember going to a conference once where the workshop leader believed he had the way to "end the worship wars." His bottom line solution was simple: refuse to object to anything someone else might choose to do in the name of worship. He was convinced that you express love to your brothers by simply being silent about the worship choices they make. Let me challenge you that until God ends the worship war, we are to "Have no fellowship with the unfruitful works of darkness, but rather reprove them" (Eph 5:11). Stand for truth even when the Ahabs of the day accuse you of being the troublemaker. Too much is at stake to look the other way.

Much of the current writing on worship seems to assume that worship begins when man performs a certain act or enters into a series of actions. Who initiates worship? Many who include themselves in either historic or modern evangelical circles (Charismatics, Pentecostals, Baptists and free churches of many varieties) advocate an approach to worship that relies on adherence to a certain sequence intended to bring the worshiper into "the presence of God." People are drawn into a certain emotional state defined as worship or "worshipful." Music (secondarily text) serves as the mover through the stages of "pre-worship." In fact "praise and worship" (P&W) are often defined as musical styles, not as specific actions[4] and not as responses to God being revealed. In the instructional section of a major evangelical hymnal the author suggests a three stage sequence:

> ...the worship service becomes a journey into His presence. Thanksgiving and praise move us into His presence. Worship occurs when we are before Him....The character of worship is one of quietness, reverence, tenderness and serenity....It is the responsibility of the worship leader to facilitate a sense of flow and continuity toward the goal of being in God's presence.[5]

Barry Liesch in his book *The New Worship* outlines what he calls a "five-phase model."[6] In this model the texts and music are selected to bring the worshiper through 1) invitation, (2) engagement, (3) exaltation, (4) adoration, and (5) intimacy. In describing this model, Liesch includes textual themes, but also gives specific instructions about what musical keys, tempos, emotions, physical postures, and activities will bring about the desired "worship." All of these elements are designed to help the worship leader organize a "worship set"[7] in such a way as to bring the worshiper along in his "journey to the holy of holies."[8] Liesch believes Psalm 95 is not only an example of this worship sequence but the biblical basis for a universal format. After his explanation of the passage Liesch declares, "How psychologically sound!"[9] I believe I understand the rationale for these choices, but I believe it is more biblically normative to emphasize seeing God and responding to Him than identifying a single pattern. For example, in Psalm 99:1 the psalmist begins with "The Lord reigneth; let the people tremble." Other Psalms present a variety of sequences that do not reflect the above mentioned three or five stage progression.

Similarly, Rick Warren advocates a five step service "flow" with the acrostic IMPACT: Inspire Movement, Praise, Adoration, Commitment, and Tie it all together.[10] This sequence is a curious combination of purely musical elements (emotion controllers) and worship elements, all of which are designed to make the service accessible to "seekers."

In my experiences in church music I have likewise heard many simplistic recommendations about worship service planning. People have said: "Pick some fast 'upbeat' numbers at the beginning of a worship service, then move to more 'worshipful' music that will get people in the mood for the preaching (or to enter into God's presence)." Often the "song service" is a loose collection of favorites selected to "prepare the heart for the Word." I am left wondering, where is the Word before the preaching?

The problem is that however "psychologically sound," pragmatically satisfying or good-hearted these approaches may be, they ignore the examples in the Scriptures of worship based on God's self-revelation. It is God who moves toward mankind by revealing Himself to them. It is God who desires to have a relationship with mankind, a relationship characterized by worship.[11] The Biblical examples we have seen demonstrate that worship begins when God reveals Himself (Isa 6:1; Ex 24:1) or is revealed (Neh 8:3; 1 Cor 14:24-25). This revelation may be a vision, a miraculous theophany, the declaration of His written Word, or simply a clear statement of truth. It is certainly not a prescribed journey through various musical styles or a spiritual journey through the various spaces of the tabernacle ending in the Holy of Holies. It is quite simply revealing God to people.

There are also some who may be described as liturgical renewalists. These leaders believe that worship is initiated through the vehicle of the organized church. Catholics, Lutherans, Anglicans, Episcopalians, and other Protestants make much of a formula approach to worship. Robb Redman describes their worship as a "kind of magic-formula approach to worship."[12] Perhaps a bit unkind, but still, there seems to be a feeling that if people perform specific rituals or use certain music styles, worship will inevitably follow. Although guitars and drums are replaced with organs and incense, the rationale of the renewalists is surprisingly similar to the church growth movement. The liturgical renewalists start with the lectionary and end with the Eucharist, believing that worship will happen. What is missing is a reliance on the power of God using His Word to reveal God and call men to a relationship of worship with Him.

To be fair, more writers in recent years have stated that worship is at its core a response to revelation. This concept of revelation-response is seen in the recent writings of Webber,[13] Peterson,[14] Redman,[15] Dawn,[16] and others. I believe we need to build our worship services on the clear presentation of truth. Then we need to make careful choices about what will help believers respond in scripturally informed ways. When trying to improve worship we should ask ourselves if a proposed change will reveal God more fully or help us respond more biblically. I am at a loss to think of any other questions worth our consideration. I reiterate, my purpose in challenging others with this concept is not to hurt but to sharpen. Others will no doubt sharpen and refine my thinking. Let's do so charitably.

Unfortunately, much of what is communicated about what "successful" worship should look like is not modeled in the Word. It is easy to focus on what "works" instead of what grows our people toward the model of the Word. We need to see the principles and practices of worship exampled in the Bible. Center the beginning of worship on revealing God and obeying His word as Elijah did and not on emotional or liturgical manipulation.

Worship is not so much about technique, style, or music genre as it is about trusting God as He is faithfully and clearly revealed to His people because, as Tozer suggests, "to know Him is to love and worship Him."[17] Worship begins when God is clearly revealed. Worship choices must be made, but always remember that our goal is to make God known, not manipulate people into getting into some kind of "worship groove" so they can enter into a new state of being. That is the stuff of Eastern Mysticism and the New Age movement.

2 Chron 20:18-22, 26, 28-29, 33 Jehoshaphat's Music and Worship
Exegetical Considerations

Before we look at the specifics of our passage, I want to remind you of a little history. Asa, Jehoshaphat's father, had to his credit led Judah away from many elements of false worship. Later in his reign, he committed the fatal mistake of making an unholy alliance with Syria. Jehoshaphat, now king, "sought not unto Baalim" (2 Chron 17:3) but "set himself to seek the Lord" (2 Chron 20:3). It is also Jehoshaphat who sends a group of Levitical teachers, including a singer, throughout Judah to teach the law (2 Chron 17:8). Unfortunately, he too made an unwise alliance with Israel later in his reign which brought the judgment of God. It is in this context of this alliance with the king of Israel that we read about Elijah requesting a minstrel, whose playing resulted in the hand of the Lord coming upon him (2 Kings 3:15).

In 2 Chronicles 20, a great host of enemies were marching upon Judah. Jehoshaphat ran to the right place; he sought the Lord and prayed (2 Chron 20:2-12). God responded by sending a messenger, whose extended lineage identifies him as a descendent of the temple musician Asaph (2 Chron 20:14). God assured the people that they would see the power of God displayed through a miraculous victory. Jehoshaphat and the people fell on their faces

The Divided Kingdom and the Disintegration of True Worship

and worshiped. 2 Chronicles 20:18 tell us, "And Jehoshaphat bowed his head with his face to the ground: and all Judah and the inhabitants of Jerusalem fell before the Lord, and worshiped the Lord." In this verse we see three words which emphasize the humble submission of the people. The word קָדַד (*qadad*) (which appears 15 times during various desperate situations), to bow down with your face to the ground, נָפַל (*napal*), used over 300 times to express falling down (or being thrown down) in submission, and the common word we have seen before, שָׁחָה (*saha*), to worship.

Next in the narrative are singers lifting up loud praise to God for his promise. Note that in this passage the sequence goes from worship to praise, not the other way. The King encouraged the people and then specifically instructed the singers to go before the army and praise in the "beauty of holiness" or in their beautiful, holy, priestly garments (2 Chron 20:21). It is not clear whether they sang the short text: "praise the Lord; for His mercy endureth forever" or whether they sang the totality of Psalm 136 or one of the other extended songs that included this phrase (1 Chron 16:34, 41; 2 Chron 5:13). As they sang, God set an ambush for the enemies without Israel fighting at all. After the battle the Israelites gathered the spoil (2 Chron 20:12), and joyfully blessed the Lord in Jerusalem with "psalteries and harps and trumpets into the house of the Lord" (2 Chron 20:26-28).

In 2 Chronicles 20:32-33, the chronicler gives us an interesting commentary on why, despite Jehoshaphat's leadership, his efforts were limited when he writes:

> And he walked in the way of Asa his father, and departed not from it, doing that which was right in the sight of the Lord. Howbeit the high places were not taken away: for as yet the people had not prepared their hearts unto the God of their fathers.

Principles to Apply

- The decisions of spiritual leaders, though not without limits, can significantly alter the course of others.

- A frequent sequence is for humble worship to turn into exuberant praise.
- Praise can be lifted up to God in faith, anticipating His blessing, or in acknowledgment of His blessing.

Applications

I think this narrative affords an opportunity to see the potential and limitations of spiritual leadership. God Himself has given us the inspired commentary on the life of Jehoshaphat: he did "that which was right in the sight of the Lord. Howbeit..." (2 Chron 20:32-33a). Jehoshaphat was blessed to the degree he did that which God revealed to him. He was not perfect, and the people he ruled did not fully follow the Lord. Yet, God blessed him for the right choices he made. If you are building in your head and heart, or perhaps on paper, a biblical model for your worship and music, you probably have times when you feel overwhelmed. I know I do. As we look around at the Christian landscape, we can become pretty discouraged. Is there anyone out there who hasn't bowed the knee to Baal? The answer is a resounding yes! You may not be able to stem the tide of false worship in an entire nation (or you just might), but if you stand for right, God will bless your efforts. In fact, God used a number of Kings in just this limited way, including Hezekiah (Isa 36:7), Jehu (2 Kings 10:19-31), Josiah (2 Kings 23:4-5, 19, 24), and Jehoshaphat's father Asa (1 Chron 14:3, 3; 15:8, 11-17). We all need to take a chance on making a difference. However large your circle of influence, you can seek the Lord and His miraculous power, cry out to Him, praise Him for what He has promised to do, and step aside to see Him win some battles for His glory. Then praise Him again for working through you for His own glory.

We talked rather candidly about the idea of some who believe worship must go rigidly through the sequence of thanksgiving, praise, and then worship. This is yet another example that breaks that mold. In fact, it is my observation that the scriptural norm is the opposite order. It starts with a humble acknowledgment of God's transcendent greatness, moves to praise, and then to a confident and familial thanksgiving. At times celebratory singing and praising more naturally follow a more formal presentation of truth. You might even think about singing more after the message than before. Radical, I know, but think about it: praise can then more naturally be a response to truth. And, the temptation to be man-centered by manipulating or cajoling through music or worship choices is lessened. Let the service order be the servant of delivering the truth about God and helping people respond in worship, praise, and thanksgiving.

On a related matter, I believe singing can be both a statement of faith and a statement of experience. I am not saying that "years I spent in vanity and pride" should be thoughtlessly sung by a choir of five-year-olds, but sometimes singing the testimony of another that is not yet my own is an investment in the future; an anticipation that "when sorrows like sea billows roll" I too can be ready for it as others have been. Jehoshaphat's musicians praised the person of God before the event and the actions of God after the event. Make a place for both kinds of worship in your life.

2 Kings 16: 3-4, 10-15 Cf. 2 Chron 28:2-5, 23-25 Ahaz's False Worship
Exegetical Considerations

The actions of Ahaz are sadly representative of many of the kings during this dark season of Judah's and Israel's histories. His spiritual compromises sent the nation headlong into spiritual adultery as he followed the lead of the northern tribes of Israel. Ahaz went so far as to sacrifice his own son (2 Kings 16:3). When faced with a siege by the king of Syria, Ahaz pillages the Temple to pay for an allegiance with the king of Assyria. While in Damascus brokering the deal, he saw an altar he felt he must have for his own worship in Jerusalem. Just like Jeroboam, Ahaz built an alternative altar, fashioned after the pagan altar in Damascus. Notice his twisted reasoning in 2 Chronicles 28:23:

> For he sacrificed unto the gods of Damascus, which smote him: and he said, because the gods of the kings of Syria help them, therefore will I sacrifice to them, that they may help me. But they were the ruin of him, and all Israel.

Unlike Jeroboam, Ahaz had his altar built by a Levitical priest, who was all too willing to cooperate. He then moved the laver out of its place to make room for his new altar and offered his own sacrifices on it (2 Kings 16:11-16). If that were not enough, he shut the doors of the house of God, peppered the streets of Jerusalem with other gods and set up high places for false worship throughout Judah (2 Chron 28:24-25). Even with this, much of what looked like pure worship continued to be practiced alongside these pagan worship practices.

Principles to Apply

- Out of the fountainhead of false worship flow all kinds of moral debauchery, even human sacrifice.
- Going to pagan worship for "creative" worship ideas is always disastrous.

Applications

Murder of the innocent, adultery, and social irresponsibility all have their genesis in false worship. Even today, the infanticide we call abortion is really a sterilized manifestation of this world's false worship. The unborn are being sacrificed on the altar of the god self; eliminating the inconvenient for the pleasure of the goddess. It differs little from the sacrifice of Ahaz.

Ahaz's fascination with the worship practices of the pagans around him is equally relevant. Sadly, the church is easily fooled into thinking that the place to go for ideas on how to worship is to survey the poor lost souls around us who are looking to believers to tell them the truth and make our worship decisions based on their ideas. How foolish to ask those who know the least about worship how it should be done. We bow before their gods, looking to them for help. Don't repeat history. Go to the Word not to the world!

2 Kings 18:4, 22; 19:18; 2 Chron 29:4-5, 7-8, 11, 14-36; 30:8, 14-22, 27; 31:1-12; 32:12 Hezekiah and Worship
Exegetical Considerations

Praise God that when Ahaz was sacrificing his children on the altars of Molech, He preserved Ahaz's son Hezekiah. The revival under Hezekiah was far reaching. Not only did Hezekiah tear down many of the altars and high places his father had set up, he also took many positive steps in reinstituting both the worship and music of true worship in Judah. 2 Chronicles 29 is an especially succinct recounting of the cleansing and reinstitution of Temple worship. Your heart will be blessed to read it yourself. Amazingly, the nation united around this worship revival and the "thing was done suddenly" (2 Chron 29:36).

The revival was so far reaching that Hezekiah was even moved to invite Israel back to observe the Passover in Jerusalem again (2 Chron 30:7-9). The response, however, was less than positive as we read in 2 Chronicles 30:10-11:

> So the posts passed from city to city through the country of Ephraim and Manasseh even unto Zebulun, but they laughed them to scorn, and mocked them. Nevertheless divers of Asher and Manasseh and Zebulun humbled themselves, and came to Jerusalem.

When the day for the Passover finally came, the sacrifices were offered by the priests rather than the traditional head of household because many who participated were not fully clean ceremonially. This would have kept them from participating at all under normal circumstances, but Hezekiah's prayer for God's mercy in this matter was answered, and the Lord healed the people (2 Chron 30:18-19). A week of feasting, teaching, and praising with singing followed during the feast of unleavened bread.

A revival of worship like this had not been seen since the time of Solomon (2 Chron 30:26) and there would not be another like it until the time of Nehemiah. The parallels between this time and the restoration service we will look at in the next chapter may be the very reason the Chronicler spends so much time on the details of this revival. Hezekiah's heart for worship, though not totally embraced by everyone in the nation, was rewarded by God. Unfortunately, he was followed by his son Manasseh who swung the nation back into apostasy.

Principles to Apply

- True revival in worship only occurs when there is both a rejection of what is false and an active pursuit of God-honoring worship.
- Anyone, at anytime, can change the direction of worship for good or evil. Still, leadership in worship may not be followed completely.

Applications

Some who read these lines will resonate with the need to stand against any hint of false worship, no matter the cost. Others will yearn with me to see more than merely the tearing down of what is false, but the building up of something truly God-honoring, truly Word-based in its place. Success, true success will not occur until both are evident.

If you've been in ministry for awhile you also realize that we live in an imperfect world. In many ways, we live in a world not unlike the world Ahaz built. If you put yourself in Hezekiah's sandals, you will realize how much he risked taking the stand he took. He could very easily have accepted the way things were and refused to upset anyone, except God. I don't know the world you live in, but in my world I know it is perilous to stand against what is false in the worship around us and try to move forward and invite people to worship in purity. There will be those who laugh and mock as they did when Hezekiah invited them back to Passover, but praise God some will join you in your journey toward more obedience to His Word in worship. Be strong in the Lord.

I confess I really don't know what to make of God "bending the rules" in the matter of the ceremonially unclean participating in the Passover meal, except that they are His rules to bend. The inspired, trustworthy Commentary gives us this insight in 2 Chronicles 30:18-19 stating:

> For a multitude of the people....had not cleansed themselves, yet did they eat of the Passover otherwise than it was written. But Hezekiah prayed for them saying, the good Lord pardon every one that prepareth his heart to seek God, the Lord God of his fathers, though he be not cleansed according to the purification of the sanctuary. And the Lord hearkened to Hezekiah, and healed the people.

Praise God for His mercy. Any honest person will thank the Lord that He does not give us what we deserve and reward us according to our iniquities. The Lord remembers that we are dust. Let us never, however, allow God's mercy to harden our hearts. I am certain the next Passover was different; they knew better. How about you? If you feel with some confidence that God has accepted your worship in the past, don't allow that acceptance to lessen your desire to know how Him better and grow in your maturity, to move more fully to the kind of worship gifts He deserves.

Isa 1:11-15; 2:8-9, 11, 17-18, 20 The False Worship of Israel is Condemned

Before you look at the exegetical section I would encourage you to take the time to read through the first two chapters of Isaiah.

Exegetical Considerations

God's heart for true worship and His disgust with adulterous false worship were clearly demonstrated by prophet after prophet. Isaiah's life and prophetic ministry spanned much of this tumultuous time. An examination of his ministry is illustrative of the ministry of many of the prophets.

It is important here to remind you that the Bible's use of the word *nabi* (mouthpiece) includes both the spoken and sung word. The father of prophets, Moses,[1] used music (Deut 31-32) as the tool for communicating God's legally binding covenant, a "covenant-treaty" that was sung and deposited in a special place after its proclamation.[2] The prophets regularly used the poetic/musical genre in communicating messages from God. Habakkuk 3:1 and 3:19 not only reflect the poetic/musical literary genre but specifically mention the musical form and instrument used. Jeremiah's Lamentation is also divided into five "dirges" that may have been sung. A similar dirge structure is also used at the deaths of Saul (2 Sam 1:17-27) and Absalom (2 Sam 3:33-34). Men and women who functioned in musical roles were often called "prophets" or "prophetesses." Seel suggests that "specific reference to 'the prophesying of the prophets with a psaltery and a harp' (1 Sam 10:5, 19:20; 2 Kings 3:15) were probably instances of improvised music."[3] As I have said before, Ulrich Leupold asserts that "poetry recited was unknown in antiquity."[4] There is no reason to think that Isaiah did anything other than sing many, perhaps most, of his messages for reasons we have discussed. It takes some fancy hermeneutical high stepping to imagine that "Now will I sing to my well beloved a song" (Isa 5:1) could mean anything other than Isaiah sang memorable, emotional, and at times lamenting songs as he delivered his impassioned messages to a largely illiterate people.

Isaiah's ministry spanned a long time period and is representative of the message of the prophets during the disintegration of worship and the downfall of Israel to the north and his own nation of Judah. He ministered during the reigns of Uzziah, Jotham, Ahaz, and Hezekiah (Isa 1:1).

The book of Isaiah begins with a song of denouncement. Although Israel continued to participate in worship and to bring sacrifices, God took no pleasure in them. God said, "I am full of the burnt offerings of rams, and the fat of fed beasts; and I delight not in the blood of bullocks, or of lambs or of he goats" (Isa 1:11-15; see also Jer 35:15). Israel's worship had become empty, heartless, and syncretic (Isa 29:13; 43:21-24; Amos 2:8; 4:4-5).[5] Their hands were "full of blood" and needed to be washed (Isa 1:15-16; Hab 1:16; Zeph 1:5-9).[6] Isaiah specifically mentioned putting away evil practices and learning to do good, caring for and protecting the poor, the fatherless, and the widow (Isa 68:6-7;

Micah 6:7-8,11-12; cf Deut 26:2-13).[7] One of the outward evidences of false worship has always been flawed human relationships. A lifestyle of thoughtful obedience must adorn any acts of worship. Isaiah also soundly condemned the overtly false worship of idols in the land which Isaiah repeatedly condemned (Isa 2:8-9; 10:10-11; 36:7; 40:19-20; 42:17; 44:8-19; 45:14-21; 46:5-9; 48:4-5; 57:3-7; 65:3-7).[8] Not only did Isaiah prophesy through song against evil in Israel, he also prophesied a message of hope: a time when God would destroy all false worship and restore Israel's worship and music (Isa 2:17-20; 12:1-6; 17:7-8; 19:19,21; 26:1ff; 27:9,13; 28:5; 30:22).[9]

Isaiah's heavenly vision also affords some insights into worship. In many ways it serves as a summary of several of the concepts mentioned above. The narrative begins with the self-disclosure of God (Isa 6:1-4). The angels were seen eternally worshiping God before His throne. God's transcendent power, holiness, and Lordship were lauded by the angels. Isaiah also fell down in worship before God and acknowledged not only God's transcendent holiness but also his own sinfulness and the sinfulness of the nation around him (Isa 6:5). God responded to Isaiah's confession and offered cleansing. His cleansing was accompanied by the symbolic touch of the coal from the altar of God (Isa 6:6-7). Because Isaiah saw the Lord and the sin surrounding him, it was clear to him what Israel's need was. God proceeded to the commissioning: "Whom shall I send...?" (Isa 6:8). Isaiah responded in submissive obedience and God gave him his specific mission (Isa 6:9-12).

Principles to Apply

- Singing can be a powerful way of delivering God's truth.
- God desires acts of worship only in the context of obedience. Hypocritical worship is actually worse than not sacrificing at all.
- Godly worship cannot coexist with false worship.
- A clear vision of God in worship results in a clear vision of sin, a heart ready to confess, and a life ready to serve.

Applications

Allow me to beat the drum once more. We are reading contemporary culture back into the text when we exclude the possibility that serious messages with significant content can be delivered through song. I would suggest that the genre Isaiah chose to deliver God's message to his original audience was *likely* singing for five reasons. First, this honors a hermeneutic that opts for a "normal reading" of the passage (conservative scholars like Walvoord[10] and Wiersbe[11] for example, also identify these as songs). Second, music was used as a memory aid in delivering information of great import throughout the Ancient Near East (Deut 31-32). Third, many in Isaiah's audience would have been illiterate. Kaiser says: "It is also true that the vast majority of people did not own any of the Scriptures, and most could not read, although literacy was more common among Jews than among the rest of the Greco-Roman world."[12] To the extent they could read, their reading material would have been limited and carefully guarded. Fourth, music was used significantly in connection with the prophetic office (1 Sam 10:5; Hab 3:1). Levites who were involved in music were referred to as exercising a prophetic role (1 Chron 25:1, 3). Fifth, Isaiah's message would have been served by the strong emotive properties of music.

Consider choosing music for a worship service based on the "big idea" of the service. Though we need simple texts that people can meditate on, there also needs to be substantive, deep truths communicated in our music. When someone presents truth through singing, they may be praying, testifying, teaching, counseling, or prophesying. Each of these roles may have a slightly different paradigm for selection. Think deeply about what may be different about each. We will look at this again through the eye of Paul in the epistles.

Does God want our sacrifices and service? Yes, but the prophets make it clear that they must grow out of a relationship of fidelity to God and relational integrity among God's children. God is clear when He says through Amos and Micah:

I hate, I despise your feast days, and I will not smell in your solemn assemblies. Though ye offer me burnt offerings and your meat offerings, I will not accept them: neither will I regard the peace offerings of your fat beasts. Take thou away from me the noise of thy songs; for I will not hear the melody of thy viols. But let judgment run down as waters, and righteousness as a mighty stream. (Amos 5:21-24)

Wherewith shall I come before the LORD, and bow myself before the high God? shall I come before him with burnt offerings, with calves of a year old? Will the LORD be pleased with thousands of rams, or with ten thousands of rivers of oil? shall I give my firstborn for my transgression, the fruit of my body for the sin of my soul? He hath shewed thee, O man, what is good; and what doth the LORD require of thee, but to do justly, and to love mercy, and to walk humbly with thy God? (Micah 6:6-8)

Truly successful worship cannot exist, however beautiful the music or popular the style, if there is not purity in lifestyle, a lifestyle that is characterized by love for Christ, love for others, justice, mercy, and humility. That is the model. I am afraid that to my shame, I have too often been satisfied to just lead nice music. Pray that God would help us worship from the inside out, and not be satisfied with just keeping the outward form as the nation of Israel did here.

Isaiah's face-to-face meeting with God changed him forever. At the end of the day seeing God clearly, falling down before Him in confession, and receiving His empowering forgiveness is the only activity that will hold back the war of the flesh that rages in the world around us and the world within. Guilt will not keep you and me pure. Human need will not keep us motivated to serve over the long haul. Erecting higher and higher fences in our lives will not fence out the evil desires within. Shame or retribution will not be enough. You and I will trust Him, live pure lives, stay motivated to serve Him only when we let God be God—only when we glorify God as God in all His fullness and become truly thankful for who He is.

Isaiah was a man whose view of God sustained him throughout his tumultuous life. He was serious about sin in his life and in the life of his people, and for a lifetime stayed motivated to trust and obey the Lord. Pray that in your next time of private or public worship you will see God and live in light of what you see. Let me add here that although Isaiah had many times of hearing the voice of God in his unique ministry, there were no doubt times when, like us, he simply served God through the blood, sweat, and tears of ministry—times when there were no dramatic visions. Stay faithful.

Before we leave this chapter, I want to express the regret that space will not allow us the opportunity to drink more deeply of the prophets. You might wonder what would be the value of digging deeper. When you read ahead to Christ's teaching on worship you will find that He saw the value in it, for He often quotes the prophets.

Allow me to mention two postscripts. You will find fascinating a study of Ezekiel 40-48 where the prophet describes for us the future Temple. I believe this to be a literal future Temple: a place where once again the nation of Israel will, in a memorial model much like communion today, perform worship acts intended to remind worshipers of the nature of God and the action of Christ on the cross (more on this when we study Revelation together).

The second postscript is the genre of the book of Lamentations. Allow me three quotes to establish the fact that this wonderful book is indeed a series of songs from Walvoord, Pfeiffer, and Keil and Delitzsch respectively:

> Rabbinic and Talmudic writers referred to the book by this title or by the name *qinot* which means "dirges" or "laments".[13]

> The five chapters of Lamentations are five beautiful and solemn elegies, or songs of mourning, expressing the anguish of the Jewish people at the sight of the utter ruin of their city, its Temple, and its population, under the conquering Babylonians in 586 B.C.[14]

The ancient custom of composing and singing lamentations over deceased friends (of which we find proof in the elegies of David on Saul and Jonathan, 2 Sam. 1:17ff., and on Abner, 2 Sam. 3:33ff., and in the notice given in 2 Chron. 35:25) was even in early times extended so as to apply to the general calamities that befell countries and cities; hence the prophets often speak of taking up lamentations over the fall of nations, countries, and cities; cf. Amos 5:1, Jer. 7:29; 9:9, 17f., Ezek. 19:1; 26:17; 27:2, etc.[15]

I know I have barely scratched the surface in this chapter. Be a student of the Word and study on; you will not regret it.

Chapter Ten
Exile and Restoration

In the passages to follow, we find described the most detailed examples of worship in the whole Old Testament. McConville in his commentary suggests, "We have in these verses one of the most graphic portrayals of Israel at worship in the Old Testament."[1] By understanding this time period, you will have a greater grasp of the worship world that Jesus Himself encountered. It is definitely worth the study.

1 and 2 Chronicles were written during this period and set the backdrop. I think it is significant that the chronicler spent so much time detailing the music and worship of the united and divided kingdoms. As the nation returned to the land, they needed to reinstitute godly worship and learn from their history: a history peppered with the failures of false worship. They also needed a clear model for the task of rebuilding the infrastructure of worship. The immensity and complexities of rebuilding the nation's worship and the needs of the people often caused the work to grind to a halt.

Studying this time period will also give you many insights into doing ministry when it seems like there is little hope of success and the job is overwhelming. It would have been easy for the leaders to look at the worship landscape around them, throw up their hands and give up. Learn well the lessons of these brave spiritual leaders.

Cyrus's motives for sending the Israelites back to rebuild the Temple were likely not entirely pure. We read he wanted the Temple restored so "they may offer sacrifices of sweet savours unto the God of heaven, and pray for the life of the king, and of his sons" (Ezra 6:10). Whatever the human motivations may have been, God intervened and singularly blessed those who returned. They were given ample resources, Temple furnishings, and many people were willing to leave the relative comfort of their lives to return to the rubble of what had been their beloved Jerusalem (Ezra 1:2-4).

1. Ezra 1:3-7 Decree by Cyrus to reinstitute worship in the Temple with the vessels taken by Nebuchadnezzar
2. Ezra 2:41, 65, 68-70 Musicians and offerings listed
3. Ezra 3:2-6 Sacrifices reinstituted
4. Ezra 3:10-31 Music ministry restored and praises sung at the laying of the Temple foundation
5. Ezra 4:2 Zerubbabel encouraged the people to sacrifice to the Lord.
6. Ezra 5:14-17 Defense letter for the reinstitution of worship as decreed by Cyrus
7. Ezra 6:3-12 Confirming letter by Darius
8. Ezra 6:16-22 Dedication of the rebuilt Temple.
9. Ezra 7:1, 7, 14-17, 24 Monies provided for the sacrifices, musicians go to Jerusalem under Artaxerxes.
10. Ezra 8:25-30 Dedication of the priests and offering of Israel
11. Ezra 9:1-2 Commitment to separate from the false worship of the surrounding nations
12. Ezra 10:1, 19 Ezra fell down before God, sin offering is given
13. Neh 1:11 Reference to fearing the Lord as a synonym for worship
14. Neh 4:2 Desire to sacrifice mentioned
15. Neh 5:13 People affirm their obedience and praise the Lord
16. Neh 7:1, 44, 67, 73 Musician families listed
17. Neh 8:1-9:38 Worship service at the rededication of the Temple
18. Neh 10:28-39 Responsibilities of the musicians, priests and their families
19. Neh 11:17, 22-23 Musician/priest families
20. Neh 12:24-30, 35-38, 41-47 More details about the rededication of the Temple
21. Neh 13:5, 10-18 Musicians and priests not taken care of properly, others judged for defiling the Sabbath
22. Dan 1:2 Reference to false worship
23. Dan 2:19-23 Daniel worships God
24. Dan 2:46-48 Daniel refused the worship of Nebuchadnezzar and gave God the glory
25. Dan 3:5-28 False worship of Nebuchadnezzar
26. Dan 4:34-37 Nebuchadnezzar's psalm of praise

27. Dan 5:2-4, 23 God judged the false worship done with the sacred instruments of the temple
28. Dan 6:10 Daniel's faithful worship
29. Dan 6:18 King used music to relax
30. Dan 6:26-27; 7:10, 14, 27 Darius calls people to tremble and fear before God
31. Dan 8:1-2, 15-18; 10:5-12, 16 Daniel's visions and his response before the Angel of the Lord
32. Dan 9:27 The desecration of worship
33. Dan 11:31, 38-39 God judged His people because of false worship
34. Haggai 1:4-5, 8-9 Priority of worship over self-gratification, call to build the Temple
35. Haggai 1:12 People fear the Lord under Haggai's ministry
36. Zech 2:10 Zion should sing and rejoice
37. Zech 6:12-15 The promise of the Messiah cleansing worship
38. Zech 7:5-11 True worship must be accompanied by justice and mercy
39. Zech 10:2 False worship rebuked
40. Zech 13:2; 14:16-20 All must worship the King in His kingdom
41. Mal 1:6-14 Fearing and honoring God in worship
42. Mal 2:11-13; 3:3-4 God promised to purify the sons of Levi so they can offer pure worship
43. Mal 3:8-10, 13-15 Robbing God and viewing worship as a weariness
44. Mal 3:16-18 God promised to reward those who seek to worship Him in purity

Ezra 3:2-6, 10-13; Nehemiah 8-10 Reinstitution of Worship
Exegetical Considerations

Using the template of worship from Israel's history, Ezra was blessed with the return of singers (Ezra 2:41, 65), other worship personnel (Ezra 2:68-70), and many of the resources needed to rebuild and reinstitute true worship (Ezra 1:4-6). Jeshua and Zerubbabel led their brothers in setting up the altar and beginning the sacrifices once again. The term "seventh month" is unclear as explained in this entry from *The Bible Knowledge Commentary:*

> The seventh month may refer to the seventh month after the people left Babylon or to the seventh month after they arrived in Jerusalem. This was in September-October. In years past, the seventh month had been a great month religiously for Israel. Three religious festivals were held in the seventh month: the Feast of Trumpets on the 1st day (Lev. 23:23-25), the Day of Atonement on the 10th day (Lev. 23:26-32), and the Feast of Tabernacles on days 15-21 (Lev. 23:33-36, 39-43; Num. 29:12-39; cf. Ezra 3:4).[2]

Note that they accomplished this great deed even though "fear was upon them because of the people of those countries" (Ezra 3:3). Courage is not the absence of fear; it is the fortitude to obey in the midst of fear. It is silencing the fears of what might happen to us with a greater fear of the Lord. Ezra made it clear in Ezra 3:2 that what drove them to overcome their fear was their desire to obey: "as it is written in the law of Moses." The daily sacrifices had begun, feasts were being observed, and offerings were being given, even though "the foundations of the Temple of the Lord was not yet laid" (Ezra 3:6).

During the second year, when the foundations were finally finished, the priests dressed in their priestly apparel and with their trumpets and cymbals led in praise to the Lord following the ordinances of David (Ezra 3:7-10). They did so "by courses," taking turns as their families had done before the exile. They sang again the songs of dedication the nation had sung many times before: "because He is good, for His mercy endureth forever toward Israel" (Ezra 3:11). As in the first Temple dedication, the short version we read here may have actually been the entire dedication song as we discussed before (read it again in 2 Chron 5:13ff).

The pattern of full congregational participation is exampled in the people's response. "And all the people shouted with a great shout, when they praised the Lord" (Ezra 3:11). As we discussed before, the "shouting" may have been loud singing. The positive response was not universal, however, since many who had seen the

Temple in its original glory were weeping; weeping mixed with joyful shouting (Ezra 3:12-13).

Consider now the parallel passage in Nehemiah 8-10. Notice the wording of verse one of chapter eight.

> And all the people gathered themselves together as one man into the street that was before the water gate; and they spake unto Ezra the scribe to bring the book of the law of Moses, which the LORD had commanded to Israel.

It was the people who requested the ministry of the Word from Ezra. They were not among those who Malachi rebuked when they responded to worship by saying, "Oh, what a weariness!" (Mal. 1:13). Instead they echoed the words of David, "I was glad when they said unto me, Let us go into the house of the Lord" (Ps. 122:1). The hearts of these people were further revealed by their unity: they came together "as one man" (Neh 8:1). It was not Ezra who pleaded with the people to come and listen to the Word, but the people who desired Ezra to teach them from his wooden pulpit (Neh 8:4).

The people were gathered together to hear the Word and were helped to understand it. Beginning worship by reading and explaining the Scriptures is an often repeated sequence as we have seen. This particular reading of the law lasted all morning, perhaps five or six hours. All those who could understand were "attentive unto the book of the Law" (Neh 8:3). There was such reverence and thirst for the Word that the people stood when the Law was opened. As Ezra "blessed the Lord, the great God" (Neh 8:5), the people affirmed the truths being read by answering:

> Amen, Amen, with lifting up their hands *(a physical response that indicated innocence or purity)* and they bowed their heads, and worshiped the Lord with their faces to the ground" *(a physical response of humility and surrender)* (Neh 8:6) *(italics mine)*.

Ezra read while Levites and priests stood by to help with the teaching ministry. The phrase "read in the book in the law of God distinctly, and gave the sense" (Neh 8:8) may have been the act of either explaining the text (as I suspect), or perhaps because the Hebrew language may have been a second language or the Aramaic dialects may have influenced their understanding, making sure all the listeners comprehended the meaning of the text.

Having heard the law, the people responded with great weeping. The leaders encouraged the people to stop weeping, accept the blessing of the Lord's joy, and instead enjoy a feast. They were instructed to "make mirth," send gifts to each other, and later celebrate the Feast of Tabernacles (Neh 8:10, 12, 14-16). "There was very great gladness" among the people (Neh 8:17).

Thus the centrality of the Word (Neh 8:18) set the stage for what was to follow. Notice how the people responded at the beginning of the Feast of Tabernacles in Nehemiah 9:1b-3:

> (They) assembled with fasting, and with sackclothes, and earth upon them. And the seed of Israel separated themselves from the strangers, and stood and confessed their sins, and the iniquities of their fathers. And they stood up in their place, and read in the book of the law of the Lord their God one fourth part of the day; and another fourth part they confessed, and worshiped the Lord their God.

What follows in the rest of chapter nine is a psalm of praise very similar in content and structure to Psalm 105. At this rededication of the Temple, two groups of Levites (Neh 9:4-5) antiphonally led the congregation in song as they instructed the people to "Stand up and bless the Lord" (Neh 9:5b). This text is not unlike the texts we read in Exodus 15 (after the nation is redeemed from Egypt), Deuteronomy 31-32 (the song Moses instructed the nation to sing before entering the promised land), 1 Chronicles 16 (at the moving of the ark into Jerusalem), and 2 Chronicles 6 (at the dedication of the first Temple). It seems likely that this text was sung because of the content (the history of the nation which the people were to remember) and the purpose (to encourage the people in corporate praise and reciting together the history). Having sung the song, it was sealed as a written document and preserved (Neh

9:38), as were other covenant-treaties. This is strikingly similar to the content and purposes of Deuteronomy 31-32.

It is obvious that this event was more than just an emotional worship service with little connection to lifestyle. In the chapters to follow were life-changing commitments to separation (10:28-30), Sabbath observation (10:31), financial offerings (10:32-33), care for the Levites and priests (10:34-39), and ongoing commitments for the reconstruction of the city.

Principles to Apply

- Successful worship is dependent on the sincere desire of the worshiper to please the Lord.
- True worship must be centered on the clear exposition of God through the Word.
- The comfort or pleasure of the worshiper does not determine success in worship.
- Responses in worship can include a variety of emotions and can be physical, verbal, and volitional.

Applications

As I mentioned in the introduction for this chapter, attention to detail regarding music and worship in the Scriptures written during this period is purposeful. God was restoring the Temple for those who would seek Him and return to Jerusalem and was preparing the nation for the coming Messiah. Musicians were being recommissioned as their lineage was confirmed, as were the priests who would serve as mediators in worship. Each group was given the full support of the leadership and the nation as a whole. The reconstruction was accomplished with great attention to the detailed commands of the Law.

How about you? I am convinced that you too are endeavoring to grow in your understanding of worship in your church and in your personal life. I realize it is difficult to stand tall when so often success in church ministry is measured in terms of "satisfied customers." But unlike the local fast-food establishment, in worship, the "customer" is not always right. Worship can be successful even when it breaks the rules of commercial endeavors. Think about it: what marketing guru in his right mind would suggest that a worship service should start with an all-morning reading of the Law? To have successful worship in God's eyes, you may at times have to disappoint people. And, how utterly misguided it is to let those in the world who know the least about God and His Word determine how we worship.

The hallmark of successful worship must be the Word of God and the full exposition of God's acts and attributes. These godly people desired worship that was obedient to the Word as God had revealed it to them in the Law. They insisted that their leaders went to the Word and were willing to sacrifice their comfort and pleasure to bring back to God the worship of which He alone was worthy. Ezra, Nehemiah, Zerubbabel, Jeshua, and the other leaders heroically gave them what they called for—a Word-centered worship. We have already seen the example of many godly men and women who called the nation to forsake false worship and follow the Lord. A few of these servants experienced a measure of success, but this time people were crying out to their leaders to give them the Word. I believe that today some people, like these believers, are weary of the consumer-driven worship glitz and are once again calling us to give them the Word. Don't fail them. Dig into the Word yourself and let success be measured by obedience to the Word no matter what the sacrifice.

Look over the "service order" of this event. It is noticeably different than much of what we see in Christianity today.

- The Law is read for five or six hours.
- The leader blessed the Lord as the people affirmed the truth and responded with physical actions that reflected purity, humility, and submission.
- The people stood in honor as the Law was read and then received further instructions from the Levites.
- They were given time to weep.
- Later they were called to rejoice, fellowship, and obey by observing a specific memorial celebration (Feast of Tabernacles).

- Again they fasted and responded with physical actions which showed true contrition and hatred for sin and the ways of the sinner.
- They read the Word, confessed their sins, and worshiped.
- They sang (I am convinced) together the great acts and attributes of God.
- They committed to actions of obedience and service.

This order of service puts revelatory elements *before* responsorial elements of worship. They sang and acted because they knew what God had said, how He had acted in the past and how He wanted them to live now. I am not suggesting that you begin next Sunday with six hours of Scripture reading and exposition, but I am suggesting that the biblical model links worship response to truth. If we attempt to lead people into "worship" when they have no content for their worship we are doomed to be manipulative, or trite, or thoughtlessly emotional, or thoughtlessly emotionless. Look at your order of service and ask the question, "What am I asking these people to praise the Lord for?" What is the content of your worship? Is it the Word?

Before I challenge you with this next concept, allow me a confession. I confess that I am too often a person given to reaction. I am, at times, so fearful of what man may think of me that I fall into the snare of disobedience. I am afraid I might look like someone with whom I disagree. Because I am not wildly charismatic, I fear showing emotion. Because I am not distantly neo-orthodox, I fear embracing the reality of God's inscrutability. Because I am not necessarily "high church," I fear worship that may take some contemplation. Because I do not believe we must do penance, I fear taking the time to understand the ugly darkness of my sin and what it cost my Savior. Pray along with me that God would help all of us resist the temptation of becoming reactionary, but rather strive to worship with heart, soul, mind, strength, and will. Notice that in their responses there was a balance of sobriety and festival, godly sorrow and rejoicing. Make room for all of these responses in a couple months of worship services. Not every service can be a fitting display of every possible emotion. As God works in your life to obey His Word more fully, do so no matter what others may call you. The people in this narrative obeyed the Word in the midst of their fear.

Malachi - False Worship Exposed
Exegetical Considerations

Malachi is four short chapters, less than three pages in my Bible. I would encourage you to read it through quickly both before and after you read the exegetical considerations. The exact time of Malachi's ministry in relationship to the worship we looked at in the last section was likely later, by several years. This explains many of the rhetorical questions Malachi presents in the book, as we will see.

God, through Malachi, begins by affirming His love for His people. It is in this context that the somber messages to the spiritual leaders (the priests) were framed. Beginning in Malachi 1:6 he appeals to the nation's relationship to Jehovah as Father by saying, "if then I be your Father, where is my honor? And if I be a master, where is my fear?" The concepts of honoring, fearing, and relationship in worship are here restated. Love, honor, and fear are not mutually exclusive concepts or emotions. They are multiple sides of what it meant for the Israelites to fully see and worship the Lord.

The next part of the verse is directed specifically at heart attitudes that were reflected in worship practices. Malachi 1:6b-7a asks,"...where is my fear? saith the Lord of hosts unto you, O priests, that despise my name. And ye say, wherein have we despised Thy name? Ye offer polluted bread upon my altar." The priests are saying by their choices and actions, "the table of the Lord is contemptible" (בָּזָה *baza – to lightly esteem*) (Mal 1:7b). Their wicked hearts were demonstrated in offering sacrifices that did not meet the qualifications of the Word. Even the governor deserved better than what was being offered to the Lord (Mal 1:8). Carson gives the following insight into the reason God refuses to accept such worship (see Mal 1:10):

> Apparently they had deluded themselves into thinking that when it came to worship or offerings, something was better

than nothing, lukewarm was better than cold. In fact, the Lord would prefer that such slovenly, irreverent, hypocritical worship would cease altogether (v 10; cf. Is. 1:11–15; 29:13; and Rev. 3:15–16).[3]

Malachi 1:11 has been the topic of disagreement among Bible scholars. Keil and Delitzsch have a very helpful historic consideration of the issues surrounding this verse.[4] For my part, I think the most natural reading leads to the understanding that this is the future fulfillment and desire of God to bring all the nations, indeed, all of creation to worship Him (Ps 50:1; 113:3; Isa 45:6; 59:19).

Returning to the dialog between God and the priest, God not only refused to accept their polluted worship, He added that the priests looked upon pure worship as a "weariness" and "snuffed" (וְהִפַּחְתֶּם *napah*) at it (Mal 1:13). This inner heart and outward act of "sniffing" at or letting a blast of air out is still all too common in our world. The outward acts (blemished, torn, inferior sacrifices) were directly tied to inward attitudes (contempt, disrespect, self-centeredness) which in turn showed up in their emotions ("snuffing").

The priests are then rebuked for not giving glory to God (Mal 2:2) but forsaking their godly heritage (Mal 2:4-5), refusing to be truth-centered (Mal 2:6-9). "Ye have not kept my ways, but have been partial in the law" (Mal 2:9b). Instead, Israel had "profaned the holiness of the Lord which he loved, and hath married the daughter of a strange god" (Mal 2:11b). Even in the midst of their unfaithfulness to the Word the priests wondered why the hand of God was not on them (Mal 2:13). The prophet reminded them of their need for relational integrity in marriage (Mal 2:14-16), and confronted them about the sin of saying evil is good, and finally, their belief that God would not judge (Mal 2:17).

Chapter three reminds the Israelites that God, whom they said they wanted, would indeed come, but would come in judgment with an expressed purpose. Malachi 3:3-4 says,

> He shall purify the sons of Levi, and purge them as gold and silver, that they may offer unto the Lord an offering in

righteousness. Then shall the offering of Judah and Jerusalem be pleasant unto the Lord.

The prophet goes on to call for relational integrity and faithful giving (Mal 3:5-11). The priests were instead self-serving, communicating instead that it was vain to serve God and that it was an unpleasant thing to obey God's Word. The proud are truly happy, the wicked are "set up," and "they that tempt God" are delivered from destruction (Mal 3:13-15).

But even in the middle of this bleak picture we see God's mercy and provision for the minority who would fear the Lord. Mal 3:16-17 promises:

> Then they that feared the Lord spake often one to another: and the Lord hearkened, and heard it, and a book of remembrance was written before Him for them that feared the Lord, and that thought upon His name. And they shall be mine, saith the Lord of hosts, in that day when I make up my jewels; and I will spare them, as a man spareth his own son that serveth him.

Principles to Apply

- As with other spiritual disciplines it is easy for worship actions to become mundane.
- God appeals to His own character and our relationship with Him as the motivation for pure worship.
- Though ungodly attitudes in worship can be denied, wrong attitudes are manifested in discernable actions.
- Costly, undefiled sacrifices are the only sacrifices worthy of our God.
- Word-centered worship should be the standard for success, not the feelings of the worshiper.
- God desires to purify His people so they can offer pure worship to Him.
- Even in the midst of apostasy in worship, the remnant of true worshipers will be blessed by God.

Applications

Malachi's message stands in sharp contrast to the wonderful example of worship we studied in the last section. The battle for pure worship rages on throughout history as it will until God, once for all, silences all that is false in this universe. It is only natural that the Israelites would have responded with religious fervor when they initially returned to Jerusalem. Everything was so new; they saw themselves as so needy, so vulnerable, and they were exposed to preaching that they had not heard before. As time went on, however, what was new and exciting became mundane and later, just plain boring. As our text describes it, worship became "a weariness." As I said, this is natural. The nation was in decline, as we studied in the last chapter. They often looked to outward changes in the headlong pursuit of their own pleasure: mixing elements of false worship with pure worship. They reasoned that cheap worship that was not quite obedient was somehow okay. Worship that was obedient to the Word and for God's pleasure alone just didn't seem like it was quite enough.

I confess, I understand this bent to boredom. None of us want a boring... well, anything. A boring activity or relationship is something we work to avoid. If, tragically, you would describe your marriage as boring you should seek to do something about it. But what? The problem we face in marriages today is that the world around us is willing to do almost anything to avoid boredom, including divorce (specifically mentioned in Malachi), unfaithfulness, and even cruel, twisted perversion. Is your greatest motivation for making changes in your marriage so you won't be bored? You see the analogy I am about to make, I'm sure. I am not saying that you should not make worship choices that stimulate interest. There *are* things that can be done within the parameters of the Word to deliver the Word in creative ways, both verbally and musically. But trying to out-entertain or out-amuse the world in an effort to keep from being "boring" in worship cannot be our goal. Pray with me that God would help us to believe in our hearts that God and His pleasure are enough in worship. How can we become bored with bringing pleasure to God?

In the prophet's blistering rebuke, God appeals to His own character and the relationship He has with each believer as the reason they should come back to Him. God says, I have loved you, I am your Lord, Father, and Master (Mal 1:2, 6). Praise God those things can be said of any child of God. As a practical application, I would suggest that you center the speaking and/or musical elements of your services on a specific act or attribute of God. People will take home with them more than just someone else's spiritual experience but more profoundly a clearer understanding of the Lord.

Moving to the core of Malachi's message, we see clearly that although attitudes are certainly deniable they are just as certainly evident in the worship choices people make. In post-modern America I frequently hear, "don't judge, you can't tell what is on the inside." True, Jesus did say, "Judge not according to the appearance, but judge righteous judgment" (John 7:24). He also told us just as clearly to judge fruit when in Matthew 7:15-19 we read:

> Beware of false prophets, which come to you in sheep's clothing, but inwardly they are ravening wolves. Ye shall know them by their fruits. Do men gather grapes of thorns, or figs of thistles? Even so every good tree bringeth forth good fruit; but a corrupt tree bringeth forth evil fruit. A good tree cannot bring forth evil fruit, neither can a corrupt tree bring forth good fruit. Every tree that bringeth not forth good fruit is hewn down, and cast into the fire. Wherefore by their fruits ye shall know them.

God rebuked the Israelites for attitudes that they in turn denied. His answer to them was to point to the shoddy, disobedient worship choices they made. I know we can't see into people's hearts, and that final judgment is the Lord's business, not ours. We can, however, tell much about a person, movement or ministry by the worship choices they make. Be bold, discerning, upfront, and above all, loving as you take your stand for God and against the false worship around you.

I made the point above that costly worship, from the very beginning of time is the kind of worship that honors God. Though no act of worship can ever be fully worthy of God's greatness, our goal should be continual growth. We must avoid the temptation to reserve our best resources for ourselves and give God our leftovers. Let the Word be your standard for success, and ask the Lord what costly worship should look like in your life.

On another matter, we need to realize that God's purpose for our purity is so we have the privilege of offering our gifts to Him unhindered. "He shall purify the sons of Levi, and purge them as gold and silver, that they may offer unto the Lord an offering in righteousness" (Mal 3:3). God wants us to commit to purity so that we can offer the gift of our worship to Him in righteousness. Would you pray for me, as I pause to pray for you, that together we would honor the Lord by offering our worship to Him out of pure lives?

I want to end this section by giving you the hope God gave Malachi's audience. If you fear the Lord and take to heart God's message, God will remember you like he remembered those few who worshiped in sincerity during this tumultuous time. And, let's encourage other likeminded worshipers and "speak often one to another" as we read in Malachi 3:16-4:4:

> Then they that feared the LORD spake often one to another: and the LORD hearkened, and heard *it*, and a book of remembrance was written before him for them that feared the LORD, and that thought upon his name. And they shall be mine, saith the LORD of hosts, in that day when I make up my jewels; and I will spare them, as a man spareth his own son that serveth him. Then shall ye return, and discern between the righteous and the wicked, between him that serveth God and him that serveth him not. For, behold, the day cometh, that shall burn as an oven; and all the proud, yea, and all that do wickedly, shall be stubble: and the day that cometh shall burn them up, saith the LORD of hosts, that it shall leave them neither root nor branch. But unto you that fear my name shall the Sun of righteousness arise with healing in his wings; and ye shall go forth, and grow up as calves of the stall...Remember ye the law of Moses my servant, which I commanded unto him in Horeb for all Israel, with the statutes and judgments.

Regrettably, I leave this chapter without dealing in detail with many passages that have been the source of strength for me over the years. In summary fashion I offer these last few paragraphs before we move on to the New Testament.

The prophets ministering during this period reinforced the messages of the pre-exilic prophets we looked at briefly in the last chapter. The people were rebuked for following dumb idols (Zech 10:2-3), and judgment was promised (Mal 2:2-3, 11-13). Costly, selfless worship was God's demand in each of the prophets (Zech 7:5-7; Mal 1:6-14; 3:8-10, 13-15; Hag 1:4-9). Relational integrity is once again stated as both a prerequisite and a result of God-honoring worship (Zech 7:5-11). The restoration of Israel's worship was promised (Zech 2:9-11; 6:12-15; 13:2; 14:16-21; Mal 3:3-4; 3:16-18).

Even while the nation was in exile and enduring the judgment of God, some individuals sought to worship God in truth. The Israelite children (Shadrach, Meshach, and Abednego) and Daniel worshiped God and refused to bow down and worship Nebuchadnezzar (Daniel 2:19-20, 23; 3:5-18, 28). Instead they actively worshiped God before their heathen captors (Dan 2:19-23; 3:17-18, 28; 6:10). Even Nebuchadnezzar and Darius (perhaps under the coaching of Daniel) penned songs of praise (Dan 4:34-27 and Dan 6:26-27). Daniel's heavenly vision, much like Isaiah's, reinforced the future place of worship in God's eternal plan (Dan 8:11-18; 10:5-19).

Chapter Eleven

Christ on Worship

If for your own reasons you have decided to turn here to begin your study, I would encourage you to rethink your decision. Jesus Himself said, "Think not that I am come to destroy the law, or the prophets: I am not come to destroy, but to fulfill" (Matt 5:17). When Christ read the Word, His Scriptures were those we refer to as the Old Testament. He often referred to worship in the Old Covenant and quoted the Prophets. As our example, He faithfully worshiped in obedience to the rigors of the Law into which He was born.

In this transitional period between the Testaments, Christ functioned in three ways: (1) as a faithful example of true worship, (2) the divine teacher on worship and, (3) and, as the God-man, the object of all true worship. Because of His person and ministry, Christ brings into sharper focus those concepts which are truly transdispensational and transcultural. I am going to organize this chapter by putting our usual format of exegesis, principle, and application within the context of one of three sections: Christ's example as a worshiper, Christ's teaching on worship, and Christ's acceptance of worship.

Christ's entrance into the world, His incarnation, showed us His worship practices, gave us the opportunity to hear His teaching on worship, and gave us many examples of the kind of worship He accepted. Christ was co-creator with the Father, yet He obediently worshiped the Father. Christ willingly offered Himself as the supreme sacrifice for sin (Phil 2:6-8; Luke 2:32-33). The very act of Christ becoming the God-man taught us that God in the person of Christ initiated the way for a worship relationship between God and men to begin. And, from the very advent of Christ, He accepted the worship of the angels, the shepherds, Simeon, Anna, and eventually the Wisemen (Luke 2:9, 13-14, 20, 27-32, 38, Matt 2:2-11).

1. Matt 2:2-11 The worship of the Wisemen
2. Matt 4:8-10 Temptation of Christ, cf. Luke 4:7-8
3. Matt 5:16 Purpose of good works
4. Matt 5:23-24 Relational integrity before worship
5. Matt 6:9-13 "Lord's" Prayer, cf. Luke 11:2-4
6. Matt 8:2-3 A leper worshiped Christ, cf. Mark 1:40; Luke 5:12
7. Matt 8:27 Marvel, fear, and wonder at the miraculous stilling of the sea, cf. Mark 4:41; Luke 8:25
8. Matt 8:28-30 Demoniac of the Gadarenes fell down and worshiped, cf. Mark 5:6, 20; Luke 8:37-39
9. Matt 9:8 Multitude marveled and glorified
10. Matt 9:13 Christ on sacrifices quotes Hosea 6:6
11. Matt 9:18 Jairus worshiped then asked to heal his daughter, cf. Mark 5:22; Luke 8:41
12. Matt 9:23 Music involved in mourning; the lament song is still used
13. Matt 10:37-38 Command to love the Lord supremely, cf. Luke 14:26-27
14. Matt 11:17 Reference to music and dance, cf. Luke 7:32
15. Matt 11:25 Jesus thanked the Father in prayer
16. Matt 12:2-8 Explanation of Sabbath observation and the law, cf. Mark 2:23-28; Luke 6:1-5
17. Matt 14:6 Dancing of Herodias, cf. Mark 6:22
18. Matt 14:33 Jesus walked on the water; disciples respond in "worship," "fear," "astonishment," and "wonder," cf. Mark 7:51; John 6:19
19. Matt 15:7-9 Jesus on form and heart quotes Isa 29:13, cf. Mark 7:6-9
20. Matt 15:25 The worship of the Canaanite woman
21. Matt 15:30-31 Jesus healed those who fall at His feet and they glorify God
22. Matt 15:36 Jesus gave thanks to the Father
23. Matt 17:5-8 Transfiguration, cf. Mark 9:2-10; Luke 9:29-35
24. Matt 17:14 The man with a lunatic son bowed before Christ
25. Matt 18:10 Angels always beholding the face of God in worship
26. Matt 18:20 Using the language of Exodus 29:41, Christ promised His special presence when believers gather

27. Matt 18:26-29 Servant who owed and fell down before the king in worship
28. Matt 20:20 Mother of Zebedee's children worshiped Christ
29. Matt 21:9-16 Triumphal entry and the second cleansing of the Temple, cf. Mark 11:9-10, 15-17; Luke 19:37-40, 45-47; John 12:13. Christ quotes Jer 7:11; Isa 56:7
30. Matt 21:37 Parable of the wicked stewards who would not reverence the son, cf. Mark 12:6
31. Matt 22:30 Believers are "as the angels" in heaven, cf. Mark 12:25
32. Matt 22:37-38 Jesus quotes Deuteronomy 6:5, the greatest commandment, cf. Luke 10:27-28
33. Matt 23:17-23 Jesus discussed the temple, altar, and tithe and the importance of doing worship acts within the context of judgment, mercy, and faith; Christ alluded to Hos 6:6 and/or Amos 5:21-25, cf. Luke 11:42
34. Matt 23:35 Reference to the slaying of Zacharias in the Temple
35. Matt 24:1-2 Jesus predicted the demise of the earthly Temple, cf. Luke 19:44
36. Matt 24:30 Christ will return showing His glory
37. Matt 25:31 Christ will manifest His glory on His throne with the angels
38. Matt 26:7-13 Alabaster box sacrifice, cf. Mark 14:3-8; Luke 7:36-50
39. Matt 26:17-30 Jesus observed the Passover and lead in the singing of the Hallel, cf. Mark 14:12-26; Luke 22:7-20
40. Matt 26:49 The kiss of Judas, cf. Luke 22:47
41. Matt 26:39, 42, 44 Jesus prayed, falling on His face, cf. Mark 14:33, 35, 39; Luke 22:41
42. Matt 26:64 Reference to Jesus sitting in the place of worship
43. Matt 27:29 Soldiers mockingly "worship" Jesus, cf. Mark 15:19; Luke 22:63-65; John 19:3
44. Matt 27:51 The Temple veil was torn, cf. Luke 23:45
45. Matt 28:8-9 Resurrection elicited "fear and great joy," the disciples worshiped at Jesus' feet
46. Matt 28:17-20 The great commission given in the context of worshiping disciples
47. Mark 2:12 Healing of the lame man

48. Mark 3:11 The unclean spirits fell down before Christ
49. Mark 5:33 Woman worshiped after being healed of the issue of blood, cf. Luke 8:47; Matt 9:20-22
50. Mark 5:42 People "astonished" at the miracles of Christ
51. Mark 7:25 Woman worshiped and asks for her daughter's healing
52. Mark 9:49 Jesus quotes Lev 2:13 and Eze 43:24 now referring to believers as sacrifices that are all salted
53. Mark 10:17-21 Prospective disciple bowed in worship before Christ
54. Mark 12:29-33 Greatest command and holy living is more important than sacrifice
55. Mark 12:41-44 Jesus commended the sacrificial worship in giving of the widow cf. Luke 21:1-4
56. Luke 1:8-12, 20 Zacharias's vision and worship in the Temple
57. Luke 1:46-48 Mary's worship
58. Luke 1:64-65, 67-79 Zacharias's song of praise is called "a prophecy"
59. Luke 2:9, 13-14, 20 Angels' and shepherds' praise
60. Luke 2:24 Worship of Mary and Joseph
61. Luke 2:37-38 Anna "served" in the Temple
62. Luke 5:8-11 Peter's "Isaiah experience"
63. Luke 5:25-26 After Christ's miracle people glorified God and were amazed
64. Luke 7:16 Fear and glorifying Christ after a miracle
65. Luke 8:45-47 Worship of the "sinful" women
66. Luke 10:21 Jesus gave praise to the Father
67. Luke 10:39-42 Mary worshiped, Martha served
68. Luke 13:1 Reference to Pilate mingling the blood of Galilaeans with their sacrifices
69. Luke 13:13, 17 Glorifying God
70. Luke 14:10 Word "worship" is used of mundane praise
71. Luke 15:7, 10 Joy in heaven over repentance, refer to Zeph 3:17
72. Luke 15:24-25 Music at the feasting of the prodigal
73. Luke 16:13 Comparison between serving God or serving mammon
74. Luke 17:15-16, 18 One of ten lepers returned to worship

75. Luke 18:10-14 Worship of the Pharisee and publican contrasted
76. Luke 18:43 Blind man healed, people praise God
77. Luke 21:27 The glory of the return of Christ
78. Luke 23:47 Centurion glorified God by describing Christ as righteous
79. Luke 24:5 Disciples worshiped at the open tomb
80. Luke 24:50-53 Worship at the ascension of Christ
81. John 1:14, 17 The ministry of Jesus was all about revealing the fullness of God's grace, truth, and glory
82. John 1:29, 36 Christ's place as the lamb of God based on the concepts of OT worship
83. John 2:11 Purpose of Christ's miracles to show the glory of God
84. John 4:20-24 Worship and the Samaritan woman
85. John 5:20, 23 Purpose of miracles is to honor the Father
86. John 9:31, 38 Man blind from birth is healed, he worshiped and God was glorified
87. John 11:4, 32 Lazarus is raised again so that God might be glorified; Mary worshiped
88. John 12:3-8 The sacrificial gift of Mary as she anoints Jesus feet
89. John 12:20 Worshiping Greeks seek Christ
90. John 12:26 Jesus called His disciples to "serve" Him and the Father
91. John 12:43 Jesus condemned those who sought the praise of men more than the praise of God
92. John 13:31-32 Jesus desire to glorify the Father
93. John 14:13 The Father is glorified in the Son
94. John 15:8 The Father is glorified by believers bearing fruit
95. John16:14 The Spirit will glorify the Son
96. John 17:1, 4-5, 10 Christ's prayer demonstrated the importance of glorifying the Father
97. John 18:6 Soldiers fell down at the words of Christ
98. John 21:19 Purpose of Peter's death was to glorify God

Christ as Example

From childhood, and most notably at His baptism and temptation (Matt 3:13-17), Christ demonstrated that He was the perfect example of a life of obedient worship (Luke 2:49; John 2:23). Christ came to be the completer, the fulfillment of pure worship outlined in the Mosaic and Davidic covenants (Matt 5:17). Christ proclaimed, even while faithfully teaching in the Temple, that He was the *new* Temple (Matt 12:6-8; Luke 2:19, 21), the Lamb of God (Luke 1:29, 36). As the new Temple, He came to be the Temple Cleanser (Matt 21:9-16; Mark 11:9-11, 15-17; Luke 19:45-47; John 2:14-17).

It is difficult to underestimate the influence and importance the Temple and Synagogue played in the worship of Christ's day and even during this church age. You will see later how these institutions influenced the infant church in the book of Acts. Here I would like to underscore the importance of the Synagogue in the life of Christ. Notice the constant practice of Christ during His life and ministry. "Jesus answered him, I spake openly to the world; I ever (πάντοτε *pantote,* always, continually) taught in the synagogue, and in the temple" (John 18:20). We see several references that confirm Christ's practice (Matt 4:34 [cf. Mark 1:21; Luke 4:15]; Matt 9:35; Matt 12:9 [cf. Mark 3:1; Luke 6:6]; Matt 13:54 [cf. Luke 4:44; Mark 6:2]; John 6:59). Phillip Schaff suggests this would have been His weekly practice and identifies the locations Paul visited as well.

> As our Lord himself in his youth and manhood worshipped in the synagogue and the temple, so did his early disciples as long as they were tolerated. Even Paul preached Christ in the synagogues of Damascus, Cyprus, Antioch in Pisidia, Amphipolis, Beraeea, Athens, Corinth, Ephesus. He "reasoned with the Jews every sabbath in the synagogues" which furnished him a pulpit and an audience.[5]

Later, as Jesus led worship during Passover He declared He was indeed, *the* sacrificial Passover Lamb (Matt 26:26-27, 30; Mark 14:22-26: Luke 22:19-21). As the perfect Passover Lamb,

His own sacrificial death established Him as the true and "fleshy" Tabernacle/Temple of God. It was God Himself in the person of Christ who entered as the eternal High Priest so that "the veil of the temple was rent in twain" (Mark 15:38; Luke 23:45). Christ's very life is a perfect example of obedient, revelatory worship; a worship that would have been fully informed by the teaching, singing, and Scripture reading that was Synagogue worship.

Matt 4:9-10; Luke 4:5-8 Temptation of Christ
Exegetical Considerations

In the beginning of Christ's public ministry Satan tempted Him to bow down in false worship. In Christ's response to Satan, Jesus used the two predominate terms for worship we see in the New Testament. First, Christ used the Greek term προσκυνήσεις, *proskuneo* (worship) when quoting Deuteronomy 6:13 where the Hebrew term is יָרֵא *yare* (fear). Christ used the word "worship" (προσκυνήσεις, *proskuneo*) when referring to this Hebrew term for "fear" even though in the LXX (the Septuagint, is a Greek translation of the Hebrew Scriptures) *yare* is translated φοβηθήσῃ, *phobethese* (fear) in other OT passages. Christ recognized the interrelationship between worship and fear that we have already seen in our OT study.

The second significant New Testament term, λατρεύσεις, *latreuseis* (to serve), is also used in this narrative. Newman and Stine argue that "In the present context *worship* and *serve* are used with the same meaning, the second verb forming a parallel to the first."[6] Jamison, in his commentary says, "In the *Hebrew* and the *Septuagint* it is, 'Thou shalt *fear*;' but as the sense is the same, so 'worship' is here used to show emphatically that what the tempter claimed was precisely what God had forbidden."[7] Christ underscored the truth that worship involves God-consciousness and appropriate outward actions of service. I will address the implications of this in the application section.

As I stated in the introduction, when Jesus taught on worship He often did so by reaffirming concepts revealed in the Old Testament. It is significant that Satan aimed his temptation at the object of worship as he has always done. Satan approached Jesus with an offer to give up his own dominion over the world if Jesus would only fall down before him and make him His object of worship.

It is also significant that in this early narrative Christ affirmed His deity by insisting on the worship of God alone and just as purposefully encouraged people to worship Him. Blomberg adds:

> Jesus' insistence on worshiping God alone makes the characteristic Matthean theme of worshiping Jesus (e.g., 2:2; 8:2; 9:18; 14:33; 15:25; 20:20; 28:17) all the more significant as evidence for his divinity.[8]

Principles to Apply

- Worship involved a proper fear of the Lord and service for God; both inward and outward elements.
- Christ insisted that all worship be directed at the triune Godhead.

Applications

Much can be learned in this brief account of Christ's temptation. First is Christ's use of the word "worship" when Deuteronomy uses the word "fear." I recall having a conversation with a pastor who took exception to my admonition to live in the fear of the Lord. He insisted that because of the work of Christ we need no longer fear the Lord. We have already discussed the difference between godly and ungodly fear. Although we do have confidence as believers, that should not lessen our resolve to approach God with a balanced understanding of His transcendent greatness.

I also think it strange that some have suggested that the ideas associated with the word *proskuneo* (to bow or kiss toward) are concepts that do not apply to the believer today.[9] I have heard it preached that now our lives should be centered on activities denoted by the word *latreuō* (to serve). Christ confirmed in this encounter that our worship need not exclude either formal acts of worship or lifestyle. In fact, as far as word usage is concerned, *latreuō* is used 86 times in the LXX to refer to a number of formal Mosaic worship acts. It is in the New Testament the concept of "service" is expanded to mean something more than a worship act. Yet, today it seems people imagine "serving the Lord" has nothing to do with what might happen in a formal worship time (a worship act) and only with what happens outside of it. Consider Anna who "served God with fastings and prayers night and day" (Luke 2:37). In the biblical model, service to the Lord in no way excludes actions designed for the pleasure of God alone in a specific act like praising through singing or speaking. "Service" need not be thought of as exclusively human in its orientation. Yes, service certainly includes giving a cup of cold water in the Savior's name, but it does not exclude bowing and singing a song together as a "sacrifice of our lips" to God (Heb 13:15).

Notice as well that in the narrative, Satan's temptations center on taking the focus of worship off of the Lord God and onto other things. Calvin had it right: our hearts are "a perpetual factory of idols" (*Institutes* 1:108). We must always remain vigilant in our effort to center worship on the Lord, no matter what "successes" another center may offer. Looking deeper at the heart of the temptation, Satan simply wanted Christ to speed things up. Satan's temptation amounted to an appeal to fudge on the object of worship so that success would be more immediate. After all, Christ could bypass the stigma and agony of the cross if He would only compromise on this matter of worship. Isn't it all about the end and not the means anyway? Doesn't God want Christ to rule the kingdoms of the world? Don't be deceived; when it comes to "successfully" bringing about Christ's "exaltation," bowing before Satan even for a moment brings certain ruin.

Matt. 21:12–17; Mark 11:15–19 Lu 19:45–48; John 2:13–22, The Two Cleansings of the Temple
Exegetical Considerations

To begin our discussion of this narrative I need to tell you that a minority opinion suggests there was only one cleansing of the Temple since none of the gospel writers mention both. You may wish to research it further, but I am convinced we see Christ cleansing the Temple on both His first and last trips to Jerusalem. By doing so He dramatically illustrated His desire for pure worship: a desire we have seen often repeated in the prophets. These two cleansings served as bookends to His public ministry in Jerusalem. Between them were many times when He taught in the Temple, foreshadowed by His youthful declaration that He was to be in the Temple about His Father's business (Luke 2:49). For this reason Jesus often and openly taught in the Temple to those who would listen to Him (Mark 11:11, 27; 12:35; Luke 19:47; 20:1; John 7:28; 8:2, 20; 18:20). Jesus' own testimony before the Sanhedrin is that He was "daily in the Temple" teaching the people (Matt 26:55; Mark 14:49; Luke 19:47; 22:53).

We will begin by looking at His first cleansing recorded in John 2. Jesus entered Jerusalem and responded with great passion when He saw what worship had become. His dramatic actions were a direct fulfillment of the prediction of Malachi 3:1-2: Messiah was prophesied as the one who would come to "purify the sons of Levi, and purge them as gold and silver, that they may offer unto the Lord an offering in righteousness" (Mal 3:3). Finding the worship of God tarnished by commercialism (the money changers and merchants) and seeing the compromise inspired by convenience (some were making use of a "shortcut" through the temple court), Jesus took aggressive action to drive out the animals, overturn the tables of the money changers, and stop those who made the temple a thoroughfare (John 2:14-15). As I mentioned in the introduction, Jesus quoted the prophets we studied in the last chapter. Here Jesus says they had made the Temple a "house of merchandise" (John 2:16). Seeing Christ's zeal, the disciples were immediately reminded of Psalm 69:9: "For the zeal of thine house hath eaten me up" (see John 2:17).

In the second cleansing, Jesus uses even stronger language, specifically mentioning Jeremiah 7:11: "Is this house, which is called by my name, become a den of robbers" (Luke 19:46 cf. Mark 11:17; Matt 21:13) and Isaiah 56:7 "for my house shall be called a house of prayer." By this act of cleansing, Jesus established His authority and declared war on the false worship of the religious elite.

When questioned by the Temple leaders, Jesus answered by predicting His own death and introducing the idea which would be more fully developed later, namely that He was the reality of the Temple. Christ said, "'Destroy this Temple, and in three days I will raise it up.' Then said the Jews, Forty and six years was this Temple in building, and wilt thou rear it up in three days? But he spake of the Temple of his body" (John 2:19-21). The Temple building may have become an object of worship itself instead of the reminder of God's glory that it was intended to be. Christ transformed the meaning of "Temple" because He *was* the manifest glory of the Father, a concept more fully developed in the book of Hebrews.

Christ's second cleansing of the Temple was combined with His triumphal entry. Wiersbe says:

> Jesus investigated the temple and then returned the next day to cleanse it. He had cleansed the temple early in His ministry (John 2:13–22), but the religious merchants came back again. Mere outward reformation does not last unless the heart is changed. What began as a service to foreign Jews (who needed to change money or purchase sacrifices) had become a business that had no place in the house of God. People used the temple as a shortcut from the Mount of Olives (v. 16), and the stalls and tables cluttered up the Court of the Gentiles where the Jews should have been witnessing about the true God to their Gentile neighbors. In His indictment against the leaders (v. 17), Jesus quoted Isaiah (56:7) and Jeremiah (7:11), both of whom had condemned the nation for its sins in the temple (Isa. 1; Jer. 7). A "den of thieves" is the place thieves go to hide when they have committed a crime. The religious leaders were using the worship of God as a cover for their sins![10]

In just a few hours, God Himself would rip the veil that had separated so many from the holy of holies. Christ Himself cleared the Temple building so it would be ready for this holy act.

Principles for Application

- Christ desires worship that is pure. He is passionate and zealous to protect the integrity of worship.
- Worship should center on the Lord, just as prayer should be centered on the Lord, not on the one praying.

Applications

Think about the times in Israel's history when God showed His wrath most powerfully; He was guarding the integrity of worship. These events in Christ's ministry underscore the Trinity's unbending insistence on pure worship; not worship that centered on the profit or convenience of the worshiper. God must be worshiped, and He must be worshiped on His terms.

If you are understanding that the essence of worship is what (or ideally Who) your center and source for all things is, then you also understand how imperative it is that worship *forms* carefully picture God. Many around Christ, even the religious leaders of His day, saw nothing wrong with what was going on in the Temple's outer court. Whether they stood idly by for financial gain, to fulfill the desires of the people, or simply to preserve the status quo, we do not know. Perhaps they, like so many today, felt it was all about culture—it was just not worth getting involved. Jesus thought differently.

Jesus was not casual about what was happening in worship around Him. Tell me, should we be? Follow Christ's example with all that is in you; strive to make gathering in Christ's name about meeting with God on His terms. It is very right for us to defend the integrity of God in worship. We can and should compromise what are our liberties to give away, but we dare not prostitute the integrity of worship. God's honor is not ours to give away or compromise. May God give you strength to kindly and firmly stand for the honor of His name in worship. Anger at false worship is justified, but keep it focused on problem solving and directed toward concrete solutions.

Christ's Teaching on Worship

I will give you in the next few paragraphs a summary of Christ's teachings on worship and then will deal with a specific passage. Much of Christ's teaching was done by His life. Although in striking ways Jesus changed the face of worship forever, we also see continuity in His teaching. Along with Jesus' quotes during His temptation and temple cleansing we see some other ways in which He reinforced concepts we have already seen in the OT. For example, in Matthew 9:13, Christ rebuked the Pharisees by quoting from Hosea 6:6, "For I desired mercy, and not sacrifice; and the knowledge of God more than burnt offerings." Jesus made it clear that although sacrifice was a part of worship in the OT (see similar passages: 1 Sam 15:22; Ps 40:6; 50:7–15; 51:16; 69:30–31; Prov 21:3), God has always insisted on mercy in the worshiper's relationships and increasing the knowledge of Himself in worship acts. We also see Jesus restated Isaiah's stinging rebuke in Matthew 15:7-9 (cf. Mark 7:6-9), when he quotes Isaiah 29:13: "Wherefore the Lord said, forasmuch as this people draw near me with their mouth, and with their lips do honor me, but have removed their heart far from me, and their fear toward me is taught by precept of men." Christ taught nothing new when He identified the tendency for people to fixate on the outward and substitute men's teachings for God's.

On another occasion Christ repeated the need for relational integrity that we see so clearly in the ministries of the Old Testament prophets (Matt 5:23-24; 9:13; Mark 12:3-33; 23:23). "But go ye and learn what that meaneth, I will have mercy, and not sacrifice: for I am not come to call the righteous, but sinners to repentance" (Matt 9:13). Christ desires true heart change in our relationships, not just outward sacrifices (Matt 15:7-9; cf. Mark 7:6-9; Luke 11:42; 18:10-14).

Not only do we see Christ reinforcing OT teaching about worship, we also see instances when Jesus expanded on well-known worship practices. For example, in Mark 9:49-50 Jesus said "...every sacrifice shall be salted with salt. Salt is good: but if the salt have lost his saltness, wherewith will ye season it? Have salt in yourselves, and have peace one with another." Jesus quotes

Leviticus 2:13 and Ezekiel 43:24 and further extends the meaning of salted sacrifices by likening believers to the salt that was applied to sacrifices. Another example of expanding definitions, although not explicitly taught, is the promise that just as the Tabernacle and the Temple (Ex 29:41) were places where God's unique presence dwelt, so now when two or three gather in Christ's name, there God's unique presence once again is evident (Matt 18:20). Certainly Christ's teaching during the Passover meal observed with the disciples is a clear example of how an OT worship practice, the Passover, is infused with NT meaning (Matt 26:17-30).

I also see as enlightening Christ's instructions to his disciples about prayer in Matthew 6:9-13 (see also Luke 11:2-4). His pattern for prayer demonstrated a priority in worship by beginning and ending with affirmations of God's character: "hallowed be Thy Name" and later "Thine be the kingdom, and the power, and the glory, forever" (Matt 6:9, 13). Consider as well the request we make of God that His "will be done in earth, as it is in heaven." Heaven is the place of God's special presence (Matt 6:9) where worship is a continual activity. It is God's will for the worship activities of heaven to be continually occurring in heaven. Craig Blomberg comments on this phrase.

> "Your kingdom come, your will be done on earth as it is in heaven" expresses the desire that the acknowledgment of God's reign and the accomplishment of his purposes take place in this world even as they already do in God's throne room. The first half of the prayer thus focuses exclusively on God and his agenda as believers adore, worship, and submit to his will before they introduce their own personal petitions.[11]

Christ states that in eternity believers would be "as the angels of God in heaven." Primarily Jesus is addressing the fact that they would not marry (Matt 22:30 cf. Matt 18:10; Mark 12:26); however, John Nolland has expanded the discussion by suggesting, "The core thought is that resurrection involves 'progress into a new mode of being' that transcends present limitations."[12] Simply stated, worship is the eternal activity of heaven, something believers should pray for and desire here on earth.

In the gospels Christ reiterates the truth of Zephaniah 3:17, stating: "The Lord thy God in the midst of thee is mighty; he will save, he will rejoice over thee with joy; he will rest in his love, he will joy over thee with singing." Christ says there is joy in heaven *in the presence* of the angels. "Likewise, I say unto you, there is joy in the presence of the angels of God over one sinner that repenteth" (Luke 15:10). God Himself rejoices with joyous singing! Romans and Hebrews also teach that Christ Himself sings among His brethren, other believers (Rom15:9-11 and Heb 2:11-12).

We also see that Jesus taught the reason men should do good works, even the good works of the miraculous, was to glorify the Father (Matt 5:16; 9:8; 15:31; Luke 18:43). Finally, Christ accomplished His greatest "work" by glorifying the Father and humbly bowing (Matt 26:39) and submitting to the death of the cross (Phil 4:8).

Notice also Christ's response to the question of the greatest commandment. As discussed above, the first four commandments of the Decalogue focus quite pointedly on worship. Yet, Christ summarizes these commands with the positive restatement of the greatest command: love the Lord (Deut 6:5). Christ's answer demonstrated that the essence of true, pure worship is to love the Lord. And, as He further teaches, to love the Lord within the context of relational integrity is reflected in the last commandments which He summarized with the command to love your neighbor as yourself (Mark 12:28-33; Luke 10:27-28).

The transfiguration revealed several concepts illustrated in other Old and New Testament passages. Peter, James, and John would soon see Jesus' human weakness, submission, even humiliation in the upcoming crucifixion. This event allowed them to see Him in His transcendent divinity. I believe we are reminded here, as surely the disciples were, that Christ is fully God and must be seen in the fullness of His person. We too must worship Christ always appreciating and picturing Him accurately in His fullness.

In the transfiguration Christ initiated worship by revealing Himself (Matt 17:2; Mark 9:2-3; Luke 9:29-32). Second, those who observed this miraculous glimpse into His kingdom responded by bowing in fear (Matt 17:6; Mark 9:6; Luke 9:34). Third, the humble worshipers were "touched" by God (the response of Divine Trinity to all those who humble themselves in His sight (Isa 6:5-7; Rev 1:17-18 and others), and fourth, these worshipers were directed to specific service (Matt 17:7-9; Mark 9:9-10; Luke 9:35-36). Transdispensational worship components we have studied together in the OT abound in this passage and will be seen again in Revelation.

I also want to remind you that although the disciples had an amazing experience here in the mountain, it was not the "normal" experience of life for them. Though they desired to set up tabernacles and live continually in this extraordinary worship environment, Christ had other tasks for them to do. In the Scriptures, such Isaiah-like experiences were most often once in a lifetime. Peter in his epistle recounts this event and says that although he was privileged to be an eyewitness of the majesty of God, even hearing the audible voice of God in this amazing worship event, he had "a more sure word of prophecy" in the written Scriptures (2 Peter 1:19). The events and emotions of a single worship experience must always remain subordinate to the excellence of the Word. The Word must remain supreme.

In Christ's last words to His disciples before His ascension, He gave what many have called the "great commission" (to make disciples, Matt 28:19-20). This commissioning to further service was given in the context of the "great command." Notice the preceding context: "And when they saw him, they worshipped him" (Matt 28:17). Christ gave the command to reach the nations within the context of worshiping disciples (Matt 28:17-20; Luke 24:52). Similarly, Isaiah, Ezekiel, and other OT servants were also "commissioned" within the context of worship (Isa 6:1-8; Ezekiel 1:28-2:3).

John 4:20-24 The Woman at the Well
Exegetical Considerations

One of the most frequently quoted texts regarding worship is Christ's exchange with the unnamed Samaritan woman described in this passage. In this narrative the object of true worship and the essential ingredients of true worship are clearly delineated. In the beginning of the dialog we see the woman's focus: the place of worship. Christ redirected her focused to the Person of worship (John 4:20-22). Christ wanted her to understand that true worship was about having a relationship with the Father through the person of the Messiah, as revealed through the Jewish Scriptures (John 4:22), not the place or religious activity of a certain people group. Donald Guthrie gives this insight:

> Although neither Jerusalem nor Mt. Gerizim were relevant in this matter, the Jews were nevertheless superior in their understanding of God. Since the Samaritans were restricted to the Pentateuch, they lacked the theological richness of the revelation of God in the rest of the OT. When Jesus says *salvation is from the Jews* (22) he is not saying all Jews will be saved, but that through the Jews came the knowledge of that salvation in the Scriptures.[13]

Edwin Blum concurs and adds:

> "Salvation is from the Jews" in the sense that it is available through Jesus, who was born of the seed of Abraham.[14]

In this passage Christ also made it clear that God was not seeking worship per se, for all of creation and the multitude of holy angels already worship the Trinity. What God is actively seeking is worshipers: people with whom He can have a relationship of worship (John 4:23-24). The woman wanted to talk about worship activities and places; Christ wanted to talk about the Person of worship: "the Father."

This passage also outlines that true worship *must* be characterized by two essential elements: spirit and truth (John 4:24). D. A. Carson believes this verse is primarily reinforcing the need to be Christ-centered in worship. He says "to worship God 'in spirit and in truth' is first and foremost a way of saying that we must worship God by means of Christ."[15] Jesus personifies spirit and truth, and because He is One with the Father He is the rightful recipient of all worship. I also believe that this statement addresses the need for worship to be characterized and refined by spirit and truth. This is nothing new, as we have seen. Truth and spirit are characteristics of godly worship that are both complementary and balancing. Jesus showed once again His ability to succinctly communicate the essence of truth on any topic. Hughes says:

> The term "spirit" refers to the sphere of worship. True worship happens when a believer's spirit is connected with God's Spirit, not when a believer is in any particular physical place like Jerusalem or Samaria. God's Spirit is everywhere, therefore worship can happen anywhere. The term "truth" implies that the human worshiper is open and conforming to God's revealed ways of worship and life, specifically Jesus' call to repentance and honest, spiritual worship.[16]

Principles to Apply

- The object of worship is of primary importance.
- Worship must be centered on a relationship with God who is seeking worshipers.
- Worship must be characterized by spirit and truth.

Applications

The place of worship and the traditions of different worship groups were addressed by Jesus in this passage. Jesus corrected the misconception that worship should be focused on a place or the practice of a particular group. Instead, Christ insisted that worship must be based on a relationship with God as revealed in the Hebrew Scriptures. He said, "Ye worship, ye know not what: we know what we worship: for salvation is of the Jews" (John 4:22). I believe this statement also combats the post-modern idea that worship concepts and practices can be legitimatized simply because a group of people agree that they are permitted. Jesus pointed instead to the objective truth that salvation would come through the Jews and was regulated by God's Special Revelation. Worship should be centered in the truths of the revealed Word. It is not enough to accept any and all worship practices with a trite "well, that's just their culture, that's how they worship." Christ calls every "group" to obey the Word revealed through the Jewish authors of the Scriptures. Just as profound is the realization that Messiah *has* come though the Jewish race as He promised, and all worship is by, through, and for Him.

John 4:22 also reminds us that God has always desired a relationship with mankind that was characterized by worship. God is seeking worshipers, not simply worship. My heart breaks when I see those who seem to be caught in the deadness or emptiness of worship practices and do not understand that worship is about a relationship with the God of the universe and cannot be defined as simply a list of activities. Worship is about a relationship with God that is reflected in actions of adoration and service; it can never be defined merely as a list of rules or specific liturgy.

Next I believe we must see again the truth that worship is deeply and sincerely spiritual while being clearly truth-centered. If we worship without a sincere inner spirit, we have missed the mark. We just a surely miss the mark if we show great passion in our worship only to drift into empty sentimentality because it is not filled with substantive truth. God wants it all: spirit and truth.

Christ Accepted Worship

Probably no greater evidence of Christ's equality with the Father is revealed than by the fact that Christ without reservation accepted the worship due only to the Godhead. While Christ accepted people's worship, He also clearly taught that God was a jealous God and that He alone must be worshiped as Master, confirming His own deity, "Ye cannot serve God and mammon" (Matt 6:24; 10:37-38; Luke 16:13). As Christ revealed Himself and manifested His divine Godhead before the world, many responded in humble worship. In the synoptics we see Christ accepting the worship of a leper (Matt 8:2-3), a ruler (Matt 9:18), the disciples (Matt 14:33; Mark 4:41), the Gentile woman (Matt 15:22-28), an unnamed man (Matt 17:14), the disciples after His resurrection (Matt 28:9), the crowd (Mark 2:12), a demoniac (Mark 3:11) and many others (Matt 5:6, 20, 22, 33, 42; 6:51; 7:25, 37; Mark 10:17, 26, 32; Luke 5:8-11, 12, 25-26; 7:16; 8:25, 28, 41, 47; 9:43; 17:15-19). Christ accepted and eternally commended the costly worship of Mary

(Matt 26:7-13; cf. Mark 14:3-9; Luke 7:37-38; John 12:3-9). This concept of costly worship being accepted by Christ was also evident in Christ's commendation of the sacrificial worship of the unnamed widow and her offering of two mites (Mark 12:41-44; Luke 21:1-4).

Finally, Christ Himself promised that He would come again, manifesting His "power and great glory" and receive men's worship at His return (Matt 24:30; 25:31; Luke 21:27). It will be then that Christ will accept the eternal worship of His entire creation.

Matt 14:33; Mark 6:51; John 6:19 Jesus Walking on the Water
Exegetical Considerations

Because of the brevity of the text I would like to discuss, I will give you all three synoptic accounts in the AV.

Then they that were in the ship came and worshipped him, saying, Of a truth thou art the Son of God. (Matt 14:33)

And He went up unto them in to the ship; and the wind ceased: and they were sore amazed in themselves beyond measure, and wondered. (Mark 6:51)

So when they had rowed about five and twenty or thirty furlongs, they see Jesus walking on the sea, and drawing nigh unto the ship: and they were afraid. (John 6:19)

The variety of verbs used to describe the reaction of the disciples to Christ's miraculous display of His power enlightens our understanding of New Testament worship. First, Matthew uses προσεκύνησαν (*prosekunesan*), a common verb for worship meaning to bow or kiss before. Remember that in the context of Judaism, they would have understood this verb with the same broadness as they did the term for bowing in the Old Testament. *Proskeneo* is how the LXX almost exclusively translates הִשְׁתַּחֲוָה (*shachah*).[17] Both words represented a physical action (bowing toward or bowing to kiss) and a heart response of humility and submission. The words came to represent either the action or the attitude. Keener further explains:

> The term *worship* was applied to homage offered to pagan kings as well as that offered to deities. Although it could indicate prostration as a sign of respect (e.g., 1 Sam 24:8; 25:23), it is an unusual term to express Jewish disciples' amazement at a human teacher, even in miracle stories. Ancient miracle stories (including many in the Gospels) often concluded with the observers' awe and praise.[18]

It is logical that the disciples should react to this particular miracle with worship, repeating the same pattern we have seen in the Old Testament. Having seen Christ's power and authority clearly evidenced, they responded. The other gospel writers use words that help further describe this response. Mark, for instance, uses a unique phrase referred to in these word studies:

> **They** were **sore amazed in themselves** (λιαν ἐν ἑαυτοις ἐξισταντο [*lian en heautois existanto*]). Only in Mark. Imperfect tense picturing vividly the excited disciples.[19]

> **Sore** amazed (λίαν ἐκ περισσοῦ ἐξίσταντο). Lit. *exceedingly beyond measure*. A strong expression peculiar to Mark. ἐξίσταντο, *were amazed.*[20]

The word group to which ἐξίσταντο (*existanto*) belongs is used several times by the synoptic gospel writers. It is often used to describe the reaction of those who had seen Christ perform a miracle. "He healed him, insomuch that the blind and dumb both spake and saw. And all the people **were amazed**" (Matt 12:22-23); "he arose, took up the bed, and went forth before them all; insomuch that they were all **amazed**, and glorified God" (Mark 2:12); "and straightway the damsel arose, and walked; for she was of the age of twelve years. And they were **astonished with a great astonishment**" (Mark 5:24). (See also Luke 2:47; 8:56, and 24:22;

and how Luke uses the term as people responded to miracles in Acts 2:7, 12; 8:9, 11, 13; 9:21; 10:45 and 12:16).

In John 6:19, John describes the response of the disciples as one of fear (ἐφοβήθησαν, *ephobethesan*). Since we have already discussed "fear" extensively, I will refer you to a helpful article in TDNT (*Theological Dictionary of the New Testament*) in the endnotes.[21]

Principles to Apply

- Christ builds upon the concepts and commands of the Old Testaments when defining worship for believers.
- Fear, amazement, astonishment, and awe are all words that help describe the godly response of worshipers to Christ and His ministry.

Applications

The Word reveals a wonderfully balancing view of worship involving both attitude and action. Still, there seems to be an either/or battle raging among some of my friends. Worship should involve both attitudes of reverent awe and amazement, and actions of sacrificial service. One should not substitute for the other in any relationship, certainly not in our relationship with our All in All. I join you, however, in opposing the extremes of sappy religiosity unconnected from a life of service, or heartless, slavish service devoid of times of amazing and astonishing pleasure in the presence of the Savior. It is tempting to be drawn to only those Bible passages that fit our comfort zone without letting the balance of the Word wash over us. Never let your propensities toward one blind you of your need for both.

We need not drum up emotions in an effort to get people into a "worshipful mood." We need a clear vision of God and the work of Christ, and then we need to stay amazed at what we see. How distressing that we can think on Christ and be bored. How can I think for a moment that I need anything more than a good look at my Savior for worship to be "enjoyable." The tragedy of Malachi's time was that because worship form didn't change radically enough for the people, worship became "a weariness." Don't let this world, so entertainment-crazed, so over-stimulated, bring us to the point that we are no longer amazed at the all-sufficient work of Christ. It is wonderful to be creative, clear, and fresh in presenting the truths of God in Christ, but we must fight the tendency in all our hearts to simply introduce the new and novel to "spice up" what we should never grow bored of—the truth.

If we are sufficiently convinced that entertainment is not the goal, what should our attitude be? Did Christ take away the need for godly fear? Although He certainly did take away the need to fear men and the utter terror that awaits the unredeemed, He replaced it with a reverent confidence in His finished work on the cross. There is still room today for the fear of the Lord. Consider these verses from the Epistles:

> Wherefore we receiving a kingdom which cannot be moved, let us have grace, whereby we may serve God acceptably with reverence and godly fear: For our God is a consuming fire (Heb 12:28-29).

> Thou wilt say then, The branches were broken off, that I might be graffed in. Well; because of unbelief they were broken off, and thou standest by faith. Be not highminded, but fear (Rom 11:19-20).

> Wherefore, my beloved, as ye have always obeyed, not as in my presence only, but now much more in my absence, work out your own salvation with fear and trembling. (Phil 2:12).

When Paul was explaining what moved him, he mentioned two motivators within a couple of verses of each other. He said, "Knowing therefore the terror of the Lord, we persuade men" (2 Cor 5:11) and "For the love of Christ constraineth us" (2 Cor 5:14). The New Testament does not introduce us to another god nor does it say we may stop having a godly fear of the Lord. Instead, the NT encourages us to have confidence as we approach God's throne, accepting the forgiveness we have in Christ while acknowledging the transcendence of our Father God. Conformityto the completeness of the Godhead is our goal: growing into the fullness of the stature of Christ.

All moral flaws ultimately come from a flawed view of God. We must commit to "looking unto Jesus," to staying amazed and living full of wonder at His matchless beauty. Only then will we have the joy of being gradually changed into His glory. Only seeing the Lord in His fullness as we worship, only in making musical choices focused on the goal of a balanced presentation of the Godhead can we hope to see this miraculous work accomplished.

Chapter Twelve
Worship in the Early Church

Acts is a wonderful book to interact with when considering the purposes and practices of the NT church. Not only do we find in Acts transitional information between the Testaments for the nation of Israel, but we also find how OT worship concepts and practices informed Gentile believers. Much can be learned.

1. Acts 2:11 Content of the message of Pentecost was the "wonderful works of God"
2. Acts 2:41-47 Elements of the Apostles' worship ministry included doctrine, fellowship, the Lord's supper, baptism, prayer, and continual public praise
3. Acts 3:8-10 Lame man leapt and praised God for all to see
4. Acts 3:13 God glorified His Son Jesus
5. Acts 4:21-33 Worship in the early church included lifting up in one accord Christianized psalms, speaking the word, fellowship, witnessing to the resurrection
6. Acts 5:11 Fear came on the church after the judgment of Ananias and Sapphira.
7. Acts 7:32-33, 40-44 Reference to Moses' worship and false worship in Israel's history
8. Acts 7:48-49 The description of the eternal temple as the dwelling place of God
9. Acts 8:27 Ethiopian given more revelation in the context of his worship
10. Acts 9:4-6, 31 Paul's salvation and Isaiah experience
11. Acts 10:25-26 Peter refused the worship of Cornelius
12. Acts 10:46 Gentiles magnified God as evidence of the Holy Spirit
13. Acts 11:18 Glorified God for the salvation of the Gentiles
14. Acts 12:23 God judged Herod because he did not give God the glory

15. Acts 13:2 Barnabas and Saul were commissioned in the context of worship (λειτουργέω leitourgeo, used in the LXX for cultus of the OT priests and Levites)
16. Acts 13:26 True followers of God referred to as those who "fear God"
17. Acts 13:48 Believing Gentiles glorified the Word of the Lord
18. Acts 14:11-18 Paul and Barnabas put down the false worship of the residents of Lystra
19. Acts 15:20, 29 Gentile believers called to distance themselves from idol worship
20. Acts 16:14 More revelation given to Lydia as she worshiped God
21. Acts 16:25-29 Paul and Silas sang and praised in prison, jailor responded in worship
22. Acts 17:16, 23-29 Athenian false worship and the Mars' hill worship sermon
23. Acts 18:7 Justus worshiped God
24. Acts 18:13 Paul accused of worship contrary to the law
25. Acts 19:17 Fear fell on the Ephesians when demonic fell on Sceva.
26. Acts 19:24-27, 35 Worship of Diana threatened
27. Acts 21:20 Church glorified God when they heard of Gentile salvation
28. Acts 21:25 Gentiles warned to keep separated from things offered to idols
29. Acts 21:26-28 Paul participated in ceremonial temple purification and was accused of polluting the temple
30. Acts 24:11, 14-15 Paul defended his worship of Christ before Felix
31. Acts 27:23 Paul testified of his worship (λατρεύω latreuo) of God

Just as Christ interacted with Temple and Synagogue worship, the Apostles in the early church also interacted with the worship concepts and practices we read in the OT. Jesus taught on worship to the woman at the well by telling her that "salvation is of the Jews" (John 4:22). So, in the early church the influence and heritage of the OT, seen in the Temple and Synagogue, are evident in the teachings of the Apostles. Although the need for sin sacrifices had been rendered completely unnecessary after the sacrifice of the Perfect Lamb, Christ, the church continued "daily with one accord in the temple" (Acts 2:46) involving themselves in the prayer and teaching times. Consider the testimony of Peter and John as they went to the Temple "at the hour of prayer" (Acts 3:1). Just as Christ's regular practice was attendance and participation in the Synagogue (Mark 1:21-28; 3:1-6; 6:2ff; Matt 6:23; Luke 4:15-31ff; 6:6; 13:10; John 6:59; 18:20), so Paul and others regularly visited the Synagogue on their missionary journeys (Acts 9:20–25; 13:5, 14, 46; 14:1; 17:1–2, 10; 18:4, 19; 19:8).

There is much that can be learned from a study of Synagogue worship that we don't have time to investigate. As a basic starting point, you might refer back to Ezra and Nehemiah where the practice of praise, prayer, and Bible instruction served as a template for the Synagogue of the Apostles' time. Ralph Martin's book, *Worship in the Early Church* (Eerdman, 1964), and Phillip Schaff's book *History of the Christian Church* (Logos reproduction, 1997) are among many helpful resources in this area.

Because of the influence of the music of the Synagogue, specifically Psalm singing, music was an important part of early church practice. Walter Elwell points out how pervasive that influence was in the early church in the *Tyndale Bible Dictionary:*

> By the time of Christ, the synagogue had become the chief place of worship for the Jewish people. It began as a place for study of the law but gradually became the center of worship for Jews unable to attend the temple. The liturgical service of the temple could not be duplicated in the synagogue as there was no sacrificial rite, and the music could not be exactly reproduced as there were no trained Levitical singers. Scholars do not agree about the amount of continuity between the music of the temple and the music of the synagogue, but there is evidence that certain musical practices did remain constant between the two places of worship.
>
> Information on the customs and rituals of the synagogue come from Talmudic writings. The musical elements of worship in the synagogue were the chanting of Scripture,

psalmody, and spiritual songs. The choral singing of the temple was replaced by a single cantor. The cantor was a layman who, according to tradition, had to have the following qualifications: "He had to be well educated, gifted with a sweet voice, of humble personality, recognized by the community, conversant with Scripture and all the prayers; he must not be a rich man, for his prayers should come from his heart." His most important job was the cantillation of the Law and the Prophets. A series of accents and punctuations, forerunners of actual musical notation, were indications for the cantor in the musical interpretation of the Scripture.

Psalm singing was gradually transplanted from the temple to the synagogue, which in turn influenced the early Christian church.[1]

Allow me to highlight the importance of music in the entry above. Guard yourself from ignorantly believing that music was not an important part of the ministry of the Word in this time period. Now let's look at some specific passages.

Acts 4:21-33 Worship in the Early Church
Exegetical Considerations

First I believe it would be helpful to understand the elements included in the worship of the early church we see mentioned in this passage. Later, we will deal with the way in which these elements may have been exercised.

I remind you that the word for "saying" (λέγω, *lego*) is used in the NT to convey the general idea of proclamation. In Revelation 5:9 we read how they "sang a new song saying" (καὶ ᾄδουσιν ᾠδὴν καινὴν λέγοντες·). The language allows for more than just "speaking." Believers "said" something to the Lord in prayer when they sang. Adhering to a normal hermeneutic, it is my opinion that the text we read in Acts 4 was likely sung by this group for two main reasons.

First, the inclusion of the phrase "in one accord" (ὁμοθυμαδόν, *homothymadon*) combined with the phrase "lifted up their voice" (ἦραν φωνὴν, *airo phone*) seem most naturally and best understood as singing together. I don't think that they lifted up their voice in unison in some "spiritual" sense. It would seem very natural that they sang this together. In fact, I cannot imagine how they could have literally voiced this together without singing.

Second, this united and audible text is clearly an edited version of Psalm 146:6 and Psalm 2, and these Psalms were sung throughout Israel's history. Richard N. Longenecker introduces this section and describes it as "a spontaneous outburst of praise, psalmody, and petition."[2]

Archibald Robinson, in his commentary suggests "'By the mouth of our father David' (του πατρος ἡμων δια πνευματος ἁγιου στοματος Δαυειδ) from Psa. 2:1 f. [is] here ascribed to David. Baumgarten suggests that the whole company sang the second Psalm and then Peter applied it to this emergency."[3]

John Polhill's comments below could also be taken to mean speaking or singing. His comments on this passage could apply to the common practice of singing by the liturgical leader. What he describes as the liturgical practice of "praying a phrase," music historians refer to as "lining out" a song as liturgical leaders *sang* each phrase which was then repeated. He asserts:

> Together they lifted their voices in praise to God. That they offered an occasional prayer of this nature in unison is unlikely. Luke was simply expressing that the whole community joined together in this prayer. (Marshall (*Acts*, 103) suggests they may have followed the Jewish liturgical procedure of using a leader who prayed a phrase at a time, with the others repeating phrase by phrase.) God was addressed as "Sovereign Lord," a common designation for God in the Old Testament and appropriate to this gathering of Jewish Christians....The Scripture is in the exact Septuagintal rendering of Ps 2:1–2 and is presented as a prophecy, spoken by God through David under the inspiration of the Holy Spirit. Most likely originally relating to God's triumph over Israel's enemies through the anointed king, the Christians came to see it as in a real sense prophetic of Christ. All the details of these first verses of the

psalm were applicable to the passion of Christ, and the Christians did so in their prayer (v. 27). The raging nations represented the Gentile rulers and their cohorts, the soldiers who executed Jesus. The people of Israel were those who plotted in vain. Herod represented the "kings of the earth"; Pilate, the "rulers"; and Christ, the "anointed" of God.[4]

When referring to the musical nature of this passage, Loerdes Montgomery suggests:

> In music as well as other aspects of their developing liturgy, early Christians closely modeled their services on synagogue practice, and the early church adopted many ritual elements from the synagogue. It is thought that many of the prayers used in the first three centuries of Christian worship were taken directly from or adapted from prayers used in the synagogue. One thing that we know about the use of psalmody in synagogues in the early Christian centuries is that psalms were often sung in alternation between a soloist and the congregation. As this practice was used later in Christian worship, it came to be known as *responsorial* psalmody. Though this was possibly the most common method of delivery, there were other ways of singing the psalms in Jewish liturgy. In one type, which we call *antiphonal* psalmody, alternate verses were sung in turn by two choruses.[5]

I believe it is also important to note that singing here illustrated ways in which worship concepts, and even the specific worship practice of Psalm singing, demonstrated continuity and discontinuity with OT worship. This song was built on the common concepts of the Psalms and infused with NT concepts. The form of the Psalms was used with a new text. As the believers met to pray, comfort, and instruct one another, they did so with the corporate affirmation of truths through music. This was a continuation of teaching through singing among the people of God that would be further developed for the church age in the epistles. The pattern for music in the NT was in this case, the Psalms—the very Word of God.

Notice as well that Acts 4:31 ("when they had prayed") described this event as a prayer. "Lord, thou art God, which hast..." (Acts 4:24b). As before, songs addressed to God are clearly seen as prayers and not separate events. For that reason singing was not so much an element of worship as a vehicle for an element of worship. In much the same way speaking is not an element of worship but a vehicle for elements of worship. Believers said something to the Lord by singing it to Him.

Notice as well the order of events in this passage. They saw the mighty working of God work on their behalf (Acts 4:23), they lifted up their voice to God in one accord as they lifted up Psalms (Acts 4:24-30), they were "all filled with the Holy Spirit" (Acts 4:31a), and they went forth boldly proclaiming the greatness of God (Acts 4:31b).

Principles to Apply

- Unity among believers can manifest itself in proclaiming truth through music.
- Sacred music compositions should find their template in the songs of Scripture.
- The normal pattern for worship is seeing the acts and attributes of God, offering up praise and adoration for those actions among the people of God, evidencing the presence of the Holy Spirit, and boldly proclaiming the gospel.

Applications

I have spent some time making the point and quoting some substantive scholars to reinforce the idea that the early church, like believers from other dispensations, readily incorporated music into their public worship. Believers have always sung the truths of God in a corporate setting. It is also clear that the content of the song was substantive; you might even say the text was a bit challenging. Although we should sing simple songs of affirmation, we should balance them with substantive songs that require thought as we see modeled in the Word.

If you object to the idea that we should say substantive truth through music in our gatherings the burden of proof really rests on you. History, specifically Biblical history, word usage, and the application of a natural hermeneutic all argue for the probability that these substantive truths were sung together in the early church.

Allow me to ask you to think again about where your template for music comes from. The early church looked to the Psalms and songs they read in the Word for their template. Although it is wise to understand the musical and textual vocabulary of our place and time, we must be driven primarily by the Scriptures for our pattern. The song pattern we read in Acts was built on God's inspired Word. We should do the same. In fact, I would say some of what is labeled "traditional" music, music of the last hundred years or so, is woefully lacking when compared to biblical song texts. If we are honest we must confess that much of our music is patterned after things far inferior to the Scriptures. Compare your song texts with the Word, making the Word your standard. We should not be satisfied with being "slightly better than" what others may be doing.

We also see in this passage that proclaiming truth through music was both a natural response to the working of God on their behalf and a way of affirming the truths of the gospel in a memorable way. Music infused the truth with emotional passion. Gathering together to sing the truths of God has been the practice of believers since the beginning. To see it here again in Acts is no surprise. We too can build unity and express it as we sing the truths of God among His people. The fact that music today has become a tool of disunity is sad indeed. Worship music should be a tool for building unity around the truths of God, not the divisive, self-focused thing it has often become. In this narrative, believers demonstrated again that seeing God, singing praises to the Lord, being filled with the Spirit and going out in the power of the Spirit to proclaim the truth was the natural and normal sequence of activities in worship.

Acts 16:25 Paul and Silas Sang and Praised in Prison
Exegetical Considerations

I have selected this passage because it illustrates once again the vertical and horizontal elements of music and worship. God, worshiping believers, and unredeemed people all surrounded this impromptu worship "service." Take note of how believers were singing *to* God in prayer *among* the unredeemed. In fact, *Word Studies in the New Testament* renders the text (προσευχόμενοι ὕμνουν) literally "*praying, they sang hymns*. The praying and the praise are not described as distinct acts. Their singing of hymns was their prayer, probably from the Psalms."[6] Once again in this passage singing and praying were not separate elements. Singing was a vehicle for prayer.

Paul and Silas chose to sing to God while others listened and while they were in the midst of pain and degradation. This in itself was no doubt a powerful testimony. Although it would be a stretch to directly connect the actions of the jailor and the other prisoners with their singing alone, (there was the matter of the earthquake), I think we can say as a minimum that their singing added credibility to their gospel testimony. "Then he *(the jailor)* called for a light, and sprang in, and came trembling, and fell down before Paul and Silas, and brought them out, and said, Sirs, what must I do to be saved?" (Acts 16:29-30). The faith of Paul and Silas, so clearly seen in their positive praise of God, became an amazing testimony to those who heard them. A.T. Robertson suggests these grammatical insights:

> **About midnight** (κατα δε μεσονυκτιον [*kata de mesonuktion*]). Middle of the night, old adjective seen already in Mark 13:35; Luke 11:5 which see. **Were praying and singing** (προσευχομενοι ὑμνουν [*proseuchomenoi humnoun*]). Present middle participle and imperfect active indicative: Praying they were singing (simultaneously, blending together petition and praise). ὑμνεω [*Humneo*] is an old verb from ὑμνος [*humnos*] (cf. Isa. 12:4; Dan. 3:23). Paul and Silas probably used portions of the Psalms (cf. Luke 1:39, 67f.; 2:28f.) with occasional original outbursts of praise. **Were listening to them** (ἐπηκροωντο αὐτων [*epekroonto autōn*]). Imperfect middle of ἐπακροαομαι [*epakroaomai*]. Rare verb to listen with pleasure as to a recitation or music.[7]

Singing their prayers, Paul and Silas lived their relationship with God before others as they sang and spoke to the Lord. As a wonderful byproduct to their praise, the other prisoners listened, even perhaps, intently.

Paul and Silas were directing their singing primarily to God, though it is clearly evident that others heard them as they sang their prayers. As they sang "...the prisoners heard them" (Acts 16:25b). I am reminded of the sequence we read in Psalm 40:3, "And he hath put a new song in my mouth, even praise unto our God: many shall see it, and fear, and shall trust in the LORD." Paul and Silas were not driven in their prayer of praise to impress the lost around them; their sung prayer was a sincere expression of their heart to God, not to men.

Principles to Apply

- Singing and prayer should be openly practiced before the unredeemed.
- As believers worship the Lord openly, their worship will certainly impact others.

Applications

Our praise should be public. Over and over in the Psalms believers are commanded to sing to the Lord before the heathen. "I will sing praises unto thee among the nations" (Ps 108:3b). "Therefore will I give thanks unto thee, O LORD, among the heathen, and sing praises unto thy name" (Psalm 18:49 and many others). Now in Acts, we see again the power of public praise for the testimony of Christ. Yet, openly praying and praising is something rare today. To be honest, this is something that is difficult for any of us to do. What would people think? But before we excuse ourselves from this practice commanded in the OT and practiced in the NT, I would call you (and challenge myself again) to remember that if we want to be truly Word based, then we must swallow hard and ask God for the grace to be publically worshiping believers. These dear brothers were. If they sang their prayers (or sang and prayed) in the midst of their pain, during public degradation, and among people who were, after all, the criminal element of their day, then we too should commit to being public in our praise and prayer. This world is dying to meet a believer who has the joy of the Lord in their life and is not afraid to let it out! God help us to open our eye and take a good look at the hand of God in our lives, to see Him so clearly that praise and prayer is not stopped by pain or injustice, but rather becomes a song of praise that is not silenced by what others might think about us.

To provide some balance regarding our public prayer and praise, and since we are here in the application section, I would also ask you to think again about the difference between singing (or praying and praising) for the pleasure or approval of the "human audience" and singing primarily for the pleasure and approval of God. In Matthew 6:5 Jesus told his audience, "When thou prayest, thou shalt not be as the hypocrites are: for they love to pray standing in the synagogues and in the corners of the streets, that they may be seen of men. Verily I say unto you, they have their reward." Worship done for the commendation of men is empty indeed. Worship done "out loud" for God's ears has a tremendous impact on those who observe us. I am not saying that somewhere in our decision-making process our human audience is not to be considered (Paul addresses this in 1 Corinthians 14), but that our primary audience is the Lord and not men.

Acts 17:23-25 Paul's Mars' Hill Sermon Addressing Worship in Athens
Exegetical Considerations

I want you to see first in this passage that it was the Athenians' false worship that arrested Paul's attention. "His spirit was stirred in him, when he saw the city wholly given to idolatry. Therefore disputed he..." (Acts 17:16b-17a). In fact, the grammatical structure gives the sense that it was precisely the sight of this false worship that motivated Paul to "discourse" (διαλέγομαι, *dialegomai*, from which we get our word dialog). Paul dialoged not only in the synagogue, and with other religious people, but also in the market place and eventually with the philosophers of Athens.

This worship conversation happened with two distinct groups of people, the Epicureans and the Stoics. Vastly different from each other, the Epicureans taught that the purpose of life could be achieved simply by pursuing with abandon all the pleasures life could possibly provide. The Stoics on the other hand believed that fulfillment was achieved by enduring life with its pain and suffering without complaint and accepting whatever "fate" brought along. Neither school believed in the monotheistic God of Israel. The Athenians took great pleasure in hearing new things (Acts 17:21) and filled their city with tens of thousands of gods and god-like images. It is this interest of the Athenians in worship that Paul used as a platform to confront their idolatry. Paul said "I perceive that in all things you are too superstitious" (very religious, NASB) (Acts 17:22).

Paul recognized that there was no lack of worship activity among these people and that their pluralism included the worship a Divine Creator God. It was this God whom the Athenians ignorantly worshiped. Remember that Christ also acknowledged the worship of the unnamed woman at the well and likewise concluded that she actively worshiped, but in ignorance; "ye worship, ye know not what" (John 4:22).

Paul addressed their ignorant false worship by presenting three central truths. (1) The great sufficiency of God as Creator and Provider (Acts 17:24-25). Because of this God is not in need of whatever "service" (θεραπεύεται, *therapenetai*) man may bring Him. (2) As Creator of all mankind He is Lord of all and not a distant deity (Acts 17:25-28). (3) Because He is Lord, men should not attempt to make an idol for Him but rather repent, accepting Christ ("that Man (Christ) whom He (God) hath ordained" and "hath raised Him from the dead" vs. 31; see Acts 10:42) as Judge and giver of life (Acts 17:29-31). One might summarize the content of Paul's message as a focus on the attributes and then the actions of God in Christ, which should cause false worshipers to repent of their false worship, and worship God in truth by accepting the lordship of Christ and His gift of resurrection.

Principles to Apply

- Looking past the outward manifestations of sin, it is the false worship of people that should move believers to action.
- Believers should confront false worship in the world with the positive teaching of God's attributes and actions in the person of Christ.

Applications

False worship is the fountainhead of all sin. Although Paul doubtless saw the sinful actions of the Athenians all around him, what really grabbed his attention was the fountainhead—the object of men's worship. Paul knew what we often forget; the process of change toward godliness must start with a frank and open addressing of the issue of *who* stands as the object of men's worship. Remember, we become what we worship, and the immorality of Athens could only be addressed after the worship of Athens was corrected. So it is today. We can only address the sinful addictions of our day when we address the worship of our day. Worship really does matter. What is it that breaks your heart when you think about your town? Is it their false worship? What issues bother you in your local church, your ministry, your family, or your own life? Change, permanent change must be based on *first* things: repenting of false worship and worshiping God alone. We too can fixate with disgust on the pleasure-seeking Epicureans or the fatalistic Stoics and miss their true need. Athens was not so different from the place you and I live.

Paul gives a wonderful model for addressing the false worship around us. You will notice he goes to the synagogue, interacts with religious seekers, freely converses in the market place, and addresses the philosophically elite. In each case he addresses their ignorant worship by giving them the truth of the Word more completely. He was not bashful about telling people that they did not worship God with knowledge. Instead, Paul was vigilant to battle error by clearly presenting the truth about the person and work of God in Christ. It is here that evangelism must begin.

Think about the Epicurean culture that we live in today; it easily gives rise to an easy-believism. Our modern day Epicureans want to avoid the unpleasantness of hell and gain the pleasures of heaven. People are eager to escape the punishment that their sin demands, but not so eager to leave the sin Christ came to redeem them *out* of. Further, I find that people may embrace the need to forsake the sin that is destroying their lives, but they are often reluctant to dethrone the idols of their hearts and show their repentance by worshiping the God who created them. "Help me overcome this sin but don't tell me how to worship" they say. I am convinced, however, that we see so much failure in our "evangelism" because we fail to address the fundamental problem: people are false worshipers. They ignorantly worship themselves. Only when they learn to set their affections on the Lord will they ultimately be delivered from the false worship that gives rise to their sin and ultimately their damnation. Only when our relationship with the lost addresses this issue will there be true conversion. Only when we all address our own worship will there be consistent holy living.

The book of Acts introduces several important elements for the worshiping church that are further explained in the rest of the NT. In our next chapter Paul expands upon the practices of the church and lays out for us many important practices and principles.

Chapter Thirteen
Pauline Epistles

Before you read what I pray will be a stimulating chapter, consider writing down ideas for your own New Testament model for worship and music. Especially as you read the passages in Paul's Epistles. It is my prayer that you will let God work in your heart and consider putting on paper what you believe to be a biblical model for worship and music, a model for both your personal life and the life of your church. You might think about organizing your thoughts into three sections.

1) Write down what you think the ideal worship and music program should look like from the Scriptures you are reading. Include both mandates and principles. Even though this model might not (let's be honest, will never) exist in its totality in our broken world, it is important to start with a thoroughly biblical model. Dream big; build a great model. For example, in my perfect model everyone who ministers through music in the church is fully conscious of what they are teaching.

2) Now, as mandates and principles occur to you from the passages in the Epistles that will govern your worship and music choices, write them down in a second section or in combination with the biblical model you are developing. For example, because I want everyone who ministers through music in the church to be fully conscious of what they are teaching, I will not ask people to sing something they don't understand. This governing principle refines and sometimes limits who might be involved in a music leadership role or what I might ask them to sing.

3) Last, start a "scattergram" of ideas for programs or procedures that might help you to be a doer of the Word and not a hearer only. Ask the question, "What can I do that will help me move toward a more biblical model in my worship and music?" For example, I might ask those involved in special music to put in their own words the song they intend to sing in church. Because I want everyone who ministers through music in the church to be

fully conscious of what they are teaching, I will call three weeks ahead of time those who are going to be singing in the public service and discuss with them what they are going to share. Several other ideas or programs should come to mind that will help you accomplish the task of living out your model.

I believe you will have the greatest success "doing theology" in the arena of worship and music by gaining an understanding of the model of scripture and working out from there. This approach requires more honest wrestling than simply answering specific questions, but I believe it is a more holistic way of understanding any topic in the Word.

I am praying God will help you think deeply and biblically about worship and music and that your study of the Word will make you a better leader. Build a biblical model of worship and music, assess your strengths and weaknesses, ask God for wisdom and endeavor to make gradual and edifying progress toward the model. Drink deeply of God's Word, gain biblical wisdom, live real!

1. Rom 1:20-32 Results of false worship
2. Rom 2:22 Robbing the temple is contrasted with idolatry
3. Rom 9:4 Paul used the word "service" (λατρεία, latreia) to refer to the worship cultus of the OT priests
4. Rom 11:3-4 Reference to bowing the knee to Baal
5. Rom 11:33-36 12:1-2 A sacrifice acceptable based on the great mercy of God
6. Rom 14:6 Admonition to give thanks to God in choices regarding dietary considerations
7. Rom 14:11 Promise that all will bow before Christ one day
8. Rom 15:6-11 Music and unity in Christ ("one mind and one mouth") Christ the singer, cf. Psalm 18:49; Gentiles and Jews together praising God
9. Rom 15:16 Paul infused OT cultus language to describe Gentile access
10. Rom 16:17-18 Motives, fruits and techniques of false teachers (including musicians)
11. 1 Cor 1:29-31 God alone is to be glorified
12. 1 Cor 3:16-17 Paul called the church at Corinth the NT temple

13. 1 Cor 5:7 Christ is named as the Passover sacrifice for NT believers
14. 1 Cor 5:10-11, 6:9 Idolatry is named as an evidence of a lost condition
15. 1 Cor 6:19-20 Individual believers are called the NT temple of God, the touch point and revealer of the glory of God
16. 1 Cor 8:1-13 Meat offered to idols
17. 1 Cor 9:13 Temple worship ministries used as an illustration
18. I Cor 10:7 Paul calls NT believers to flee idolatry and learn from the false worship of Israel
19. 1 Cor 10:14-31 Command to flee idolatry, avoid association with idol worship and do all things to lift up Christ
20. 1 Cor 11:4-5 Regulations for public prayer and prophesying
21. 1 Cor 11:27-30 Cautions about worshiping unworthily
22. 1 Cor 12:2 Gentiles were carried away in idolatry
23. 1 Cor 14:7-8,15-16,25-26 Paul on public worship and music
24. 1 Cor 15:25, 27-28 Christ will be worshiped
25. 2 Cor 1:3 Paul blesses God
26. 2 Cor 2:15 Paul uses OT cultus language to refer to NT believers
27. 2 Cor 3:14 Christ is the One who did away with the veil
28. 2 Cor 4:6,15 Man's purpose is the lifting up of God
29. 2 Cor 5:1, 4 Believers referred to as "tabernacles"
30. 2 Cor 6:16-7:1 Believers referred to as the temple of God, called to be separate from idols and be pure
31. 2 Cor 9:11-12, 14 God's great acts inspire Paul's thanksgiving
32. 2 Cor 10:17 Command to glory in the Lord
33. Gal 1:5, 9, 24 Paul greets the church with the command that Christ is to be glorified forever
34. Gal 4:8 Reference to doing service to things that are not truly God
35. Gal 5:20 Command to avoid idolatry
36. Gal 6:14 Paul's personal commitment to glory only in God
37. Eph 1:3 Paul's opening praise
38. Eph 1:6 Salvation is to the praise of the glory of His grace
39. Eph 1:12,14 Believers should, in turn, be to the praise of His glory
40. Eph 1:16 Paul does not cease to give thanks

41. Eph 1:22 All things are under Christ's feet, an allusion to universal worship
42. Eph 2:6-7 Believers are raised to the place of worship in Christ so that they might show forth His glory
43. Eph 2:21-22 Jewish and Gentile believers are joined together as a temple (dwelling place) of God and are the "habitation of God through the Spirit"
44. Eph 3:14 "For this cause" Paul bowed the knee in worship κάμπτω τὰ γόνατά
45. Eph 3:21 Christ is to be glorified in the church.
46. Eph 5:2 Christ is referred to in OT worship cultus terms as the sweet smelling sacrifice
47. Eph 5:4 "...but rather giving of thanks," should characterize the believer
48. Eph 5:5 Covetousness is called idolatry
49. Eph 5:18-21 The Spirit and music
50. Phil 1:11 Fruits of righteousness are to the glory and praise of God
51. Phil 2:9-11 Every knee will bow in worship, every tongue will confess Christ's glory
52. Phil 2:17 Paul uses OT cultus language, "offered," (σπένδω, spendo) to describe his life as a sacrifice or service of worship
53. Phil 3:3 Characteristics of true worship are worshiping in spirit, rejoicing in Jesus, and not trusting in the position of the flesh, Gentiles are now part of the circumcision
54. Phil 4:6 Prayer should be accompanied by thanksgiving
55. Phil 4:8 This text could possibly have been written as a song, as it was later used
56. Phil 4:18 Paul uses OT cultus language to describe the offering of the Philippians
57. Phil 4:20 Benediction
58. Col 1:3, 12 Paul expressed his thanksgiving
59. Col 1:15-20 Song text of worship
60. Col 2:7 Believers admonished to abound in thanksgiving
61. Col 2:16-18, 23 False worship described
62. Col 3:5 Covetousness is described as idolatry
63. Col 3:15-17 The place of the Word and music in teaching and admonishing

64. Col 4:2 Admonition to watch for Christ with thanksgiving
65. 1 Thes 1:9-10 Salvation experience described as turning from idols to the living God
66. 1 Thes 5:16, 18 Rejoicing and thanksgiving commanded
67. 2 Thes 1:3; 2:13 Paul thanked God for the Thessalonians
68. 2 Thes 1:10, 12 Christ will be glorified and admired at His coming, which is His purpose for all people now
69. 2 Thes 2:3-4 The son of perdition is revealed as the one who opposes the worship of God alone and exalts himself
70. 2 Thes 3:1 The Word is to be glorified
71. 1 Tim 1:12 Paul thanked Christ publicly
72. 1 Tim 1:17 Verse of praise
73. 1 Tim 2:1, 8-11; 3:15 Paul's instructions regarding public worship
74. 1 Tim 3:16 Early Christian hymn text
75. 1 Tim 4:3-4 Meats are to be received with thanksgiving
76. 1 Tim 6:15-16 Verses of praise
77. 2 Tim 1:3 Paul publicly thanked God
78. 2 Tim 4:6 Paul used OT cultus worship language σπένδω spendo to describe his sacrificial service
79. 2 Tim 4:18 Ending benediction
80. Philemon 4 Paul publically thanked God

I am very excited about finally arriving at this portion of the book. As I sit to write this chapter, I am again overwhelmed with the opportunity and responsibility to dig deeply into the Word for what God can say to us today. Again I realize this chapter could be a book in itself. God has so many wonderful and challenging truths for us from Paul's pen and much that must be considered to make it real in our lives. First, I want to remind you of some introductory truths.

As obvious as this might seem, I feel compelled to remind you that Paul was a zealous Jew who would have been very much at home with the worship and music practices of Temple and Synagogue and well schooled in all the Hebrew Scriptures. Paul would have known more fully the many millenniums of Israel's worship and music history we have studied together. And, even though he was the special apostle to the Gentiles, he regularly used OT worship terminology assuming and building upon their knowledge of the OT worship cultus. This fact will become important when we consider some of the passages below.

Just as we have seen in some of the OT passages, some passages in the NT, even in the epistle, are also hymn texts. You will remember we explored the interjection of music and the poetic structure in several OT texts. The prophet or "forthteller" would naturally and with some regularity use music in his delivery. Music was often used to recount the most important events and concepts in Israel's history (Ex 15; Deut 31-32), a fact of which Paul would have been well aware. No doubt he too sang Israel's history just as orthodox Jews use musical chant to aid in their memorization of vast portions of Scripture even today. It is no surprise that Paul would also use musical structure in some of his writings and commanded music to be used in the church's teaching and counseling.

Although there is not complete agreement on which portions of Paul's epistles were hymn texts and which were not, recent attention to genre studies have yielded at least some consensus. The TDNT suggests Eph. 5:14; 1 Tim. 3:16; Phil. 2:6–11; Col. 1:15–20 as a start.[1] The *New American Commentary* (Broadman and Holman, 2001) agrees. "Recent studies have addressed the presence of hymns in the New Testament and found them in many places, such as Col 1:15–20 and Phil 2:5–11."[2] Others have expanded these passages. Donald Guthrie, for example, suggests that 1 Timothy 3:14-16 is a hymn.[3] Conservative scholar Roy Zuck says,

> In fact, Ephesians 1:3–14 is one of the longest psalms of the New Testament, and it is a praise psalm in its form. Paul raised this upbeat note, because God has taken and is taking the initiative in forming His new community and providing them with a vast array of spiritual blessings in Christ, blessings whose source is heaven (1:3). Throughout the hymn (as in the doctrinal section of Col. 2:6–3:3), the phrases "in Him," "through Him," or "in Christ" appear, showing that Jesus mediates those blessings. The hymn gives the general praise in Ephesians 1:3 and then mentions three specifics in verses 4–14.[4]

It is hard to discern what sections are indeed hymns and which simply became hymn texts early on in church history. Some scholars have also suggested that 1 Peter 3:18–20, 1:20 and 2:21–24 may also represent hymn fragments.[5] Certainly as the church's worship and music developed, many passages of Scripture were set to music or chanted, the common practice of both Testaments. Now let's turn our attention to some specific passages that address worship and music.

Rom 1:20-32
Exegetical Considerations

In the opening verses of Romans, Paul introduces his letter by discussing how God is revealed in the gospel and creation. In salvation, God shows His "power" (Rom 1:16), His "righteousness" (Rom 1:17), and His "wrath" (Rom 1:18). In creation, God demonstrates His "eternal power" (Rom 1:20), and "Godhead" or divine nature (Rom 1:20). As God reveals Himself He expects men to "glorify" (ἐδοξασαν, *edoxasan,* from which we get our noun doxology) Him and respond with thankfulness (ηὐχαρίστησαν, *eucharistesan,* from which we get our word Eucharist, meaning celebration) (Rom 1:21).

Paul then explains the connection between false worship and wickedness. The moral debauchery Paul lists in Romans 1:29-31 are evidences of the natural outworking of false worship. Notice the cause-effect relationship in the grammar of Romans 1:21-24: "Because that, when they knew God, they glorified Him not as God neither were thankful...God gave them up...." Look later in verse 26 where Paul again makes this connection: "For this cause God gave them up to their vile affection...." Thomas R. Schreiner observed this cause-effect relationship. He says,

> Both the content of verses 18-32 and some structural clues contained therein indicate two major subsections. First, Paul argues that God's wrath is righteously revealed because people suppress the truth about the one true God and turn to idolatry (vv. 18-23). Then in verses 24-32 he specifies the

consequences of idolatry in terms of the moral disintegration of human society.[6]

Not only do we see a cause-effect relationship between false worship and immorality; false worship also causes men to become "vain in their imaginations," have their "foolish heart darkened," and "become fools" (Rom 1:22). All of this occurred because men's worship focused on corruptible man and not the eternal God. Men "worshiped (ἐσεβάσθησαν, *esebasthesan*, used only once here) and served (ἐλάτρευσαν, *elatreusan*, a form of the general term for serve) the creature more than the Creator, who is blessed forever. Amen" (Rom 1:25).

Paul makes it clear that this false worship is built upon a foundation of error about the person and work of God. Men "changed the glory of the uncorruptible God" (Rom 1:23), and later, "changed the truth of God into a lie" (Rom 1:25). It is the inaccurate picturing of God, twisted by men's false worship and driven by men's desire to worship and serve self, which results in man falling into the trap of sin. As God allows man to follow his own desires, sin becomes its own punishment.

Principles to Apply

- God has initiated worship by revealing Himself to man. He then expects his creation to respond by glorifying Him and expressing thankfulness.
- False worshipers are characterized by foolishness, darkness, and moral debauchery. Sin is the natural outworking of false worship.
- The only solution for moral debauchery is true worship of the Creator God.

Applications

How should we begin worship? Worship should start by focusing on the person and work of our Redeemer and Creator God. The way to stimulate godly worship is to accurately and fully reveal the nature of God in the gospel and creation. It is the Christ of the gospel and the person of God revealed in creation Who must be our focus today and will continue to be the theme of our worship in the eternal state. To imagine that the best way to begin worship is to manipulate people musically, or in some other way, to trick them into a certain "mood" is to move away from the model of the Word and rely on the impotent power of the creature. Paul was careful to build his ministry on the clear presentation of truth. He wrote in 1 Corinthians 2:1-5:

> And I, brethren, when I came to you, came not with excellency of speech or of wisdom, declaring unto you the testimony of God. For I determined not to know anything among you, save Jesus Christ, and him crucified. And I was with you in weakness, and in fear, and in much trembling. And my speech and my preaching was not with enticing words of man's wisdom, but in demonstration of the Spirit and of power: That your faith should not stand in the wisdom of men, but in the power of God.

Paul wanted people to see the Lord, clearly and fully. That should be our goal in each of our worship and music choices. Our question should always be, what will help people to understand who God is and what He has done? We must not bow at the altar of human desires. When we do that, when our worship and music planning is driven by what people like, whether conservative or trendy, we are worshiping and serving corruptible man instead of the incorruptible God.

As God is revealed or exposed in our services, it is only natural that we should glorify Him for who He is. As we present a picture of God in our worship and music, we must be careful not to present a caricature of His true Person. Our theology proper, who we know God to be, must be the guardian of our music choices. The best safeguard for appropriate music will be good theology. Most people will read over that last sentence without much thought. But I believe this is the reason that those who make musical choices need to do everything in their power to know and live in light of a clear theology. Does the person or people responsible for balancing the music selections of your ministry have the tools they need to understand the person and work of God? What is their theological training? What is yours?

When considering the details of your music, let me ask you to think about the last six weeks of music and worship choices in your church. How balanced is your view of God and His work in light of your music? Is your theology the ever vigilant guardian of your musical choices? How about the music in your personal life? Are you glorifying God for who He is? Or are you allowing, either by commission or omission, a gradual exchange of the truth for a lie?

Godly worship should be centered on presenting God, glorifying Him for who He is, and then developing an appropriate musical vehicle for giving thanks to Him. On this point I am constantly convicted. We are called upon to be worshiping, praising, thankful believers. If we fail to worship, if we fail to show thankfulness in our lives, we will inevitably fall into the trap of Satan. It may not seem like "such a big deal," but if we fail to worship and be thankful, we will certainly be doomed to moral collapse. Yes, it is true that Jesus said "if these *(people)* should hold their peace, the stones would immediately cry out." It is true that God will be praised with or without us. But if we refuse to be thankful, it will be our loss; it will be our lives that will eventually crumble into corruption. Commit to glorifying God for who He is and embrace the truth of His character by being truly thankful for the God you seek to see and portray more clearly.

Rom 11:33-12:2 Offering Ourselves in Worship
Exegetical Considerations

Most believers are familiar with Paul's appeal for sacrificial worship in Romans 12:1-2. Many have not considered however that this call to sacrifice was made in the context of his own exuberant praise of God in the end of chapter 11.

> O the depth of the riches both of the wisdom and knowledge of God! how unsearchable are his judgments, and his ways past finding out! For who hath known the mind of the

Lord? Or who hath been his counselor? Or who hath first given to him, and it shall be recompensed unto him again? For of him, and through him, and to him, are all things: to whom be glory for ever. Amen. (Rom 11:33-36)

Carson points out that this section is "a hymn of praise to the God whose ways are beyond our understanding and criticism."[7] The call to sacrifice is made in the context of considering God's nature, character, and actions. This beautiful doxology closes the doctrinal half of the book and serves as the foundation upon which the practical life of the believer is now to be built. It would be hard to underestimate the importance of this transitional hymn of praise. It is the believer's motivation for right living, as we will see in the rest of Romans. Paul so eloquently extols God's character and actions that the believer's complete sacrifice of all he might hold dear is deemed only reasonable. The believer's worship is based on God's greatness just as Psalm 29:1-2 states, "Give unto the LORD the glory due unto his name; worship the LORD in the beauty of holiness."

Not only is the sacrificial worship of total surrender the natural response of the believer, Paul also lists several qualifications for our sacrifice. First, the word "present" (παριστημι, *paristemi*) is used with OT worship in mind. Wuest quotes Vincent when he explains, "'It (παριστημι) is the technical term for presenting the Levitical victims and offerings. See Luke 2:22. In the Levitical sacrifices the offerer placed his offerings so as to face the Most Holy Place, thus bringing it before the Lord.'"[8]

Next Paul explains that the temple of the Holy Spirit, the believer's body is a *living* "sacrifice" (θυσία, *thysia*). The Hebrew מִנְחָה (*minha*) is often translated θυσία, (*thysia*, "sacrifice") in the LXX (Amos 5:22 ff.; Hos 6:6; Isa 1:10 ff.; Jer 7:21; 1 Sam. 15:22 and others). Paul uses OT worship language infused with NT meaning to implore the believer to respond to the character of God by offering his body as a sacrifice of worship. Paul uses this term elsewhere to refer to the sacrifices of false worshipers (1 Cor 10:18), to Christ's sacrifice (Eph 5:2), the sacrificial service of believers (Phil 4:18), and to his own sacrificial service (Phil 2:17).

This offering is not just any offering, but an offering that is "holy" (ἅγιος, *hagios*), that which is "set apart for God." Only this holy offering is "acceptable" (εὐάρεστον, *euareston*) to God, well pleasing to Him.

We have discussed the word "service" (λατρεια, *latreia*) before. To the non-Jew, "service" would have meant anything rendered for hire. The Jew, familiar with the LXX, would have seen it used to refer to the OT service of God by the priest or Levite. Wuest suggests,

> Doubtless, in the thinking of Paul, the word was used here to speak of the believer-priest's sacred service, not as the Levitical priests, offering a burnt sacrifice which was apart from themselves, but a living sacrifice which was not only part of themselves but also entailed the giving of themselves in connection with the giving of their bodies to the service of God.[9]

Paul further qualifies this holy sacrifice of the believer by stating that the sacrifice of worship should not conform to the thinking of this present world but be transformed by the work of God (Rom 12:2). Believers are to stop patterning their lives after the culture (forms, mannerisms, styles, speech, music, and habits) of this present age (αἰων, *aion*), but instead, allow themselves to be changed (μεταμορφοομαι, *metamorphoomai*) by the Lord. This same word is used in Matthew 17:2 to describe the transfiguration of Jesus. The action of transformation is performed by God in each believer as he is continually "beholding as in a glass the glory of the Lord, [being] changed into the same image from glory to glory, even as by the Spirit of the Lord" (2 Cor 3:18). Of course, this truth must have important implications on our worship and music choices. As you look further in Romans 12 you will notice that Paul developed the practical importance of relational integrity in light of this sacrificial worship.

Principles for Application

- The call for sacrificial worship is made in the context of the praise of God's mercy and wisdom.
- Sacrifices, even the sacrifice of one's life, must be given to God on His terms.

Applications

Those of us who are in spiritual leadership of any kind as friends, parents, or pastors call on others to change the way they are living or acting. Sometimes we are in the position to call upon others to make tremendous sacrifices. We would do well to learn from the many examples of Scripture illustrated in this specific passage. Paul, under the superintendence of the Holy Spirit makes the appeal to great sacrifice, to holy living, and to transformation in the context of his own praise of God. I have often heard appeals to such sacrifice based on need or guilt instead of the person and work of God. Ultimately, the only sufficient motivation for the kind of sacrifice Paul is calling the Romans to make is the indescribable greatness of God. Remember that verse and chapter breaks, even the punctuation we have, would not have been present in the original letter. Paul's audience would have heard or read the appeal of chapter 12 while the hymn of praise was still ringing in their ears. It certainly makes sense to tie your call for sacrifice to the attributes and actions of our eternal Father. I think our preaching is often powerless because we fail to carefully present and appeal to the excellence of the Godhead in the events leading up to our application of truth.

At the conclusion of Paul's doxology, he begins the practical section of the Epistle by using OT worship language; he calls redeemed believers to act as living sacrifices. I can't help but think back on the sacrifice of Abraham of his beloved son Isaac on the altar. As in the Genesis account, the sacrifice walks away still very much alive. Paul himself talked about "dying daily," yet being a living sacrifice for Christ (Phil 2:17).

Perhaps like no other passage in the NT, believers are confronted with the truth that as important as a single act of worship may be, all of life should be seen as an act of worship. Presenting your body as a living sacrifice makes even clearer the all encompassing nature of our lifestyle of spiritual worship.

Paul's audience would have understood the importance of every offering being "holy, (and) acceptable to God." The believer's sacrifice of himself in holiness, as if he himself were the spotless sacrifice laid on the altar, is a sacrifice acceptable to God. Unquestionably, specific acts of adoration and praise should reflect that same holiness. Make personal holiness your first priority when making any worship decision, especially those made in public worship.

Paul now draws a contrast between sacrifices that are conformed to the world (αἰῶνι, *aioni,* present age) and those that are transformed (μεταμορφοῦσθε, *metamorpsousthe,* completely transformed or transfigured). Paul warns believers to be careful not to allow the thinking process of the pagan world system to influence our ideas; certainly we should not get our ideas about how to worship the Lord from this world's system. Generations of false worshipers have done this as we have seen (consider Jeroboam, 1 Kings 23:26-33). A marketing survey that decides how we worship is repugnant to God. Our minds must be renewed by the Word. We must go to the Scriptures to see the Lord in His fullness and then with great carefulness make worship and worship music selections that wisely and fully communicate the truth of His character. Accuracy is our highest goal. Our music and worship choices must be driven by the desire to see the Lord more clearly and offer to Him the gifts, especially the gift of ourselves, the way He desires. It is only then that our worship will prove to a watching world what is truly acceptable to Him. We will "prove what is that good and acceptable and perfect will of God" (Rom 12:2b). Worshiping on our terms with a bent toward conforming to this world's system, seeking to please ourselves, proves we have slipped off the altar for a more comfortable seat on the throne.

Many challenging and practical passages in Romans have implications for our worship and music. Before we leave Romans, I draw your attention to chapter 15 where Paul calls for unified praise to illustrate the great mystery that both Jews and Gentiles are one in the church. In a figurative sense, it is Christ who is singing *through* both Jews and Gentiles (Rom 15:6-11). Singing is possibly the only activity that could explain *how* the church could "with one mind and one mouth glorify God," (Rom 15:6). Thomas R. Schreiner offers this fuller explanation:

> It is also noteworthy that the word "glorify" (*doxasai*) is explained with parallel terms: "praise" (*exomologesomai*) and "sing" (*psalo*) in verse 9; "rejoice" (*euphranthete*) in verse 10; "praise"(*aineite*) and give praise (*epaine-satosan*) in verse 11. The glorifying of God by the Gentiles occurs in worship, when the name of God is lauded and praised. We note again, then, that the central theme of the book, the honor and praise of God's name, reaches its fulfillment when Jews and Gentiles worship together harmoniously.[10]

What a beautiful picture of our oneness. What a wonderful activity singing can be when it is done with the transformed, renewed minds of yielded believers.

Eph 5:18-21 Music and the Spirit
Exegetical Considerations

Paul opens up the epistle to the Ephesians in verses 1:3-14 with an exaltation of the Godhead given in hymn form. In verses 1:6, 12, 14 Paul uses the term "to the praise of His glory" (εἰς ἔπαινον δόξης, *eis epainon doxes*). Paul's statement makes it clear that the reason for doing anything is to bring glory to the Lord. Later in the epistle he clearly states that the purpose of the church should be the glory of God; "unto Him be glory in the church" (Eph 3:31). In fact, the church united is referred to as "an holy temple in the Lord: In whom ye also are builded together for an habitation of God through the Spirit" (Eph 2:21b-22). As Paul nears the end of the doctrinal section, he gives a personal testimony of what motivates him in ministry and worship. Notice "for this cause" (Eph 3:1) and "for this cause I bow my knees" (Eph 3:14). He then ends the doctrinal section with a doxology.

> Now unto him that is able to do exceeding abundantly above all that we ask or think, according to the power that worketh in us, unto him be glory in the church by Christ Jesus throughout all ages, world without end. Amen. (Eph 3:20-21)

As in Romans, the bridges between the theological and practical sections of the letter are divided by a hymn of praise. Carson in his commentary suggests:

> The doxology formally closes and rounds off the first half of the letter with an invitation to thankful worship, just as it began (1:13–14). It provides a transition between Paul's prayer and teaching section and his consequent direct exhortations (chs. 4–6; cf. Rom. 11:33–36 which has a similar function).[11]

In Ephesians 5 Paul develops the practical importance of building the new man through the Spirit. In 5:18 Paul uses two finite verbs: the prohibition "be not drunk" (μεθύσκεσθε, *methysko*), and the positive command "be filled" (πληρόω, *pleroo*) "with the Spirit" (Eph 5:18). The next adverbial participles referring to music appear as subordinate phrases to these main commands. Whether the participles are to indicate means or results could change particular applications, but undoubtedly there are several significant principles about worship and music ministry in the church that can be demonstrated from these verses. First, it is significant that Paul uses the word "speak" (λαλοῦντες, from the root *laleo*) to refer to the psalms, hymns, and spiritual songs he lists next. Paul uses this same word 61 times in his epistles, including 23 times in 1 Corinthians 14 alone. Whether Paul is talking about singing, prophesying, or other communication, he uses the general word "speak." In our present culture, the musical activities of believers are often considered less important than other "speaking" activities in the public assembly. Paul clearly did not communicate this here in his choice of words. Peter O'Brien in his commentary says flatly, "The apostle is not referring to two separate responses of speaking in songs and singing, but is describing the same activity from different perspectives."[12] Whether "speaking" the "oracles of God" (1

Pet 4:11) verbally or "speaking" the "word of Christ" using "psalms, hymns, and spiritual songs," the Word from God has been powerfully communicated. If you would like to do further research on this, please refer to the longer treatment of this in TDNT by looking up ᾄδω (*ado*) and read there about the interrelationship between "speak" and "sing" explained in detail. In summary, I give you this single quote from the larger entry:

> Between the spoken word and song the distinction is fluid... In the NT we have the phrases: ᾄδειν (τὴν) ᾠδήν (Rev. 5:9; 14:3; 15:3), and also: ᾄδειν τῷ θεῷ (τῷ κυρίῳ) (Col. 3:16; Eph. 5:19). The same idea is also conveyed in Revelation by λέγειν, as in Rev. 5:13: λέγειν φωνῇ μεγάλῃ (cf. also λαλεῖν in Eph. 5:19).[13]

Second, the grammatical structure of the verse includes both the vertical and horizontal elements of worship music ministry. Note that the believer is both speaking to others ("yourselves"), himself ("in your heart"), and to God ("to the Lord") (Eph 5:19). Though the primary audience of worship is the Lord, others are edified or even evangelized when they "overhear" worship addressed to the Lord (see also Acts 16:25; 1 Cor 14:25).

Third, multiple musical text genres are mentioned in the passage. Many scholars suggest that, "In the NT there is still no precise differentiation between ᾠδή, ψαλμός, and ὕμνος, e.g., in Col. 3:16 or Eph. 5:19."[14] Psalms, (ψαλμός, *psalmos*) could refer specifically to the singing of the book of Psalms, but it could also refer to instrumental music or singing accompanied by instruments, since it literally means, "a striking, twanging, or striking the chords of a musical instrument."[15] Hymns (ὑμνοις, *humnois*) were praises to God. Spiritual songs (ᾠδαις πνευματικαις, *oidais pneumatikais*) were a general description of any song of a spiritual nature. Robertson suggests, "The same song can have all three words applied to it....The verb ᾄδω [*aido*] is an old one (Eph. 5:19) for lyrical emotion in a devout soul."[16] I believe Paul used these terms to refer to the totality of worship music. However, it is important not to excuse the church from singing a variety of texts and especially the Scriptures, specifically the Psalms. Paul desired a hymnody that was broad in textual scope. Otherwise, he would have simply used the least specific term (spiritual songs) and not included Psalms and hymns at all. Further, it is the singing of Psalms that is specifically mentioned in 1 Corinthians 14:26 and James 5:13.

Fourth, Paul reinforced the need for heartfelt worship music directed, "in your heart to the Lord." We see in this passage worship and music elements that are intensely personal, community conscious, and vertically focused.

Last, the AV translates later in verse 19 the same root word for psalm in its verb form (ψάλλω, *psallo*), (verb, literally "psalming") as "making melody" to the Lord. This melody making, quite possibly of instrumental music as mentioned above, continued to be a part of the worship music of New Testament believers in both Ephesus and Colosse.

Principles for Application

- Practical living should be motivated by and built upon a clear understanding of God's acts and attributes. Hymns of praise are a fitting bridge between doctrine teaching and practical living.
- Believers are called to "speak" to each other through singing.
- Music is both an outward manifestation of the Spirit's presence and a means by which the Spirit is able to control the believer.
- Textual variety is an important part of private and public worship music.
- Music has personal, communal, and devotional implications. It is both vertical and horizontal in its impact.

Applications

In this Epistle once again we see the practice of focusing the attention of believers on the attributes and actions of God in a worship hymn before addressing the topics of practical living. Acts of worship and praise in response to clear revelation is an order we have seen throughout several passages: exposition – praise – application. Perhaps, by including transitional hymn texts, Paul is simply taking a break from his propositional teaching to call upon his readers to offer up praise to the Lord. It is also possible that Paul intended these other hymnic portions to be sung by the Ephesians:

- "There is one body, and one Spirit, even as ye are called in one hope of your calling; One Lord, one faith, one baptism" (4:5-6).
- "He ascended up on high, he led captivity captive, and gave gifts unto men" (4:8).
- "Awake thou that sleepest, and arise from the dead, and Christ shall give thee light" (5:14).

It seems Paul might have used singing as a means of reinforcing truth, as a venue for infusing truth with the emotional power of music, and as a way of breaking up verbal teaching, something we might experiment with today. As a minimum, consider conscientiously selecting the music to coordinate with what you are hoping to bring home to your family or congregation.

Now, consider some specific teachings of Ephesians 5:18-21. I think it is instructive that this long sentence, which begins at verse 18 and may extend all the way to verse 24, begins with the central idea of being controlled, not by wine, but by the Spirit. I would suggest that we apply this concept broadly. We should not be controlled by anything other than the Spirit.

Some believe that what follows in this passage are the outward evidences of people who are truly controlled by the Spirit: singing, giving thanks, submission, and relational integrity. This is certainly consistent with what we have already seen in the Word. It is my observation that those who are controlled by other outside influences, wine, drugs, sex, even certain kinds of music, evidence heartless singing, critical apathy, a disdain for leadership, and little concern for the kind of relationships in the body that are truly edifying. Bear in mind, this passage comes on the heels of a wonderful passage focusing on the beauties and purposes of a local church (Eph 4:11-16). In the immediate context we are called to walk, not as children of the darkness, but as children of the light. Being thus empowered by the Spirit we manifest His fruit in choices we make (Eph 5:1-17).

Equally convincing is the view that this passage describes actions that are not just evidential but causative. We are able to say no to outside influences like wine when we are speaking to ourselves with godly music, are actively thanking God, and are submitting ourselves to the authorities God puts in our lives. This position asserts that Paul is saying we ought to be filled with the Spirit *by* using the tool of music for controlling our thoughts, actively praising and thanking God, and submitting ourselves to the work of God through our leaders. I think there is room for the idea that God intends us to see the passage as both a reflection of the Spirit and the means by which the Spirit does His work. In either case what follows in the passage has significant implications.

We are unquestionably commanded to practically use music in the ongoing effort to build the new man and "reckon as dead" our old nature. There is no exception clause for those who may not enjoy singing, or don't think that singing is their thing, or marginalize its importance. Singing is for everyone. For those who plan services I would call you to consider the need to invite everyone to participate. We can do that by carefully selecting music for the congregation to sing and by giving sufficient time and place for this significant activity. Even when we are listening to others sing, we must stay engaged and "participate" in what is being sung.

Having considered the command, let's move to considering the multiplicity of texts Paul mentions. As I mentioned above, I believe God intends us to sing a variety of texts. Scripture, specifically the **Psalms**, **hymns** of praise and adoration that are declarations of truth both creedal statements and testimonies, and other **spiritual songs** that accurately teach a balanced view of the Christian experience. I have heard it suggested that this list may represent an order of priority: Scripture songs first, songs about the Godhead, and lastly, songs of testimony and the Christian's walk. Consider your personal and corporate music looking for just such a balance. Consider whether your music has a balance between concrete and abstract; first person prayer and first person testimony; deeply reflective vs. simple; confident in forgiveness yet regarding the awfulness of sin; etc. Only as we consider the need to balance singing in our personal lives and the life of the church can we hope to accurately portray our beautiful Savior.

As we make choices about portraying our God, the intriguing question of instrumental music comes to mind. It is my opinion that instruments can help us in our communication of the many sides of God. They can also distract as churchmen have argued for centuries. We all need to weigh in on whether instruments help or hinder infusing the text with God-honoring emotion and perspective. The writers I have read that take the position that instrumental music should be excluded do so mainly because some church father or denominational leader made that call. I think the fact that Paul includes the word *psallo* (lit. to touch with the fingers) in this passage would at least allow for instrumental music in the church. I also think it a rather extreme dispensationalism that observes instrumental music in both the OT and the eternal state and yet excludes it from the church. Still, each church leader needs to wrestle with what musical elements will best show the fullness of the Godhead and what musical elements will build up the body, always in that order. In my opinion, instruments carefully chosen and well played can be used both as a fitting representation of Who God is and a fitting response by His people as they offer their praise. It is here that the sounds, uses, and even the associations of various instruments must be considered. I repeat again that it is a ridiculous argument to say that since drums are in the Bible the way in which they are played is inconsequential. Use instruments and play them in a way that pictures God accurately and does not enflame the flesh.

I end this application section reinforcing the need to understand that when you sing, you first of all sing to yourself. A friend of mine once told me that this is something white believers struggle with and most African-Americans understand. First, we sing to ourselves. When we are truly speaking to ourselves, we powerfully speak to others. Others truly are impacted by what we speak to them through our music. Speak carefully. Most importantly we must always speak to the Lord in our music. Someday we will stand before God's throne and join the song of the ages in praise to our God and Savior. In the meantime, let's use our sanctified imagination and enter His throne room with full assurance as we "come before His presence with singing!"

Col 3:16
Exegetical Considerations

If I could only share one passage with someone about the place and importance of music in the life of the believer, it would be this passage. I am convinced that the concepts in this verse are what many Bible believers today "just don't get" about music generally and worship music in particular. In understanding the truths in this passage we can unleash the power of a long neglected tool in the believer's life.

Again, I would like you to consider the greater context of the whole book of Colossians. Paul directs his listeners to remember the greatness of Christ, who in all things is to have "the preeminence" (Col 1:18). This is found in what most conservative commentators believe is an early hymn (Col 1:14-20) and serves as a wonderful template for a hymn that is a statement of doctrine or a creedal song. Believers are encouraged to remember that their "life is hid with God in Christ" (Col 3:3) and to "mortify" the old desires and "put on the new man" (Col 3:5, 10). An important part of putting on and putting off is letting God's Word take up residence in the believer by using the powerful tool of music. Paul talks about music in the context of the practical living, just as he does in Ephesians. I am grieved that many have neglected the intensely practical tool of music in discipleship.

Begin first by considering the command to let the Word "dwell" (ἐνοικείτω, *enoikeito*), take up residence, or inhabit the life of the believer. This cardinal truth is something Paul often emphasized and is a major teaching throughout the NT. Jesus prayed, "sanctify them by thy truth, thy word is truth" (John 17:17). Peter said that if one is fruitful "in the knowledge of Christ," growing in the Word of truth, he would "never fall" (2 Peter 1:8-10). In 2 Corinthians 2:18, Paul says it is by "beholding as in a glass the glory of the Lord, *(that we)* are changed into the same image from glory to glory, even as by the Spirit of the Lord." It is through the Word "richly," (πλουσίως, *plousios*) or abundantly inhabiting our lives that sanctification and growth occur.

In light of the importance of this command, Paul implores the church to accomplish the task of teaching and admonishing with great wisdom (σοφία *sophia*). I believe the punctuation we read in the AV is unfortunate. Allow me to explain with a homey illustration. Consider the sentence "A woman, without her man, is nothing." Now compare the same words with different punctuation "A woman: without her, man is nothing." Since there was no punctuation in the original, we are left with wrestling whether Paul meant "Let the Word of Christ dwell in you richly in all wisdom;" thus tying the word wisdom to what the Word is able to bring to the believer's life. Or whether Paul intended to communicate "Let the Word of Christ dwell in you richly, in all wisdom teaching and admonishing in Psalms..." For help with this and some other concepts I will introduce below, I would draw your attention to a very similar text in Colossians 1:28 where the grammar and syntax is comparable. When Paul describes his ministry of "preaching" (καταγγέλλομεν, *kataggellomen*, the AV translates this word as "preach" 10 times, "show" three times, "declare" twice, "teach" once, and "speak of" once)[17] he states his desire to teach and admonish "in all wisdom." The emphasis here is more clearly upon the action of teaching and warning or admonishing. I believe Paul in 3:16 is commanding the believer to be wise in how he teaches and admonishes using musical mediums.

This universal need to have the Word abundantly dwell in our lives, this deep desire of every true believer, is accomplished when believers are involved in two activities: teaching (διδάσκω, *didasko*) and counseling (νουθετέω, *noutheteo*). When Paul preached, he taught and admonished; when believers sing, they "teach and admonish." The implications of the aspects of music must be considered. Other references to warning (νουθετέω, *noutheteo*) include an explanation of Paul's ministry overall (Acts 20:31; 1 Cor 4:14; 1 Thes 5:12) and Paul's encouragement for believers to be involved in admonishing others (Rom 15:14; 1 Thes 5:14; 2 Thes 3:15). Melick gives this insight:

> Admonishing differs from teaching. Admonishing has the element of strong encouragement. It is generally practical and moral, rather than abstract or theological. It is the way teaching is reinforced in the lives of the hearers. Such orderly arrangement of truth and strong practical encouragement are to be done in wisdom. Among other things, that means the person exercising these gifts will understand, in the will of God, how to exercise them appropriately. It also means that their exercise will be distinctly Christian in motivation and method...Singing effectively teaches and encourages. In 3:16, the pastoral function Paul claimed for himself in 1:28 is broadened to include the entire congregation and the medium of music. Few activities have such ability to teach, prompt recall, and encourage, and they have always been a vital part of Christianity.[18]

References to the importance of teaching and teachers for the NT believer are almost too numerous to mention.[19] All of the NT writers address the need for good teaching and learning and sternly warn about the influence of false teaching. Since music is used as a teaching and counseling tool, musicians are indeed teachers and counselors. We live in a day when technology makes the impact of musical teachers unprecedented.

I am not saying that speaking and singing do not linguistically and practically differ, just that they *overlap* semantically. For example, the songs of Scripture are largely prayers, testimonies or proclamations (statement of fact or creed). The examples of speaking in the Scripture tend to be more didactic and/or propositional in nature. It is probably overly simplistic, but generally I see music as more volitional and affective in its impact and speech more suited to didactic and propositional delivery. This is why speaking and singing are, or should be, powerful partners in the teaching and admonishing of biblical truth. Paul makes it clear that when we sing and are sung to, it has the potential for positively getting the Word in our hearts, heads, and actions. By extension, we must also understand, as did the believers at Colosse, that the influence of musical teachers is profound.

We have already discussed the reference to Psalms, hymns and spiritual songs as we looked at Ephesians, but allow me to draw your attention to Richard Melick's comments on the trio of song types:

> Although there is a consensus that the terms have significant overlap and cannot be distinguished sharply, there is some help in seeing where they most differ. "Psalms" are, no doubt, the psalms of the Old Testament. The word "hymn" occurs only twice in the New Testament, here and Eph 5:19. It may describe a "festive hymn of praise." Recent studies have addressed the presence of hymns in the New Testament and found them in many places, such as Col 1:15–20 and Phil 2:5–11. In Scripture, however, they are never called hymns, and the use of the term reflects modern church worship more than is necessarily true of the first century. "Spiritual" songs seems to describe other musical compositions, perhaps like gospel songs. Whatever they were, Paul cautioned that they must be spiritual, not secular. Together, these three terms address the entire scope of musical expression in early church worship.[20]

So there is no confusion about the importance of singing and not just listening to what others may sing, Paul repeats the command to be continually "singing (ᾄδοντες, *adontes*) with grace in your hearts." Here, Paul is not only reinforcing the need to actively participate in singing the truths of God, but uses the OT word "heart" to represent the totality of the person. Nothing teaches and admonishes more effectively and permanently than heartfelt, grace-filled singing. Once again Paul underscores the vertical and horizontal elements of worship music and ends the verse with a command for heartfelt, gracious singing to the Lord first and foremost.

Principles for Application

- Music is a powerful tool to allow the Word to dwell in the believer.
- Teaching and admonishing through music must be done with great wisdom.

- Musicians become powerful teachers and intimate counselors. This can be both a blessing and a curse.
- Singing should be heartfelt and full of grace.
- Singing should always be done for the ears of the Lord first and foremost even while speaking to others or yourself.

Applications

In the introduction I said I believe this is a most critical passage. I can think of no greater prayer in my heart for the people in my congregation than that the Word of God would take up residence in their hearts. Even greater is my desire to see the Word be truly at home in my life and the life of my family. If my people truly became people who were constantly taught and admonished by the Word as they lived their lives, they would shine as bright lights in my town. That is why this worship and music issue is such a big deal to me. It really *does* matter what believers sing and have sung to them not only in church, but all week long. In fact, I would rather have an influence on what plays in the minds of my congregation the approximately 110 waking hours a week they are *not* in church than the 3 or 4 hours they are in church. I am not saying that believers must sing hymns every waking hour, but the music that tends to circle in our heads at any given time has such an influence in how we think it often undoes the godly thoughts we so long to live out at the end of the last sermon we heard. Let me ask you a question. What *is* playing in your head right now? What is "dwelling" in your heart right now? If the Word of Christ is not permeating your thinking it may be that you are allowing too many negative influences in, or you may be neglecting the powerful influence of godly music in your own discipleship.

If this truth has gripped your heart, you will understand why we must exercise great wisdom as we go about teaching and admonishing in our songs. I must tell you that I am disappointed that some of my friends do not exercise this much needed wisdom. I fear they thoughtlessly endear impressionable young believers to musical teachers with little knowledge about what these musical teachers believe or what their agenda may be. I must regress a bit and talk about this in more detail. If you are thinking through how to apply the truth that musicians are teaching and admonishing us, you understand that this is not a simple proposition. Let me suggest some concepts to consider illustrated in the following chart.

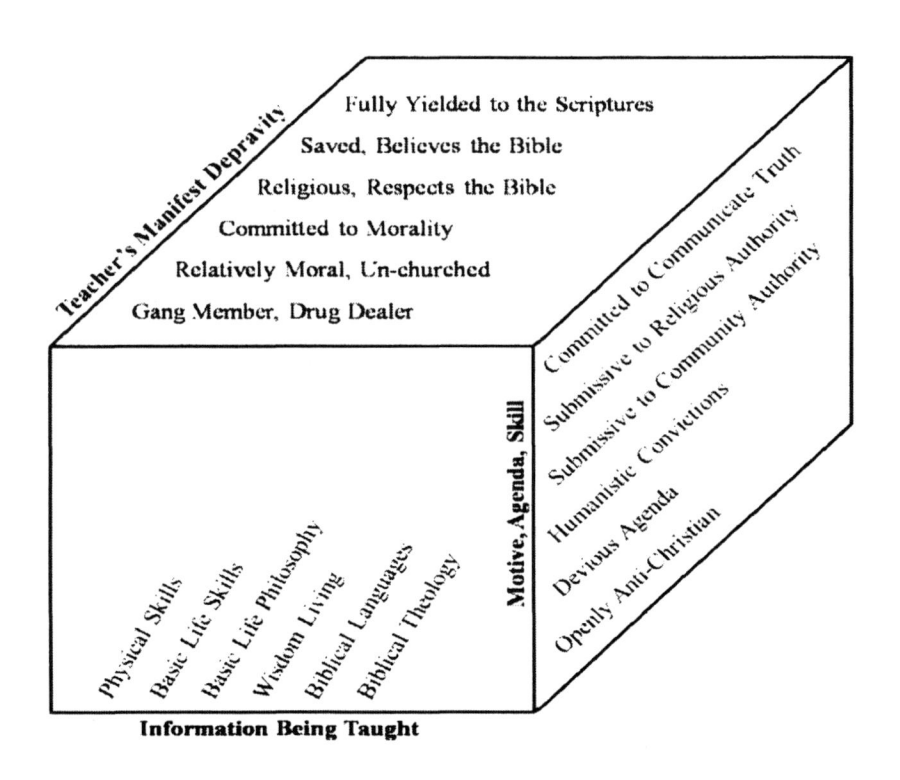

Teacher's Manifest Depravity (axis)
- Fully Yielded to the Scriptures
- Saved, Believes the Bible
- Religious, Respects the Bible
- Committed to Morality
- Relatively Moral, Un-churched
- Gang Member, Drug Dealer

Motive, Agenda, Skill (axis)
- Committed to Communicate Truth
- Submissive to Religious Authority
- Submissive to Community Authority
- Humanistic Convictions
- Devious Agenda
- Openly Anti-Christian

Information Being Taught (axis)
- Physical Skills
- Basic Life Skills
- Basic Life Philosophy
- Wisdom Living
- Biblical Languages
- Biblical Theology

I believe we need to think three dimensionally about this thorny issue. Although the diagram above is not perfect and certainly not inspired, it may serve to stimulate your thinking. First, I think we must understand that there are levels of information that are being taught. For example, a musical teacher may simply be teaching me about life around us as reflected in the natural order of things. Or, he may be trying to accurately tell me what the Scriptures teach on a certain subject. He may be intentionally or inadvertently twisting what the Scriptures teach about the nature and character of God: how God feels or thinks about something.

Second, we must consider the teacher's manifest morality. The musical teacher may be openly rebellious to any morality, or committed to human goodness, or submissive to human government, or submissive to Christian morality, or attempting to be yielded to the Scriptures.

Third we must also consider the musical teacher's agenda, motivations, and even his or her skill in communication. In thinking through this, you can see how even an unredeemed person *could* be committed to a level of integrity in communication that allows him/her to teach something of value. On the other hand some musical teachers are so twisted in their agenda, so influenced by their demonic counterparts that they are not to be trusted on any level. As hard as it may be to think through this paradigm, no matter how much deep thought it requires, no matter our thirst for the simple answer, we are called to exercise great wisdom.

Let me stir up your mind by quoting some passages that we must apply to the prophets and teachers who use the language of music as they communicate to us and our people.

> Beware of false prophets, which come to you in sheep's clothing, but inwardly they are ravening wolves. Ye shall know them by their fruits. Do men gather grapes of thorns, or figs of thistles? Even so every good tree bringeth forth good fruit; but a corrupt tree bringeth forth evil fruit. A good tree cannot bring forth evil fruit, neither can a corrupt tree bring forth good fruit. Every tree that bringeth not forth good fruit is hewn down, and cast into the fire. Wherefore by their fruits ye shall know them. (Matt 7:15-20)

> Now the Spirit speaketh expressly, that in the latter times some shall depart from the faith, giving heed to seducing spirits, and doctrines of devils; Speaking lies in hypocrisy; having their conscience seared with a hot iron; Forbidding to marry, and commanding to abstain from meats, which God hath created to be received with thanksgiving of them which believe and know the truth. For every creature of God is good, and nothing to be refused, if it be received with thanksgiving: For it is sanctified by the word of God and prayer. (1 Tim 4:1-5)

But there were false prophets also among the people, even as there shall be false teachers among you, who privily shall bring in damnable heresies, even denying the Lord that bought them, and bring upon themselves swift destruction. And many shall follow their pernicious ways; by reason of whom the way of truth shall be evil spoken of. And through covetousness shall they with feigned words make merchandise of you: whose judgment now of a long time lingereth not, and their damnation slumbereth not...But chiefly them that walk after the flesh in the lust of uncleanness, and despise government. Presumptuous are they, selfwilled, they are not afraid to speak evil of dignities. Whereas angels, which are greater in power and might, bring not railing accusation against them before the Lord. But these, as natural brute beasts, made to be taken and destroyed, speak evil of the things that they understand not; and shall utterly perish in their own corruption; And shall receive the reward of unrighteousness, as they that count it pleasure to riot in the day time. Spots they are and blemishes, sporting themselves with their own deceivings while they feast with you; Having eyes full of adultery, and that cannot cease from sin; beguiling unstable souls: an heart they have exercised with covetous practices; cursed children: Which have forsaken the right way, and are gone astray, following the way of Balaam the son of Bosor, who loved the wages of unrighteousness. (2 Peter 2:1-3; 10-15)

Beloved, believe not every spirit, but try the spirits whether they are of God: because many false prophets are gone out into the world. Hereby know ye the Spirit of God: Every spirit that confesseth that Jesus Christ is come in the flesh is of God: And every spirit that confesseth not that Jesus Christ is come in the flesh is not of God: and this is that spirit of antichrist, whereof ye have heard that it should come; and even now already is it in the world. (1 John 4:1-3)

For the time will come when they will not endure sound doctrine; but after their own lusts shall they heap to themselves teachers, having itching ears; And they shall turn away their ears from the truth, and shall be turned unto fables. (2 Tim 4:3-4)

Now I beseech you, brethren, mark them which cause divisions and offences contrary to the doctrine which ye have learned; and avoid them. For they that are such serve not our Lord Jesus Christ, but their own belly; and by good words and fair speeches deceive the hearts of the simple. (Rom 16:17-18)

For such are false apostles, deceitful workers, transforming themselves into the apostles of Christ. And no marvel; for Satan himself is transformed into an angel of light. Therefore it is no great thing if his ministers also be transformed as the ministers of righteousness; whose end shall be according to their works. (2 Cor 11:13-15)

The teaching and counseling power of music is something I believe the contemporary church has not shown wise caution about. As a practical matter, I usually start with those musical teachers who are the most akin to my biblical presuppositions; those most committed to the Scriptures, and then work cautiously out from there. Yes, I have found some truthful, helpful material among those who believe very differently than me and when associations are not an issue I believe that music can be used. Sometimes material can be usable with a simple disclaimer. Simply say that although you do not endorse everything this author or artist has written, you have found this piece to be edifying. Many times this is all that is necessary to keep your people from buying that CD that you and they will regret purchasing.

I also believe that music is a powerful tool we have not fully utilized. I encourage you to consider taking your next series of messages or mission conference or special meetings and teach some Scripture songs that will allow your people to take the truth of God to work with them. Sing songs to yourself that are full of the truths of the Word so they will be with you in the heat of the spiritual battles you are facing from day to day.

I would also challenge you to take a good hard look at what we are really teaching our children with the musical choices we are making for them. Not only are we handicapping our young people by teaching silly drivel that makes little sense to them, we are also missing a wonderful opportunity to bring the powerful tool of music to bear in their lives. Certainly we must be age appropriate, but that does not mean we have the liberty to denigrate our God with songs like "Father Abraham." If you want to sing some silly songs about spiders or whatever to get the wiggles out, go ahead, then transition to simple, reverent songs that accurately portray the God they need a lifelong relationship with. If we tie God to the silliness of some of what passes for children's church music in some circles, we run the risk of having them leave their relationship with the Lord behind with their Barney sheets. Again, take an objective look at what your children are learning about God in their music and teach them wisely.

1 Corinthians 8-10 Associations with Idolatry
Exegetical Considerations

Before we look in detail at these particularly important passages in 1 Corinthians, I think it is important to outline the general mood and worship themes of the entire book. Surprisingly, though Paul is writing to Gentile believers in a pagan culture, he uses OT worship terminology throughout. In 1 Corinthians 3, when Paul is talking about building the church, he refers to it as "God's building" (1 Cor 3:9) and asks rhetorically,

> Know ye not that ye are the temple of God, and that the Spirit of God dwelleth in you? If any man defile the temple of God, him shall God destroy; for the temple of God is holy, which temple ye are. (1 Cor 3:16-17)

Later, referring to the purity essential for individual believers, he again uses Temple terminology: "What? know ye not that your body is the temple of the Holy Ghost which is in you, which ye have of God, and ye are not your own?"(1 Cor 6:19). Paul also assumes the Corinthians' knowledge of the Passover as he makes reference to Christ's sacrifice:

> For even Christ our Passover is sacrificed for us: therefore let us keep the feast, not with old leaven, neither with the leaven of malice and wickedness; but with the unleavened bread of sincerity and truth. (1 Cor 5:7-8)

Peppered throughout Corinthians are admonitions to avoid idolatry (1 Cor 5:9, 10; 6:9; 10:7; 12:2). Paul offers practical help in making certain of this by giving believers several principles about idolatry and those things clearly identified with them.

First, unlike America today,[21] the problem of idol worship and meat offered in worship to those idols was a real one in Corinth.[22] The prohibition to the early church in Acts 15:20 and 29 was designed not only to preserve testimony, but also, as seen in 1 Corinthians 8 and 10, to encourage believers to actively "flee from idolatry" (1 Cor 10:14). Paul warns that if believers fellowship with idols in any way they provoke God to jealousy. "Do we provoke the Lord to jealousy? are we stronger than He?" (1 Cor 10:22). Paul makes the following line of argument when addressing the thorny issue of associations in these two chapters.

- Idols are nothing and this meat is innately good, but such knowledge can lead to pride (1 Cor 8:1-2; rhetorically again in 1 Cor 10:18).
- Believers should live by a higher standard than just knowledge-based decisions. Believers should move toward love-based decisions (1 Cor 8:2-3; 1 Cor 10:24).
- Idols are nothing, but some people could not move beyond the identification these idols had with the meat at that time (1 Cor 8:4-5; 1 Cor 10:25-27). There is a place for "educating" those who may have a conscience that is unduly sensitive, but that is not the primary solution to the immediate situation in this passage.
- The believer should not use things or do things that would cause a brother to violate his conscience and fall into false worship again (1 Cor 8:7; 1 Cor 10:25, 29).
- The believer should ask himself if the inclusion of this element is truly important (1 Cor 8:8; 1 Cor 10:32-33).

- Care must be taken not to cause a spiritual disaster by emboldening a brother to slide back or lean into error. Garland says, "Their minds are still infused with old conceptions that spring up involuntarily."23 In fact, Paul says that if a brother is defiled, there has been a sin against Christ Himself (1 Cor 8:9-11). The believer should lovingly choose to forfeit his "rights" forever, if need be ("while the world stands"), if doing that act which a brother associates with evil emboldens him to move toward paganism or endears him to a system that would lead him back into the world (1 Cor 8:12-13).

Principles for Application

- Idolatry is serious and must be avoided at all costs.
- Making decisions about elements that might be identified with pagan idolatry should be others oriented and individual "rights" should not be selfishly held.

Applications

In applying this passage, it is important to remember that worship music is not specifically in view here. Instead, Paul is addressing meat as it may be eaten in one's home. I would suggest that if Paul were talking about bringing this meat into church for a love feast of some kind, the idea would have been completely rejected. A second important consideration is to remember that music and meat are fundamentally dissimilar. Meat is not mood-altering nor does it influence volition and personality as music does. Meat does not teach. These passages are dealing with associations more strictly. Also, we are dealing with a "thing" in the passage, an inanimate object. We are not discussing a method of communication between two moral beings. For that reason, when applying this passage we might better talk about musical instruments than about musical style. Certainly style has associations but making applications regarding style is an application by extension and not primarily in view here. The shortest trip up the "abstraction ladder" would call for one to make the application to inanimate objects such as guitars, or maybe electric guitars with flames and trap sets rather than style of communication. Or, if we bring Romans 14 into the discussion, the place some musical instruments, perhaps organs or tambourines may have had in a former religious tradition. Since I did not address Romans 14 specifically, let me reference it here.

Romans 14 deals primarily with practices associated with Judaism. Perhaps by abstraction, some might apply this to religious practices from a new believer's former religious heritage. The line of reasoning might look something like this:

- Believers should stop judging a brother about having or using instruments (possibly organs or tambourines) or traditions from a former religious heritage (Rom 14:1-2).
- Believers should leave final judgment of other believers to God (Rom 14:3-4).
- Believers should come to a definite conclusion for themselves, for each believer will answer to God for his own choice and how he made that choice (Rom 14:5, 12).
- When a believer makes a liberty choice, that liberty choice should not cause someone to stumble back into the error of a previous religion because of the "baggage" associated with the choice (Rom 14:13).
- Believers should make decisions, "as much as lies in (them)," that promote peace, unity, and Christian growth (Rom 14:19).
- If the believer's conscience condemns him, he should "cease and desist" (Rom 14:23).

In 1 Corinthians 8 and 10, as well as Romans 14, Paul's stance is not one of promoting his own agenda or "rights," but one of humble service to others, all with a careful commitment to avoid any associations with the pagan idolatry around him. I think it is so ironic that one of the hit television shows of our day is "American Idol." I wonder what Paul would say about using the music styles which are so much a part of the temples of false worship overrunning our country today. Yes, associations do change over time, and there may be musical instruments, forms/styles and specific songs that we deem to be innately acceptable, even beneficial, that in their own time and way will lose their close identification with the paganism of our day. However, we must commit to choosing carefully and lovingly.

Since I will not deal with the meat question in detail when it appears later in our Revelation study, I think it is important to reference an intriguing passage in Revelation 2:14, 20. Twice Christ mentions meat offered to idols and fornication. First, He references Balaam (Num 22-24) who "cast a stumbling block before the children of Israel, to eat things offered to idols, and to commit fornication." Second, He condemns the church at Thyatira: "thou sufferest that woman Jezebel, which calleth herself a prophetess, to teach and seduce my servants to commit fornication, and to eat things sacrificed to idols." Further, as I have mentioned, Acts 15:29 and 21:25 call upon Gentiles to keep from this idol-meat which was strictly forbidden for OT Jews. I am committed to the inspiration and unity of the Scriptures, so I know there is no contradiction between Paul, Luke and John. The concern of God expressed by these writers is that there be great caution about using or doing things associated with idolatry in any way. I must also conclude that there is a close association between this lack of caution over separation from idolatry, illustrated by the idol-meat eaters, and fornication. Those who are unconcerned with associations easily fall prey to immorality. Whatever conclusions you may come to in reading 1 Corinthians regarding your liberty to use an instrument or musical style associated with the idolatry of the world make sure you consider the whole of Scripture. Please, proceed with great care.

I am going to take this opportunity to launch into the culture question as it relates to the application of this general principle of associations. I recently ran across an article that in the opening paragraph said culture was a "gift of God" and later that "culture is in itself amoral." Later in the paper several definitions for culture are given which included these two. "Culture is the texts and practices of everyday life."[24] "Culture is the sum of all that has spontaneously arisen for the advancement of material life, and is an expression of spiritual and moral life. It comprises language, habits, ideas, beliefs, customs, social organization, inherited artifacts, technical processes and values."[25] I confess I have some difficulty making sense of this. I would guess that this is confusing for more than just me, for putting these ideas together; I believe what is being said is that "an expression of spiritual and moral life" is "amoral." Or that the "texts and practices of everyday life" are "amoral." Can it be that the expressions and practices of moral agents are amoral? Even Tillich, the self-professing existentialist of the past generation was convinced that culture was an expression of morality. He said:

> The fact that every act of man's spiritual life is carried by language, spoken or silent, is proof enough of this assertion. For language is the basic cultural creation. On the other hand, there is no cultural creation without an ultimate concern expressed in it. This is true of the theoretical functions of man's spiritual life, e.g. artistic intuition and cognitive reception of reality and it is true of the practical functions of man's spiritual life, e.g. personal and social transformation of reality. In each of these functions in the whole of man's cultural creativity, an ultimate concern is present. Its immediate expression is the style of a culture. He who can read the style of a culture can discover its ultimate concern, its religious substance.[26]

Culture in its many expressions is a demonstration of a belief system. As one anonymous Indian said of his Hindu culture "Culture is the fruit, religion is the root."[27] What a group of people believe is borne out in their culture.

We must embrace the fact that "every *creature* of God is good" (1 Tim 4:4). That *"things"* which can be attributed to the creation of God are in themselves capable of being used for moral and immoral activities. Marijuana as a plant is good. Its very existence brings glory to God by manifesting the creative diversity of God. But can we say that all the ways men may use marijuana is morally neutral or amoral? I am prepared to say that the elements that make up music (pitch, tone, duration, timbre, etc) are, in some abstract sense, neutral elements, but when they are combined into any organized intelligent statement they reflect moral character. They communicate in a way that reflects the character of God, or not. How else are we to understand Paul's admonition that "Whether therefore ye eat, or drink, or whatsoever ye do, do all to the glory of God" (1 Cor 10:31)? Eating and drinking are rather "homey" parts of human cultures and yet we have the capacity to glorify God in how we eat or drink, or not. How else are we to understand Paul's admonition to think about that which *is* lovely? (Phil 4:8).

If what is being said by my dear brother is that the *fact* that culture exists is an "amoral" or a morally neutral *fact,* then I would suggest that almost all thinking people agree. Culture exists because people inhabit the earth. But to go further and say that because culture exists everywhere equally, therefore every individual culture in every way equally reflects God's intention for culture is an enormous leap.

Perhaps what is being attacked is that Christians have been opposed to everything in the world that is not produced by Christians. But I have yet to meet that straw man. I believe he does not exist. The *fact* of culture is of course the intention of God. He created more than one person and expects them to interact with each other. This interaction results in them manifesting their culture in ways that reflect God's character or are in rebellion to it. I am unrelentingly opposed to saying culture is morally neutral or amoral.

As politically incorrect as it may sound, I believe an examination of various human cultures reveals that some cultures may be closer than others in reflecting the fixed norm of Kingdom culture (how things will be when Jesus is King) in various areas. That is why it is dangerous to reason from culture back to the Scriptures. Instead we should endeavor to build the best biblical model for worship and music as we can and then go to the culture in which we find ourselves and look to stimulate progress toward that model. Let me give you some examples. Meekness may be more highly esteemed (though perhaps for all the wrong reasons) in one culture over another. Though all cultures may value and respect elders, some cultures may have a tendency to value elders in a more biblically normative way. Even the musical building blocks used by individual cultures may reflect a more natural order (and I would argue a more biblical order) than others. A people group's understanding of what is beautiful or ugly may be based on the desire to reflect the beauty of God: a beauty that we are not told to self-define, but are told to observe and think on (Psalm 27:4; Phil 4:8). Or an aesthetic may be based on and defined by men who may not be looking to God as their standard. The answer to the question "Is beauty arbitrary or objective?" should have its basis in the Bible, not strictly humanly devised logic. God calls Himself the standard of beauty. We are to understand, appreciate and then submit ourselves to God's ideal(s) of beauty even as we admit that we will in some ways fall short. It follows then that some cultures will do a better job than others in reflecting God's beauty.

Let me review some material I introduced in chapter 3. I believe there is something refining in understanding that the standard for culture exists outside of man. In all fairness, I am sure a great deal of unanimity on this point exists among people who are writing and speaking on the topic of culture. Most people agree that believers need to be discerning about what areas of any culture they embrace. The article I referenced and many others like it goes on to embrace (quite well I might add) this very point. Many, perhaps most, are quick to add very helpful concepts in acting discerningly and redemptively toward contemporary culture. I would suggest you give some thought to the idea that outside of "kingdom culture," the way things would be if Jesus were King, every culture is in some ways sub-ideal. I would go further and suggest that this is what Christ showed us in the beatitudes; some of what "kingdom culture" looks like. We all long for what life will be like when King Jesus rules supreme. In the mean time let's commit to seeking to know and reflect Christ-like culture as best we can.

Allow me to regress once again. I am not to saying that music is completely universal in all its meanings. I am saying that even though we have no Special Revelation to quantify beauty at this time, we are given hints of what God's definition of beauty may be as we observe His creation. It is the existence of such an objective standard of beauty outside of mankind that is refining and disciplining: refining, because it calls people to a process; disciplining, because it makes God the "bench mark" of beauty and not man himself. We should be cognizant of the need to grow into reflecting God's beauty in our music more completely as we seek to serve Him.

Admittedly, culture does have some bearing upon our perception of beauty in music. Musical symbols go through subtle associational changes as people are exposed to them. Music is perceived differently by different people because of the change in "associational baggage" that accompanies the referent and also because of the desensitization that results from man's depravity and his constant exposure to sinful practices. Music is really only performed once. Every subsequent time and place music is performed it goes through subtle changes in nuances of meaning because of the associations tied to it.

Some universals in both language and music are shared. The very fact that one can define and translate from one language to another is testimony to some universals in language.[28] This is apparent in music when physical motions (dance, marching, etc.) are observed. Age and location seem to have little or no effect on how a person responds to rock music, for instance. John Makujina puts it well when he says:

> Whereas one may argue that a certain combination of musical elements can take on various meanings (and I think these meanings are far more restricted than most), it is rather difficult to find a non-sexual or otherwise wholesome connotation for the flexions of rock-related aphrodisiac dancing and stage acrobatics.[29]

Emotions are understood and expressed quite uniformly between cultures, and music that reflects these emotions is usually correspondingly understood between cultures. This is even further reinforced in light of the world wide influence of Hollywood. As we leave this discussion I remind you that interacting with culture, specifically as it is manifested in music will need the wisdom and direction of the Holy Spirit, the wisdom God has promised to give those who seek Him. God "that giveth to all men liberally and upbraideth not" (James 1:5).

1 Corinthians 14 Music and Worship in the Church
Exegetical Considerations

Paul gives believers overarching principles of public worship and warns us of possible abuses in the entirety of 1 Corinthians 10-14. In chapter 11 Paul gives some specific instructions and warnings about public worship. In the spirit of 1 Corinthians 10:31,

Paul tells the Corinthians to honor God when it comes to two specific areas. First, in discussing head covering, Paul's general admonition to do outwardly what best honors God and honors God's ordained authority (1 Cor 11:4-5). Second, with one of the most sobering warnings of the epistle, Paul warns believers to observe communion honorably. Once again in the context of the communion service Paul demonstrates that God, the Jealous God, still judges those who participate in worship acts "unworthily" (1 Cor 11:27-31). Next, Paul devotes time describing the mutual ministry in the body of Christ (chapter 12) and the superiority of love (chapter 13). It is in this context that Paul specifically addresses the need for clear and edifying worship and music in the church (1 Cor 14:3, 12, 26).

In previous discussions about teaching, music and the prophetic office we have talked about how ancients read the word "prophecy." When examining how the word was used in the world of the Text it is clear that the Corinthians viewed music as a part of "prophecy." They understood that these words shared semantic domains. Music was one method of proclamation. Let me share these three entries in TDNT, #G4382:

> 1) The prophet is essentially a proclaimer of God's Word. This is especially true of the prophets in Paul's congregations;
>
> 2) ...The verb προφητεύω is much more prominent in Paul. Of the 28 instances 11 are in the Pauline Epistles. Like προφήτης, προφητεύω has several meanings, a. Most comprehensively it can mean "to proclaim the revelation, the message of God, imparted to the prophet (1 Cor 11:4 f.; 13:9; 14:1, 4 f., 39).
>
> 3) ...In Paul the word has a predominantly ethical and hortatory character. It denotes teaching, admonishing and comforting (1 Cor 14:3, 31).

In general terms, the Corinthian on the street understood a "prophet" was a proclaimer. Paul used the term comprehensively as his original audience would have understood it. Remember, teaching and admonishing were accomplished though both speech and singing (Col 3:16). Anthony Thiselton also embraces a broad and singing (Col 3:16). Anthony Thiselton also embraces a broad understanding of προφητεύω, *propheteuo* agreeing that it is primarily about "forth-telling."[30] Later in *The International Greek Commentary*, Thiselton further develops this idea by including "teaching" and "admonition" as a part of prophecy.[31] The Corinthians would have understood that the purpose of speaking and singing, indeed all music making, in worship was to accurately proclaim God.

Paul now encourages the church to be understandable and edifying in their public worship (1 Cor 14:3). This clarity in revelation, knowledge, prophecy, or doctrine (14:5b) is illustrated with instrumental music, language (I believe this is Paul's use of the word tongues), and military signaling (14:7-14). In summary fashion, Paul calls upon the Corinthians in 14:12 to excel in or be zealous (ζηλωτής, *zelotus*) about edification and leave behind what is self-focused and unfruitful. Paul then calls for cognitive as well as "spirited" singing and praying to the end that all those in attendance are edified and are able to participate by giving thanks and affirming the truth by responding, "Amen" (14:15-17). As God was accurately revealed during worship, this "revelation" resulted in conviction, repentance, and acknowledgement that God was "tabernacling" within the believer (14:24-25). Ultimately, the goal of the public gathering was for God to be so clearly understood (14:15-16) that the body was built up, and unbelievers who were present were brought to a relationship of humble "worship" (προσκυνήσει, *proskynosei*) and later falling down on his face (εσών ἐπὶ πρόσωπον, *peson epi prosopon*) (14:25). Paul again reminds the Corinthians of the importance of understandable, spirited worship in all of its elements. "How is it then, brethren? when ye come together, every one of you hath a psalm, hath a doctrine, hath a tongue, hath a revelation, hath an interpretation. Let all things be done unto edifying" (14:26). Finally, worship is to be submissive to written, church and familial leadership and disciplined by decency and order (14:26-40).

Principles for Application

- Worship is primarily an offering to God, and public worship should reflect a loving desire to build up believers.
- Clarity in communication and wholehearted participation are hallmarks of godly worship.
- The desired response in worship should be godly humility and an obvious evidence of the Spirit of God in the lives of both the participants and observers.
- All public worship should be governed by submission, discipline and order.

Applications

The single overarching principle in this chapter on public worship is that all things done in the public meeting be for the purpose of building up or edifying the body as a whole. It is not inconsequential that the preceding context in chapter 13 is a restatement of the importance of love. Built on the foundation of love's superiority, Paul moves to the subject of how love is fleshed out in decisions of public worship.

Paul underscores the need to edify by being clearly understood with three interesting illustrations: musical instruments, bugle signals used in battle, and lastly spoken languages (14:7-11). I think it is interesting in our post-modern world, where people seem convinced that music itself cannot give any universally clear communication, Paul would uses music as an illustration of this very idea. "And even things without life giving sound, whether pipe or harp, except they give a distinction in the sounds, how shall it be known what is piped or harped?" (14:7). If we are observant and honest, however, we understand that music is more universal in its communication than speech and probably more so today than any time in history. The main point Paul is making should not be lost; communication should be clear and understandable. It is possible to err in making this passage say more than it should, but remember Paul is using instrumental music to make the point that clear communication should be our goal. After all, instruments give a distinction in sound as do signal trumpets. It is not a stretch to appreciate the fact that edifying communication extends to more than words alone. The goal of every music leader should be clarity in form so the message is not impeded. The end of this goal is to "...seek that ye may excel to the edifying of the church" (14:12).

Paul then moves to the specific issue, the use of unknown tongues or unlearned languages. Again Paul uses a trilogy of examples. He specifically mentions the need to be understandable and spiritual in prayers, singing, and the giving of thanks (14:13-16). Jesus' words in John 4:23-24 echo in my mind; worship must be both in spirit and truth. Paul says the one who does not know this unknown tongue will not be edified. The listener will not be able to "amen" what is being said. Any of us who have had the privilege of being in a worship service where an unknown language is being used can relate to this. You rejoice that believers are praying, singings, and praising, but you are unable to fully participate. Sounds, and the emotions that correlate with those sounds, resonate at some level as you hear other believers loving Christ in their music, but you really don't know when to say "amen" to what is being said or sung. Paul says it would be much better if you knew the language so you too could be edified (14:17).

Paul's selflessness shows itself as he reminds us again what the heart of the matter must be. He says essentially, "I have the knowledge, but I limit myself so the body can be edified" (14:18-19). Paul *does* take the time in his letter to give the Corinthians knowledge about tongues and their purpose (14:21-22) then quickly restates the over-arching principle when we are making decisions regarding public worship; Paul presses again by asking "will this edify?" He handled this similarly when addressing the meat offered to idols issue in 1 Corinthians 8 and 10. Paul says that knowledge puffs up, "we know idols are nothing," but love seeks to edify (1 Cor 8:1).

As you read 1 Corinthians 14, you will see that Paul brings the Corinthians back to the superior aspects of prophecy over tongues. In this context, he addresses a question with important ramifications for us today. Paul identifies what he considers to be a "successful" outcome when the "unchurched" come to a worship service. 1 Corinthians 14:25 says unbelievers who might be in attendance will be confronted with the truth about God and the true nature of their own heart, humbly fall down on their faces, worship, and testify that "God is really among you." I think we too often are looking for something else. My personal observation is that we may be expecting unbelievers to applaud what we do in worship. Believers may be looking for some sort of self-fulfillment in worship. I agonize over the times when I see or hear other agendas. How would you measure a successful worship service? Take some time to write down what a successful worship service looks like in

light of this passage and make that your overarching goal in service preparation.

Again Paul brings us back to center. Do what is good to edifying (14:26). Make sure that everything that is done, from language choices, to prophesy, to singing (Psalms), or to speaking (14:27-39) builds up the body. The whole service should be done in a disciplined fashion: decently and in order (14:40).

Paul wanted to build up the church by being clear in his communication. He refused to be manipulative. Paul said he "renounced the hidden things of dishonesty, not walking in craftiness, nor handling the word of God deceitfully; but by manifestation of the truth commending ourselves to every man's conscience in the sight of God" (2 Cor 4:2). He refused to lose people in language known only to himself. I believe it is important to use music and speech that is clear and understandable to the church and balance this with the supreme need to stay God-centered in our worship choices. Paul kept this balance by keeping the focus off of self and on the desire to love Christ supremely and love His Bride the church more than he did himself. In all this, we also see Paul's desire to stay uncompromisingly separate from all false worship (Acts 14:16-18).

This chapter is filled with high and lofty goals that need to become real in your church and home. Before you move on to the next chapter let me encourage you to prayerfully and carefully write down some practical ways in which you will be a "doer of the Word and not a hearer only."

Chapter Fourteen
Hebrews, James, 1, 2 Peter, 1, 2, 3 John and Jude

The book of Hebrews is *the* central book in the NT for developing an understanding of how Christ forever changed OT worship. The book demonstrates both continuity and discontinuity in worship between the Testaments. Throughout, we read about the superiority of Christ in worship practices. This book has it all: heavenly throne room worship, the worship of angels, priests, high priests, sacrifices, Sabbath, tithes, even the mysterious King/Priest Melchisedec. Although Hebrews presumes a full understanding of OT worship cultus and can be difficult to understand, it is exceedingly rich. As you interact with this book you will understand better the metanarrative of worship in the entire Bible.

I have listed the other general epistles but will deal in detail only with Hebrews and 1 Peter. Let me encourage you again, however, to consider the stern warnings of Jude and 1, 2 John and apply them to the musical teachers so powerfully positioned to influence our culture. Remember all that we have learned about music's power to teach and admonish.

1. Heb 1:3 Christ is described as the revealer of God's glory
2. Heb 1:6 The angels of God worship Christ
3. Heb 2:7-9 Christ is pictured on His throne, crowned with glory
4. Heb 2:12 Christ prophetically declares through singing His oneness with the church
5. Heb 2:17 Christ is described as the "faithful high priest"
6. Heb 3:1-3 Christ is counted worthy of more honor than Moses
7. Heb 4:4-9 NT Sabbath is contrasted with OT Sabbath
8. Heb 4:14-5:5 Christ's high priestly role as advocate is superior to Aaron's priesthood
9. Heb 5:6-10; 6:19-20-7:1-28 Christ is compared to the King/Priest Melchisedec who was greater than Abraham who paid tithes to Melchisedec
10. Heb 8:1-6 Christ's superior ministry in the heavenly Temple; fulfillment of Jer 31:31-34

11. Heb 9:1-10:12 Gifts and sacrifices of OT worship and their picturing of Christ
12. Heb 10:16 Another reference to Jer 31:31-34
13. Heb 10:19-22 Writer uses Temple terminology (holy of holies) infused with NT concepts
14. Heb 10:26 Parallel between OT sin offerings and sin in NT believer's life
15. Heb 11:4 Worship of Cain and Abel referenced
16. Heb 11:17 Worship of Abraham
17. Heb 11:21 Worship of Jacob
18. Heb 11:28 Reference to the Passover
19. Heb 12:28 NT believers are commanded to serve (λατρεύωμεν, *latreuomen*) with reverence and fear
20. Heb 13:10-16 The NT sacrifices of praise within the context of a life of worship
21. Heb 13:20 Benediction
22. James 1:26-27 Characteristics of pure religion (in Col 1:18 translated worship)
23. James 2:19 Even devils believe and tremble
24. James 2:21 Reference to Abraham's worship
25. James 3:9-10 Blessing God incongruous with cursing men
26. James 5:13 Command to rejoice by singing Psalms
27. 1 Pet 1:3 Blessing God
28. 1 Pet 1:6 Greatly rejoicing in God
29. 1 Pet 1:7-8 The purpose for trials is so believers will be found to praise and honor God
30. 1 Pet 1:11 Christ's glory will follow His suffering
31. 1 Pet 1:21 God gloried Christ at the resurrection
32. 1 Pet 2:4-10 NT believers are described using OT images; set apart to show Christ's praises
33. 1 Pet 2:12 The purpose of good works is to glorify God
34. 1 Pet 3:22 Christ pictured as the object of worship in heaven
35. 1 Pet 4:3 Idolatry described as part of the flesh
36. 1 Pet 4:11 Short doxology "to whom be praise"
37. 1 Pet 5:1 Even Peter will partake of the glory of the Son in heaven
38. 1 Pet 5:11 Concluding doxology
39. 2 Pet 1:13-14 Peter referred to himself as a tabernacle

40. 2 Pet 1:17 Reference to God giving Christ "honor and glory"
41. 2 Pet 3:18 Concluding doxology
42. 1 John 3:12 Reference to the worship gifts of Cain and Abel
43. 1 John 5:20-21 "...that we may know Him that is true...keep yourselves from idols"
44. Jude 11 Reference to the "way of Cain" and "error of Balaam"
45. Jude 25 Concluding doxology

Hebrews begins by showing Christ as the great Revealer of the Godhead: "the brightness of His glory" (1:3). Christ is superior to angels (1:4), being the Son now seated on the throne with a "scepter of righteousness" (1:8). From this exalted place He is to be worshiped by all creation, even those holy angels that minister to the Godhead (1:13-14). Though He sits as Lord and King, the writer demonstrates that Christ joins the redeemed brothers He has sanctified in declaring God's name in the church (2:11-12). Next, Christ's titles as Apostle and High Priest (3:1) show that He is more glorious than even Moses (3:2-8). This passage begins to lay the foundation for the dismantling of OT worship practices. The writer carefully lays out what elements of worship are transdispensational, crossing from one dispensation to another. Here we see what worship *practices* will be laid aside taking into account Christ's ministry. Even Sabbath (σαββατισμός, *sabbatismos*) practices, an important structure for worship since creation, are nuanced by the ongoing ministry of Christ. Now, it is Christ who gives the Sabbath rest reserved for the believer in heaven because of His finished work (Heb 4:4-9). Believers have ceased from their work and are at rest in Christ.[1] This brings us to the first passage for our consideration.

Hebrews 4:14-5:6, 10; 7:1-21 Christ's Unique High Priestly Position After the Order of Melchisedec
Exegetical Considerations

The writer begins this section by building upon Christ's high priestly role introduced in 2:17. He uses OT terminology, picturing Christ entering the new Temple, heaven itself. As we have seen in the Pauline epistles, Christ replaced the physical tabernacle/temple of God on earth (John 2:19). "We have such an high priest, who is set on the right hand of the throne of the Majesty in the heavens; a minister of the sanctuary, and of the true tabernacle, which the Lord pitched, and not man" (see Heb 8:2-3; 9:11). Now, through the ministry of the Holy Spirit, He indwells believers and has made them His temple—His dwelling place (1 Pet 2:5 and 1 Cor 3:16-17; 6:19). Early in Hebrews, the writer builds upon temple/throne room imagery (2:8-9). The OT physical tabernacle, Christ during His incarnation, and now all believers are, in actuality, simply patterns of the *real* temple which is the holy of holies in heaven; but more on this later in Hebrews 9 and 10.

It is Christ's role as high priest that gives Him the ability to be both a compassionate advocate and an effective intercessor before the Father. Stated in the negative in the AV, we might better understand it in the positive. Hebrews 4:15 teaches that, "Our high priest is touched with our infirmities, was tempted in like manner as us, yet remained sinless." This gives believers confidence as we come to ask for mercy and grace; Christ was fully man. At the same time Christ's singular holiness allowed Him to sacrifice Himself wholly for the sins of others since He Himself was sinless; Christ was fully God.

We may have a difficult time understanding why the writer spends so much time talking about Melchisedec, but the Jewish reader would have understood that Jesus was not born of Aaron's line but rather Judah's. The question of how Christ could "legally" act as high priest is answered in the unique priestly ministry of Melchisedec. The inadequate ministry of the priests in Aaron's line accounts for the need of One who did not need to sacrifice for His own sins (5:1-4). This makes Melchisedec a more suitable, though still inferior, antitype. Christ, like Melchisedec, is both King and Priest (7:1), and thus superior to Aaron and even Abraham (7:2 ff). Christ's preeminence over all things, His superiority to *any* priest or sacrifice in the past makes Him the Institutor, Mediator, Surety (down payment), and Executor of His own last "will and testament." His centrality in worship is thus established forever by His sacrifice.

Christ was the last sacrificial Lamb. He triumphantly removed every sin, from every believer, for all eternity. This sweeping removal of the need for "the blood of bull and goats" radically changed the cultus of believers. His sacrifice superseded the need for any further animal sacrifices (Heb 5:6, 10; 6:20; 7:1, 10, 11, 15, 17 see also 1 Cor 5:7). However, in the Millennial Kingdom a memorial sacrifice will be reinstituted (Eze 40-48).

Principles for Application

- Christ is lifted up as the central figure of all worship.
- Christ alone, as the great High Priest, makes worship possible through His intercession.

Applications

I am profoundly impressed again with the superiority of Christ to every creature in heaven and earth. His very person demands that He be the only center of worship. We have seen in Hebrews that He is superior to any priest and any previous sacrifice. Yes, even NT believers who can glory in their priestly position and their confidence to enter the Holy of Holies, must always remember that Christ alone is the High Priest, and we only enter because of Him. In my church, we are committed to respecting the fact that every believer is a priest and needs no intercessor except for Christ and the Holy Spirit (Rom 8:26). God forbid that the confidence we have as believer priests should ever cause us to exalt our priesthood above that of Christ Himself. What priest would ever enter into his ministry with self-fulfillment or self-aggrandizement in mind? Hebrews should punctuate in our minds once again the need to enter every worship time with our High Priest securely enthroned as the only One worthy of worship.

Bless God that Christ has made it possible to worship! We have the eternal privilege of gathering around God's throne and offering up our worship. I am becoming increasingly convinced that the value we put on our position in Christ intensely influences our sanctification. When in the darkness of the night you mutter to yourself "I am such a ...," you set a direction for yourself. If you focus on your position in Christ and your inheritance in Him, you will be struck with the outlandishness of living in either self-centeredness or defeat. If you are fixated on your own failures, even the reality of your unworthiness, you will at the same time stop looking at the Author and Finisher of your faith, our worthy, matchless Christ. Instead, we must focus on the Worthy Sacrifice who makes our worship possible. Worship and music choices that stop short of pointing to God, and most importantly to the work of God through Christ, are incomplete or manipulative. Every element of our worship should be saturated with the works and character of God in Christ. All other elements and people should melt into insignificance. As worship leaders, we should be ever striving to become inconsequential prompters so people come away forgetting our names and remembering His.

Hebrew 9-10 Continuity/Discontinuity of Worship in the Testaments
Exegetical Considerations

Continuing with what I introduced in the previous section, what we will see in these two chapters is the contrast between the earthly pattern of worship in the OT Law and their corresponding heavenly reality. Jesus is the central figure because He alone can cleanse us, present us to God, and unify us into a new habitation.

> It was therefore necessary that the patterns of things in the heavens should be purified with these; but the heavenly things themselves with better sacrifices than these. For Christ is not entered into the holy places made with hands, which are the figures of the true; but into heaven itself, now to appear in the presence of God for us. (Heb 9:23-24)

For the uninitiated, the writer gives many details about the worship cultus of the OT and describes in some detail the tabernacle and temple (9:1-7). John Drane makes this observation:

> Far from being redundant, Judaism was an essential prerequisite for the full articulation of Christian faith—and so Hebrews goes on to list a 'large crowd of witnesses' taken from the Old Testament and Jewish history, whose experience of

God is part of the ongoing narrative that culminated with the coming of Jesus (11:1–38).[2]

The Holy Spirit is credited with illuminating the way into the Holy of Holies which the blood of Christ has now made manifest (διόρθωσις, *diorthosis*, literally, to straighten) (9:8-10). Christ is once again pictured as a "more perfect tabernacle" (9:11). It is only Christ's work that allows believers to be purged from their dead works so that they can properly worship (λατρεύειν, *latreuein*) (9:14). Using the image of a testament (as we would use the phrase "last will and testament") the writer explains how Christ is both the testator (the one providing the legally valid will) and the mediator (the executor of the will) of His own "testament" (9:15-17). It was Christ's death that brought the new testament into full effect. Just as blood was literally sprinkled on the people in the OT (Ex 24:8), a pattern of Christ's future ministry, so Christ entered once into heaven to "sprinkle" the redeemed with His own blood (9:23-28). By this act Christ "put away sin by the sacrifice of Himself" (9:26b). Praise God!

The writer begins chapter 10 once again confirming that OT Law was "a shadow of good things to come" (10:1). The Law, by its very nature, was a constant reminder of man's sinful acts. God did not institute the bloody sacrifice of animals as the final remedy for sin. This is stated repeatedly even in the OT (Ps 40:6-8 [quoted here]; Ps 51: 16; Isa 1:11; Hosea 6:6) and by Christ Himself in Matthew 9:13. Hebrews 10:7 gives testimony that Christ had "come (in the volume of the book it is written of me,) to do thy will, O God." His sacrifice took away the need for the Mosaic Law "once for all" (10:10). Or as Weirsbe points out, "Only the death of Christ could tear that veil (Mark 15:38) and open the way into the *heavenly* sanctuary where God dwells."[3] After making the final offering of His own blood, Christ assumed His rightful place on the throne (10:13-15). This action gives the believer access "into the holiest by the blood of Jesus" (10:19). It is this confidence that the writer appeals to in giving three commands: (1) draw near to God, (2) hold fast to the faith, and (3) minister to other believers in the context of the local assembly (10:20-25).

Principles for Application

- Blood is the sin covering of every age. The blood of Christ is the only final remedy for sin. Animal sacrifices have always pointed forward to the final sacrifice of Christ. He is the believer's substitute.
- Drawing near to the Lord is based on the finished work of Christ and results in certain observable outcomes; namely, faithful doctrine and relational integrity.

Applications

The simple reading of these chapters underscores the discontinuity between the worship of the OT and the NT. Christ radically changed the way believers worship. Just as clearly continuity is underscored. For example, all believers in all ages are reminded that the bloody sacrifice, ultimately the bloody sacrifice of Christ is their only hope of redemption. I applaud a few recent composers who have committed to writing songs that remind us of this reality. All we are and do as believers must have its basis in the gospel. If we don't base our Christian walk on the good news of Christ's redemptive act, we run the risk of becoming mere moralizers. Make sure that your songs, and the general tenor of your worship, center on the blood. The liturgical history of communion, especially among Bible believers, has vacillated between over and under observance. The believer's service of remembrance, the Lord's Supper, must always be carefully observed and creatively crafted; it should never become routine. In all of Biblical history bloody sacrifices have been central. Even in the age to come, which we will examine more closely in the next chapter, the sacrifice of Christ is celebrated. Never shy away from songs and services that emphasize the sacrifice of Christ. His work on the cross is the only basis upon which we can "draw near to God with full assurance."

Worship in the Word is based on the clear revelation of God and the work of Christ. This is where our worship should begin. Only then can we move on to practical areas of the Christian's walk. I believe one of the most profound needs of our day is to grab hold of the people of God and remind them of who they are in

Christ. I can think of only a few songs that direct our thoughts on that centering truth. Yet our identity, who we are in Christ, needs to be the driving force in our lives. A wonderful template is the song "Arise My Soul, Arise," but more need to be written. In Hebrews we are called upon to live with confidence because of our new standing in Christ, a theme clearly seen on other epistles like Romans 5-6. As you look over your next message and the accompanying song service ask yourself these questions: "is this service built upon the solid foundation of our relationship with the Lord?" "Do my people understand who in the world they are in Christ?" He alone is our only sufficient motivation and prize. Even our testimony songs should to be built on the importance of the work of Christ in providing the gospel and not just "the way we feel about" what Christ has done.

It is no mistake that it is in this context the writer calls on believers to flesh out their relationship with Christ by coming to the Father with full assurance. Drawing near to God (10:22) in worship with songs and prayers is a wonderful way to "come into His presence." It is by abiding in this place that holding fast to the faith we have been delivered is made possible (11:23). It is also out of this rich fellowship with the Father through the blood of Christ that we find possible the motivation and tact to persistently exhort our fellow believers (11:24). Healthy body life grows out of such worship as we will see further in the next passage.

Hebrews 13:15-16 New Testament Worship Practices
Exegetical Considerations

You may wonder why a book whose central theme is the transition of worship elements in the OT to Christ and the NT would have so little to say about the actual practice of worship. A more thoughtful reading reveals, however, that certain acts of Christian worship *are* taught and assumed.

First, you must bear in mind that the writer assumes the reader's full understanding of OT worship. Worship *acts* performed in the context of a life lived as a sacrifice have other OT and NT parallels as we have noticed in our study. Sacrifices for sin have been fully paid by Christ (Heb 10:12), but believers are still called upon to make sacrifices themselves: "By him therefore let us offer the sacrifice of praise to God continually, that is, the fruit of *our* lips giving thanks to his name. But to do good and to communicate forget not: for with such sacrifices God is well pleased" (Heb 13:15-16). Notice both worship acts (verbal praise) and worship living (εὐποιίας καὶ κοινωνίας, *eupoiias kai koinonias,* doing good in the gathering) are sacrifices that continue to be God-pleasing.

The importance of giving public thanks is also reflected in Hebrews 10:28, where NASB and others translate "let us show gratitude, by which we may offer to God an acceptable service." David Peterson suggests in *The New American Commentary:*

> The proper response to God's gracious offer of *a kingdom that cannot be shaken* is to *be thankful*. Such gratitude is the basis and motivation for true and acceptable *worship*. The Greek verb here (*latreuein*) may also be translated 'to serve', as it is in 9:14. Christian worship cannot be restricted to prayer and praise in a congregational context. As ch. 13 illustrates, we are to worship, or serve, God by faithfulness and obedience in every aspect of our lives (note particularly 13:15–16; cf. Rom. 12:1). However, the writer also insists that acceptable worship is characterized by *reverence and awe*, and supports his challenge with a description of God as *a consuming fire*.[4]

Neither Hebrews nor the NT as a whole minimize public praise in worship. We have seen throughout the entire Word, even as early as the worship of Cain and Abel, that relational integrity was both the prerequisite and the result of true worship. The whole Bible reinforces the need for relational integrity in the gathering of God's people. Worship in the NT is not limited to what happens on a Sunday morning any more than it excludes the value of time spent by believers bringing their sacrifices of praise.

Hebrews 10:23-25 commands and encourages the regular assembly of believers. Though Sabbath is given its more complete meaning in chapter 4 as the rest that remains eschatologically (4:9), believers are still commanded to actively seek the assembly. Specifically, believers are to be "provoking" (παροξυσμὸν, *paro-*

zusmon, stirring up) each other to love and good deeds. This definition is reminiscent of the command to admonish one another we looked at early in the Pauline epistles (Col 3:16; Rom 15:14). The complexion of the public assembly changed between testaments, but its importance remains. We observe in Hebrews 3:13 that regular, yes, even daily exhortation between believers is commanded. Relational integrity that is nurtured in the public gathering continues to be a part of the worship of the NT. In fact, the need for such gathering is likely heightened by the absence of the OT cultus. Due punctuates this dramatic need for the public assembly when he states,

> With no temple, no priesthood or clerical hierarchy, no (visible) sacrifices, none of the outward accoutrements of formal worship that accompanied all other religions, no visible god and no future (as far as the world's estimate of things was concerned), the importance of eternal hope cannot be overstated. Hope was the life of the community of God's people....[5]

Just because the priest's ministry of bloody sacrifices was rendered unnecessary by the sacrifice of Christ did not mean that sacrifices were not commanded. Wuest comments on this in his commentary:

> The believer-priests of the New Testament are to offer, not animal sacrifices as did the Aaronic priests, but the sacrifices of praise. The Rabbis had a saying, 'in the future time all sacrifices shall cease; but praises shall not cease.' Philo says: 'They offer the best sacrifice who glorify with hymns the Saviour and benefactor, God.'
> But the recipients are cautioned that their obligations as priests are not exhausted with praise. Good deeds must also be included. The Greek word translated "communicate," *koinoneo* (κοινονεο), in this context means "to make one's self a sharer or partner" with someone else in his poverty or need.[6]

The twin commands of praise and good works are given in the context of an explanation of the Day of Atonement (13:11-13). After a description of the sacrifice of Christ, the writer calls believers to join Christ in His place outside the camp. I remind you that God calls both of these kinds of sacrifices "spiritual." Continual praises to God and the good work of sharing with the body of Christ are both gifts given to God as spiritual sacrifices (see Phil 4:10-20 and Rom 12:1-2). Our word and our works are our sacrifices for Christ. It is by Christ's sacrifice ("by Him therefore") that we are called to offer ours. And it is in these offerings of worship that "God is well pleased" (13:16).

Principles for Application

- Acts of worship performed in the context of righteousness and in light of the sacrifice of Christ, and a lifestyle of worship are balancing parts of worship.
- Healthy relationships in the church grow out of a confident worship relationship with the Father.

Applications

I have spent some time in this passage because some incorrectly conclude that because God expects us to live our entire lives in a lifestyle of worship that we are excused from specific words of praise. We still sacrifice in the NT with our words *and* our lives. Words have never substituted for actions and actions do not preclude our spoken and sung praises. You might even make an argument that the order we see in this passage is normative. First, we consider Christ's bloody, efficacious sacrifice; then, we offer up verbal praise and thanks; then we live life with relational integrity with our brothers and spiritual leaders. This is the pattern we have seen in our long journey through the Scriptures. Dear brother, show us the Lord, help us to offer our praise, and live in love with God's people. This is successful worship; this will please the Lord.

Because of Christ's work, the believer can now enter into the Holy of Holies and worship the Father in full assurance (Heb 4:16; 6:19; 7:25; 10:1,22; 11:6; see also 1 Pet 2:5,9). Conceptually, Christ's ministry was not so much about discontinuity as it was continuity. By virtue of His mission, He became the fulfillment, the continuity of worship *principles*. Practices changed radically, but the principles were made manifest as God progressively revealed His plan to replace the illustrations of the OT with The Reality; with Christ Himself. In the OT there were repeated sacrifices for sin; in the NT there is One. The centrality of the bloody sacrifice of animals in the OT is replaced by the bloody sacrifice of One. In the OT, the temple/tabernacle were central figures; in the NT, all believers can go the Holy of Holies in heaven with confidence wrapped in the bloody garment of the One. As Due puts it,

> Christian worship in Hebrews is nothing if not a replacement cultus, by which these Hebrew believers are both expressing the nature of their devotion of God through Christ in the power of the Spirit, and renouncing all alternatives, old covenant worship included."[7]

In our next chapter on Revelation, we will see with even greater clarity the glories of worship in the heavenly Holy of Holies.

1 Pet 2:4-12 NT Believers Described Using OT Worship Images
Exegetical Considerations

1 Peter is filled with descriptions of what a believer is in Christ. He is elect (1:2), begotten of God (1:3), the recipient of an inheritance (1:4-5), saved (1:5), redeemed (1:18), purified (1:22), born again (1:23), and the list goes on. Among these descriptions Peter juxtaposes OT worship imagery to explain the believer's position. He begins his line of reasoning by referring to Christ as the "Living Stone" that was rejected "but chosen of God, and precious" (1:4). In the next verse Peter calls all believers "lively stones" as well (2:4-5). Then, making an allusion to the Temple he describes the church as "a spiritual house," in the same way Paul makes that analogy in 1 Corinthians 3. Next, believers are called a holy priesthood, able to "offer up spiritual sacrifices acceptable to God by Jesus Christ" (2:5b). *Word Studies in the New Testament* defines the term ἀνενέγκαι (to offer up) as "The usual Old Testa-

defines the term ἀνενέγκαι (to offer up) as "The usual Old Testament (Septuagint) term for offering of sacrifice. Lit. *to bring up* to the altar. Compare Heb. 13:15"[8] The priest would bring his offering up to the brazen altar. We have seen both in Hebrews 13:15-16 and in Romans 12:1-2 what those sacrifices are for the NT believer. Being part of a "holy priesthood" (ἱεράτευμα ἅγιον, *hierateuma hagion*) meant not only that the believer had access and privilege, but also the responsibility of holy living, a point Peter makes quite clear in 1:14-16. Bear in mind too that these terms have a corporate sense with important implications for believing church bodies today. The term "offerings" (θυσίας, *thysias*) is used in the LXX for the cultus of the OT and in other NT passages we have studied together. (See also: Isa 56:7 Ps 4:5; 50:14; Hos 14:2; Phil 4:18.)

In the next verses (2:6-8), Peter further develops the metaphor of Christ as the Rock and His preciousness to those who believe. Verse 1:9 continues the description of the believer again using OT terminology. Peter's reference to believers being "a chosen generation" (γένος ἐκλεκτόν, *genos eklekton*), a royal priesthood (βασίλειον ἱεράτευμα, *basileion iepateuma*), a holy nation (ἔθνος ἅγιον, *ethnos agion*), and a particular people (λαὸς εἰς περιποίησιν, *laos eis peripoiesin*) would have been very important corporate identifiers for these poor persecuted, scattered believers. Certainly these descriptions informed not only their identity in the world but also their attitudes and actions in the worshiping assembly. In fact, Peter expands on this further in verses 10ff reinforcing the fact that though these believers may have felt they had no unique identity, they now had an identity as "the people of God" (2:10).

Nestled between these identities, each pregnant with meaning, is the reason for this wonderful identity. Believers have this identity so that "ye should show forth the praises of Him who hath called you out of darkness into His marvelous light" (2:9b). Just as Peter uses descriptive terms rich in OT heritage, he repeats the theme that believers are saved to praise, a theme we have seen often in our study. Consider again the reason for the Exodus, "that they might sacrifice" (Ex 8:8). Remember the example of the Psalms, "that I may shew forth all thy praise" (Ps 9:14); "O Lord, open thou my lips; and my mouth shall shew forth thy praise" (Ps 51:15); "we will shew forth thy praise to all generations" (Ps 79:13). Wilmington offers this inspiring commentary in outline form:

> *We are kings and priests!* Having been "nobodies" (see Hos. 1:10; Rom. 9:25), we are now both kings and priests:
> - kings, for we'll someday rule with Christ (see 2 Tim. 2:12)
> - priests, for we have direct access to God (see Eph. 2:18; Heb. 4:16)
>
> Israel *had* a priesthood; Christians *are* a priesthood. Believer-priests offer:
> - themselves (see Rom. 12:1; Phil. 2:17; 1 John 3:16)
> - their substance (see Rom. 12:13; Gal. 6:6, 10; Titus 3:14)
> - their service (see Heb. 13:16)
> - their songs of praise (see Heb. 13:15)[9]

Principles for Application

- NT believers fulfill many of the OT priestly roles because of the ministry of Christ.
- NT worship reflects a corporate as well as an individual dynamic.

Applications

It is true that Christians do not bring sacrifices to the Temple, but we have the awesome responsibility and privilege of offering many kinds of spiritual sacrifices. Priests bring offerings. We offer our bodies, our every act as a living sacrifice (Rom 12:1-2; 1 Cor 10:31). We bring our good works to and for others (Heb 13:16; Matt 10:42). We bring our monetary gifts (Phil 4:10-20). We bring the offering of bringing others to Christ (Rom 15:16). And we bring our verbal praise in speech and song (Heb 13:15). These are all gifts God is blessed to receive. One does not substitute for another.

I also come away from this passage impressed again with the corporate identity we are given in the NT. The entire passage reflects not only vertical elements but horizontal implications as well. Independent Baptists, of which I am one, make much of the "priesthood of the believer." What a glorious and wonderful truth. Unfortunately, some have taken this to such an extreme that they have forgotten that we have a corporate identity among fellow priests. We stand as a legion of priests washed and commissioned by our High Priest, Jesus Christ. Priests have unimpeded access to God, but they also have a ministry of reconciliation (2 Cor 5:18) and intercession (James 5:20). We must never ignore the "us" of the local church. And, we must never forget that Biblical truth calls us to live as "strangers and pilgrims," free from the lusts of the flesh that drive the lost world around us. As NT priests we are to live out our calling as salt and light, preserving and shining in our decaying and dark world.

While we are striving to be pure, we must also be overt in our praise. We are saved to worship with our lives and with our words. Have I said it enough? One will not substitute for the other. Good works and good words should be filling our lives. This world is dying to see and hear a praising Christian, a Christian unashamed to praise his God with singing and speaking that shows how great God is. We are here to shamelessly proclaim to the world the excellencies of God.

Chapter Fifteen
Revelation

No study of worship is complete without a study of Revelation. It should be instructive to anyone considering worship and church music issues to see God's worship and music plan for the future. If you have ever wondered what a worship service would look like if God designed it, you can see it here. Many of the future promises about worship and music, and many of the worship concepts taught in the prophets are fulfilled in the future Kingdom outlined here in the book of Revelation. Worship, or its verb form, προσκυνέω (*proskyneō*) is specifically mentioned 24 times. Here in Revelation, God will bring to completion His desire to have all creation worship before Him. Finally God will drive into eternal darkness all false worship (Rev 14:9-11; 19:20; 21:8). God will see His throne surrounded by all those from every nation and time, and those angelic beings who serve Him, singing and playing a new song (Rev 4:8-11; 5:8-147:10-12; 11:16-17; 14:2-3; 15:3-4; 19:1-6). The throne room, known only through visions by prophets and apostles, will be clearly seen by all who believe. Then, as never before, true worship will be characterized by both inward and outward elements.

Three overarching and summary transcultural and transdispensational concepts can be identified in this final revelation. These principles of worship and worship music should characterize the saints of all ages.

First, God will "eternally initiate" the worship of men and angels. He will finally see all elect sentient creatures wholeheartedly singing His praises in light of His holiness. The "gospel" throughout the ages is essentially that God has made a way for man to worship Him in the Person of Christ. It is the act of God that gives redeemed men and holy angels the eternal privilege of worshiping Him; it is not man's good idea (Rev 1:5-6; 7:9-12). Kistemaker celebrates this truth when he comments on Revelation 7:9-12 by saying, "The saints in heaven sing a song with one accord."[1] Finally the "worship war" will end. God called mankind to worship Him in the garden and then provided for mankind's redemption through animal sacrifices. God called the nation to worship Him when, through the Passover lamb, He redeemed His people out of Egypt. God called man to worship Him when *the* Passover Lamb was "lifted up" on Calvary. And in Revelation, God calls all nations, even all creation, to Himself so they can eternally worship Him (Rev 14:6-7).

Among the New Testament books, Revelation singularly illustrates all the people of God singing His praise in worship. The content of the song, so uniquely separate from the false worship of the beast and the false prophet, is rich in rehearsing the attributes of God, His acts as Creator and Redeemer.

Second, since the beginning of time there has been an eternal, cosmic conflict over the object of worship. Since Lucifer's fall, he has sought to "ascend into heaven,...exalt [his] throne,...sit also upon the mount,...ascend above the heights,...[and] be like the most High" (Isa 14:13-14). Throughout history Satan has called men to forsake the worship of God and follow him in false worship. When Christ came to earth in His first advent, it was worship that was at the heart of His temptation (Matt 4:9-10). When Christ comes the second time, the false worship of Satan and his followers will be crushed. It is this cosmic conflict that has been the origin of all human and angelic sin; all sin has its genesis in false worship (Isaiah 14; Romans 1).

Third, God, by virtue of His divine Person, stands completely alone as the only worthy recipient of all of creation's exuberant praise. He is worthy of worship by virtue of His creation and His act of redemption as the Lamb. It is because of God's worthiness that He alone is able to set whatever terms best reflect His own nature and character. All creation will ultimately worship God according to His standards and conditions.

Revelation worship is centered around the Trinity. God gave the Son the Revelation (1:1), yet the reader is called to "hear the Spirit" (2:7). In Revelation 4-5 the Lord God Almighty (4:8-10), the Lamb Himself (5:8-10), and the seven Spirits of God (5:6) are offered worship. The entire Godhead is involved in, and the recipient of worship on the throne.

Revelation

1. Rev 1:6 God made believers kings and priests; opening doxology
2. Rev 1:17 Seeing the throne, John assumed the posture of worship
3. Rev 2:14, 20 Things sacrificed to idols; Jezebel the prophetess
4. Rev 3:9 God will make even the unregenerate worship
5. Rev 4:8-11 Worship around the throne, the angels are still proclaiming God's holiness 24 elders join the angels in worship God's creation is for His pleasure
6. Rev 5:8-14 Worship around the throne, the new song in the eternal state, instrumental music in heaven, believers called priests, all creation worships before the Lamb, worshipers fall down before the Lamb
7. Rev 6:10 Martyrs call for justice in the context of worship
8. Rev 7:11-12 Worship around the throne, believers will assume the posture of worship, blessing, glory, wisdom, power, and might are ascribed to the eternal God
9. Rev 9:20-21 Those who would not repent of false worship are finally judged
10. Rev 11:1 The worship place of the temple is described
11. Rev 11:15-17 Worship around the throne, angels sound out the praises of God, 24 elders join the angels
12. Rev 13: 4, 8, 12, 15 Judgment pronounced on those who worship the beast
13. Rev 14: 2-3, 7-11 The new song of heaven, New song of heaven sung by the martyrs, called to fear God vs. 7, false worshipers will be judged
14. Rev 15:2-4, 8 Worship around the throne, angels with the harps of God, song of Moses and the song of the Lamb, consider the texts of revelation , temple filled with smoke at the temple cf. temple dedication
15. Rev 16:2 Judgment on false worshipers
16. Rev 18:7, 22 Babylon sets herself up to be worshiped, music is wiped away in judgment
17. Rev 19:2-4, 10, 20 Worship in the heaven, amen and alleluia exclaimed, beasts and 24 elders worship the Father, angel refused John's worship and calls him to worship God alone, false prophet, beast, and all those who worshiped them are damned

18. Rev 20:4 Martyrs who refused false worship are rewarded
19. Rev 22:3, 8-9 Eternal worship, God's servants serve Him forever, Angel refused John's worship and calls him to worship God alone

Sixteen hymn or hymn fragments are found in the book of Revelation (12:10-12; Rev 13:9-10; Rev 14:4-5, 7, 8, 9-12, 13; Rev 16:7; Rev 18:2-8, 10, 14-15, 20-24 [This is a funeral dirge for great Babylon]; Rev 21:3-4). Most of the hymn sections are readily identified by their poetic structure. Walvoord suggests that there are 14 doxologies in the book of Revelation.[2] An examination of the worship text models of Revelation will be a wonderful template for us if we will prayerfully consider them.

I will mention here once again that the term speak (λέγω, *lego*) is used in the NT to convey the general idea of proclamation. For example, in Revelation 5:9 we read how they "sang a new song saying" (καὶ ᾄδουσιν ᾠδὴν καινὴν λέγοντες). Believing in the plenary inspiration of the Bible means the meaning of words makes a difference, and we take the meaning of words from the Scriptures themselves. The language shows us that the word "speaking" is broader than our narrower modern meaning. Believers "said" something to the Lord when they sang. Adhering to a normal hermeneutic, we understand that the use of this word group includes the possibility that poetic sections were sung. For example, the AV may say that the four beasts were "saying" (λέγοντες, *legotes*) "holy, holy, holy," but we understand by the poetic nature of the text and the use of the same word in 5:9 that singing is in view.

Before we look at the first passage, I would like to highlight from 2:14 and 2:20 an issue we examined in 1 Corinthians 8 and 10: the involvement with meat offered to idols and their close association with fornication and idolatry. Wherever you stand on the meat issue you must account for these verses in 2:14 and 2:20. They seem to condemn without qualifier because God says these individuals will "seduce my servants to commit fornication, and to eat things sacrificed unto idols." In several messages to the churches, believers are warned to avoid the false worship and false teachings of the unredeemed.

Rev. 4:1-11 The First Throne Room Worship Scene
Exegetical Considerations

This is the first of several antiphonal songs. In the immediate context of our first throne room worship scene we have a gracious invitation by Christ to come and "sit with me in my throne" (3:21). Then John picturesquely describes what he saw in his vision of the Temple/Throne room.

- The King of Kings is seated on His throne (4:2).
- A rainbow is encircling the throne (4:3).
- Angels and elders are seated around the throne dressed in white and wearing gold crowns (4:4).
- The central figure in worship is the Godhead in the person of the Father (4:2-4).
- Thunder and lightning resound (4:5).
- Awesome creatures minister to God around the throne, acclaiming His holiness, lordship, power, and eternality (4:6-8).
- Because of God's person the beasts give honor and thanks to God in song (4:9).
- The elders respond to all they see with the acts of bowing, sacrifice, and praise specifically centering on the manifest glory of God in creation (4:10-11).

Consider the participants in worship in this scene. Some difference of opinion exists over who these 24 elders might be. Some suggest they represent the 12 tribes and the 12 apostles; some suggest they represent the heavenly equivalent of the temple musicians of 1 Chronicles 25:1, and some believe they are simply angelic or human worshipers. I believe they represent believers from all the ages principally because in the following chapter they sing of their own redemption by the Lamb (5:9; 5:13-14). The other major participants are the four living creature who surround the throne. Their appearance seems to challenge John's descriptive ability, as well as our ability to imagine them. To our modern mind they seem monstrous, yet John describes them as "like" a lion, a man, a calf, and an eagle, covered with eyes and having six wings. Like someone who lacks the senses to see or hear, we too will struggle with what these creatures will actually look like until we will one day possess the senses of heaven.

In the heavenly throne room, the works of believers have ceased and the rewards for their faithful service are seen in the golden crowns the elders wear. Believers and angels alike center their praises on the only worthy One, God Himself. The natural response of the worshipers is to remove their crowns and cast them at the feet of the One who redeemed and empowered them to accomplish their works in the first place.

Take special note of the content of their praise: the person and work of the creator God. The four creatures begin first with the summary fact that God is "holy, holy, holy" (ἅγιος, *agios*). We need to understand that the word encompasses even more the fact that God is morally pure. Holiness carries with it the idea that God is transcendently above and separate from all of mankind in every way. Chiefly, God is the very definition, the very personification of purity and rightness. This fact profoundly sets Him apart from His created beings. Every way in which God can be described, He is wholly (holy) above any created being. Worship for this reason centers on the attributes of God and how those attributes are demonstrated in His actions. Specifically in this song, worship is centered in His acts as Creator (4:10-11).

Principles for Application

- Worship must be centered on the person and work of God and not on the needs or accomplishments of the worshiper.
- Acts and words of worship must be given in the context of humility and purity.
- The very person of God demands a natural response of worship from His created beings.
- All of creation was purposely created for God's pleasure. Our theology is framed doxologically not soteriologically.

Applications

My deepest prayer for you is that you would come to grips with the true center of your worship. Since the beginning of creation the object of worship has been a conflict of cosmic proportions. God's created beings can worship God or deflect their worship away from Him and, ultimately, onto themselves. Finally, when God once-for-all silences all false worship, we will see God as the only true center of worship. Until then the Bride of Christ must be vigilant to fight off the tendency we all have to be self-centered. Continually ask yourself if you reflect the God-centered worship we see in Revelation.

Throne room worship is admittedly something we cannot achieve in this lifetime. Unlike heaven, we live in a world that is largely ignorant of the God of the Bible. In heaven, the need to go out in the highways and byways of life and share the good news will be unnecessary. Here on earth we live in a place where believers are still shackled by the desires of the flesh and the needs of our physical bodies. There, we will no longer need to exhort, encourage, admonish, or teach other believers. Now, all of these are worthy activities that God assures us are a part of worship. There, around the throne, we will have all the energy of a glorified body for wonderful, unfettered bowing and adoring (προσκυνέω, *proskyneo*); actions that are often interrupted by other necessary service (λατρευ, *latreu*) in our fallen world. But when we can take time out of our demanding schedule to gather around the throne as a body of believers, or when we as individual believer-priests lose ourselves in the wonder of our position in Christ, we are gloriously transported to our future. I gain perspective every time I read these words and pause to soak them in. Someday, worship will finally be unhindered. In the meantime consider what principles we might take from the heavenly worship service we see here.

I think it is helpful and instructive that worship begins with a clear revelation of God on His throne. The progression of thought in the response goes from attributes to actions. Look over your worship service order. Are you letting the response of worship grow out of a clear picture of who God is? This is the order of Scripture, and certainly we see it here. A service that insists on response before articulating what people should respond to is doomed to be manipulative. Look over your service and ask yourself what you are specifically asking your people to worship, or praise, or thank God for. Or, begin your worship service preparation by asking the question: What attribute of God informs or empowers people to do what I am asking them to do in the service? You might start by looking over the wonderful texts we have in Revelation and centering your services around some of them. We have many wonderful poetic texts sprinkled throughout the Bible from which to choose, most notably the Psalms. Perhaps start by picking some of them. We may need to jettison some of the human ideas about service preparation we have enshrined in our traditions and be informed by the service models of the Word, specifically those in the perfect services we see modeled in Revelation.

Whatever you learn from this passage, I hope you will come away embracing the truth that all creatures, including you, were created by and for Him. Let's worship Him who alone is worthy!

Rev. 5:5-14 The Song of the Lamb
Exegetical Considerations

The next song in Revelation is a Christ-centered song that pulsates with thanksgiving for the work of Christ in salvation (5:5-6). The four creatures and the twenty-four elders are once again involved. This time they have harps and golden fragrant vials that represent the prayers of the saints (5:8). It would be difficult to overstate the importance of OT Temple allusions in the book of Revelations. The heavenly temple, as we saw so vividly in the last chapter with the book of Hebrews, is the reality; the OT Temple was a dim reflection.

We see in the next section that the elders held incense which was a common image for prayers in the OT (Ps 141:2). The instrumental music we see in the heavenly throne room was also prefigured in the elaborate music of the OT Temple (1 Chron 25:1, 3, 6; 2 Chron 5:12; 29:25; Neh 12:27; cf. 1 Sam 10:5). We can only assume by the context that these harps accompanied the new song that followed.

As you examine the song itself, you will notice that it is described as being a "new song" (ᾠδην καινην, *oiden kainen*). This terminology was used frequently in the Psalms (33:3; 40:3; 96:1; 98:1; 144:9; 149:1; see also Isaiah 42:9, 10) to describe something that was new in kind and character. The Greek has two words for "new:" *neos* meaning new in point of time, and *kainos*, used here, which means new in quality.

The song is a first person explanation of why the Lamb, described in the previous worship scene, is worthy to open the book and its seals. The Lamb is worthy because he was slain and by that act redeemed worshipers out of every tribe, people group, and nation (the reason I believe the elders are not angels). Not only are they redeemed, they are also given the exalted position of kings and priests, empowered to reign on the earth (5:9, see also 1:6).

In the second stanza of this song the elders and creatures are joined by an innumerable company of angels (9:11) singing now in the third person, "Worthy is the Lamb that was slain to receive power, and riches, and wisdom, and strength, and honor, and glory and blessing" (9:12). Again, the broader term "saying" (λέγοντες, *legontes*) is used of this unison proclamation with the additional qualifier "with a loud (*mighty*) voice" (φωνῇ μεγάλῃ, *phone megale*, from which we get megaphone).

Finally in the last stanza, again in the third person, we see the verbal fulfillment of Philippians 2:10-11: "That at the name of Jesus every knee should bow, of things in heaven, and things in earth, and things under the earth; And that every tongue should confess that Jesus Christ is Lord, to the glory of God the Father." This passage in Philippians and the passage here in Revelation are both hymns of praise as D. A. Carson puts forward.[3] Every creature in the universe joins in affirming the Lamb's eternal place on His throne and His worthiness to receive "blessing, and honor, and glory, and power" (9:13). To this the four beasts respond "amen" and the 24 elders once again fall down and worship (9:14).

Principles to Apply

- In Christian worship, God-centered worship is Christ-centered worship. It is Christ the Lamb that occupies the throne with the Father in the eternal Godhead.
- Christ's worthiness in worship is based not only on His creative acts but preeminently on His redemptive act.
- Many tenses are reflected in the music texts of Scripture. The worship music of believers should reflect the same variety.
- All of creation, redeemed and unredeemed alike, will one day bow the knee in worship to God.

Applications

I have found *Worship by the Book,* edited by D. A. Carson a very helpful resource. The most valuable part of the book is his insightful definition. It serves as a frame from which he interacts with many helpful concepts reflected in the Word. His definition for worship is so all inclusive I will quote it here.

> Worship is the proper response of all moral, sentient beings to God, ascribing all honor and worth to their Creator-God precisely because he is worthy, delightfully so. This side of the Fall, human worship of God properly responds to the redemptive provisions that God has graciously made. While all true worship is God-centered, Christian worship is no less Christ-centered. Empowered by the Spirit and in line with the stipulations of the new covenant, it manifests itself in all our living, finding its impulse in the gospel, which restores our relationship with our Redeemer-God and therefore also with our fellow image-bearers, our co-worshipers. Such worship therefore manifests itself both in adoration and in action, both in the individual believer and in corporate worship, which is worship offered up in the context of the body of believers, who strive to align all the forms of their devout ascription of all worth to God with the panoply of new covenant mandates and examples that bring to fulfillment the glories of antecedent revelation and anticipate the consummation.[4]

Notice specifically his line: "While all true worship is God-centered, Christian worship is no less Christ-centered." It is interesting to me that we see in Revelation both the Father and the Son occupying the throne. They are different in function and role but one in essence. We should not imagine that God the Father was alone on the throne in the OT and God the Son is now a superior figure in the NT. God has not and will not change. The whole Trinity is coequal and must be central in our worship. There is a movement today that seems to elevate Christ above the other members of the Trinity. Christ's work in redemption can cause us to develop a skewed idea that God's entire person is singularly defined by the gospel or His salvific work. God is even more than the sum total of His redemptive acts toward man. He is not monolithically concerned with saving mankind. His greater desire is to glorify Himself in *all* of His creation. Certainly the crowning action of God in Christ was the Passion Week culminating in His resurrection, but the other acts of God in creation are also a part of why we worship Him.

Technically, we understand that the *Trinity* is central, that *all* His works are worthy of our worship. Practically, we understand that being Christ-centered *is* being God-centered, for they exist as One.

Please don't misconstrue somehow, that centering Christ in our worship will leave us with nothing. We will have Christ, what greater treasure? Keep in mind that Christ is the perfectly selfless Bridegroom. Not only that, in His unrivaled care and provision for believers He has also given us the entire family of God. They act as agents of Christ. In our day they are His voice, hands, and feet. It is easy, however, to begin looking to the people in the church and lose our worship-center. God is the source, people are only resources. In heaven, if not before, all mere mortals will fade into our proper limited significance. On a very practical matter, I have been in churches where I believe people are too frequently mentioned for no apparent reason. Spend time in worship transitions endearing people to the Lord or the Scriptures and not to the people who are ministering. The few times I have been asked to sign someone's Bible I have asked them to sign mine in return. It just makes sense to me. Those of us who find ourselves in places of leadership in worship must be vigilant to mortify the pride that positions and titles lend themselves to. We who are in leadership are highly praised and highly criticized. Allow me to borrow an application from Revelation 4; lay the crowns you may receive in this life at Christ's feet often and completely. If you lose focus, if you lose your center, either pride or discouragement will rule your life. God help all of us to get used to the idea that "He must increase and we must decrease."

Let me take this opportunity to emphasize the content of the song texts we read in Revelation. I made specific note of the tense and theme variations in the exegetical section. Now I can make the practical suggestion that you balance your services with the same variations. You might think about beginning with more concrete statements of truth before asking everyone for a wholehearted testimony in song or a meditative prayer. I don't mean for this to be a legalistic formula, but I do think it can be a helpful pattern. Even in your personal worship you may need to begin by singing, saying, and praying concrete truths to God and yourself before you move to first person elements. Give thought to the overall balance of your worship texts.

Let me leave this passage by reminding you that we normally define worship in the context of redeemed people and their relationship with their loving heavenly Father. But there is a sense in which all creation will bow in worship to God. Sadly, some people will only "worship" as they bow to experience His wrath. We have the blessed opportunity to bow in submissive worship now as His adopted children. If we fail to humble ourselves now, we will be brought to our knees against our will. In either case we will be filled with awe, wonder, and fear.

Rev 7:9-17 The Worship of God for the Fulfillment of His Works
Exegetical Considerations

This group of worshipers is made up of an innumerable host of the redeemed from every nation, kindred, people group, and tongue who were saved during the tribulation (7:9). They are clothed in white and are waving palm branches as they sing "salvation to our

God which sitteth upon the throne, and unto the Lamb" (7: 10). The praise is directed to both God (τῷ θεῷ, *toi theoi*) and to the Lamb (τῷ ἀρνίῳ, *toi arnioi*). They are joined by angels, elders, and the four creatures who fall down (ἐπι τα προσωπα αὐτων, *epi ta prosopa auton*) before the throne and worship (προσεκύνησαν, *prosekunosan*) (7:11).

The opening text about salvation is followed by a second text sung by the angels, elders, and four creatures. It resembles the text we looked at in chapter 5. "Blessing and glory, and wisdom, and thanksgiving, and honor, and power, and might, be unto our God forever and ever. Amen" (7:12). Note also that separate feminine articles are used with each of the seven attributes given God, as in 4:11 and 5:12-13. After a short prose section the poetic song text continues in 7:14-17:

> These are they which came out of great tribulation,
>> and have washed their robes,
>> and made them white in the blood of the Lamb.
>> Therefore are they before the throne of God,
>>> and serve him day and night in his temple:
>>> and he that sitteth on the throne shall dwell among them.
>> They shall hunger no more,
>> neither thirst anymore;
>> neither shall the sun light on them, nor any heat.
> For the Lamb which is in the midst of the throne shall feed them,
>> and shall lead them unto living fountains of waters:
>> and God shall wipe away all tears from their eyes.

This poetic text starts with concrete statements of truth and then moves to personal testimonies about the benefits of salvation; how these truths affect the believer.

Notice that the elders are among the group who "worship" (προσεκύνησαν, *prosekunosan*) (7:11) and later the redeemed are said to "serve" (λατρευουσιν αὐτῳ *latreuousin autoi*) (7:15). Just as terms are used to describe the activities of believers in a previous dispensation, they are used here to describe eternal activity.

Principles for Application

- Believers from every people group gather to offer praise and adoration to the Trinity, specifically, both the Father and the Son.
- Song texts that express concrete attributes of God are often followed by texts that express personal testimonies.
- Worship that is characterized by both adoration and acts of service are seen in every dispensation.

Applications

As I mentioned in the previous passage, worship is Trinitarian. I tell you emphatically: all three persons of the Trinity are involved in worship. In this passage the Father and the Son occupy the throne. One person of the Trinity is not somehow more personal. "Jesus knows our every weakness" but so does the Father. Christ's friends are no less God's friends. Christ and the Spirit both stand as our intercessors (Rom 8:26, 34). Though I cannot offer many of my own solutions, since my gifts as a poet are limited, I believe we really need more good theologically sound songs about the Spirit's role in our lives. He is often ignored in our preaching and singing. Yet, the Spirit is just as fully Trinity. Make sure that you strive to keep the balance of the Trinity in your worship.

I am impressed, even a little surprised, with the fact that worship around the throne does not seem to erase racial differences (distinct peoples and nations are mentioned) but still clearly pictures a unified voice in worship. The whole NT pictures a people of God united around pure worship (Eph 2:11-22). It is so sad when Satan introduces the error that racial heritage or culture should cause divisions in our worship. Being a unified people in worship does not mean we must surrender our racial identities, but it does mean that our various identities should not hinder us from bringing one mind, the mind of Christ, and one heart, filled with the Spirit, before our common Father God. In heaven, if never before, unity around true worship will bring believers together into a single wave of praise. Unity in our worship should be our goal *through* our cultural diversity. Practical choices need to be made to build unity within cultural diversity and this happens when worshipers are united around the truth.

We see again that the text in this passage goes from concrete theology to personal experience. I am not repeating this so that you slavishly begin every gathering with the rigid format of deep theological songs and never begin with a simple testimony song. What I am saying is that this is the pattern we have seen in the Psalms, and clearly in this passage. Let this pattern inform our worship and music choices. In this text, we see salvation rightly pictured as the gift of God; it is all of Him. Then we see many of God's glorious attributes enumerated. Only after this does the text move to a description of what God has done for believers. As a minimum we should be introducing our songs by pointing to the character of the Trinity as it relates to our Christian experience.

I mentioned in the introduction that *proskuneo* or related words are used prominently in describing the worship of Revelation. Just as we saw in the gospels, people responded with this kind of worship when they saw Christ for who He was. In the epistles, we see the word *latreu* or related words used more frequently. I made the point in the gospels and again in the epistles that the use of either word is not exclusive. During this church age, we are rightfully preoccupied with the business of *latreu*. But when the Bridegroom was here on earth and when we go to Him into His throne room, we will be rightfully preoccupied with *proskuneo*. But even in the eternal state we will do more than just bow before the Lamb and sing His praises, we will also serve Him, or do "jobs" for Him. In the eternal state both words and works will be a part of our practice of worship. The balance will change but the elements will remain.

Rev 14: 2-11 New Song of Heaven Sung by the Martyred 144,000; "The Everlasting Gospel"
Exegetical Considerations

I have included this passage for one main reason: the explanation of "the eternal gospel" (εὐαγγελιον αἰωνιον, *euaggelion aionion*). In chapter 14 we see a song sung by the redeemed and martyred 144,000 witnesses. In this song they are accompanying themselves on harps. I remember someone describing heaven and saying, "It's not like we are going to be playing harps or something up there." But there are harps in heaven and the redeemed will be playing them (5:8, 14:2, and 15:2). Again music is described as a wall of sound, a voice of many waters, a great thunder (1:15, 4:5, 6:1, 10:3-4, 11:19, 14:2, 16:18 and 19:15). I believe a plain reading of the context and the literary structure informs us that this is the glorious song of those martyrs. The song itself was "a new song…and no man could learn the song except the hundred, and forty and four thousand, which were redeemed from the earth" (14:3).After a description of these individuals in 14:4-5 we read the proclamation of the "eternal gospel" by an angel:

> And I saw another angel fly in the midst of heaven, having the everlasting gospel to preach unto them that dwell on the earth, and to every nation, and kindred, and tongue, and people, Saying with a loud voice, **Fear God**, (φοβήθητε τὸν θεὸν, *phobethute ton Theon*) and **give glory** (δόξαν, *doxan*) to Him; for the hour of his judgment is come: and **worship** (προσκυνήσατε, *proskunesate*) Him that made heaven, and earth, and the sea, and the fountains of waters (**emphasis** mine) (Rev 14:6-7).

The song continues with the familiar formula of attribute and then actions. In this case they are the specific rehearsal of the actions of God in His wrath and judgment (11:18-19).

Principles for Application

- God's good news, or gospel, is His invitation to an everlasting worship relationship.
- Worship texts in the Word generally progress from God's attributes, to His actions, and then to human experience.

Applications

We have come full circle. Since Genesis, God has intended to have a relationship with mankind; a relationship that is characterized by man's worship of God. I was recently looking over a gospel tract that described Christ as the gateway or bridge to eternal life. I don't doubt the sincerity of the sentiment or the glorious truth that heaven can be our home through the work of Christ. What I find distressing is that we give the impression that the "thing" we seek is heaven, not the person of God. Since creation, God has sought to glorify Himself, and one of the ways He shows His own magnificent and glorious character is by inviting man to have a relationship with Him. Here in Revelation we understand clearly that the eternal gospel, the eternal good news, is that God invites man to have a relationship with Him.

This relationship is established by fearing God, giving God glory, and humbly worshiping Him (14:7). Carson says, "The message is called *the eternal gospel*, since the eternal blessings of the good news still remain for those who will respond."[5] Wilmington expands upon this idea and suggests that the eternal gospel is in three parts, proclaimed by three angels. The "first invites people to fear and glorify God before judgment falls (14:6–7). The second predicts Babylon's fall (14:8; 18). The third warns against worshiping the Antichrist (14:9–11)."[6] Juxtaposed against the eternal gospel is the eternal judgment awaiting those who are in league with the harlot Babylon and bow in worship to the beast (14:8-11). It is our relationship with God that allows us to be with Him, where He is—in heaven. Jesus is our gateway or bridge to God, which only incidentally, brings us to heaven.

The martyrs sing a grand and glorious sound that we have never experienced before; a song that is new in kind and character. We see around the throne our song of everlasting praise, praise focused on God's great attributes, many of which Christians today do not even know. This is such a good place to start, for all sinful temptation can be traced back to a denial of some aspect of God's person. After a clear recitation of God's great character the song text moves to recount God's great actions, even actions of judgment.

It's all about content; content that is sung, content that is sung in a way that is new in kind and character.

Rev 15:3-4 The Song of Moses
Exegetical Considerations

In this victory song, sung by triumphant saints with their harps (15:2), we see a song text borrowed from the OT. It is the song of Moses and the song of the Lamb (15:3). The first song refers to the song of Moses in Exodus 15 or perhaps Deuteronomy 32. It is possible the entire song is in view here as it was at other times when a short phrase was referenced (the Temple dedication [1 Chron 16] and rededication [Ezra 3:11]). The song is then applied to the present triumph in Revelation. It is no surprise that parallels between Israel's exodus out of Egypt and Christ's victory in the tribulation would appear together in this song.

In this song we are again reminded of God's great deeds, justice, truth, glory, and holiness. Then we read again how all the nations will worship God (Ps 2:8-9; 24:1-10; 66:1-4; 72:8-11; 86:9; Isa 2:2-4; 9:6-7; 66:18-23; Jer 10:7; Dan 7:14; Zeph 2:11; Zech 14:9). Carson insightfully observed that,

> Every line of the song is reminiscent of the prophets and psalmists. *Great and marvellous are your deeds*, *cf.* Ps. 98:1; 111:2; 139:14. *Just and true are your ways*, *cf.* Dt. 32:3; Ps. 145:17. *Who will not fear you ...*, *cf.* Je. 10:7. *All nations will come ...*, *cf.* Ps. 86:9. *Your righteous acts have been revealed*, *cf.* Ps. 98:2; Is. 26:9.[7]

The fact that the song is made up entirely of quotes from the OT shows a level of continuity in worship concepts reflected in this text. These phrases were not only a part of the OT texts but remain a part of Jewish liturgy even today.[8]

I think it is important to recognize that the worship phrases first focus on the works of the Lord and then the ways of the Lord. "Great and marvelous are Thy works, Lord God Almighty; just and true are they ways, thou King of saints" (15:3). Knowing God's works is important; knowing God's ways is essential. What follows is a rhetorical question. "Who shall not fear Thee, O Lord, and glorify Thy name?" (15:4a). What the passage is presenting is that those who understand God's works and ways naturally respond by fearing and glorifying God. Then there are three truth statements: "for Thou only are holy: for all nations shall come and worship before Thee; for Thy judgments are made manifest" (15:4b).

Principles for Application

- The continuity of worship music texts is seen throughout the Bible.
- Worship texts should reflect not only God's works but also His ways. These truths should shape the response of the worshiper.
- Even in the eternal state, worship is characterized by godly fear and active glorification of the Godhead.
-

Applications

We have new songs mentioned in Revelation yet we also have the song of Moses (Exodus 15) being sung. Some songs have contemporary application to things happening within the context of the narrative and some songs are taken from the early patriarchs of Israel. It is probably a little bit of a stretch, but I would suggest that perhaps even this might inform our choices now. No, the passage does not teach this truth, but as a model we might think about the possibility of including both songs that reflect grace age living with songs that recognize our connection with other believers in other ages. Not every song in Revelation is strictly about the ministry of Christ or the work of the church during John's day. Again, we need balance that reflects the balance of God's Word. I resist the idea that every song in the NT church must speak of a salvific act.

As I began saying in the exegetical section, I am challenged to consider the emphasis on both the works and then the ways of God. Every word God has put in His Word is important (plenary); the fact that we read "works" (ἔργα, *erga* literally, the actions of

God) and "way" (ὁδοί, *hodoi* literally, the direction God is moving) speaks to us of the need to expand our knowledge of God to include more than just what God has done, but also the direction He is moving. It is the difference between knowing random actions and understanding how a person thinks. God's works should inform us about His ways. It is in this deeper sense that God desires for us to know Him instead of simply knowing about Him. Learning Bible stories has a place, but moving beyond the story to the lesson we must learn about God's ways is much more important. Weirsbe concludes this section by saying that if "earth-dwellers ... would not praise God for His works, they would never understand His ways.[9] Teach your people God's works, and in your teaching make sure they grasp His ways. I think this is especially important when we interact with the music curriculum of our children's ministries.

As the works and ways of God are known, it is obvious that our response should be to fear the Lord and glorify Him. This is only natural. To see God and not be moved with fear and actively glorify Him is impossible. Revelation 15:4 summarizes that God alone is holy, God alone in His Lordship commands the worship of all the nations, God's judgments are manifest for all to see. If we see the Lord in all His glory and if we help those we minister with see the Lord in all His glory, worship will follow. This is essentially our "job" as leaders.

Rev 19:1-8 The Chorus of the Redeemed
Exegetical Considerations

Chapter 19 gives us the last three songs of the great Apocalypse. It is the fourfold Hallelujah of the end of time (19: 1, 3, 4, and 6). This passage is the only time that the word "hallelujah" (ἀλληλουϊά, *allelouia*) is used in the NT. Alleluia means "praise the Lord," however, which is repeated many times in the NT and the LXX. The Hallel Psalms (the title for Pss 113 to 118) derive their title from the word "hallelujah" and were sung annually at both the Feast of the Passover and the Feast of Tabernacles.

The first hallelujah begins when "a great voice of much people in heaven" (19:1a) is heard singing, "Hallelujah; Salvation, and

The first hallelujah begins when "a great voice of much people in heaven" (19:1a) is heard singing, "Hallelujah; Salvation, and glory, and honor and power, unto the Lord our God" (19:1b) because judgment was brought upon the great harlot. Revelation 19:2 is a quote taken from the larger song we read in Deuteronomy 32:34-43. Alleluia is then repeated as the smoke of judgment rises up. "Celebrating" the demise of an enemy is foreign to our culture but not to the world of John and his original audience. It also has biblical precedent; recall the song of Deborah (Jud 5) and the songs of victory of Israel (Ex 15; 1 Sam 18:6-7). In fact, this song is the commanded response to the defeat of Babylon: "Rejoice over her!" (Rev. 18:20).

Again the twenty-four elders and the four living creatures fall down before God, singing responsively, "Amen; Alleluia" (19:4). What follows is a voice coming "out of the throne, saying, praise our God, all ye his servants, and ye that fear Him small and great" (19:5). Obviously, it is not the Son or the Father calling for the worship since it is a call to worship "our" God, but likely one of the angels.

Finally, John hears "as the voice of a great multitude and as the voice of many waters, and as a voice of mighty thundering, (ὡς φωνην μεγαλην ὀχλου πολλου, *hos phonen megalen ouchlou pollou*) saying Alleluia; for the Lord God omnipotent reigneth" (19:6). What follows is a song celebrating the marriage of the Lamb and His Bride, the church. The picture of the marriage relationship between God and His people is a common image in both the OT and the NT (Isa. 62:4; Hos 2:19-21; Eze 16:1; Ps 45; Mark 2:19; 1 Cor 6:15-17; Eph 5:25-27). Pfeiffer points out the beauty of the Bride in this lovely wedding song.

> The bridal attire is noticeably different from the attire of the great harlot, for the holy bride wears only glistening white and pure linen (Rev 19:8), symbol of the righteous acts of the saints. All that the NT speaks of as relating to Christ the bridegroom and the Church the bride is now consummated.[10]

It is important to remember that the foundation of joy and gladness in this passage is the worthiness of the Lamb; it is He that has made the Bride ready (19:7). About this gladness, TDNT says "It is indeed the eschatological act of divine salvation which is supremely the theme of rejoicing, as is seen most clearly in the song of Revelation 19:7."[11] The Bride's white garments have been washed in the blood of the Lamb and her fine linen, which is the "righteousness of the saints" is white because, and only because, she has been clothed by the work of Christ (19:8). Last, other believers (OT believers and tribulation saints) are invited to the millennial marriage of Christ and His Bride (19:9).

Principles for Application

- The character and actions of God should be the basis of the believer's praise.
- Joy and gladness are blessings that Christ gives His Bride the Church. These positive emotions are the result of a right relationship with God and should motivate believers to honor Him in worship.
-

Applications

First God's character is extolled. God is to be praised because He is the author of salvation; He is glorious, honorable, powerful, just, and righteous in His judgments. It is then that we are reminded of God's actions. God brought down the harlot Babylon and avenged the blood of the martyrs. The response of the elders and creatures is to once again bow and proclaim Amen and Alleluia! The command for the throne room dwellers, both small and great, to praise our God is the natural response of glorified servants who fear the Lord. Even in heaven, balanced fear is a part of the worship of believers and so it should be with us. The call to worship we see in this worship text is fully heeded. This great company, with a communal voice that sounded like rushing water and thunder lifts up a crescendo of praise for God's omnipotent Lordship. Finally the gladness and joy of the Bride is complete. Weirsbe comments on our matrimonial relationship by saying:

The wedding feast (19:7–9) is a reference to the end of the long and sometimes painful engagement between Christ and his saints. It marks the beginning of the eternal unbroken marriage relationship of perfect fellowship and love. This vision is here to encourage the readers through their tribulations with the vision of their ultimate entrance into God's glory. The study of prophecy should witness to Jesus, giving believers a greater appreciation of His person and work (19:10).[12]

John the Baptist describes his joy as the "friend of the Bridegroom" when He points to Christ as the one who must take the higher place with the Bride (John 3:29-30). We must also continually look for ways to be the friend of the Bridegroom and endear the church to her true leader and love, Jesus Christ.

We see in Revelation models for worship that inform and challenge. Though we live in a different world with many limitations it is important to allow these perfect models to help us see more clearly the heart of our Savior and God. It is our study of the Word that will give us the models for worship and music we should use as our templates. God give us wisdom.

Chapter Sixteen
Conclusions

The NT church today must know the mandates and principles about worship and music we read in the Word. If you have jumped ahead to this chapter without having entered into the study, let me implore you to rethink your decision. You may agree with the conclusions you are about to read, but I hope you do so only because you are convinced from your own study of the Word. You are free to disagree; but again I hope you do so because of your study of the Word. Go to the Bible first, and then draw out from this wonderful, inspired Source of Truth your conclusions about worship. It is there we read that all of the Word is profitable for our daily lives. This is why we must move on to practically applying the Word in our lives. I hope this study will be a beginning for you. I assure you it represents only a beginning for me. My study has led me to shed some dogmas I once held and feel a growing passion about concepts I only casually held before. Truth does that in our lives. I hope as you interact with the truth of God's Word you too will be refined and purified. As I reread the manuscript in preparation for this final chapter, I made several changes. I am quite sure that if I read it several dozen times more I would continue to see concepts I wish I had stated differently. But the time has come. I am writing this brief chapter to bring to the surface one more time concepts that I believe we need to wrestle through in our time.

I begin by stating the cornerstone truth that God alone is worthy of all worship and that He, for His own glory, created moral beings to celebrate His greatness in worship. This worship is only made possible when God reveals Himself and initiates a relationship so men can be empowered to bring a gift back to Him, showing Him their honor and love. Because He is supremely worthy, all moral agents, including angels, must make the choice to enter into a worship relationship with God. True worship happens only when we worship on His terms and for His pleasure; true worship is characterized by spirit and truth, heart and understanding. Any other worship is false worship. Any other worship is essentially self-worship.

Because God's express intention is to have this worship relationship with His creation, He endowed sentient beings with the gift of communication, specifically the gift of music. Music is not the creation of human culture but a reflection of it. Ultimately, the fact that God is a musical God and has shared with angels and man this musical gift must temper every conversation about music's moral character. It makes a difference that God, and not man, is the Author of music. I also see in this "truth of first importance" profound implications about the spirit world. We wrestle with spiritual forces who are also musical beings. We cannot be ignorant of Satan's devices, nor can we ignore the work of his henchmen in this world. We also understand that music is a powerful force in the world of men today because God intended it so. Music's power, intended to be a blessing to mankind, can also be twisted into a force for evil. To ignore its power for good or evil is foolish. The influence of music has certainly been intensified by the unprecedented technological advances of our day.

Throughout the Word we see music as a divinely ordained tool to communicate first to God and then to others many different kinds of information. Music is a memory aid, a teaching method, a constant admonisher, and an emotion-charged tool for celebrating human and divine attributes, characteristics, acts and ideas. Music is a wonderful communication tool that will go on for eternity. Never let the efforts of some in our time minimize music's biblical role in your life and ministry. I believe we live in a time when music is unfairly relegated to the trivial world of the entertainer. Many in the church labor under the misconception that important truths belong to the preacher alone who must be the sole speaker of truth. The Word on the other hand also calls the congregation, individual believer priests, to speak, teach, and admonish through singing as well as through speech. Because of the teaching and counseling power of music, because of the God-given power of music to affect our will and emotion, musicians are more than entertainers; they are powerful proclaimers of or detractors from truth. Many today are deceived into thinking that it doesn't matter who their musical teachers are. Not only that, many ignore the positive benefits of a life filled with music that builds the Spirit and causes the Word to richly dwell in the believer's life.

The Word teaches us to transform our own minds using the wonderful tool of music privately and it also gives us mandates and principles for the use of music in the church. Our musical choices in public worship reveal God. We must strive for the goal of picturing the Godhead accurately in all His transcendence and eminence. Our goal is clarity in presentation, wholeheartedness in participation. Only as we strive in our worship choices to reveal God in His completeness can we hope to see Him formed in us.

We must also embrace just as completely the truth that we are seeking to lead God's people to respond with wholehearted, selfless praise in a musical vocabulary that reflects simplicity and complexity, transcendence and eminence. We seek both to reveal God and to offer appropriate responses to Him in worship. Both the innate characteristics of music and the associational characteristics of the music must be wisely and lovingly considered. This kind of balance, so desperately needed, will only be accomplished within the context of the totality of our worship choices. Wisdom for the practical application of this lofty goal can be ours as we humbly seek God.

The goals of our church music program will be reflected in our practice. We must plan with great care. We have the mandate of Scripture to critically examine the balance and direction of our musical choices and allow the model of the Word to determine whether our balance is successful or not. Make an ongoing list of what you are presenting musically and ask the question of balance with your church staff or several who are involved in the worship ministries of your local church. This is obviously paramount when it comes to corporate praise in congregational singing, what I consider the most important element of the musical delivery of the Word. I think it is also important when leaders in worship (what we commonly call "special music") pray, testify, or declare a truth about God through music. Soloists, accompanists, choirs, Scripture readers, and even those making announcements must understand the importance of their role and demeanor as they partner with the senior pastor in modeling biblical worship. Musicians should be brought in as partners in the presentation of truth. They should be reminded of their responsibility of teaching and admonishing in light of the whole service and not just sing whatever strikes them at the time. All music should be prayerfully selected in light of the overall theme of the service.

We must also wrestle each week with centering and connecting all the aspects of the service, both spoken and sung. This can be either thematic or sequential but must always be logical. The "big idea" of the service, driven by the Bible text of the spoken message, should bring along the musical elements of the service. The propositions of some Bible texts are best served when the application is built on the foundation of a specific act or attribute of God in worship. For example, sequentially moving from God's mercy to the need for believers to share the gospel with others could be an effective way to present the big idea of outreach. Both speakers and singers must be committed to the clear exposition of the Word; it is paramount that unity be maintained. When we consider the actions of Baptism and the Lord's Supper or our physical responses in worship, our supreme desire should be the edification of the body.

The goal of personal music choices must reflect the truths of the Word as well. Every believer should be overt in his spoken and sung praise of our Savior. Personal worship is the theme of many of the worship narratives we studied together. Our personal worship profoundly influences the direction and effectiveness of corporate worship. Consider asking these questions when making personal music choices:

A. Understanding Yourself
- Is this controlling me in any way? Why am I listening to this? 1 Cor 6:12; Rom 6:12
- Are spirit-controlled emotions expressed and encouraged? Gal 5:24
- Is this feeding the old man or the new man? Col 3:5-6,10
- Am I fully convinced this is acceptable to the Lord? Is He glorified? Rom 14:23; Eph 5:10-11
- Is this music advancing my growth? 2 Pet 1:5-8

B. Understanding Your Musical Teachers and Counselors
- What is this musical teacher's motivation and agenda? 2 Pet 2:1-2
- What fruits are identified with this music? What character is being revealed? 2 Tim 3:1-5
- Is this teaching consistent with Phil 4:8; Prov 4:23-27; and 2 Cor 10:5?

C. Understanding How My Musical Choices Affect Others.
- What impact will this have on others? Rom 14:15; 1 Cor 8 and 10
- Am I acting in love or flaunting my liberty? 1 Cor 8:12-13
- What is identified with this music for others? 1 Cor 10:31-33
- Is this making for peace and edifying? Am I preferring others? Rom 12:10; 14:19
- Is this building up my local church and pastor? Heb 13:17

D. Understanding Music Ministry in the Church
- Are the Lord and the Christian experience accurately portrayed? Col 3:16
- Does this selection advance what Pastor is trying to achieve in this service? 1 Cor 14:26
- Does this music endear people to the right teachers? Eph 5:11
- Does the singer or the style distract from or obscure the message? 1 Cor 14:7-12

Someday believers and angels alike will forever worship Him who alone is worthy. God-centered worship continues to be the greatest need and worship choices continue to be the most controversial issue of the church today. My desire is for you to move forward and let the Word have the preeminence in all your thinking about worship and music. My desire is for you to move away from false worship which so insidiously plagues the church. "Have no fellowship with the unfruitful works of darkness, but rather reprove them" (Eph 5:11). Until we all bow before the Lamb to worship without hindrance, may God alone be your final thought, may you draw near to Him in full assurance, may God alone be your center and may God's Word be your final authority for worship and music.

Chapter 1- endnotes

[1] Strong, James: *The Exhaustive Concordance of the Bible: Showing Every Word of the Text of the Common English Version of the Canonical Books, and Every Occurrence of Each Word in Regular Order.* Ontario: Woodside Bible Fellowship., 1996, S. G3008

[2] Process theology teaches that God "grow(s) and develop(s) like the rest of the universe" (Milard Ericson in *Christian Theology* [Grand Rapids, Michigan: Baker Book House, 1984] 264.) I am opposed to the process theologian's view of God, specifically as it may be applied to the worship of God in the church today.

[3] Cultus or cult is an increasingly common word in worship writing that is used in this book to refer to the actual practices of worship.

[4] William Wickes, *Two Treatises on the Accentuation of the OT* (New York: KTAV Publishing House, Inc., 1970), 1.

[5] You may want to refer to John Frame's more detailed work on this subject in *Worship in Spirit and Truth*, pp. 111-122. Although there are several matters on which Dr. Frame and I would disagree, I desire to do so charitably, accurately, and to acknowledge where I believe he contributes to the discussion. Although I have attempted to communicate with him via email he has not responded at the time of this publication.

[6] Duane L. Christensen, *A Song of Power and the Power of Song* (Winona Lake, IN: Eisenbrauns, 1993), 6. Christensen says that because music is such a powerful form of communication in some cultures, some Wycliffe Bible translators are considering abandoning written translation altogether in favor of musical forms.

[7] John Piper, *Don't Waste Your Life* (Wheaton, IL: Crossway Books, 2003), 162.

[8] Matt Redman, ed., *The Heart of Worship Files* (Ventura, CA: Regal Books, 2003), 13.

Chapter 2 – endnotes

[1] This word is used in its formal sense. It refers to the organized practice of a religious system. For instance, the Mosaic sacrificial system is the "cultus" of Israelite worship.

² R. L. Harris, G. L. Archer, and B. K. Waltke, *Theological Wordbook of the Old Testament* (Chicago: Moody Press, 1999, c1980). All footnotes of this work will use the abbreviation TWOT. Exact locations will be given using TWOT number or Scripture passage. Either can be referenced in Logos or Bibleworks. TWOT # 2131a.

³ TWOT

⁴ J. F. Walvoord and R. B. Zuck; Dallas Theological Seminary. *The Bible Knowledge Commentary: An Exposition of the Scriptures* (Wheaton, IL: Victor Books 1983, c1985), Job 38:7.

⁵ John E. Hartley, *The Book of Job* (Grand Rapids, MI: William B. Eerdmans Publishing Co., 1988), 495.

⁶ The two Greek words most commonly translated "speak" are λέγω *lego* and λαλέω *laleo*. There are subtle differences in shades of meaning, but they are synonymous in the sense that they both refer to proclaiming something. *Laleo*, for example is most commonly translated "speak" but obviously has a broader meaning when Paul uses it to refer to singing in Ephesians 5:19. *Lego* is also used to refer to singing as it is in Revelation 5:9 (καὶ ᾄδουσιν ᾠδὴν καινὴν λέγοντες). They literally "sang saying." I believe speaking and singing can both be in view, especially when what follows is a poetic section. See further the treatment of these passages in chapter 13 - Revelation.

⁷ For a summary treatment of the argument for this dual meaning position see John F. Walvoord and Roy B. Zuck; Dallas Theological Seminary: *The Bible Knowledge Commentary: An Exposition of the Scriptures* (Wheaton, IL: Victor Books, 1983-c1985), S. 1:1284. They also take this position.

⁸ Francis Brown, Samuel Rolles Driver and Charles Augustus Briggs, *Enhanced Brown-Driver-Briggs Hebrew and English Lexicon* (Oak Harbor, WA: Logos Research Systems, 2000), xiii.

⁹ Ibid., xiii.

¹⁰ TWOT #1409. See also Holliday's lexicon, following W. F. Albright in BASOR, *Bulletin of the American Schools of Oriental Research*, No. 110.

¹¹ Rabbi Moshe Eisemann, *Yechezkel a New Translation with a Commentary Anthologized from Talmudic, Midrashic and Rabbinic Sources* (Brooklyn,

NY: Mesorah Publications, Ltd., 1988), 469. Eisemann's work agrees with this translation and then adds "which most commentators concur."

[12] TWOT #285. Used here as it is many of the 385 times to indicate God's conference of His favor on man.

[13] Gordon J. Wenham, *Word Bible Commentary, Vol. 1 Genesis 1-15* (Waco, TX: Word Inc., 1987), 76.

[14] TWOT # 1782b.

[15] Nils Wallin, Bjorn Merker and Steve Brown, eds., *The Origins of Music* (Cambridge, MA: The MIT Press, 2001), 8.

[16] Egon Wellesz, ed., *Ancient and Oriental Music* (London: Oxford University Press, 1957), 2.

[17] Curt Sachs, *The Rise of Music in the Ancient East and West* (New York: W.W. Norton and Co., 1943), 20.

[18] Wellesz, *Ancient and Oriental Music*, 231.

[19] Wallin, *The Origins of Music*, 3. See also his chapter on "Universals in Music," 23-26.

[20] For a more scholarly treatment of this issue see: John Makujina, *Measuring the Music* (Willow Street, PA: Old Paths Publications, 2002), Chapters 4, 5 and Appendix C.

[21] Herbert W. Bateman, ed., *Authentic Worship: Hearing Scripture's Voice, Applying Its Truths* (Grand Rapids, MI: Kregel Publications, 2002), 162.

[22] For a more complete treatment of the morality question, see also Kimberly Smith, *Music and Morals, Dispelling the Myth* (Enumclaw, WA: WinePress Publishing, 2005), Frank Garlock and Kurt Woetzel, *Music in the Balance* (Greenville, SC: Majesty Music, 1992), or John Makujina in *Measuring the Music: Another Look at the Contemporary Christian Music Debate* (Willow Street, PA: Old Paths Publications, 2002).

[23] Bateman, *Authentic Worship: Hearing Scripture's Voice, Applying Its Truths*, 163.

[24] John M. Frame, *Worship in Spirit and Truth* (Phillipsburg, NJ: Presbyterian and Reformed Publishing House, 1996), 111.

[25] Ibid., 112-113.

[26] Dan Kimball, *Emerging Worship: Creating New Worship Gatherings for Emerging Generations* (Grand Rapids, MI: Zondervan Publishers, 2004), vii.

[27] Ibid., vi.

[28] I will suggest only a few of the many resources available in this area. In the area of ancient music, internet sources I found helpful include an article by Thomas Cahill, accessed at http://www.randomhouse.com/features/cahill/essay5.html, William Barry, in a well researched article accessible at http://www.newadvent.org/cathen/12174b.htm, an article by Jewish scholars Emil G. Hirsch and Wilhelm Nowack at http://www.jewishencyclopedia.com/view.jsp?artid=1021&letter=M and several sites too numerous to mention here under the search question "ancient Hebrew poetry was sung."

Printed works of value include Louis A. Burkhalter, *Ancient and Oriental Music*, Vol. I Oxford History of Music, (London: H. S. Stuttman Co.; distributed by Doubleday, 1968), 25ff., C.C.J. Polin, *Music of Ancient Near East*, (New York: Vantage, 1954) especially p. 73. and Braun, Joachim, *Music in Ancient Israel/Palestine: Archaeological, Written and Comparative Sources*. (Grand Rapids, MI: William B. Eerdmans Publishing Co., 2002). In addition, although I do not agree with all her conclusions, the work of Suzanne Haik-Vantoura, *The Music of the Bible Revealed* (Trans. by Dennis Weber) (John Wheeler, ed.; BI-BAL Press/King David's Harp, Inc., 1991) also addresses the issue of sung Hebrew poetry.

[29] Ulrich S. Leupold, "Worship Music in Ancient Israel: Its Meaning and Purpose" (*Canadian Journal of Theology*) xv (1969), 180.

[30] Enhanced Strong's Lexicon: 4503 מִנְחָה Hereafter all footnotes of this work will use the abbreviation ESL. Exact locations will be given using ESL number or Scripture passage. Either can be referenced in Logos or Bibleworks.

[31] On the word order (conjunction + subject + verb) see Matthew Henry, *Matthew Henry's Commentary on the Whole Bible; Complete and Unabridged in One Volume* (Peabody, NY: Hendrickson 1996, c1991).

[32] Brown, Driver and Briggs, *Enhanced Brown-Driver-Briggs Hebrew and English Lexicon*.

[33] I use the term worship event to give the broadest possible definition. This includes both public, corporate events like temple worship, or the formal

worship of Cain and Abel in Genesis 4 as well as private worship times like Abraham's worship with Isaac.

[34] Charles Hodge, *Systematic Theology Vol. 3* (Oak Harbor, WA: Logos Research Systems, Inc., 1997), 363.

[35] Henry, *Mathew Henry's Commentary on the Whole Bible; Complete and Unabridged in One Volume*, S. Ge 6:8.

[36] Walvoord and Zuck *The Bible Knowledge Commentary: An Exposition of the Scriptures*, S. 1:37.

[37] TWOT #1624 suggests, "Thus, the whole animal is brought up to the altar and the whole is offered as a gift (*minha*, q.v.) in homage to Yahweh."

Chapter 3 - endnotes

[1] Tremper Longman, *Immanuel in Our Place* (Phillipsburg, New Jersey: P and R Publishing Co., 2001), 16.

[2] Earlier (Genesis 17:3, 17) the phrase "fell upon his face" is also used.

[3] David Peterson, *Engaging with God: A Biblical Theology of Worship* (Downers Grove: Intervarsity Press, 1992), 63.

[4] Noel Due, *Created for Worship, From Genesis to Revelation to You* (Geanies House, Scotland: Christian Focus Publications, Ltd., 2005), 50.

[5] Walvoord and Zuck, *The Bible Knowledge Commentary: An Exposition of the Scriptures*, S. 1:58.

[6] James M. Freeman and Harold J. Chadwick, *Manners and Customs of the Bible Rev. ed.* (North Brunswick, NJ: Bridge-Logos Publishers, 1998), S. 24.

[7] Robert Webber makes a strong case for this. See Robert Webber, *Evangelicals On the Canterbury Trail: Why Evangelicals Are Attracted to the Liturgical Church* (New York: Morehouse Pub. Co., 1989). For a succinct treatment refer to the encyclopedic work he edits. Robert Webber, ed., *The Complete Library of Christian Worship. Vol. 6, The Sacred Actions of Christian Worship* (Nashville, TN: Star Song Publishing Group, 1993), 73-76.

⁸ Calvin M. Johansson, *Music and Ministry, A Biblical Counterpoint*, (Peabody, Massachusetts: Henderson Publications 1984), 51.

⁹ Ibid., 59-60. Note that Johansson also supports jazz as a legitimate medium. I disagree at this point for two reasons. First the associations and origins of jazz make it highly suspect. Second from observing the sexual fruits associated with its use. Secular jazz players give testimony to this effect on their listeners.

¹⁰ David J. Hesselgrave and Edward Rommen, *Contextualization* (Grand Rapids: Baker, 1989), 162.

¹¹ John Makujina, Unpublished paper delivered at the National Leadership Conference, Lansdale, PA, 1999. 8.

¹² Barry Liesch, *People in the Presence of God* (Grand Rapids, MI: Zondervan Publishing House, 1988), 235-239. This chapter is entitled, "Why Seminaries Should Teach Music and Worship."

Chapter 4 - endnotes

¹ D. A. Carson, *New Bible Commentary: 21st Century Edition 4th ed.* (Leicester, England; Downers Grove, Ill., USA: Inter-Varsity Press, 1994), S. Dt 16:21.

² See also J. H. Kurtz, *Offerings, Sacrifices and Worship in the Old Testament* (Peabody, Massachusetts: Hendrickson Pub. Inc., 1998), 35-36.

³ Walvoord and Zuck, *The Bible Knowledge Commentary: An Exposition of the Scriptures*, S. 1:294.

⁴ Ibid., S. 1:302.

⁵ Robert Jamieson, A. R. Fausset and David Brown, *A Commentary, Critical and Explanatory, on the Old and New Testaments* (Oak Harbor, WA: Logos Research Systems, Inc., 1997), S. Dt 22:11.

⁶ Brown, Driver, and Briggs, *Enhanced Brown-Driver-Briggs Hebrew and English Lexicon.*

⁷ Jamieson, Fausset and Brown, *A Commentary, Critical and Explanatory, on the Old and New Testaments*, 69.

[8] Frank E. Gaebelein, ed., *The Expositor's Bible Commentary, Vol. 2* (Grand Rapids, MI: Zondervan Publishing House, 1990), 480.

[9] Keil and Delitzsch, *Commentary on the Old Testament*, S. 1:466.
[10] Ibid. S. 1:468.

[11] Eugene Merrill, *The New American Commentary: An Exegetical and Theological Exposition of Holy Scripture NIV Text Vol. IV* (Nashville: Broadman and Holman Publishers, 1994), 402.

Chapter 5 - endnotes

[1] Keil and Delitzsch, *Commentary on the Old Testament*, S. 1:285-286.

[2] Freeman and Chadwick, *Manners and Customs of the Bible Rev. ed.*, S. 102.

[3] Warren W. Wiersbe, *Be Strong* (Wheaton, IL: Victor Books, 1996, c1993), S. Jos 5:13.

[4] Walvoord and Zuck, *The Bible Knowledge Commentary: An Exposition of the Scriptures*, S. 1:351.

[5] Paul J. Achtemeier, *Harper's Bible Dictionary 1st ed.* (San Francisco: Harper and Row, 1985), S. 448.

[6] M. G. Easton, *Easton's Bible Dictionary.* (Oak Harbor, WA: Logos Research Systems, Inc., 1996, c1987).

[7] For helpful studies of Hebrew prose and poetry respectively see Alter, *The Art of Biblical Narrative;* id., *The Art of Biblical Poetry* (New York: Basic Books, 1985).

[8] Block: *Judges, Ruth; The New American Commentary* 6, S. 213. Some would also add the Song of Moses, Deuteronomy 32

[9] Daniel Isaac Block, *Judges, Ruth* (Nashville: Broadman and Holman Publishers, 2001, c1999), (Logos Library System; *The New American Commentary* 6), S. 149. That this phenomenon is attested in extrabiblical writings see especially the Egyptian prose and poetic accounts of the Battle of Kadesh, in A. H. Gardiner, *The Kadesh Inscriptions of Rameses II* (Oxford: Oxford University, 1960)..

[10] Walvoord and Zuck, *The Bible Knowledge Commentary: An Exposition of the Scriptures*, S. 1:389.

[11] Larry Richards, *The Bible Reader's Companion* (Wheaton, Ill.: Victor Books, 1991), S. 163.

[12] Carson, *New Bible Commentary: 21st Century Edition 4th ed.*, S. Jdg 5:1.

[13] Block, *Judges, Ruth; The New American Commentary* 6), S. 216.

[14] G. Kittel, G. W. Bromiley and G. Friedrich, ed., *Theological Dictionary of the New Testament Vols. 5-10* compiled by Ronald Pitkin (Grand Rapids, MI Eerdmans: 1964-c1976).

[15] Liberal scholars (See Wood [below, 37-56] for a list of these scholars and a critique of them.) have conjectured that Saul was involved in some kind of ecstatic experience in this narrative; that perhaps music was used to bring the prophets into such an ecstatic state. See further Leon J. Wood, *The Prophets of Israel* (Grand Rapids, MI: Baker Book House, 1979), 103-104. Given the use of the word *nabi* and its relation to music I believe it is more likely that Saul was involved in spontaneous praise using music and joined the other prophets in their singing.

Chapter 6 - endnotes

[1] David F. Payne, *I and II Samuel* (Louisville: Westminster John Knox Press, 2001, c1982 The Daily Study Bible Series), S. 84.

[2] Carson, *New Bible Commentary: 21st Century Edition 4th ed.*, S. 1 Sa 16:14.

[3] Robert D. Bergen, *1, 2 Samuel* (Nashville: Broadman and Holman Publishers, 2001, c1996) (Logos Library System; *The New American Commentary* 7), S. 184.

[4] Francis Bacon is the father of the modern scientific method. Although the scientific method is helpful in determining truth in some arenas, modern man has often enthroned the scientific method as the only method for determining truth.

[5] Keil and Delitzsch, *Commentary on the Old Testament*, S. 3:510.

[6] Jeremy Montagu, *Musical Instruments of the Bible* (Oxford: Scarecrow Press, 2002) 48-50, 81.

[7] P. Kyle McCarter, Jr., *2 Samuel, A New Translation with Introduction, Notes and Commentary* (Garden City, NY: Doubleday and Co., 1984), 188.

[8] Walter C. Kaiser, *Hard Sayings of the Bible* (Downers Grove, Il: InterVarsity, 1997, c1996), S. 221. See also: Makujina, John, *Measuring the Music*, 291-303.

[9] J. A. Thompson, *The New American Commentary Vol.* 9 (Nashville, TN: Broadman and Holman Publishers, 1994), 176-177.

[10] Carson, *New Bible Commentary: 21st Century Edition 4th ed*, S. 1 Ch 25:1.

[11] Richards, *The Bible Reader's Companion*, S. 275.

[12] For a helpful summary see further Liesch, *People in the Presence of God*, 180-191.

[13] J. A. Thompson, *1, 2 Chronicles* (Nashville: Broadman and Holman Publishers, 2001, c1994), (Logos Library System; *The New American Commentary* 9), S. 170. See also McConville, *I and II Chronicles*, 93.

[14] J. G. McConville, *I and II Chronicles* (Louisville: Westminster John Knox Press, 2001, c1984 The Daily Study Bible Series), S. 92.

[15] Paul Lee Tan, *Encyclopedia of 7700 Illustrations: A Treasury of Illustrations, Anecdotes, Facts and Quotations for Pastors, Teachers and Christian Workers* (Garland TX: Bible Communications, 1996, c1979).

[16] Thompson, *1, 2 Chronicles; The New American Commentary* 9, S. 227.

[17] Keil and Delitzsch, *Commentary on the Old Testament*, S. 3:593.

[18] Thompson, *1, 2 Chronicles; The New American Commentary* 9, S. 229.

[19] McConville, *I and II Chronicles*, S. 136.

[20] Jamieson, Fausset and Brown, *A Commentary, Critical and Explanatory, on the Old and New Testaments*, S. 1 Ki 11:4.

[21] Warren W. Wiersbe, *Wiersbe's Expository Outlines on the Old Testament* (Wheaton, IL: Victor Books, 1993), S. 1 Ki 9:1.

[22] Paul R. House, *1, 2 Kings* (Nashville: Broadman and Holman Publishers, 2001, c1995), (Logos Library System; *The New American Commentary* 8), S. 167.

[23] Ibid., S. 167.

Chapter 7 – endnotes

[1] "A knowledge of the Psalter by heart was required of candidates for ordination. St. Gennadius, Patriarch of Constantinople (A.D. 458-471), refused to ordain as priest anyone who had not been diligent in reciting the Psalter. St. Gregory the Great inquired if Rusticus, who had been elected Bishop of Ancona, knew the Psalter by heart, and refused to allow John the Presbyter to be consecrated as metropolitan of Ravenna on account of his ignorance of the Psalter. The second Canon of the second Council of Nicaea (A.D. 587) laid it down that no one was to be consecrated bishop unless he knew the Psalter thoroughly, and the eighth Council of Toledo (A.D. 653) ordered that "no one henceforth shall be promoted to any ecclesiastical dignity who does not perfectly know the whole Psalter" (Can. 8)."
http://www.christianleadershipcenter.org/504/dvot504worship.htm. Accessed on 06-07-2007. Luther refused to ordain those who could not, from memory, sing the entire Psalter. (see L. W. Bacon and N. H. Allen, *The Hymns of Martin Luther* [New York, 1883]).

[2] Kimball, *Emerging Worship: Creating New Worship Gatherings for Emerging Generations*, vii.

[3] Ibid., vi.

[4] For one entry among others see Jamieson, Fausset and Brown, *A Commentary, Critical and Explanatory, on the Old and New Testaments*, S. Ps 119:54

[5] TWOT #613.

[6] TWOT 1022a.

[7] Walvoord and Zuck, *The Bible Knowledge Commentary: An Exposition of the Scriptures*, S. 2:735.

[8] Craig S. Keener, *The IVP Bible Background Commentary: New Testament* (Downers Grove, Ill.: InterVarsity Press, 1993), S. 1 Ti 2:8.

[9] George Angus Fulton Knight, *Psalms: Volume 1* (Louisville: Westminster John Knox Press, 2001, c1982 The Daily Study Bible Series), S. 289.

[10] Henry, *Matthew Henry's Commentary on the Whole Bible: Complete and Unabridged in One Volume*, S. Ps 63:3.

[11] http://www.challies.com/archives/000394.php accessed on 3/1/2007

[12] R. Laird Harris, Gleason Leonard Archer, and Bruce K. Waltke, *Theological Wordbook of the Old Testament* (Chicago: Moody Press, 1999, c1980), S. 979.

[13] Timothy Friberg, Barbara Friberg and Neva F. Miller, *Analytical Lexicon of the Greek New Testament* (Grand Rapids, Mich.: Baker Books, 2000 Baker's Greek New Testament Library 4), S. 158.

Chapter 8 - endnotes

[1] Carson, *New Bible Commentary: 21st Century Edition 4th ed.*, S. Job 1:1

[2] Robert L. Alden, *Job* (Nashville: Broadman and Holman Publishers, 2001, c1993), (Logos Library System; *The New American Commentary* 11), S. 61.

[3] Keil and Delitzsch, *Commentary on the Old Testament*, S. 4:278-279.

[4] Christo H. J. vanderMerwe, Jackie A. Naude and Jan H. Kroeze, *A Biblical Hebrew Reference Grammar* (New York: Sheffield Academic Press, 1999), 139.

[5] Warren W. Wiersbe, *Be Patient* (Wheaton, Ill.: Victor Books, 1996, c1991 An Old Testament Study), S. Job 1:20.

[6] Harris, Harris, Archer and Waltke, *Theological Wordbook of the Old Testament*, S. 399.

[7] Ibid., S. 399.

[8] K.T. Aitken, *Proverbs* (Louisville: Westminster John Knox Press, 2001, c1986 The Daily Study Bible Series), S. 14.

[9] H. L. Willmington, *Willmington's Bible Handbook* (Wheaton, Ill.: Tyndale House Publishers, 1997), S. 349.

[10] Duane A. Garrett, *Proverbs, Ecclesiastes, Song of Songs* (Nashville: Broadman and Holman Publishers, 2001, c1993), (Logos Library System; *The New American Commentary* 14), S. 365.

[11] Ibid., S. 378.

[12] Ibid., S. 378.

[13] Jamieson, Fausset and Brown, *A Commentary, Critical and Explanatory, on the Old and New Testaments*, S. So 1:1.

Chapter 9 - endnotes

[1] House, *1, 2 Kings*, S. 184. House quotes a plethora of sources in this commentary on this particular issue.

[2] Walter A. Elwell and Philip Wesley Comfort, *Tyndale Bible Dictionary* (Wheaton, Ill.: Tyndale House Publishers, 2001 Tyndale Reference Library), S. 347.

[3] Carson, *New Bible Commentary: 21st Century Edition 4th ed.*, S. 1 Ki 18:20.

[4] See Robb Redman, *The Great Worship Awakening* (San Francisco, CA: Jossey Bass, 2002), 22-46 for an in-depth description.

[5] Ken Barker, ed., *Songs for Praise and Worship, Worship Planner Edition* (Grand Rapids, MI: Word Music, 1992), 474-475.

[6] Barry Liesch, *The New Worship* (Grand Rapids MI: Baker Books, 1996), 47.

[7] Ibid. p 71-86. This term is also used as a chapter heading by Andy Parks, *To Know You More* (Downers Grove, IL: InterVarsity Press, 2002), 171.

[8] Ibid., 61.

[9] Ibid., 56.

[10] Rick Warren, *The Purpose Driven Church* (Grand Rapids, MI: Zondervan Publishing House, 1995), 240.

[11] Although Elmer Martens, *God's Design* (Grand Rapids, MI: Baker Book House Co., 1981) does not specifically use this terminology he does defend as "Yahweh's purpose" the redemptive act for the purpose of an ongoing relationship. It is outlined on pp.17-20 and expanded upon throughout the volume to include all the dispensational periods.

[12] Redman, *The Great Worship Awakening*, 91.

[13] Robert Webber, *Ancient-Future Faith* (Grand Rapids, MI: Baker Books, 1999), 102-106.

[14] Peterson, E*ngaging with God, a Biblical Theology of Worship*, 26.

Endnotes

[15] Redman, *The Heart of Worship Files*, 13.

[16] Marva Dawn, *How Shall We Worship* (Wheaton, IL: Tyndale House Publishers, Inc., 2003), xi.

[17] Tozer, *Whatever Happened to Worship.*, 121.

Chapter 10 - endnotes

[1] Willem A. VanGemeren, *Interpreting the Prophetic Word* (Grand Rapids, MI: Zondervan Publishing House, 1990), 28-29. VanGemeren describes Moses as the "fountainhead" of the prophetic office.

[2] For a more in depth treatment see Gaebelein, ed., *The Expositor's Bible Commentary, Vol. 2*, 193.

[3] Thomas Allen Seel, *A Theology of Music Derived from the Book of Revelation* (Metuchen, New Jersey: The Scarecrow Press, 1995), 52-53.

[4] Leupold, "Worship Music in Ancient Israel: Its Meaning and Purpose", 180.

[5] See also Isa 58:2-7, 13-14; Jer 10:2-5, 14-15; 11:10-17; 13:10-11; 19:4-6; Ez 8:5-15; 14:3-8; 18:5-6; 20:7-9; 22:26; 23:30,37-39; Joel 1:13.

[6] See also Jer 14:12; 16:11-13; 17:1-2; 32:29, 35; 44:3-6, 8, 15-26; Lam 2:6-7; Ez 5:11; 6:4-6; 44:12; Hos 8:4, 11-14; 10:1-8; 13:1-4; Amos 5:21-27; Nahum 1:14.

[7] See also Jer 7:1-11, 17-23; Hos 6:6; 14:2-3, 8.

[8] See also Jer 2:11, 20, 23, 27-28; 2:6, 9-10; 5:7, 19; 7:30-32; 8:2,19; 9:14; Hos 3:1; 4:13-19; Hab 2:18-20; Zeph 3:4.

[9] See also Jer 31:7, 12-13; 33:9, 11, 18-22; 43:12-13; 50:2; 51:47-48,52; Ez 30:13; 37:23; 40:39-44; 44:15-16, 23-24, 27; 45:4, 17; 46:2-3, 9; 48:9-11; Joel 2:26; Micah 1:7; 4:5; 5:12-14; Zeph 3:9.

[10] Walvoord and Zuck, *The Bible Knowledge Commentary: An Exposition of the Scriptures*, S. 1:1032.

[11] Warren W. Wiersbe, *Be Comforted An Old Testament Study* (Wheaton, Ill,: Victor Books, 1996, c1992), S. Is 5:1.

[12] Kaiser, *Hard Sayings of the Bible*, S. 404.

[13] Walvoord and Zuck, *The Bible Knowledge Commentary: An Exposition of the Scriptures*, S. 1:1207.

[14] Charles F. Pfeiffer, *The Wycliffe Bible Commentary: Old Testament* (Chicago: Moody Press, 1962), S. La 1:1.

[15] Keil and Delitzsch, *Commentary on the Old Testament*, S. 8:465.

Chapter 11 - endnotes

[1] McConville, J. G., *Ezra, Nehemiah, and Esther* (Louisville: Westminster John Knox Press, 2001, c1985 The Daily Study Bible Series), S. 115.

[2] Walvoord and Zuck, *The Bible Knowledge Commentary: An Exposition of the Scriptures*, S. 1:658.

[3] Carson, *New Bible Commentary: 21st Century Edition 4th ed.*, S. Mal 1:6.

[4] Keil and Delitzsch, *Commentary on the Old Testament*, S. 10:641.

[5] Philip Schaff and David Schley Schaff, *History of the Christian Church* (Oak Harbor, WA : Logos Research Systems, Inc.), 1997.

[6] Barkley M. Newman and Philip C. Stine, *A Handbook on the Gospel of Matthew* (New York: United Bible Society, 1988) 87.

[7] Jamieson, Fausset and Brown, *A Commentary, Critical and Explanatory, on the Old and New Testaments*, S. Mt 4:10.

[8] Craig Blomberg, *Matthew* (Nashville: Broadman and Holman Publishers, 2001, c1992), (Logos Library System; *The New American Commentary* 22), S. 85.

[9] *The Dictionary of Biblical Languages With Semantic Domains* defines προσκυνέω (*proskyneō*): **1.** LN 53.56 **worship**, bow as an act of allegiance or regard (Mt 2:2); **2.** LN 17.21 **prostrate oneself before**, kneel down before as an act of reverence. *Proskyneo* occurs 25 times in the gospels and is translated both as bow/prostrate/fall before and worship. It indicates both a posture and an attitude of worship.

[10] Warren W. Wiersbe, *Wiersbe's Expository Outlines on the New Testament* (Wheaton, Ill.: Victor Books, 1997, c1992), S. 130.

[11] Blomberg, *Matthew*; *The New American Commentary* 22, S. 119

[12] John Nolland, *The Gospel of Matthew: A Commentary on the Greek Text* (Grand Rapids, MI: William B. Eerdmans Publishing Co., 2005), 905.

[13] Carson, *New Bible Commentary: 21st Century Edition 4th ed.*, S. Jn 4:4.

[14] Walvoord and Zuck, *The Bible Knowledge Commentary: An Exposition of the Scriptures*, S. 2:286.

[15] D. A. Carson, ed., *Worship by the Book* (Grand Rapids, MI: Zondervan, 2002), 37. See also Richard E. Averbeck in his two chapters dealing with spirit and truth and also in Herbert W. Bateman, ed., *Authentic Worship: Hearing Scripture's Voice, Applying Its Truths* (Grand Rapids, MI: Kregel Publications, 2002), 79-133.

[16] Robert B. Hughes, J. Carl Laney and Robert B. Hughes, *Tyndale Concise Bible Commentary* (Wheaton, Ill.: Tyndale House Publishers, 2001 The Tyndale Reference Library), S. 470.

[17] Kittel, Bromiley and Friedrich, *Theological Dictionary of the New Testament*, S. 6:760.

[18] Craig S. Keener, *The IVP Bible Background Commentary: New Testament* (Downers Grove, Ill.: InterVarsity Press, 1993), S. Mt 14:33.

[19] A.T. Robertson, *Word Pictures in the New Testament* (Oak Harbor: Logos Research Systems, 1997), S. Mark 6:51.

[20] Vincent, *Word Studies in the New Testament*, S. 1:iii-197.

[21] Kittel, Bromiley, Friedrich, *Theological Dictionary of the New Testament*, S. 9:209.

Chapter 12 - endnotes

[1] Walter A. Elwell and Philip Wesley Comfort, *Tyndale Bible Dictionary* (Wheaton, Ill.: Tyndale House Publishers, 2001 Tyndale Reference Library), S. 922.

[2] Richard N. Longenecker, *Expositor's Bible Commentary Vol. 9* (Grand Rapids, MI: Zondervan, 1981), 308.

[3] Archibald Robinson, *Word Pictures in the New Testament* (Nashville, TN: Broadman Press, 1930).

[4] John B. Polhill, *Acts* (Nashville : Broadman and Holman Publishers, 2001, c1992), (Logos Library System; *The New American Commentary* 26), S. 148.

⁵ Lourdes Montgomery, *Singing Psalms in the New Millennium* http://www.npm.org/Articles/SingingPsalms.pdf. Accessed 10-27-2007.

⁶ Vincent, *Word Studies in the New Testament*, S. 1:iii-535.

⁷ Robertson, *Word Pictures in the New Testament*, S. Ac 16:25.

Chapter 13 - endnotes

¹ Kittel, Bromiley and Friedrich, *Theological Dictionary of the New Testament*, S. 8:500-502.

² Richard R. Melick, *Philippians, Colossians, Philemon* (Nashville: Broadman and Holman Publishers, 2001, c1991), (Logos Library System; *The New American Commentary* 32), S. 304.

³ Guthrie, *New Testament Introduction 4th rev. ed.*, S. 653.

⁴ Roy B. Zuck and Darrell L. Bock; Dallas Theological Seminary, *A Biblical Theology of the New Testament* (Chicago: Moody Press, 1996, c1994), S. 309.

⁵ Guthrie, *New Testament Introduction 4th rev. ed.*, S. 799.

⁶ Thomas R Schreiner, *Romans,* (Grand Rapids: Baker Books, 1998), 83.

⁷ Carson, *New Bible Commentary: 21st Century Edition 4th ed.*, S. Ro 11:33.

⁸ Kenneth S. Wuest, *Wuest's Word Studies from the Greek New Testament: For the English Reader* (Grand Rapids: Eerdmans, 1997, c1984), S. Ro 12:1.

⁹ Wuest, *Wuest's Word Studies from the Greek New Testament: For the English Reader*, S. Ro 12:1.

¹⁰ Schreiner, *Romans,* 757.

¹¹ Carson, *New Bible Commentary: 21st Century Edition 4th ed.*, S. Eph 4:7.

¹² Peter T. O'Brien, *The Letter to the Ephesians* (Grand Rapids: William B. Eerdmans Publishing Company, 1999), 394-395.

¹³ Kittel, Bromiley and Friedrich, *Theological Dictionary of the New Testament*, S. 1:164.

¹⁴ Obrien, *The Letter to the Ephesians*, 395.

[15] Strongs #5568.

[16] Robertson, *Word Pictures in the New Testament*, S. Vol. V c. 1932, Vol VI c. 1933 by Sunday School Board of the Southern Baptist Convention.

[17] James Strong, *The Exhaustive Concordance of the Bible: Showing Every Word of the Test of the Common English Version of the Canonical Books, and Every Occurence of Each Word in Regular Order* (Ontario: Woodside Bible Fellowship., 1996), S. G2605.

[18] Melick, *Philippians, Colossians, Philemon*, S. 304.

[19] An electronic search of *Englishman's Concordance* yields 97 occurrences of διδάσκω *didasko*.

[20] Melick, *Philippians, Colossians, Philemon*, S. 305.

[21] Meat offered in false worship remains an issue in India and other countries today.

[22] See also, Anthony Thesilton, *The New International Greek Testament Commentary* (Grand Rapids, MI: William Eerdmans Publishing Co., 2000), 617.

[23] David Garland, *1 Corinthians* (Grand Rapids: Baker Book House, 2003), 380.

[24] John Storey, *Cultural Studies and the Study of Popular Culture* (Athens, GA: University of Georgia Press, 1996), 2; as cited in T.M. Moore, *Redeeming Pop Culture* (Phillipsburg, NJ: P and R Publishing, 2003), 18.

[25] Ken Myers, *All God's Children and Blue Suede Shoes* (Wheaton: Crossway, 1989), 34.

[26] Paul Tillich, *Theology of Culture* (New York: Oxford Press, 1959), 42-43.

[27] Comment relayed by Dr. Monty Buhdahl on 12/13/2006 from a teaching tour in India, July, 2006.

[28] David J. Hesselgrave and Edward Rommen, *Contextualization* (Grand Rapids: Baker, 1989), 162.

[29] John Makujina, Unpublished paper delivered at the National Leadership Conference Lansdale, PA, 1999. 8

[30] Anthony Thesilton, *The New International Greek Commentary* (Grand Rapids: William Eerdmans Publishing Co., 2000), 956.

[31] Ibid. 960.

Chapter 14 - endnotes

[1] For an excellent treatment of Hebrews see Due, *Created for Worship*, 153-182.

[2] John William Drane, *Introducing the New Testament Completely Revised and Updated* (Oxford: Lion Publishing plc, 2000), S. 421.

[3] Wiersbe, *The Bible Exposition Commentary*, S. Heb 10:19.

[4] Carson, *New Bible Commentary: 21st Century Edition 4th ed.*, S. Heb 13:1.

[5] Due, *Created for Worship*, 169.

[6] Wuest, *Wuest's Word Studies from the Greek New Testament: For the English Reader*, S. Heb 13:13-15.

[7] Due, *Created for Worship*, 178.

[8] Vincent, *Word Studies in the New Testament*, S. 1:iii-643.

[9] Willmington, *Willmington's Bible Handbook*, S. 770.

Chapter 15 - endnotes

[1] Simon Kistemaker, *New Testament Commentary, Exposition of the Book of Revelation* (Grand Rapids: MI: Baker Book House, 2001), 254.

[2] Walvoord and Zuck, *The Bible Knowledge Commentary: An Exposition of the Scriptures*, S. 2:966.

[3] Carson, *New Bible Commentary: 21st Century Edition 4th ed.*, S. Re 6:1.

[4] Carson, ed., *Worship by the Book*, 26.

[5] Carson, *New Bible Commentary: 21st Century Edition 4th ed.*, S. Re 15:1.

[6] Willmington, *Willmington's Bible Handbook* , S. 803.

Endnotes

[7] Carson, *New Bible Commentary: 21st Century Edition 4th ed.*, S. Re 15:1.

[8] See further: William Barclay, *The Revelation of John: Volume 2* (Philadelphia: The Westminster Press, 2000, c1976 The Daily Study Bible Series, Rev. Ed), S. 118.

[9] Wiersbe, *The Bible Exposition Commentary*, S. Re 15:1.

[10] Pfeiffer and Harrison, *The Wycliffe Bible Commentary: New Testament*, S. Re 18:1.

[11] Kittle, Bromiley and Fiedrich, *Theological Dictionary of the New Testament*, S. 1:20.

[12] Robert B. Hughes, J. Carl Laney and Robert B. Hughes, *Tyndale Concise Bible Commentary* (Wheaton, Ill.: Tyndale House Publishers, 2001 The Tyndale Reference Library).